THE YEAR
CHINA
CHANGED

To Franklin Huang
with best wishes,

Tom Seovel
6/16/13

司德華

THE YEAR
CHINA
CHANGED

by TOM SCOVEL

MEMORIES OF
REMARKABLE EVENTS
AND EXTRAORDINARY PEOPLE

TATE PUBLISHING
AND ENTERPRISES, LLC

Published by Tate Publishing & Enterprises, LLC
127 E. Trade Center Terrace | Mustang, Oklahoma 73064 USA
1.888.361.9473 | www.tatepublishing.com

Tate Publishing is committed to excellence in the publishing industry. The company reflects the philosophy established by the founders, based on Psalm 68:11,
"The Lord gave the word and great was the company of those who published it."

Published in the United States of America

ISBN: 978-1-62510-864-7
1. Travel / Asia / China
2. History / Asia / China
12.11.16

for Janene

ACKNOWLEDGEMENTS

Writing and publishing a book is similar to many of life's weighty endeavors; it can only be accomplished with the help of others, some whose names you can readily recall well afterwards, and others who may have helped just as much but even whose faces have faded into time. For their able and most recent assistance I am indebted to the good people at Tate Publishing who welcomed this manuscript from the very beginning, who facilitated and expedited the book's production, who demonstrated unflagging zeal and creativity in marketing the work, and who ultimately published a better product than their author originally offered them. Publishing a book is a long, arduous, and collaborative process, but good things take time, and I am deeply grateful to everyone I worked with and much appreciate their energy, talent, and grace.

Since I view this book as more about China and her people rather than about my experiences there, I feel compelled to express my great debt of gratitude to all the Chinese who assisted me and my family during our year of residence. Many of them are named in the book, and it is obvious from the respective narratives I have spun how generous they were, especially given the socioeconomic constraints they were subjected to and the political oppression they had undergone and, in many cases, were still experiencing. I offer special thanks to our home institution, the Tianjin Foreign Languages Institute: to the leading cadres for their flexibility and openness (well, most of the time!), to our faculty colleagues who were in many ways wonderful students and in others magnificent teachers, and to all the students in our classes, seminars, and special lectures. Their love of learning was both contagious and inspiring.

Without intending to slight any of those just thanked as a group, I have chosen to mention several individuals whose friendship and benevolence were extraordinary. Zhang Jintong ("Xiao Zhang") was more a didi than our interpreter and constant companion, and as a little brother, he became part of our family: an older sibling to our two children, a teacher and facilitator to Janene, and the harried but faithful arbitrator between the institute's sometimes conservative hierarchy and the two crazy Americans to whom he was assigned. Wang Zhanmei was the invisible member of the dissertation committee for Janene's eventual doctoral thesis on English Language Teaching and political change in China, but he was more than just an academic advisor. He spent many hours detailing the vagaries of a teacher's life under the Communists and bravely told us story after story that few would dare to mention. Because of our common love of pedagogy, I also enjoyed working with him, and for both Janene and me, Wang was a rare colleague and an uncommon friend. Our son's piano teacher was another special soul for he literally brought music into our lives, training our son Derick to be an accomplished and confident pianist and also assuring that he would be a well-trained trombonist. Xu Laoshi was also one of the first Christians we met, and the stories of his faithfulness and that of his family in times of persecution were humbling. Pursuing your faith in America is almost too easy; in China at that time and especially during the immediately preceding Cultural Revolution, it could be a matter of life or death. Because we went to China as teachers, it is fitting that I conclude this short list of names named with that of one of our students, Yang Bing. Technically, he was Janene's student, one of the brightest of her remarkably luminous class, but he later worked briefly with me as a graduate student and over the years has become our unofficially adopted son. During our year in China, Bing stood out as an unusually brilliant and open-minded young man, and Janene felt blessed to have been his teacher. Now, several decades later after he came to seek his fortune in America, we have enjoyed seeing him gain a profession, get married, raise a family, and succeed in ways we would've thought inconceivable when we first saw him as a skinny scholar who loved playing basketball. He has been incredibly generous to us, and he remains to this day a living link to our remarkable year in China.

Of course I cannot conclude these acknowledgements without referring to my family. Although it is obvious that neither this book nor my China experiences would exist without my parents, they are much more than just the author's sine qua non. Fred and Myra Scovel raised all six of their children to be intellectually curious, to value the weight of words, to love China and her people, and above all to strive to be Christ's disciples. Time and time again as I was writing this manuscript, I became aware of the legacy they left me, and my admiration for their years of service deepened immeasurably. When Janene and I returned to the States after our time in China, we asked them several times how they were able to endure the hardships they faced, challenges far more onerous than the inconveniences that constantly annoyed us. They would smile almost wistfully and reply simply, "but the people, the people." My parents died years ago and except through my mother's writing, they no longer serve as references for me, but my siblings, especially my two gege have proved invaluable sources of information. My older brothers, Jim and Carl, have the most vivid and accurate memories of China and were especially useful in providing me with details of my early life in Jining, the Weifang internment camp, and other family experiences. As with any piece of writing, if my accounts or memories differ from the information they or others have provided, I alone am responsible for the discrepancies.

I wrote this book to fulfill a promise I made to my wife, and so like my parents, she is the raison d'etre for this work. For all of

1979, Janene kept a diary detailing our life in China, often written in tiny but legible entries in order to squeeze all her observations and reactions into the space allotted for that day's events. Her attention to names, dates, and facts, and her keen and often frank comments about what we experienced served as the major reference for this book and helped balance and complement my own notes and memories. In addition, Janene pored over the draft of every chapter, spotting many infelicities of spelling, style, and substance, and giving me the ultimate gift any author can receive, making me aware of not what was written, but of what was read. I also want to thank our son, Derick, our daughter, Christine, and once again especially Janene for spending that year in China with me. It was not their ancestral home, and in 1979, it was an inhospitable and challenging place for an American family to live, but they suffered through the worst and enjoyed the best as much as I. The opportunity to teach in China and to return to my roots was rare indeed, but because my family was willing to share that opportunity with me, my experience was enriched beyond measure. To them, and all who made that year so exceptional and this book possible, I express my ultimate gratitude.

TABLE OF CONTENTS

The surprising invitation to teach in China/ a brief flashback to my boyhood experiences during the Communist revolution/ culture shock after arriving in Beijing/ sightseeing, acculturation, and a chance to witness a historical celebration

The challenges of settling in at our residence in Tianjin/ welcoming in the Chinese New Year/ the difficulties in arranging for our children's education/ adjusting to our duties at the institute and winning over our students and colleagues/ questions and controversies in classes and conversations as we acculturated to different approaches to learning and teaching

The devastation left by the 1976 earthquake/ adjusting to life in a hotel and meeting strange guests/ friendly encounters with the People's Liberation Army/ hosting Tianjin's "first" Fourth of July Party/ witnessing life on the city streets up close and personal/ continual political constraints, limitations on personal freedom, and pervasive sickness

Introducing eight extraordinary Chinese/ the diminutive paleontologist who revealed an amazing secret about our institute/ the "Korean" Jin raised by GI's and an expert on American culture in the forties/ the Russian Jin loyal supporter of the Party/ the Chinese Jin- a scholar without peer/ three remarkably different women representing three generations and worldviews of modern China/ our dear friend Wang- brave, friendly, bright, and tragic

The return of the native- a rare chance to visit my birthplace in Shandong/ climbing historic Tai Shan/ a return to the village in Anhui where I lived during the civil war just before the Communist victory in 1949/ a summer visit to sophisticated Shanghai/ hilarity and frustrations during two weeks at the famous summer resort of Qingdao/ a marvelous opportunity be the first former prisoner to return to the WW II internment camp at Weifang

A glimpse at how Chinese history is fundamentally forged by its geography and how her people are united by a unique writing system/ demonstrating how Confucianism has shaped Chinese culture right up to the very present/ a look at how the Taiping Rebellion violently disrupted centuries of imperial rule and how the Communists finally united China a century later after decades of civil war/ ways in which Chinese maps create intriguingly different mental maps of the nation and the world/ boyhood recollections of the Communist victory and its immediate effects on the life of the Chinese and also on the Scovel family

Mao Zedong's rise to power and the extraordinary ways in which he was venerated in 1979, two years after his death/ the absolute fealty demanded by the Party despite many incongruous and hypocritical contradictions/ heart wrenching stories told to us of suffering during the just concluded Cultural Revolution/ the suppression of civil liberties and the repression of religion/ the brutal death of a family friend/ the reopening of the Tianjin church and the first public worship service

Economics is at the heart of Communism and during 1979, major economic reforms were promulgated at the local and national levels/ costs for goods and services were often incomprehensible and inequitable/ a Chinese system of apartheid/ ways in which the Communist "work unit" replaced the traditional system of clans/ further reforms and relaxation of restrictions took place almost weekly

Sporting activities and what they revealed about Chinese society at that time/ autumn celebrations, banquets and final trips to the countryside/ deeply personal stories and reflections told by Chinese friends as we were about to leave/ hints that China would soon dominate America with exports/ final farewells to students and friends and one last act of filial piety

A PROLEPTIC PROLOGUE

三十年河东，三十年河西

sanshi nian he dong, sanshi nian he xi

For thirty years, the river flows east;
then for another thirty, it flows west.

Many years ago and long before I retired from academia, my wife extracted a commitment from me, a promise that culminated in the book that you are about to read. "Tom," she observed one day after scanning one of my scholarly publications, "you're a great writer, but the stuff you produce is so boring. Promise me that when you retire, you'll write a book about our year together in China." I was initially taken aback by her somewhat tart observation, but on reflection, I had to agree that there are no shelves in any bookstore stocked with texts about psycholinguistics or treatises on second language acquisition. I also had to admit that I've never once spotted a fellow passenger ever settle into a book on these topics to while away the hours of a long-distance flight. Accepting her observation as well as her compliment, it was equally easy to accede to her request, so I promised that I'd write a China book for her upon retirement. After all, I was in the middle of a lengthy career as a linguistics professor, and my future life as a retiree seemed far away, lost somewhere in the mists of a new and distant millennium. With uncommon speed, however, the future became the present, and at the age of seventy and after a forty-seven-year teaching career, I sat down to fulfill the promise I had made decades earlier.

I was born and raised in China and was fortunate enough to survive times of hardship during World War II, when the

Japanese Imperial Army controlled China and her people, and times of equal difficulty during the subsequent revolution, when the Chinese themselves bitterly fought each other. I was equally fortunate to be able to recall so many of my childhood experiences and to remember them without regret. After my family left China, I had always wanted to return, but the Cold War climate that froze relations between the United States and the People's Republic of China prevented me from realizing this dream, and I was afraid that I would live forever as an exile. Through a sequence of surprising events beginning with the Nixon-Kissinger negotiations with the Chinese in the midseventies, my wife and I were invited by the PRC government itself to spend a year teaching in my homeland, and just before the two governments normalized relationships, Janene and I left our home in America with our two kids to spend all of 1979 in the land of my birth. It was the most difficult, challenging, exciting, and ultimately rewarding year of our lives, and this is precisely why Janene extracted the promise from me to record these memories permanently upon my retirement. But when I sat down to begin writing, I was initially struck with remorse. It was 2009, and thirty years had passed since that eventful sojourn in China. Surely, too much time had slipped by. So many memories had evaporated, and the People's Republic of China back then had now been transformed into a completely new nation, virtually unrecognizable when compared to the place and people we remembered. Yes, Janene was right in insisting that I should turn the events of that year into a book, but I really should've responded to her request when she first asked, a year or so after we had just returned to the States. Now it was too late!

I lamented my situation for a few days until slowly it dawned on me that the timing was apt if not ideal. Sixty years earlier, the revolution was complete, and the People's Republic of China was formed. Sixty years earlier, I was a young witness to the civil war and the eventual Communist victory. Those sixty years could not have been more neatly divided by our year in China for 1979 served as the perfect fulcrum, balancing the many memories I had of the war-torn years of my childhood with the amazing transformations that have taken place in contemporary China. For thirty years after the Communist Revolution, the river of Chinese history flowed eastward and inward, hewing tightly to its narrow Asian banks and stubbornly adhering to its own independent course, but during the year we were there, things began to change, and the river started to course ever more swiftly westward and outward, flooding the country with innovation and modernity. The year 1979 split those sixty years right down the middle, half reminiscent of prerevolutionary China and half harbinger of things to come. It was also a year of remarkable experiences that I was privileged to witness as a participant-observer, and it was a time when I discovered that irrespective of all that we see today, much has remained unchanged and that the superficial trappings of modernization hide an inner Chinese psyche that has survived several millennia of history. Thus comforted by the realization that time was actually my ally, I embarked on my quest to fulfill my promise and began writing this story.

Little did we know, when we accepted the sudden and surprising invitation to go to China in the autumn of 1978, how much that decision would transform our lives. When I left China at the age of twelve, I was quite certain that I would never have a chance to return, and though there were times when I came physically close to the land of my birth, this very proximity served only to heighten a sense of exile. The first opportunity came during treks near the Chinese border when I attended high school in the Himalayan foothills. Later, during years of residence in northern Thailand, I lived only a day's drive away from Yunnan Province just north of us. Finally, on trips to Hong Kong on the mainland of China itself, I came tantalizingly close to fulfilling my childhood dream. Then at midlife, at the age of forty, I not only had a chance to visit my homeland, but to do so with my family and to reside there for a year with time and opportunity to retrace my roots and visit every single place where I had once lived. These opportunities filled me with great joy, and it was equally rewarding to return to the States after our year of residence to share these experiences with my siblings, who had the same China heritage as I, and with my parents, who were still living. Of course they were the ones who created this legacy through their decision to serve as medical missionaries there for more than twenty years. However, it was only after returning to America and witnessing the remarkable changes in the People's Republic that I began to appreciate what we experienced during our incredible year in China.

Time after time, it became apparent that 1979 was not just a chronological fulcrum from which to leverage the story of my boyhood and our life there as one of the first American families to return to that Communist nation. That year was also the moment when the entire nation pivoted culturally, changing direction from east to west and roaring toward modernization with a speed and ferocity never seen before in history. Yet looking back with three decades of hindsight, I can spot the seeds of change that sprouted almost imperceptibly while we were there: the normalization of diplomatic relations between the PRC and the United States, the creation of the first special economic zones, the enforcement of an early retirement policy to stimulate institutional change with new and younger blood, the transition to a market economy, the adoption of the one-child policy, and the lifting of prohibitions against public religious worship.

If via the magic of a time machine you were able to be transported back to Tianjin to meet me in 1979 and had described any one of the myriad of transformations China would undergo during the next thirty years, I would have ridiculed you unmercifully. I remember seeing one of the political slogans on a billboard promulgating the then popular Four Modernizations, and it read "Catch Japan by the Year 2000!" I recall remarking sarcastically to a Chinese colleague something like, "China will be lucky to catch up to one of the poor African nations by then." Little did I know that not long after the new millennium, China would far surpass Japan in terms of imports to the United States. Never did I dream that the economy of my native province, Shandong, which was at that time comparable to that of Swaziland, would be on a par with that of Switzerland in thirty years time. Not even in my wildest imagination would I have ever guessed that in three decades, Chinese cities would swarm with hordes of automobiles; teem with glistening shopping centers, nightclubs, world-class sports venues; and that Starbucks, McDonald's, and Pizza Huts would sprout up like weeds at every nook and corner. I would have roared with derision if you told me that the Chinese would build golf courses left and right, that the country would become the largest market in the world for Louis Vuitton handbags, that Chinese tourists would be flooding Disney World, Universal Studios, and every other popular travel site around the globe, that four out of the world's ten largest banks would be Chinese, and that the PRC would come in a close second only to the United States in terms of its percentage share of the global economy. Even the less dramatic changes in family life would have left me gaping with incredulity. In 1979, virtually no one owned their own house or apartment; almost no one had a personal or home phone or a car or a pet, and very few people were plump. Thirty years ago, it was almost unimaginable that, in today's China, millions would have their own place of residence, have a car, and that phones would be more common than fountain pens. Pets abound, and alas, so does obesity and with it diabetes. Yet looking back on our stay and reflecting on all our experiences, it is apparent that 1979 was the year the nation started to change direction, and like a boat that had been chugging slowly eastward upstream, China made a U-turn and, once caught in the westward current downstream, continued to gain speed and momentum until it transformed itself into the nation we are familiar with today.

All these very visible trappings of commercialism, materialism, and modernity are deceiving, however, especially to Americans, who are deluded into believing that somehow blue jeans, nightclubs, pop music, and fast-food chains have westernized, globalized, and Americanized the average Chinese city dweller into contemporary clones of themselves. Nothing could be further from the truth! Boats and rivers can change direction, but the water remains the same. During our year in China, from the events we witnessed, in our many travels, and through innumerable and intimate conversations with Chinese friends, we were able to discern that deep down, the spirit, character, and worldview of the people have remained, for the most part, steady and invariable, and thus the yin of change is balanced by the yang of stability, and only when both are recognized as equal and complementary forces can modern China be adequately understood and appreciated.

Since other disciplines have appropriated terminology from linguistics over the years, turnabout is fair play, and thus I choose to borrow a concept from theology to capture the essence of what we experienced that year in China and a term that simultaneously foregrounds what you are about to read. *Prolepsis* is used to describe the pre-actualization of future events, the invasion of the present by the power of what is yet to come. In a sense, it reverses the traditional view of history: rather than seeing the past as prologue, prolepsis asks us to view the future as the present. Only with hindsight have I come to realize that our year in China was not simply a remarkable and overwhelmingly significant personal encounter, the fulfillment of a lifelong ambition, it was also a proleptic experience. The events that unfolded in front of us in 1979 were almost daily manifestations of the powerful changes that would consummate in the future China that we recognize today. Consequently, with a proleptic vision that could only stem from sixty years of witnessing the ebb and flow of modern Chinese history, I now share with you memories of remarkable events and extraordinary people during the year China changed.

CHAPTER 1

千里之行，始于足下

qian li zhi xing, shi yu zu xia

A journey of a thousand *li*
begins with the first step.

I am no stranger to China. She is my birthplace, the cradle of my earliest memories, the schoolhouse of my elementary education, and the incubator of my personality. I slurped noodles with chopsticks before I became adept with knife and fork, and to this day, I prefer rice to potatoes and stir-fried chicken to a charcoal-grilled T-bone. I once spoke Chinese almost as well as English although it is much to my embarrassment as a linguist that I have lost much of the bilingual skill I once possessed. Finally and most significantly of all, I lived in large part in a Chinese world. We dwelt in comparative luxury to be sure, and our missionary family was sheltered in many ways from direct exposure to the more authentic China outside our compound, but I grew up with Chinese habits, ideas, and people. Except for our nuclear family, I lived by and large in a community of Chinese faces, and I felt so comfortable with this Asian home, despite the suffering that surrounded us, that it took many years to get used to life in America.

After completing his training in medicine, my father set out for China with my mother and their firstborn on a slow boat to serve under the Presbyterian board of foreign missions in the land of my father's childhood dreams. All but the eldest and youngest of the six of us were born in China, and during my parents' more than two decades of service there, they taught each of us to accept China as our home and to cherish the Chinese as our friends.

We lived in three different provinces: Shandong, Anhui, and Guangdong, and in each place, we were flooded by the torrents of change that spilled across the land and inundated every crevice of society during those troubled years before, during, and after World War II. We were imprisoned in a civilian internment camp by the Japanese Imperial Army. We lived in a superficially tranquil village during the postbellum conflict between the Communist and Nationalist armies. We were welcomed as true friends of China by the Party after Liberation in 1949. And finally, we were incarcerated again as American spies before our final release by the Communists in 1951.

From that time on, I had waited for an opportunity to return to my native land, but never as a tourist or casual visitor on a state-sponsored tour. I wanted the chance to return to my former homes, to renew old acquaintances, but most of all, to have the opportunity to live among the people and witness what had changed and what had remained impermeable. Most of all, I wanted to savor a life that once was and might once again still be. That opportunity came with unexpected abruptness in the form of a telephone call one Thursday evening in late October 1978 as I was eating dinner in our Pittsburgh home. It took a moment to identify the caller, the vice provost in charge of development at my university, and before I even had time to wonder why an administrator of such exalted stature was phoning a lowly assistant professor like me, the motivation for his call suddenly took me back to the land of my birth. "I've just been on the phone with the liaison office for the People's Republic of China in Washington, and they have asked me to contact you immediately to see if you are willing to go to China to teach under the auspices of the Chinese government. As far as we know," he added, "you're the first American to be officially invited back by the PRC." A phone call with a woman at the Chinese Liaison Office in Washington the next day confirmed the veracity and gist of the vice provost's call and convinced me that my aspirations to return were no longer the stuff that dreams were made of, but were a sudden and tangible reality.

The next two months were consumed by frenzied preparation: arranging for someone to rent our house, making our peace with friends, relatives, students, and colleagues, and dealing with matters momentous and miniscule. It was sixty days of letters, phone calls, weekend trips, purchasing, and packing. All of these proceedings were particularly vexed by the apparent naiveté of the liaison office and the annoying lack of details they seemed capable of providing. They were surprised to learn that I was married, had two children, and was unwilling to commit to teaching for more than a year. In those tentative early years of direct contact between the two nations, the Chinese consular staff appeared either unaware of or unconcerned with such weighty capitalistic matters as family responsibilities, contracts, mortgage payments, and professional obligations. But after learning that Janene was a certified and experienced teacher, they quickly agreed to offer her a position as well and allowed us to bring our son and daughter along for a one-year commitment. We eventually learned that we would be teaching in Tianjin, that they would pay the round-trip airfare for the four of us, and that we would receive a monthly salary on top of free accommodation. What we would teach, how much we would make, and many other details would be taken care of once we arrived in China, and I was ultimately left with an oral contract and had to trust the voice on the other end of the phone just as she, in turn, was forced to rely on my word.

Around Christmas, we were buoyed by President Carter's announcement that relations would soon be normalized between the United States of America and the People's Republic of China (PRC) and that beginning in January, the two Pacific giants would shake hands across the sea that had separated them for so long. This news gave us added momentum and publicity and, much to our children's delight, gained us notoriety in the press and appearances on radio and television.

Still, there were days of doubt; most palpable was the evening we learned that the school board for my wife's school district had voted not to grant Janene a leave of absence from her permanent teaching position in our suburban neighborhood. She eventually lost that job to accompany me to China, and bitter though that decision proved to be, it is to her credit that she never allowed this personal disappointment to quell her enthusiasm for our venture.

With brusque swiftness, preparations and farewells were completed, and we were on a 747, chasing the sun across the Pacific, and even our four-year-old daughter, Christine, knew that something strange and adventuresome was in the wind. As the plane plowed against the winter jet stream toward our ultimate destination, I thought about my parents, for when they first sailed to China in 1930, they docked at the port city of Tianjin. Now, half a century later, in a vessel far speedier than theirs, we were heading for the same destination. And when I bade farewell to my native China in 1951, I was a boy of twelve. Now, a full generation later, I was returning to China with my own twelve-year-old dozing innocently in the seat next to me. Am I recapitulating my parents' life? Is Derick my reincarnation? The circles of time were closing.

Even though China had been open to Americans ever since the Nixon-Kissinger diplomacy of the early seventies, in those early days of rapprochement, virtually all foreigners visiting China were routed through Hong Kong, both on arrival and departure. Because only a limited number of international air carriers had direct egress to China, Hong Kong was a natural point of embarkation and disembarkation since it was already a tourist mecca and a hub of international transportation. In keeping with the Chinese tradition of walls and gates, British-ruled-but-Chinese-dominated Hong Kong represented a safe and narrow gate into the People's Republic. It also struck me that our entry via Hong Kong was in keeping with traditional

Chinese cosmology, where south represents the earth and north signifies heaven. This is why you enter from the south gate when visiting the former imperial palace, the Forbidden City, in Beijing, and why the emperor's main quarters are in the northern section of those large palatial grounds. On a grander scale, it is fitting that Beijing (*bei jing*, the northern capital) dominates all of China from the north. When the Communists finally defeated their civil-war foe in 1949, they surely accomplished one of the greatest acts of one-upmanship when they made Beijing the capital, geographically and cosmologically trumping the Nationalists' capital of Nanjing (*nan jing*, the southern capital). So here we were, barbarians at the southern gates of the great people's empire, bound for Beijing, the center of power, on our way to our new home up north in Tianjin.

We spent two days celebrating the new year in the southern warmth and luxury of capitalistic Hong Kong and then, on the morning of January 7, 1979, took the short train ride north to the creek that separated the earthy British colony from the socialist heaven to the north, the land that would be our home for the next twelve months. Almost as an intentional symbol of the truncation between Mother China and its tiny pretension of an offspring to the south, occupied by a white queen and draped with the vestiges of a century of foreign imperialism, there was no direct train traffic across this border. Even though the tracks ran right over a bridge where any train could theoretically continue all the way through to the northern capital, none were allowed to cross. Every train in either direction had to stop at this bridge, and passengers lugging their baggage were forced to walk the few hundred yards to the other side, where they would board an awaiting train that continued on to either Hong Kong or Canton, the first Chinese city to the north. As our train pulled to a halt, I could hardly wait to hop out and catch sight of the bridge I had waited so long to see again, for I was never able to forget another January morning twenty-eight years before.

After a period of incarceration in a Japanese civilian concentration camp in Shandong in the early forties, my family was repatriated by the International Red Cross and eventually arrived in the United States. Immediately after the conclusion of World War II, my parents returned to their mission work in China, and after a few years in Anhui Province in the late forties, they were reassigned from Anhui and Shandong, where they had worked as medical missionaries for many years, to a Presbyterian-supported missionary hospital in Canton far to the south. In the fall of 1949, as the People's Liberation Army (PLA) swept rapidly southward, despite admonitions from the US consulate for all Americans to leave China, my parents felt called to stay and continue their work under Communist rule just as they had felt challenged to do so under the Japanese occupation.

At first we continued with our normal lives in the large hospital compound where we lived, and I can recall studying an American curriculum with my mother every morning and playing with my two younger sisters and with Chinese friends in the afternoons. In those early days after Liberation, my father even received a commendation called the Golden Fountain Pen from the local Party leadership for his service to the people as a foreign friend of China. However, the winds of change suddenly blew in a completely different direction, and as so often happens in the life of modern China, friends became enemies, and the Communist government decided not to look any longer at my parents as instruments of solidarity with China but as tools of American imperialism. Thus, because of the Chinese entry into the war that was being waged in Korea far to our north, we almost instantly became enemies of the state and were put under house arrest. Seeing that they were unable to continue their medical work, my parents appealed for our release, but week after week, their application to leave was denied.

My father and I, and sometimes my sisters, made these weekly Saturday-morning pilgrimages to the Canton police station to request permission to emigrate from the newly formed People's Republic. This was the only time we were allowed to leave our house during our incarceration, so we looked forward to these weekly strolls despite the perfunctory refusals that concluded each visit. We chose as many different routes through the city as we could without mustering undue attention, and I reveled in these rare moments to exercise and converse with my father. One January morning, while Dad was inside making his usual pro forma request, I stood outside, watching some kids my age play on the sidewalk. I remember they were breaking open rifle cartridges and pouring the gunpowder on the pavement to ignite. Each small explosion and billow of smoke was as captivating to me, the reputed enemy, as it was to my teenage counterparts. Fireworks have long been a symbol of celebration in China, and these miniature explosions turned out to be a propitious portent, for my father emerged from the station with unusual briskness. "Let's go home, Tommy. We're leaving for Hong Kong tomorrow morning."

A little before noon on Sunday, we disembarked from the train that had taken us from Canton to the border with Hong Kong, and we gathered our baggage to cross that same bridge and leave China forever. The bright crimson of the new China fluttered immediately behind us, and the multi-striped patterns of the Union Jack awaited us only one hundred yards ahead. My mother walked purposively across the bridge in front of me, flanked by my sisters and our cook, Ai Yang, who had chosen to leave China with us and who was also granted last-minute permission to emigrate to Hong Kong. My father and I fell into step behind. Except for a suitcase apiece, we had not been allowed to take any family belongings with us, and as a last act of humiliation, each of us were strip-searched just before we were to cross the bridge that would sever me forever from the land that was my home and the country that my parents had lived in for more than almost a quarter of a century.

We walked calmly without any visible signs of emotion or nervousness that I can recall, but just as they reached the border at the exact middle of the bridge, my mother and Ai Yang stopped, as if simultaneously cued by the burning in their hearts, embraced each other, and started to cry. It was a simple gesture, an expression of release, something that was half joy and half wretchedness, a moment I, as a twelve-year-old, failed to understand at the time. I only knew that it was embarrassing, and I remember running up to them and urging them to get across to the other side. "Don't let the Chinese soldiers see you," I remonstrated in the typical adolescent fear of being humiliated to the world by some inadvertent parental action. I looked back one more time at the PLA soldiers and the red flag waving above them. I remember this scene as vividly as if it had always been a snapshot in a family album. I wanted to wave good-bye, but I didn't.

Now a few days into 1979, due to air carrier limitations, we lugged a suitcase apiece for the year we were about to spend in China, the same restriction my family and I faced under very different conditions years earlier. And now my twelve-year-old son was walking next to me northward across that very bridge, following my wife and daughter, who strode purposively ahead of us. Yes, I was about to recapitulate my childhood, and the young man beside me was indeed a reincarnation of that same boy who years before had been forced into exile. Waiting patiently ahead of us was a PLA soldier standing at ease underneath the same red banner. I almost felt like waving a greeting to him, but I didn't. After twenty-eight years, I was finally coming home.

When we detrained after the relatively quick train ride to Canton, two blue-coated representatives of the *wai ban* (the foreign affairs office or members of the same) greeted us and whisked to a waiting room for a few hours before shepherding us to the airport for a flight to Beijing late that same afternoon. We were the only foreigners on the Ilyushin-62 that flew us northward, and immediately after takeoff, we were further alienated by the fact that we were about the only nonsmokers. When we landed hours later in utter darkness at the old Beijing airport, we were exhausted from a long day of traveling and were thoroughly fumigated by cigarette smoke. The plane appeared to have stopped in the middle of the dark runway, so we had to hike toward the dim outlines of an almost deserted terminal. Our fellow travelers rushed ahead to where the baggage handlers would eventually disgorge our suitcases, but since we were foreigners and still in a restricted area, we couldn't be greeted until we had our passports and visa checked and our luggage cleared. Because of this, we were left on our own, smoky and tired in a dimly lit airport on a dark and dismally cold night in an alien land.

The first job was to retrieve our suitcases from the pile of luggage that was eventually dumped in a shed nearby. Along with the other passengers, we scrambled up and around the pile, tugging at various suitcases to extricate our own. This was the first of many moments of culture shock that greeted us in the early weeks of our Chinese tenure, and it felt particularly odd for me to experience these feelings, for I was the one who was born and bred into this culture. So why was I so abruptly and so easily alienated by these experiences? The next step was to negotiate customs and immigration, and since our fellow fliers were all Chinese, and most probably all bureaucrats, they had long since hauled their luggage through the security barrier that separated us from the waiting area. Despite the fact we had already had our papers cleared earlier that day when we arrived in Canton, we finally completed yet another official scrutiny and decided to change some money before heading out to the dark bodies that were pressing against the security barrier.

The attempt to exchange money triggered another unexpected clash of cultures, and this time, it wasn't a collision between my American expectations and Chinese customs but between the latter and another Asian culture with which we had become comfortably familiar. When arranging our air tickets a month earlier back in Pittsburgh, we decided to use the trip to China to include a brief visit to Thailand, our previous home for seven years and the birthplace of our two children. At our own expense, we augmented our itinerary by spending four days right after celebrating Christmas in the States visiting friends in Thailand and basking in the warm hospitality for which that small kingdom is renowned. So my second culture-shock encounter was not a contrast with any American expectations but with my many experiences with the Thai, especially with the way they handle money.

Politeness counts in Thailand, and encounters with money are traditionally treated with almost reverential respect. Along with the requisite pleases and thank-yous, any substantial amount of cash is given in the same manner Thais proffer gifts: carefully with both hands or with the right hand as the left hand touches the right elbow of the extended arm. After being reacculturated to this most civil practice the previous week, imagine my astonishment when, after finally extracting the Chinese money changer's attention from her newspaper and giving her some US greenbacks to exchange, she rapidly counted up the appropriate amount in Chinese currency and tossed the bills across the counter to me with an abrupt "*Gei ni* [give you]." Perhaps it was a combination of the fatigue of the travel, the bitter, dark cold of that northern night, or the discomfort of the crowded, smoky flight, but I almost succumbed to animalistic outrage at the "insult" she had just hurled at me. Naturally, of all people, she was the least cognizant of my reaction and would, had I lost my temper, have been the most surprised and aggrieved. She had already returned to her evening paper, ignorant of the cultural wound she had scratched into the memory of one overly sensitive American. But it was time to move on, and walking to the security barrier and being the only passengers left and certainly the only foreigners arriving at the Beijing metropolitan airport that January night, it was readily apparent to us that the few figures that remained behind the security barrier represented our welcome party.

About half a dozen people eagerly greeted us, and bundled in dark clothing in that dimly lit waiting hall, it was hard even to tell the sexes apart. Several wrestled the heavy suitcases from us, and handshakes were extended all around and multiple "*Huanying, huanying* [welcome, welcome]" accompanied each handclasp. We were later able to determine that our welcoming committee consisted of at least two different bureaucracies: representatives of the wai ban of the local university—to which we were assigned and who had traveled from Tianjin to meet us—and the Foreign Experts Bureau of the state (national) council, whose office was located right there in Beijing. Because some of the officials who awaited our arrival were able to speak English, we were also peppered with polite inquiries about our flight, but we quickly heard a phrase that would pervade the conclusion of every journey, meal, or day we were to experience for the forthcoming year: "You must be tired." So frequent was this expression that we started to doubt its normal pragmatic usage in English as a polite expression of empathy inferring fatigue and began to suspect that our Chinese hosts really meant that we had no alternative but to feel completely exhausted. Be that as it may, we needed no enjoining: all four of us were truly, genuinely, and authentically bushed!

The long ride to the city was memorable in several ways. First, there was the splitting up of our family into separate cars barely before the introductory greetings ended, an event that was especially disconcerting to Janene. Years before, during our first ever visit to a Communist country when I was invited to attend an international congress of linguists in Bucharest, a Romanian official came to our hotel room to announce that I was to accompany her, stranding my wife and our infant son alone and wary on their very first morning behind the Iron Curtain. The last Janene saw of me as she peeked out the hotel window, I was being whisked away in a black sedan down the nearly empty boulevard. Since our passports had already been confiscated the night before when we checked in, Janene was bereft of arguably the two most valuable possessions any traveler to a far-off land treasures (although not necessarily in this order): her spouse and her passport. Hours later, another official came to take her to the auditorium where the opening ceremonies were convened and where she and I were eventually reunited during a reception. But her leeriness about socialist states was dissipated by the assurance that here on our first night behind the Bamboo Curtain, we were all headed to the same destination and that she and the kids would be accompanied by the entire English-speaking wai ban.

The second impression I have of that trip to city center was the ride itself. It wasn't because there was excessive speed or unholy traffic, two features that make a taxi ride from many foreign airports a nail-biting, gut-wrenching, endorphin-elevating near-death experience. Indeed, there was almost no traffic at that hour as the drivers of both cars sped down the pitch-black, tree-lined, two-lane highway that at that time was the major thoroughfare linking the international airport with Beijing. Except for a few lights winking here and there in the darkness on either side and a sporadic vehicle or two, the only other thing visible were the dim outlines of the trees whizzing by on either side for the first five feet or so of their trunks were whitewashed as if to encourage our drivers to hug the middle of the road. The darkness in itself was not frightening, it was the fact that both cars were speeding along with just their parking lights on and only with seeming reluctance would either driver switch on their headlights when they anticipated or imagined that something loomed in the road ahead. When pressed for a reason why Chinese chauffeurs drove like owls, the response that seemed to satisfy our new wai ban friends but left us even more puzzled was that the drivers knew what they were doing and were trying not to waste electricity.

The third memory I have of the final leg of that long day's journey into night was that I was chosen to sit in the monolingual car and was expected to wax eloquent in Chinese the ride in, hence the separation from my family. Because our hosts had been given some information about my background, they knew that I was born and raised in China and also had secured a doctorate in linguistics, so they logically assumed I was not only fluent in Chinese but comfortable in discussing adult topics such as academic and international affairs. Alas, they were hopelessly mistaken on both counts! For one thing, due to various factors, such as moving from China to India during my high school years and much later living seven years in Thailand, where my fluency in Thai quickly superseded my ability in Chinese, the language that was once nearly my mother tongue was greatly eroded by time and circumstance. In addition, despite my academic training and profession, I am not an exceptional language learner as evidenced by the fact that I was the only student in my American college who managed to fail the same second year French course three times in a row! Another problem I faced was what little Chinese I could extract from the white matter of my overly exhausted central nervous system was the Mandarin I knew as a little boy, and this proved to be a double curse. On the one hand, my pronunciation was excellent since I could rely on that early nurturing, but my vocabulary and grammar were exceedingly limited, both in amount and in terms of social appropriateness.

Initially deceived by my glib and ready use of Chinese chitchat, my interlocutors immediately began bombarding me with questions and topics, which rapidly exceeded my ken, and to the dismay of both parties in this peculiar colloquy, the conversation began to degenerate, and my stock started to plummet. I recall desperately trying to steer the conversation into a linguistic and topical area that I could manage. I remember when asked what the weather was like back in Pittsburgh, I seized upon a comparative pattern in Mandarin that I could still master and began bantering that "Beijing is colder than Pittsburgh, and Pittsburgh is warmer than Beijing. And Pittsburgh is smaller than Beijing, and Beijing is bigger than Pittsburgh, etc." By this time, we had already been on the road a good half hour, so I prayed that we were almost at our destination or that we might plow into an unlighted truck full of hay. But there was no such luck as the ride from the airport took over an hour, and traffic continued to be minimal. Gradually, the questioning ceased, my drivel died off, and we rode the rest of the way in embarrassed intercultural silence. I wondered if the wai ban bureaucrats sharing my ride were beginning to question the wisdom of recruiting and paying for this "foreign expert," who seemed to grow more foreign and less expert as each kilometer rolled by.

We skirted the northern edge of the city and entered the western side although Beijing itself was not much brighter than the suburbs we had been traversing. Streetlights were dim, and few lights dotted the dark windows in the monotonous rows of multistory buildings that lay block after block behind tall stone walls. Our cars slowed down and turned to wheel past the gates and ever-present gateman of one of these compounds. As we were to discover the next morning, we were guests of the Friendship Hotel, home to most of the foreign experts working in Beijing, a virtual village within that large city, and our accommodations for our first week in China. Done in by the day's odyssey, all four of us were delighted to know we could finally bed down for the night, and at that point, we would have slept as soundly on a traditional stone peasant bed as on the finest eiderdown.

But wait, whatever their station, no guests to China would be so rudely treated as to be sent straight off to their quarters without the obligatory warm-welcome feast. Thus, we were escorted up the steps of the main dining hall, ushered into the lighted corner of an otherwise dark, cavernous, and empty room, and at an hour much closer to midnight than suppertime, we were subjected to a multicourse Mandarin banquet. Again, we were separated, each car getting its own table, so Janene and I couldn't commiserate directly with one another, but fortunately, with all the food I was pretending to eat and enjoy, I didn't have to make much small talk. Looking around at my tablemates and my family and hosts seated nearby, I stumbled on a revelation that would grow in magnitude throughout our stay. It was no accident that Janene's car and table had the English speakers while I drew the monolingual contingent: the Tianjin wai ban and interpreters were with her while the Beijing administrators and other higher ups were with me. It was also no accident that the Chinese considered me the central player of that evening's drama and Janene (and certainly the kids) the supporting cast. So everyone was not equal in the People's Republic, and one of the old sayings that my parents had learned long before Liberation seemed to hold true even for this new socialist society: "The husband sings, and the wife follows." But along with this generalization, I also observed among my seatmates something contradictory but equally revelatory. The drivers of both cars were not only invited to sit with us, their ostensible bosses at both tables were overtly solicitous in serving them the choicest morsels from each dish and were anxious to ensure that their plates and bowls were full and that they had a constant supply of beer and *mao tai* (distilled rice liquor). At first, I suspected that the drivers were being lavished this attention as a reward for driving in the pitch-dark for an hour without getting any of us killed, but this practice was repeated again and again during our sojourn in China, and it quickly became obvious that in a reversal of traditional Chinese social values, academics and bureaucrats did not rank high in the socialist pecking order compared to workers, and though they did little work, chauffeurs definitely deserved a seat at any banquet table. Finally, in the waning moments of that long winter night, the feasting ended, and at that point, even our Chinese hosts seemed ready to hit the sack. We were escorted to another dark building, up a flight of stairs to two cozy rooms with drab décor, but most importantly, to beds with blankets and a place where all four of us could collapse into rapid and merciful unconsciousness.

The Friendship Hotel was much more than a hotel and more like a city within a city, a state of mind within a state, an anachronistic legacy of Soviet internationalism. Years after our China experience, when Janene and I spent part of a summer at an educational institute in Bratislava, the capital of the then new nation of Slovakia, we were told on our arrival that all of us foreigners would be lodged at the Druzba Dormitory during our stay. The institute staff was surprised when I immediately guessed that Druzba must mean friendship even though I knew not a word of Slovakian. However, the way we foreigners were immediately sequestered together in a hospitable but clearly controlled manner evoked memories of that first week in Beijing back in 1979. Our new and temporary domicile was a giant quadrilateral, squared by walls approximately half a mile long on each side, and housing five large, multistoried apartment buildings and an even larger central edifice, where an auditorium, dining halls, and other facilities were located. Like a self-contained village, the Friendship Hotel boasted a dispensary, library, theater, swimming pool, small store, gymnasium, bank, post office, garage, barbershop, and several offices, including the Foreign Experts Bureau. Being a city within a city, superficially it resembled the fabled palace of former emperors, the famous Forbidden City, located in downtown Beijing several miles to the southeast of us. Like the emperor's family, we foreigners were viewed as a unique species and were well protected from facile contact with the general public by the surrounding walls, well-monitored front gate, and overly protective staff. But there, all similarities ended. For one thing, although it was a square within the traditional squared city of Beijing, the Friendship Hotel did not square with traditional Chinese cosmology. The main gate faced east, and hence, its central access and axis was east-west and not north-south. Further, our status as foreign experts was naturally far less exalted than that of the emperor and, truth be told, much more similar to the former court eunuchs.

In the early 1950s, during the heyday of PRC-USSR partnership, a great many Soviet specialists were invited to China to help in the construction of a new socialist state and in the reconstruction of a nation that had been devastated by the anti-Japan war and the subsequent civil strife with the Nationalists. The Friendship Hotel in Beijing, as well as many other similar places around the country, was erected to house all the Russian and Soviet bloc teachers, engineers, technicians, and bureaucrats who had come as foreign experts. Although the tiled roofs and gently curving eaves gave these buildings a distinctly Chinese look, the dull blocks of apartments and even duller atmosphere that seemed to perfuse the entire campus betrayed the stolid influence of Soviet urban architecture. Although the residents could go and come each day, this place was neither a tourist hotel nor an ordinary apartment building. All traffic out of and into that main gate was well monitored, and most of the time, the foreign guests as well as the Chinese who worked within the walls were ferried to and fro by specific vehicles to specific destinations and only for specific and official purposes.

It all reminded me of the USSR embassy just up the street from where we once lived in Bangkok, when Janene and I were teaching in Thailand in the mid-sixties. The embassy had a high and aptly colored red wall behind which peeked an inordinately large number of radio antennae and transmitters and was fronted by a semicircular driveway into two front gates marked Entrance and Exit in Thai. The first half of the driveway and entrance gate were well swept and obviously well used, but the other half of the driveway and exit gate had been long covered with leaves and debris and obviously had not seen any traffic for many a moon. The entrance gate was open every day; the exit gate had remained locked for years. I always thought that this was a fitting metaphor for what I imagined transpired during those hot days of the Cold

War: people, ideas, and information easily immigrated into the Soviet Empire, but only rarely did they manage to emigrate back into the free world. I had a similar feeling about our temporary residence in Beijing. The Friendship Hotel was built not so much to forge friendships as it was to keep us in and the Chinese out.

If you can only make a first impression one time and if this claim is accurate for people, it certainly is equally true for places. The events during those first few days in China's capital had a considerable impact on us, for we were highly impressionable. Although I had never been there before, Beijing seemed to evoke deep, perhaps subliminal memories harking back to Jining, the northern city where I was born and raised. Dark browns, ochers, and grays painted all the streets, walls, buildings, and leafless trees. Sunlight could barely suffuse through the cloudy, slate skies, and in the dry cold of that northern winter, no snow softened this daylight gloom with splashes of brightness. And since these were the shortest days of the year, darkness predominated, and even an Andrew Wyeth portrait would be a riot of color in contrast. As the days progressed and the longer we stayed, our eyes started to adjust to a wider spectrum, and we noticed, for instance, that though most people were dressed in uniformly dark blue, some were clothed in gray, and the ubiquitous soldiers stood out in almost glaring khaki olive.

Another impression was the way people flooded almost every available space during the day: bicycles crowded the streets, sidewalks spilled pedestrians, and stores and offices sheltered throngs from the cold. Again a childhood memory came to mind, although this one was very clear and specific. With no radio, TV, movies, and certainly with none of the electronic entertainment that is now at the fingers and thumbs of young people, during our Chinese childhood, my siblings and I grew up largely in a world of play and books, and one of the latter that I remember vividly was a yellow-jacketed edition of *Ripley's Believe It or Not*. Among depictions and descriptions of such oddities, as a cylinder of steel penetrating Phineas Gage's skull, was a picture of a horde of grim-faced Chinese coolies marching with inexorable resolution like human lemmings. "If all the Chinese in the world were to march four abreast past a given point," the caption read, "they would never finish passing though they marched forever and ever." Irrespective of the dubious veracity and the covert racism of this claim, China never seemed to be terribly crowded to me as a child except for the packed trains, but Beijing was teeming everywhere we looked.

Any mention of Beijing invariably invokes a gripe I have about the way Americans speak about Beijing, specifically the way they pronounce the name of China's capital city. This mispronunciation was especially conspicuous during the 2008 Olympics, when broadcasters and laypeople alike misspoke the name incessantly. Forget the tones and focus solely on one consonant. *Peking* is an Anglicization of the Chinese name and is about as different from the indigenous pronunciations of Munich or Bangkok from how these cities are pronounced in German or Thai. Such articulatory latitude is common and understandable, so I have no quarrel with "Peeking." For reasons I find unfathomable however, Americans have taken up the fashion of calling the city "Bay Zhing" instead of "Bay Jing." That is, instead of a *j*, as in *jingle*, they use a consonant borrowed from French—*zh*, as in the final consonant of *rouge*. I might seem overly peevish and pedantic about this, but I cannot understand why my fellow English speakers replace a sound that is found in *both* Chinese and English with a sound that is *not* found in Chinese, and all this in an attempt to make "Beijing" sound *more* Chinese! Maybe in the cultural mind-set of most Americans, France and French are the default representatives of anything foreign or exotic, and this is why the French consonant gives the pronunciation of the Chinese capital a certain panache.

Within a few hours of our first morning at the Friendship Hotel, we were already meeting other foreigners, and quite naturally, they were eager to share some of their cross-cultural acumen with those of us who were fresh and naïve arrivals, especially since in early 1979, there were very few American foreign experts in China. One new acquaintance who has since become a lifelong family friend was Karel, a bright bundle of words, ideas, and energy, who escaped from his native Czechoslovakia during the not-so-velvet revolution against the Soviet invasion in the sixties and now was working as a foreign expert for Beijing Radio. We had barely finished breakfast in the large dining hall our second morning when Karel grabbed me and, mentioning something about my being a linguist not wanting to miss getting one of these, hustled me across the campus to the bookstore. There was already a scrum of people crowding the counter where purchases were made, but with seeming lack of respect for queues, Chinese, or decorum, he wedged himself and me into the front of this anxious crowd. "How many do you want?" he half yelled at me as he prepared to place his order. I struggled to get some cash out of my pockets all the while trying to discover what rare commodity I and all the others were fighting to purchase. Finding out that they were dictionaries, I ordered a half dozen, thinking of my future Chinese colleagues and linguist friends in the States who would especially appreciate this obviously popular edition. After our purchases were complete and we were finally free of the crowd, I saw that I was now the proud owner of *A Chinese-English Dictionary*, recently compiled and published by the Beijing Foreign Languages Institute after years of research. It served us well not only during that year in China but in the decades since, and I never reach for that olive-green volume without thinking of the spontaneous burst of speed-shopping that accompanied its acquisition.

I acquired much more than a valuable linguistic reference, however. Karel's ability to respond quickly to a rumor and to sniff out a crowd was something we also gradually learned to employ. Back then, there were no advertisements, virtually no commercialism, and the more important the news was, the more it seemed to be hidden from the masses. That "Black Friday" sprint for the bookstore during our first few days in Beijing was, therefore, a conditioned response to the environment that existed in China as well as in most other Communist countries at that time. If you ever see people queuing up anywhere anytime, jump into line first then try to find out what you're in line for. The dictionary was sold out by that afternoon, and I never recall ever seeing another copy for sale anywhere in China after my lucky morning with Karel. *Carpe dictionarium!*

Our second day turned out to be a series of ever more intriguing experiences and exemplified one of Janene's favorite aphorisms about living in Asia: Each day is different. We were taken to see the second most coveted tourist site in Northern China, the Forbidden City, the former imperial palace and home to the emperors of the Qing dynasty. Entering through the south gate on that bitterly cold January morning, we felt like the frozen chosen as the palace grounds were virtually deserted. It would've been almost impossible for us to believe that in the not-too-distant future, this site would be packed with tourists, foreign and domestic, and that all the dilapidated, unpainted structures would be restored to colorful grandeur, attracting the admiration of all foreign visitors and national pride from the Chinese themselves. But on that January morning, however fabled the palace was historically, we were surprised to see chipped bricks and tiles strewn about and weeds growing with abandon, and the predominant memory the four of us had of the visit was of the cold. In fact, Christine, who already had a cough from the dry air, complained enough for Janene, who was bone-chilled as well, to rush ahead to the northern exit and wait for us in the warmth of the car. Fortunately, we had a chance later in the year to return in the summer and enjoy a much more leisurely, informative, and distinctly warmer tour.

That afternoon, we were driven eastward down the city's broadest boulevard, Chang An Avenue, to the embassy district, where we informally registered at the United States Liaison Office. Because diplomatic recognition between the two nations was still in process, like its Chinese counterpart in Washington, this was neither an embassy nor a consulate, and the small facility cluttered with boxes and furniture was clearly a place in transition. There my status as the son of "old China hands" came into play, for despite the fact we walked in unannounced and had no connections at all with the US government, the chargé d'affaires, Stapleton Roy, gave us a friendly greeting and graciously invited us to his home for dinner later in the week. Like me, Stape was China bred, his parents having served under the same Presbyterian board of foreign missions as mine, and because he attended the brother school of my sister's boarding school in Massachusetts, he even remembered she sang in *Patience*. Both he and I were then old China hands in both senses of the term. We had grown up, lived in, and had affection for the pre-Liberation years of old China, and since virtually no Americans had been living in the People's Republic of China for a full generation, our hands and bodies were certainly no longer youthful. Not being a China watcher or someone with professional interest in Chinese-American affairs, I didn't realize that even back then, there was a near cottage industry of American Sinologists, which would eventually burgeon into a commercial enterprise. For instance, there is now the Old China Hand Press devoted to the production of volumes written by, about, and for the Roys and the Scovels of this world. Little did we appreciate on that busy afternoon what an important contact Stape would become for he was especially helpful in supplying us with materials from the embassy after it opened and in helping us at the end of our stay when we had trouble booking a flight home. The alliance worked for him as well since our presence in nearby Tianjin allowed him to pay an unofficial visit to a place outside of the capital later in the year.

In April, after we had been living in Tianjin for several months, on a return trip to Beijing, we decided to pay a visit to the Royal Thai Embassy because Christine, our adopted Thai daughter, carried a Thai passport and, unlike the other members of our family, could not be registered with the Americans. Even though Thailand already enjoyed full status as an embassy, their consulate was tiny compared to the US liaison office that we saw during that first week; furthermore, our visit completely surprised the tiny staff. They were shocked to find two white foreigners speaking fluent Thai and even more astounded when these strangers displayed a four-year-old Thai girl and asked if she could be registered with them for her one-year stay in China. After several minutes of trying to find an appropriate sheet of paper to log in her name, passport number, and place of residence in the PRC, they admitted that she was the first Thai citizen to officially register with the embassy. Our family thus became binational and bicultural representatives to China that year.

Later, we discovered that there were Thais living in China, even right there in Beijing, but these were the few dissidents who had fled Thailand largely for political reasons and were working directly or indirectly to support the cause of international Communism. Once, on a visit to Beijing Radio, I met a Thai who was helping to produce anti-American, anti-Thai government broadcasts to Thailand, and we had a pleasant conversation even though I was a symbol of the very imperialistic forces he was regaling his far-off countrymen against. The most enduring memory I have of that meeting was trying to get the conversation started in Thai. It was still winter, and we were bundled up against the Beijing cold, and the context and environment were so alien to the colorful, affable warmth of Thailand and her people, it took me several minutes to overcome the strong tendency to speak in Chinese. Once our conversation got rolling, however, we both enjoyed that rare opportunity to converse in a language we knew well but which was distinctly foreign to those we lived and worked with.

We found out we were in for a big surprise the evening of our second day after our return to the now more familiar confines of the Friendship Hotel. As we were to learn after we had become more accustomed to our new life, the Chinese were not great about letting you know what was about to happen. In that hazy ride from the airport a few days earlier, I vaguely remember even vaguer details about what we would do in Beijing: a week of sightseeing, a visit to the Foreign Experts Bureau, and then finally, a train ride to Tianjin, our home for the coming year. There was no mention of a gala celebration in the Great Hall of the People and schmoozing with a famous astronaut. Late in the afternoon, after we had returned from touring the former imperial palace, one of the wai ban came to our room to tell us that we were invited to a banquet that evening to celebrate the official signing of the restoration of full diplomatic relations between the PRC and the USA, the culmination of the work that began with the visits by the Nixon-Kissinger team earlier that decade. This reception would take place in the Great Hall of the People, a holy of holies in modern Chinese history and a place where only the chosen are allowed to enter or be entertained. During our frenzied preparations back in Pittsburgh, we had anticipated dressing for the bitter cold and the humid heat, but knowing that bourgeoisie clothing was not appreciated in the People's Republic, we had not brought any formal wear. Sensing that this was a rare event, the four of us dressed up as best we could and hopped downstairs to wait for a minibus with the few other Americans who had been tapped for this singular occasion.

We were driven to Tiananmen Square at the very heart of the city, where we disembarked at the steps of our imposing destination. True to its name, the reception was a great hall filled with round tables and, with the exception of an occasional foreign figure, bevies of Chinese cadres. This word quickly became common parlance in the English we heard throughout our stay in China, but when we first heard it spoken, we were a bit confused because the Chinese pronounced it "carter," flip-flopping the medial consonant cluster. So why did Chinese bureaucrats share the same name as our current American president, we wondered. The four of us sat down at an assigned table on the periphery of the assembled host of more important guests and munched on nuts and tasted a variety of drinks, the quality of these a cut above the fare provided us at the Friendship Hotel. For the first hour or so, there was a lot of small talk and milling around, and since we were seated close-by, at first we enjoyed watching and listening to the PLA band playing background music. We couldn't identify most of the marches and other pieces they presented, but all four of us recognized the American music they played in honor of the occasion. No, they weren't Sousa marches but enduring folk ballads like "Turkey in the Straw" and "Home on the Range."

Noticing that several people were using this time to leave their tables to greet other guests, Janene and I got up and moved toward the front and center of the hall to see if we could meet some of the visiting American dignitaries. When we got closer, among the four US senators present, we instantly recognized John Glenn, our most famous astronaut and the well-known senator from Ohio, Janene's home state. Partly due to his friendliness but largely because she was the only one of his constituents living in China, the two of them chatted amiably, and he seemed to enjoy finding out about and meeting her as she him. Seizing the opportunity, I started talking to one of the younger-looking cadres in a well-pressed, gray suit standing nearby. Genial and quietly impressive, he turned out to be the newly appointed mayor of Beijing. I wondered how effective he would be and how long he would last. I also was intrigued by the contrast between the status of the two politicians we were conversing with. Although Senator Glenn won his elections quite easily, how much more he would probably have appreciated the Democrats simply appointing him to represent Ohio, assuming, of course, it was the only party in the United States and in complete control of every aspect of national life. In contrast, how much this Chinese cadre would lament the task of actually running for his office, scrutinized by a free press, pandering to countless constituents for money, kissing squirming babies, giving ceaseless strings of speeches, and shaking an unending parade of hands coming at him in waves, four abreast at a time.

We went back to our table to banquet on a buffet of Chinese delicacies, all of which were among the most exquisite dishes we were to taste that year and any one of which we would have gladly chosen over the many monotonous and tasteless meals that would be fed to us in Tianjin that winter. Once again, we returned to our rooms at the Friendship Hotel late at night overfed and exhausted, but this time, we were starting to feel comfortable with our new surroundings. What a day! From a morning tour of the home of former emperors to an excursion to America (at least via their diplomatic sovereignty) to an evening reception honoring contemporary leaders; truly, this day was different.

Our worldviews trigger the first and most salient symbols that spring to mind when we think about countries and cultures other than our own. For many of the Chinese we met during that year, America was first and foremost the Golden Gate Bridge and Niagara Falls. I could certainly understand the first image for, after all, tens of thousands of Chinese had emigrated to the United States beginning with the Gold Rush and the bridge is emblematic of San Francisco, the west coast port through which most of these immigrants arrived. But Niagara Falls? Perhaps because the latter predates the former geologically and culturally and thus was one of the natural wonders early American missionaries talked and taught about during their two centuries of work in the hundreds of mission schools scattered throughout China. Conversely, whenever Americans are asked to conjure up images of the Middle Kingdom, the most enduring and spontaneous symbol is the Great Wall. And again, for Americans, at least for most of the nineteenth and twentieth centuries, accounts of this grand edifice were certainly part of the lore about the Middle Kingdom shared by thousands of China missionaries on their return to the United States. Ironically, as a kid growing up in Jining, the Great Wall was as much an exotic destination for me as it was for my American compatriots an ocean away, and like so many other people around the globe, to see it in person was a cherished and lifelong dream. Naturally, this dream was shared by my American-born wife and our two Thai-born children, so all four of us were excited the morning we were to visit this world marvel. Knowing that the day's excursion would be spent outside in the bracing cold, we bundled up after breakfast in our warmest clothes, including long johns, one of our wisest predeparture purchases back in Pittsburgh. We then clambered into a large, black Russian-built sedan, which had two jump seats to accommodate all the overdressed bodies. Besides our family and the driver, Lao Shen and Xiao Hu also accompanied us since they served as our constant companions in all activities that week in Beijing. They represented our home institute's wai ban in Tianjin and were our guides, translators, and new compadres.

Shen was the head of our institute's wai ban and, naturally, was older and male. He looked in his midforties and had a ready smile and gestured easily, and since he spoke almost no English, his constant flood of Mandarin, often backed up by Hu's heavily accented English translations, was a boon for resurrecting and enhancing my latent knowledge of the language. Throughout our stay in Tianjin, he remained a solid help and steady companion although we didn't quite realize during that first week of affable sightseeing together in Beijing that he was one of several bosses that would dictate what we could and could not do. Like the majority of men we were to encounter that year, he enjoyed his cigarettes. Hu was his assistant and was naturally younger and female. Like most of the unmarried women of that era, she wore long pigtails, and these made her look more like a teenager than a recent graduate of the institute. She was slightly bug-eyed, which when compounded with her natural enthusiasm for a week's vacation of sightseeing in the capital city (all on the wai ban's expense account) made her appear to gush with excitement during our jaunts together.

The titles *lao* and *xiao* were telling. First of all, in a society that had just been pretty well stripped of all superficial class distinctions by the Great Proletarian Cultural Revolution, it was surprising that any titles were used at all. *Tongzhi* (comrade) was the default and omnipresent appellation positioned after the surname, so it wasn't incorrect or uncommon to refer to our fellow travelers as Shen *tongzhi* and Hu *tongzhi*. Nevertheless, they referred to each other with Lao Shen and Xiao Hu, and these traditional titles peppered all the conversations and speeches that caught our ears. It intrigued me that fragments of the traditional, Confucian culture in which I was raised had survived the vicious onslaughts against this very heritage launched by the just-concluded Cultural Revolution, which, after all, was against the Four Olds. As an American, I was similarly fascinated by the contrast between the typical American distaste for the aging process with this transparent and venerable respect for age in China. *Lao* means old, and *xiao* literally means little, thus young. And if you are still uncertain which title has higher status in Chinese culture, simply remember that Chen was the man and Hu was the woman, *small*—as in cute and feminine. Again, there were early hints that all comrades were not created equal in the People's Republic.

During that first week in Beijing, we were absorbing and accumulating large amounts of information and were acclimating and assimilating to our new environment, but in large part, all this transpired without our being directly aware of the process. Only with hindsight did we begin to appreciate how much we had been learning and how much we had been acculturating. Take Chen and Hu's weeklong presence with us for instance.

Officially and in reality, they were there to greet us, help us with our initial needs, and act as our tour guides as we adjusted to the time, climate, and culture of our new environment. While this was all true, we began to sense that our new friends were getting as much out of the wai ban expense account as we were. After all, they were there for all the banquets, sightseeing, and excitement, and it appeared that, at least for Hu, this was her first time in Beijing, and by the time of our arrival in Tianjin a few days later, Hu started to play a minor role in any of our affairs with the wai ban and was replaced by a young man. As for Chen, who obviously had visited Beijing many times and had met several foreign experts before us, wouldn't it have been a tad dull and repetitious to carry out this weeklong assignment once again, especially in the dead of winter? Perhaps not, considering the companion he had chosen for this trip away from the knowing eyes at work and home. Whatever might have transpired or not, what happened in Beijing stayed in Beijing.

But warmed by the thickly layered bodies in the car, despite our many differences, all of us were united in our excitement to see the Great Wall that January morning. The two-hour drive itself was worthwhile as it afforded us the first glimpses of the countryside. We motored past donkey- and horse-drawn carts with truck wheels bearing their loads just as I had seen as a boy. Our route was checkered by brown fields and gray villages, the latter filled with well-dressed peasant families and small outdoor markets. Our kids got a kick out of seeing toddlers suddenly squatting down and peeing through the slits conveniently placed in the crotch of their trousers. Manual labor dominated the landscape: men and women digging into the frozen ground with heavy pickaxes, pulling heavy loads with the aid of straw shoulder harnesses, loading or unloading carts and trucks with their bare hands. This was a very different place and people from what we had been seeing the previous five days. No soft, effete, long-finger-nailed hands out here. No, here was the real China of calluses as hard as the rocks they lifted; here were the workers but alas not their paradise.

But if the journey was worthwhile, the destination was doubly so, and except for a few other tourists that wintery Wednesday, we had the Great Wall pretty much to ourselves. Away from the coal dust and smog of Beijing and aided by a brisk wind from the north, we reveled in an absolutely gorgeous day: bright sun, a clear azure sky, and the wall winding up and down in front as if inviting us to stretch our legs for as long as the cold would allow. It was an amazing experience, especially since there were so few people and virtually no commercialism, and we could hardly believe that we had been in China less than a week and already were enjoying its most iconic monument.

Like any world wonder, several myths should be unpackaged about this edifice. The Chinese call it *chang cheng*, the long wall, or to be more specific, the long city wall. Most towns and cities had walls until the founding of the PRC, so the Great Wall was constructed to separate all of these from the barbarians to the north. Even though the Communists were responsible for tearing down almost all these walls after Liberation, not much of the Great Wall remained, and what was left was not destroyed but even refurbished in some places like it had been at the site of our visit. It stood proudly as a national symbol: "The People's Liberation Army is China's great wall of steel." It was beyond the wildest realms of our most vivid imagination to guess that decades later, a "Great Wall of China" would be built in cyberspace and, unlike its historical predecessor, would stand as an almost impervious barrier to any barbarian attack! The wall was never as long as the US-Canadian border as some have imagined, but more like half that length. It isn't now and never was a great wall, but mostly a series of connected walls, but since Chinese do not mark singulars or plurals, *chang cheng* can be conveniently interpreted either way, and certainly the image of one tall continuous barricade of stone punctuated by watchtowers snaking up and down mountains is much more impressive than one of a series of walls scattered helter-skelter across the northern landscape. I've also heard the claim that the Great Wall is the only unlit man-made edifice that astronauts can see with the unaided eye from space. If this is true, what happened to the Suez and Panama Canals? Maybe this claim holds up if we define man-made as made exclusively by human hands, like those of all the manual workers we saw on our drive up. The bulk of the making was done two centuries before Christ by Emperor Huang Shi-Di, who had a short but influential reign. However, it could be argued that his even greater legacy is the fact that he was the one who founded the Qin (Chin) dynasty from which Europeans derived the name of his empire, the name that we still use for this great nation to this very day.

Despite our best winter clothing, after an hour or so of clambering about in the cold, we had lost all sensation in our extremities, so we retreated to the hospitality of a waiting room warmed by a woodstove. There we lunched on the sandwiches prepared ahead of time by the hotel and that left our Chinese comrades singularly unimpressed with the dry bread and even drier meat of this American picnic. We assured them that we found the food equally unappetizing. Our afternoon destination was the Ming Tombs, which were built much more recently than the wall in a much more modern era of Chinese history, about the time Columbus discovered America. We approached these mausoleums down a long corridor of animal statuary that led to a palatial valley of the dead where thirteen emperors had been entombed. There we toured a deep crypt and unguarded rooms filled with magnificent collections of gold headdresses and ornaments, ancient coins, and precious stones rivaling any pharaoh's tomb. All of this was imposing indeed, but the sites failed to compel our attention like the Great Wall, and because they involved an even longer trek outdoors on that cold afternoon, they were a denouement to our climatic morning tour. Once again, we returned to the warmth of our car for the drive back to the city. Of the many events we experienced that year, that early opportunity to see the Great Wall of China shines brightly in our collective memory, and for me especially, it was an enduring moment. It was my fortieth birthday.

We spent three more days in Beijing, but they began to feel anticlimactic. Either it had increased or we were more affected by it, but the smog seemed to worsen, a particularly virulent winter version of the seasonal stuff that envelops Beijing for the majority of the year. Our previous days of sightseeing had taken us back into the Ming and Qing dynasties, literally the eras of bright and clear, but the skies in contemporary, postimperial China were neither. Bituminous coal is the winter fuel that cooks the meals and warms the homes of almost all Chinese in the north, and it leaves a brownish, darkish haze that is only compounded by the emissions from the many factories surrounding every city. When there is precipitation, it is only a slight exaggeration to say that it comes in the form of acid rain or coal flakes, and probably because we had now been exposed to this pollution for several days, our throats were sore, and since she wore contacts, Janene's eyes were growing more and more irritated.

There was more sightseeing: Zhou Enlai's memorial, the Chinese History Museum, the Temple of Heaven, and a visit to the Institute of National Minorities. At the first site, we began to become aware of the degree to which Premier Zhou had been lionized and to foresee the manner in which, in some ways, he played the good cop to Mao's bad. The history museum was depressingly dull especially when compared to the Palace Museum in Taipei that has been filled with the best Chinese antiquities preserved/stolen by the Nationalists when they retreated to their island kingdom of Taiwan. By far my favorite site, equal to if not surpassing the Great Wall, was the Temple of Heaven (*Tian Tan*, the altar of heaven). It lies south of the center of Beijing surrounded by a spacious park, and from a distance, where only the roof is visible, it looks like a gigantic blue parasol topped by a golden ball. Originally built in the early Ming dynasty, seventy years before the Europeans discovered the New World, it has been rebuilt and expanded into a large temple surrounded by lesser structures, and for centuries, it served as the altar where the emperor would come to pray for bountiful harvests. As you enter a series of gates and ascend a series of stairs, you are drawn upward and inward into the central building itself, a towering circular edifice constructed entirely of wood and from which a clear day reveals a sweeping vista of the southern half of the city. The entire complex is alive with symbolism. Square walls and terraces represent the world of man; circular walls, terraces, and the central temple itself signify heaven, the abode of the gods. Although the temple was in poor repair at that time, the faded reds, golds, greens, and blues all held symbolic value. Even the steps, beams, pillars, terraces, and the stones comprising the central altar are designed to display numerical significance. For example, nine pervades this extensive numerology so that the steps leading up to the four entrances to the temple are all multiples of nine. The most popular site at the Temple of Heaven is the Echo Wall, and like the other places we visited in Beijing, since it was mid-January and the middle of the week, we practically had the place to ourselves, and the children could hear me whisper messages on one side of the great circling wall that they could catch a hundred and eighty degrees away.

Having lived in Southeast Asia and studied about tribal languages, I jumped at the chance to visit the Institute of National Minorities when we were asked if we had any special requests before leaving Beijing. After listening to one of the institute's functionaries deliver a tedious introductory lecture about the benevolence the Party had bestowed on all non-Han (non-Chinese) people groups and the importance of basing anthropological classifications on Stalin's essays on the subject, things became much more interesting when we were allowed to meet with a small group of students and teachers representing the various Tai minorities. One of them immediately stood out. He was from southern Yunnan, not too far from where we had once lived in northern Thailand, and had a ready smile, a soft-spoken charm, and spoke a dialect close to the Thai we knew. The Han officials in the room seemed a bit uncomfortable as we got more and more engaged in conversation, for here were white foreigners from a capitalist nation chatting amiably in a language closely related to the minorities who ostensibly were indebted to them and the institute.

There was a much enjoyed Chinese meal at the Roys' that night, some shopping in a regular and a Friendship Store, and several conversations at the Friendship Hotel with old China hands who had lived in Communist China a tad too long and whose patience to share useful information with us about the PRC was a bit too short. Either due to the smog, the indolent life of perpetual tourism, or our own longing to get to Tianjin and pursue the profession we loved, we were more than ready to move on. We had come almost halfway around the world, but compared to what we were about to learn and experience, we had barely taken the first step. Nevertheless, the journey of ten thousand *li* had begun.

CHAPTER 2

一言不中，万言无用

yi yan bu zhong, wan yan wu yong

If one word doesn't hit the mark,
neither will ten thousand.

On the morning of our departure for Tianjin, four cars pulled up to ferry the five wai ban, our family, and all our baggage from the Friendship Hotel to the Beijing Railway Station. The evening before, we met Xiao Zhang, who had come in from Tianjin to accompany us to our new home in China and, as we were only later to discern, to replace Xiao Hu as our primary wai ban. Zhang was immediately likable: short, lively, and engaging with both us grown-ups and the kids. He turned out to be the person we spent the most time with and ultimately became an extended member of the family. Although we basically had a suitcase apiece and our Chinese colleagues seemed to be able to survive the week in Beijing with only a small briefcase, getting this luggage into the trunks of four cars was an amusing encounter with class and space, one that we would observe repeatedly during our stay. In a society where workers, peasants, and soldiers were venerated and, until recently, academics and lower-level cadres had been scorned, our worker-drivers ranked higher than any of us and thus remained in their front seats, puffing on their cigarettes and occasionally shouting out commands to those wrestling with the luggage. Confusion was compounded because we were foreign guests, and Chinese hospitality dictated that none of us were allowed to carry or move our own bags, even those of us who were younger and stronger than our hosts. It may have been our imagination, but on our frequent trips that year in China, the repeated struggle our non-working-class colleagues had when they tried to fit any of our baggage into a car trunk strongly suggested that they lacked a basic understanding of the physics of three-dimensional space. They almost instinctively chose the largest suitcase first and stuffed it into a position where it would occupy the most space, often blocking the trunk from completely closing, and this would be followed by a second attempt that often ended up as badly as the first. Success came only after much squeezing and shoving or when the disgruntled driver would leave the warmth and comfort of his seat and, with a few flings of bags and curses, would rearrange everything to fit easily.

Finally, we were leaving Beijing and none too soon as the pollution that morning seemed to thicken. We were a bit concerned about missing the train to Tianjin after the long tango our fellow passengers had had with our luggage. "Ah, we have plenty of time," exclaimed Zhang quite confidently at 8:26 a.m. "We are almost at the station." We were not as relaxed as he, having already been told that our train was to leave at 8:34 a.m. A few minutes later, the four cars braked abruptly in front of our destination, and all of us suddenly erupted from them like circus clowns, grabbing our luggage and plunging into the cavernous interior of Beijing's central station. Up a giant escalator we all scrambled, then hurrying a hundred yards or so down a corridor, we tumbled down the stairs to the platform, and just after we hurtled into the nearest carriage, the train began its slow pull out of the station. Whew! Was Zhang just trying to be reassuring or were our wai ban friends as challenged by the physics of time as much as they appeared to be by that of space?

At first, our ride provided views of Beijing we hadn't seen, such as a large dump yard of abandoned vehicles, but gradually, urban development gave way to row houses in the suburbs and then to the rural scenes we had caught during our trip to and from the Great Wall, and after about an hour, we left the municipality of Beijing and entered that of Tianjin. Besides thirty-four provinces and autonomous regions, there were also three independent municipalities in the PRC at that time, quite similar to the district of Columbia in status though larger in size: the two most famous Chinese cities, Beijing and Shanghai, and our destination and home for the year, Tianjin. The name means heaven's ford, a fancier way of stating that it served as the port city for Beijing some eighty miles northwest, but given that Tianjin was a distant third in status among the three municipalities, in a stretch, it could be referred to as heaven's spit since this is another meaning of *jin*. Only a few weeks before our departure back in the States, we finally learned from the Chinese liaison office in Washington that we had been assigned to a foreign language institute in a city called Tianjin. Even we had to look it up on the map although it turned out to have a population roughly equivalent to New York City. Gradually, our departure from Beijing repeated itself in reverse, and the country gave way to the suburbs that rapidly transformed into the large and crowded edifices of a major metropolis. Although we had entered China a week earlier, in all actuality, this was the moment when we felt we were actually there.

The train had barely pulled to a stop when an entourage from the institute was upon us in the carriage to greet us and to wrest away our bags. After all the obligatory "warmly welcomes" and "you must be tireds," we were escorted to a fleet of cars of assorted vintage and driven the short distance to what we expected to be our domicile for the year, the No. 1 Hotel. Now, it is a fact that the Chinese have always liked numbers, and their history is replete with numerical naming, but the Communists seemed to have carried this to the extreme and have counted just about everything. There were three wastes, the infamous Gang of Four (who opposed the Four Modernizations), the five evils, a No. 6 Cotton Textile Mill, the July 7 Incident, *ba yi* or "eight one" (August 1, the founding of the People's Liberation Army, the

PLA), *chou lao jiu* or the Stinking Old Nine, and so on and so forth. There were even numbers within numbers. For example, almost all the abominations of the Cultural Revolution were blamed on the infamous Gang of Four, but since two of them wore glasses and one was a minor player, the major trio was cleverly referred to as the Ten-Eyed Three. In Communist China, everything counts! As for our hotel in Tianjin in 1979, there were no Sheratons, Hiltons, or other such accommodations; they were to be found only in capitalist countries, and they didn't count.

All of us were disappointed when we were shown the two rooms where we'd be living for the next twelve months, but Janene in particular was aghast at the decrepit furniture, cracked walls, and pervasive dust and couldn't hold back tears of dismay. We plunged into negotiation with the institute's wai ban and asked if there was an alternative to this establishment. Phone calls and consultations were made during lunch, and to our good fortune, our request was granted, and we were driven over to what had been the English concession and to what was to become our home that year, a place with the unnumbered but accurate name, the Tianjin Hotel. We found out later that this place had an even more exciting name and history, but on that afternoon, all we cared about was that we had found a home in China.

Before we had left the No. 1 for our upgrade and while negotiations about our change of venue were still carrying on, a mini disaster struck. Bothered partly by the dirty air and her tears of disappointment, Janene had gone into the dark No. 1 bathroom to remove and rinse out her contacts over the sink when the left one slipped out of her fingers and fell directly into the drain. Her spirits plummeted as fast as the lens, for she knew that contacts were irreplaceable in China. Several of the staff were immediately summoned, and using Zhang as the interpreter, she tried to explain to them what it was and how she lost it. Meanwhile, I walked into the dark bathroom and, fumbling for the light switch, turned the light off. Yes, off! It seemed that in a prudent but ill-illuminated attempt to conserve the supply of national power, the Chinese did not use lightbulbs brighter than around forty watts, so it wouldn't be much of a stretch to say that before I inadvertently turned off the light, the bathroom was dimmed by something roughly equivalent to a night-light. After some discussion, the hotel staff summoned a frail handyman armed with a few tools and, most importantly, a flashlight. He listened somewhat incredulously to a description of what the tall foreign woman had lost and wondered how a pair of glasses had disappeared down the drain. No, he was told, it was a tiny piece of glass that was stuck in her eye and had fallen out. He winced and wondered why she would want it back. But after continued interrogation, he seemed to understand and began to carefully unscrew the drain trap.

Fortunately, Janene had brought along an extra pair of hard lenses but was obviously worried about losing one of them now that one pair had only survived the first week. Since we were moving to another hotel, we left while the dismantling of the sink was in full swing, but our intrepid plumber promised to let us know if he would be successful in finding what he didn't know he was looking for. Quite amazingly, the next day, he showed up at our new accommodations proudly brandishing a tiny circle of clear plastic on his fingertips. He discovered the mysterious object as he was reassembling the trap to the sink, and how he found it in that dark room with no exact notion of what he was searching for is a small testimony to two indomitable traits of the Chinese: curiosity and perseverance. His visit was greeted with great surprise and even greater gratitude, and ironically, Janene spent the rest of the year without ever losing another lens, even on the darkest of days.

The Tianjin Hotel was in an older section of town that hugged the right bank of the *Hai He* (River to the Sea), which running roughly north to south, divided the city from the older and more cosmopolitan western half from the newer and more industrial eastern. In 1860, under the Treaty of Tianjin, one among many unequal treaties Europeans forced upon China, foreign concessions were established in various port cities, and thus the area bordering the river was carved into districts owned, controlled, and administered by whatever imperialistic power was in charge. The Tianjin pie was carved into five pieces, a slice each going to England, France, Germany, Japan, and Russia, and the laws of these nations ruled each concession, and each had its own separate commercial enterprises, cultural institutions, and political systems. In a fortuitous alignment of geography, the *Western* powers had concessions on the western side of the river with only the Japanese concession located in the east. These urban colonies lasted until the Japanese Imperial Army invaded China in the 1930s, when in a bizarre irony, the Chinese were finally freed from the bonds of European imperialism only to have them replaced by the Japanese, who coerced them into joining the so-called Greater East Asian Co-Prosperity Sphere. As Americans, we were pleased that the United States never had any official concessions in China, but this did not absolve our nation from a long legacy of commercial exploitation of China or of her immigrants who labored under brutal conditions in California and other states in the nineteenth and early twentieth centuries. After Liberation, when China was finally unified and independent, almost all remnants of this imperialistic era were erased except for the urban architecture, and especially in Tianjin, this relic of colonialism gave the city a certain panache. Thus our drive from the No. 1 to our new establishment was not just a trip to another section of town, it was a historical journey backward in time from the boring utilitarian buildings of modern China to the varied architecture of the past. Straight lines, symmetrical windows, and unadorned entranceways gave way to arches and circles, crenulated cornices, and inviting gateways. When our car pulled up to the hotel that would be our home that year, we didn't have to rely on any numerical naming to appreciate that it was a much more attractive domicile than the one to which we had originally been consigned.

Granted, we had already become inured to the drab, dreary, and depressing landscape of a Beijing winter, and we would soon find that Tianjin had even worse scenes to confront us, but initially, we were delighted with our new digs. Our new place was a moderate-sized, three-storied building of white and orange bricks marked by large windows, standing at an intersection with one of the main roads, *Jie Fang Lu* (Revolutionary Street). Led by the *fu yu ren*, our white-jacketed hotel staff, we made a grand entrance via a short, semicircular staircase through a small revolving door that spun us into a lobby adorned with dark wood instead of cracked plaster. For an establishment with such an unpretentious exterior, it breathed an almost palatial atmosphere inside, at least compared to what we had seen that morning. We were shown a corner sitting room on the second floor, overlooking the main intersection, which provided both entertainment and annoyance throughout our residence. The street scenes below occasioned many moments better than reality TV in depicting the human condition. On the other hand, the policeman in the kiosk that controlled the intersection commandeered a loudspeaker, and beginning with an early morning wake-up call, the days and evenings were punctuated with commands like "*Guo lai, guo lai* (get over here)."

The room was spacious, toasted by steam radiators, and its tall windows allowed the winter sun to stream through with its light and warmth. Next to it were two small bedrooms, each with two single beds and bathrooms as dark as the one that had swallowed up Janene's contact lens earlier in the day. None of these three rooms were connected, so the public hallway was our access for the year, but at least each of us would have our own bed, and we were soon to discover that our accommodations were luxurious beyond measure when compared to our colleagues' at the institute. There was no kitchen or even a place to heat water, so all our meals would be taken downstairs in the hotel restaurant. In response to our request for more furniture to cover the twenty-by-twenty-foot suite, the *fu yu ren* expediently brought up some desks, lamps, and even a sofa, and by the time we filled the wardrobes with clothes, stacked our books and school supplies on to the desks, and hid our now empty suitcases from view, we felt snug and settled. A week later, I was able to buy a two-hundred-watt lightbulb, and stacking one desk on top of another, I was able to climb high enough to reach and replace the dim ceiling light so that the room actually glowed after sunset. This refurbished lounge would now serve as our study, the kids' schoolhouse, and a place where hundreds of guests would be welcomed. We had a home, and at last, we had truly arrived.

In retrospect, it was rather transparent why we were first assigned coach and then upgraded to business. When we left the States, we had no written contract and were given no specific details about our accommodations or our responsibilities, but only a rather nebulous oral commitment that the institute in China would pay for our room and that we were to pay for our board from our Chinese salary, whatever that would be. In spite of all the smiles and friendly conversations in Beijing, Lao Shen, as head of our wai ban, like any prudent administrator, wasn't going to deplete his annual budget on accommodations for one family, and my guess is that the move from No. 1 substantially increased the housing expenses that he had originally projected for us. On the other hand, compared to the amount of work the two of us expended that year and the prestige the institute garnered in having the first pair of American foreign experts ever invited to Tianjin, he likely broke even despite our upgrade, and over the course of time, after knowing him a little bit better, my sense was that Lao Shen was clever enough to come out slightly ahead in any transaction.

First a flash backward then one forward. A few weeks into our stay, we noticed that some of the old silverware in the restaurant was not stamped with the name of the Tianjin Hotel but the Astor House. After some inquiry, we learned that because our area of town was part of the British concession, all the names were in English, so during this prerevolutionary period of the city, *Jie Fang Lu* was named after the English monarch under whose empire the sun never set, Victoria Avenue. Much to our incredulity, the small square across the street from us that was crowded with squatters' huts was, under the days of the Raj, the Rose Garden. Now speed ahead to 1991, a dozen years after our time in China. Janene and I were leading a group of American friends on a tour of the PRC, which included a day in Tianjin. Janene paid a visit to the hotel where a few of the former *fu yu ren* were still working and who were happy to have her survey the now refurbished and modernized facilities. Imagine her astonishment when upon being ushered upstairs to view our former home, there on the door to the sitting room was a brass plaque commemorating its place in history. To my slight disappointment, it had not been named the Thomas S. Scovel Lounge but was called the Zhou Enlai Suite. And to think that for all of 1979, we were living in a room where the beloved former premier had once stayed, yet this important moment of Chinese history was never once brought up while we resided there. It makes me wonder if, like George Washington, the beloved former premier's reputation for having slept around exceeded the actual number of places where he had in reality spent the night. Any uncertainty about the historical authenticity of this claim was doubtlessly superseded by the profits the hotel could garner from this, their most expensive room. Already money was beginning to trump dogma, but in 1979, we were living in a still very different China, and it was simply the Tianjn Hotel and the room was no more than our accommodations for the year.

Having found a place to lay our heads, our next assignment was to get a set of wheels to take us to and from work, specifically a set of two apiece. Like for all other citizens of the city, except for a few higher ups in the Party, bicycles were the most common mode of transport, and since Tianjin was situated on a plain, cycling even long distances was not particularly daunting. Twelve-year-old Derick was in his element immediately, but it had been many years since Janene and I had used a bicycle, but luckily, old habits die hard, and we were soon used to pedaling in dense traffic though barely managing to stay upright when snow, sleet, and mush made the going more treacherous. In those early days, we had no inkling of how tightly the economy was controlled and how much this impacted daily life. You just couldn't walk into a store and purchase a bike; you first had to get a *piao* or coupon specifically designated for the acquisition of a bicycle. Furthermore, only your *dan wei* or work unit had permission to dispense these coupons. Our institute gave us three as Christine was too little to ride a bike herself, and armed with these permission slips, with the assistance of the wai ban, we eventually bought three secondhand Flying Pigeons, the standard working-class vehicle of choice in the city and a cut below the more prestigious Red Flags.

At approximately $113 a piece, our purchases appeared unusually expensive for when I computed their price in terms of months of an average teacher's wage, the cost of a bike in China was comparable to the expense of a new car in the States. All three bikes were very basic models with hand brakes on the front handlebars, and with their high seats, we had to ride bolt upright, a cold and difficult task on the frequently windy days. I was taken aback by their weight for they seemed to be made of cast iron, and since none of them had gears, it took some effort to get them moving and even more to carry them up and down stairs. The latter was necessary because bicycles were stolen easily and frequently, so except for parking lots, where you paid to have your bike watched, owners would carry them into their offices even if they were upstairs. Every time we returned to the hotel, we had to lug ours up one flight of stairs and park them overnight in the safety of the back of the lobby. They had flimsy locks for the back wheel, so to ensure a bit more safety, I pasted little medallions of American flags on the front and rear fenders, and this seemed to scare off any potential thieves for the year. Our Chinese colleagues had several stolen during the year, even from second- and third-story offices, but ours were never touched.

Whenever we ran errands in the city, we would park our bikes in one of the many outdoor parking stalls, and after cramming them next to hundreds of other cycles, we'd pay a few cents to the attendant, who would loop a numbered bamboo token over the handlebars and hand us another with the matching number. When returning to retrieve our bikes, we'd confirm that the numbers matched and handed both tokens to the attendant. For the first week or so, we were amazed that thousands of people could almost effortlessly spot their cycles within the massive maze of black frames and wheels confronting them, but learning to remember roughly where we had left them in the gaggle of metal and quickly acquiring the ability to spot tiny details that separated one Pigeon from another, like our fellow commuters, we too reclaimed our bikes with ease. A few years after our stay in China, a former colleague from Tianjin visited us in Pittsburgh, and after a shopping trip to a large suburban mall, as we started to return to our car, he stopped in amazement to survey the large parking lot in front of us and wondered how on earth Americans could ever find their vehicles in that vast sea of metal!

Our freshly acquired knowledge about the importance of protecting our bikes from thieves introduced one of many contradictions between the idyllic accounts American travelers had been giving about life in China after brief visits to the PRC in the seventies and the realities we saw and faced during our year of residence. Many foreign visitors would return to their homelands with stories about how honest the Chinese were and how even insignificant items carelessly left in hotels or on trains would be quickly and safely returned to their foreign owner.

How wonderful, they would muse, there is little or no theft in the People's Republic! Although their conclusions were amiss, there was nothing about these tourist accounts to disbelieve. We experienced similar incidents as well during our stay. I remember one time during a trip, when we were waiting for the train after having checked out of our hotel and while standing on the station platform, we noticed a cyclist in the distance. He was riding furiously toward us, waving his left hand and shouting something too distant to understand. The closer he came, the more he captivated our attention, and by the time he had braked to an abrupt skid and jumped off the seat, we knew he had retrieved something valuable to return to us. "Our foreign guests left this in the bathroom," he gasped, thoroughly winded from his attempt to catch us before we had disappeared for good. We all huddled around him as he pulled a handkerchief out of his pocket and unfolded it carefully. There in the middle of his hand was a piece of soap! Yes, it was ours, and there were murmurs of approval from our accompanying wai ban and smiles from us as we thanked him for his thoughtfulness, but the whole scene struck me as a tad melodramatic. Considerate though his gesture was, it was a touch too politically correct. What we learned that year was that the Chinese are no less human than any other race and are tempted to take what isn't theirs if need dictates and opportunity arises. Thievery was punished in China just as it is in the States, but bikes and cars are pinched all the time in both nations. The big difference was that stealing a fellow citizen's bike was a simple felony in the PRC, but taking anything from a foreigner was a political crime, and the consequences were draconian. So our bikes were protected by our status as guests of the Party, and all three survived our stay safe in our alien custody.

During our time in China, except for a couple of minor instances of pilfering, we never had any unhappy encounters with lawbreakers, and unlike America, we always felt safe wherever we went, even late at night and even when Janene was out alone.

Again, this does not mean that China was a criminal-free utopia at that time, for though we never sought out the bad news that dominates the American media, off and on we heard stories that demonstrated quite unsurprisingly that the Chinese are no different from anyone else. Desperate and unprincipled people do desperate and violent deeds. One such tale emerged in one of the rare trials that was opened to foreign reporters and involved the eternal saga of revenge over love scorned. It seemed that a factory worker in the Beijing area fell in love with one of his colleagues, and not only did she refuse his advances, she ridiculed him in front of their fellow workers. Unable to stand the shame and rejection, he took a cleaver, murdered her, and then fled south to Shanghai. There he was quickly apprehended by the police not because of a well-coordinated national alert (remember, this was before the days of cell phones, the Internet, and massive electronic databases), but because the locals immediately recognized his northern accent and rightly suspected he did not have a residence permit. Just like us, every Chinese at that time was required to carry identification that confirmed their place of residence and had to secure permission to travel or move to any another city. Once arrested for being an alien to Shanghai, his name eventually popped up on the national most wanted list, and he was whisked back up to Beijing, where he was quickly tried and sentenced. According to the report of his trial, the presiding judge of the troika of magistrates that adjudicated this case delivered a two-part sentence. Number 1, the unhappy lover was sentenced to life imprisonment. Number 2, his cleaver was confiscated from him forever. After hearing this story, we were told that ordinary citizens could purchase kitchen knives only up to a modest length, and I couldn't help wondering what a howl advocates of the Second Amendment would bellow if even simple cutlery were restricted in a similar manner back in the States.

We had arrived, been domiciled, and had even purchased our means of transportation, but after a fortnight in China, we still had not seen our institute or been introduced to our students and fellow teachers. Strange, we thought that in a nation where workers were kings, our work seemed to matter so little. Only after we had been in Tianjin a few days did we find out that students were taking examinations to complete their first term and that classes would not resume until February 12, after festivities were concluded for Spring Festival (Chinese New Year). We wondered why we were urged to arrive in China in early January, a solid month before our work began, and our Chinese hosts gave the impression that they were unduly solicitous of our need to have enough time to acculturate to our surroundings and for our family to take care of the necessities of daily life before the start of a new term. The long hiatus may have also resulted from a lack of coordination among the Chinese liaison office in Washington, the Foreign Experts Bureau in Beijing, and the wai ban at our home institute in Tianjin.

Our first official contact with the institute was a lavish banquet, already the third since we entered the country, this one hosted by the institute's leadership at the No. 1 Hotel restaurant. We sat with some administrators, whom we were to see only rarely that entire year, and between the nine appetizers and nine courses, there were innumerable toasts with sweet red wine and *mao tai*, the volatile clear spirit that lubricates many a Chinese gathering. In keeping with the sumptuousness of the occasion, we feasted mostly on meat, and even the kids willingly sampled the dishes of chicken, duck, fish, pork, and beef that circled before us, but they literally turned up their noses when the fish stomach came around. Janene and I moistened our lips with at least ten toasts with different combinations of guests and to such lofty themes as friendship between the Chinese and American people, the joy of normalization between our two nations, and the desire to work together in harmony. By the end of the meal, our well-lubricated friends urged us to sing, so the two of us offered a duet we had learned in college, and then all four of us brought down the house with a rendition of "Getting to Know You" from *The King and I*. Now fully inspired and inebriated, several teachers got up and sang one or two Stephen Foster ballads in English as well as two spirited renditions of "Home on the Range." The most memorable part of the evening, at least for us, was when a student representative stood up and sang "My Country 'Tis of Thee," a brave and touching expression of welcome for his new teachers from America. Such an act would have certainly extracted severe punishment had he done this three years earlier during the waning days of the Cultural Revolution. More than all the delicacies, the toasts, and the official greetings from the assembled cadres, it was the melody that this student chose that warmly welcomed us to our new workplace, the Tianjin Foreign Languages Institute.

During those first few weeks, I was already aware of changes in the language that I had remembered from my childhood, but it was at this welcome banquet when an anachronism I unwittingly used in Chinese made me fully conscious of the fact that the social transformations effected by the Party had direct linguistic consequences. From our first day in Beijing, I was careful to use the classless address form *tongzhi*, a term that was absent from the China of my childhood, but in the new China in which we now lived, everyone was a "comrade." During one of my first return trips after our 1979 residence, I suddenly discovered that *tongzhi* was yesterday's news, and for the younger generation, it was almost an insult and not just a quaint aphorism. The waitress serving me in the eighties was now a *xiao jie* (miss), an address form that was too bourgeois during our stay in China, when everyone was still a comrade-in-arms for the revolution. In my little thank-you speech at the welcoming banquet hosted by our institute, I provoked smiles of startled amusement when I referred to Janene as my *tai tai*. When I was a boy, all married women were addressed *tai tai*, and my mother was always called *Si Taitai* (Mrs. or more elegantly Madam: *Si*, the monosyllabic Chinese surname given to our family to approximate the sound of the first syllable of *Scovel*). Baffled by the response I received, I quickly found out that *tai tai* was also too bourgeois a title for working-class China and was used, if at all, in negative connotations, such as Chiang Taitai (Madame Chiang, the despised wife of the equally unloved Chiang Kai-shek, the leader of the Nationalists). Instead, I was told to use a term I found much more endearing, *ai ren*, literally "loved one" but here meaning husband or wife or even sweetheart. Ironically, I rarely heard my Chinese colleagues refer to their spouses as *ai ren*, though on formal or public occasions, the term *fu ren* (married woman) was usually employed, and around the institute or at people's homes, more colloquial titles like *qi zi* were used by married folk. But for the rest of the year, Madame Scovel became my sweetheart and has remained so to this very day.

It is with utmost restraint that I as a linguist resist the many temptations while writing this book to delve into long and exquisite analyses of Chinese, English, or any other language that is even tangentially related to this narrative for that matter. In the main, I believe I have succeeded in not letting a story about my China years get hijacked by an endless succession of academic discourses about picayune linguistic details or lengthy expositions into the nature of human language. Nonetheless, since so much has been written about the differences between Chinese and languages like English and since so much of it is so bad, I feel responsible about setting the record straight as a language specialist and to do so early in the book rather than at the end or, worse yet, not at all. Given the amount of junk science now spewing out of the Internet, it is the responsibility of specialists in any field to share their expertise and to separate the substantive wheat from the chaff of pop science. I have limited myself then to just two observations about the Chinese language, and I hope these will deepen the appreciation of the experiences I have recorded here as well as enrich any understanding of the Chinese people.

All languages borrow words from other languages, and English is spectacularly profligate in harvesting an enormous number of loanwords from a wide variety of languages over an extended period. Chinese is at the other end of the borrowing continuum and is reluctant to borrow any foreign vocabulary at all. Clearly, if you've been around for about four millennia and come from a rich culture that has continuously dominated East and Southeast Asian history, you're more in the lending than the borrowing business. Be this as it may, compared to neighboring languages like Japanese and Thai and most certainly in contrast to English, Chinese is exceedingly picky when it comes to adding vocabulary from other tongues. And if it does take in a foreign word, it translates it rather than transliterates the new item, and this is especially true of all the new vocabulary that has spread from English over the past few decades of rapid globalization and technology transfer.

Among the few loanwords from English, my favorite was coined back in the thirties when a famous American soft drink was first marketed in China. Some unknown Chinese clerk probably working for an advertising firm in Shanghai came up with this gem that brilliantly transliterates the English brand name so that it is immediately recognizable to any English speaker. Hence, it is one of the clear but rare examples of an English loanword. However, this anonymous wordsmith also Sinicized the name so that it has a unique but appropriate Chinese meaning; that is, when you read the Chinese characters out loud, they sound like the English word for this ubiquitous beverage, but at the same time, the characters convey an attractive Chinese meaning. The name of this product transliterated into Chinese is *ke kou ke le*, and when translated, the four characters mean delectable (and) pleasurable. Can you think of a better way to brand Coca-Cola to a market of one billion thirsty consumers? But Coke is the exception that proves the rule: it stands out because there are so few loanwords like this in Chinese compared to many other modern languages.

When you hear native speakers of Japanese or Thai talk about technology in their mother tongues, it is relatively easy to pick out English loanwords like *computer*: they sound like a heavily accented version of the way an English speaker would pronounce the word. The same goes for the written form of loanwords like this, assuming that you could sound out the Japanese or Thai writing systems. With few exceptions, this simply doesn't work for Chinese. Knowing only the English word, you would never guess that when Chinese speakers start talking about *ji suan ji* (electric calculating machine) that they were referring to computers. This contrast goes for many other words like *television* or *vitamin*. Although it's dangerous to assume that linguistic differences invariably lead to contrasts in the way people think, I don't believe it's accidental that, except for the very recent present, during the past two centuries, China has been reluctant to accept ideas from outside its borders whereas these two neighbors of the Middle Kingdom, Japan and Thailand, have by and large embraced alien concepts and cultures over that same span of time.

Having just suggested that the lack of loanwords in Chinese might correlate with a reluctance among Chinese speakers to accept alien ideas, following the warning I just gave as part of this observation, let me turn around and cite just one of many illustrations of how linguistic differences do not seem to relate to contrasts in cultural perceptions. In my experience, the most pervasive and persistent misconception about the Chinese language is that because it differs so radically from English (at least in the minds of laypeople), this leads invariably to radically different ways of thinking and perceiving between these two large populations. This belief, technically known as the Sapir-Whorf hypothesis or linguistic relativity, is virtually universal, and I have had many debates over the decades with speakers of Thai, Japanese, French, and so on about how their native languages have created a different worldview from English speakers because of the perceived stark contrasts between their mother tongues and English. Again, this conviction is so common and so strong it seems impervious to the long history of research in linguistics, anthropology, and cognitive science that goes against it, and many times I simply have to shrug my linguistic shoulders and accept defeat when once again I fail to convince people to the contrary.

These speculations about Chinese on the part of English speakers are numerous and most are downright silly. English has three to twelve tenses (depending on how Latinate you want to make English grammar); Chinese has none. Therefore, Chinese people don't care about time or have a sense of history. Yeah, right! English constantly distinguishes between singular and plural nouns; Chinese doesn't, so *tamen de pengyou* can be either "their friend" or "their friends." Given this linguistic contrast, it seems logical to infer that English-speaking pupils are better with numbers than their Chinese-speaking counterparts. Sure! In English, there is an important distinction between definite noun phrases (I found *the* book upstairs) and indefinite ones (I found *a* book upstairs); Chinese makes no such distinction. This surely implies that Chinese speakers must find it hard to be specific or precise. Really? Just look at the tens of thousands of Chinese graduate students in fields like engineering, accounting, computer science, or molecular biology in both Chinese and American universities!

When it comes to pronouns, *ta* in Mandarin can substitute for *he*, *she*, or *it* in English; there is no gender distinction in Chinese. Unless you use the plural *they*, it is extremely difficult to avoid using *he* or *she* in either spoken or written English, and thus there lurks the suspicion that somehow English is more chauvinistic than Chinese because traditionally, when we talk about people or professions generically, English speakers refer to them as *he* whereas Chinese uses the genderless *ta*. Isn't it then logical to assume that Chinese speakers live in a culture where women are treated with more equality? Let me quote from one woman's account of a practice perpetrated on tens of millions of Chinese women for almost a thousand years, a practice that I was witness to as a small boy, and a barbaric cruelty that was the cultural norm among all those who spoke a language that did not distinguish between *he* or *she*.

> They did not begin to bind my feet until I was seven because I loved so much to run and play. Then I became very ill and they had to take the bindings off my feet.... When I was nine they started to bind my feet again and they had to draw the bindings tighter than usual. My feet hurt so much that for two years I had to crawl on my hands and knees. Sometimes at night they hurt so much I could not sleep. I stuck my feet under my mother and she lay on them so they hurt less and I could sleep. But by the time I was eleven, my feet did not hurt and by the time I was thirteen I was finished. The toes were turned under so I could see them on the inner and under side of the foot. They had come up around. Two fingers could be inserted in the cleft between the front of the foot and the heel. My feet were very small indeed. A girl's beauty and desirability were counted more by the size of her feet than by the beauty of her face. Matchmakers were not asked, "Is she beautiful? but "How small are her feet?"
>
> —Ida Pruitt, *Daughter of Han*, from John Fairbank, *Chinabound: A fifty year memoir.* pps. 54-55.

Crushed and hobbled, Chinese women became obsequious servants to their husbands and sexual slaves to this vile form of foot fetish, yet both the oppressed and the oppressor shared the same pronoun. Obviously, there is a disconnect between differences in cultural behavior and contrasts in linguistic structures. Just as individuals differ in quirky and unpredictable ways, so do languages and cultures, and the connections among them are far from clear.

Spring Festival still remained the major Chinese holiday, and the country basically shut down for almost a week to celebrate the new zodiacal year, which happened to be the year of the goat (or sheep) in 1979. Like other institutions, our hotel practically closed shop during this time, and for a few days, we were the only guests, and except for the bright red banners and bunting framing the entrance, the place looked virtually uninhabited. Following a tradition I remembered well from my boyhood, all four of us joined the few *fu wu ren* and cooking staff in making *jiaozi's*, and the starchy smell of these dumplings steaming in the pot on the stove is a gustatory memory indelibly buried in my midbrain. Partly because he felt sorry for us, all alone and away from relatives on this most festive occasion, but largely because of the generous sense of hospitality that so many Chinese extended, Lao Zhou, the academic head of the English Department, invited us to his apartment to celebrate Chinese New Year's Eve. Since he lived about six miles from our hotel, he arranged for an institute car to take us out to his place. Even though it was only about 5:00 p.m., it was already dark when we arrived at a set of slate-gray apartments that looked more like warehouses than living quarters. Up three flights of stairs and down a narrow corridor lit by a bare forty-watt bulb was the simple apartment of our boss, a middle-level cadre. Here he lived with his wife and three children in two rooms separated by a hallway and crowded with beds, stools, tables, books, old newspapers, and a few chests stuffed with family belongings. Throughout the evening, it seemed as if every tenant in the building came in to greet us and take a peek at the celebrity visitors. Christine was bundled off to play with some young neighbors, and Derick immediately flew off with a group of boys his age to light firecrackers. We squeezed together with our host family and other guests to chat, sip tea, and munch on peanuts and sunflower seeds. When dinner was ready, we moved across to the other room and sat together on stools, chairs, packing crates, and a bed around a table filled with what was probably the assembled crockery and silverware of all the households of the building's third floor. As for our New Year's dinner, delectable it wasn't, but we were thoroughly impressed with the amount, variety, and enormous expense of the meal our hosts so kindly provided. Fish, two kinds of shrimp, chicken, crab, beets, cabbage, one-thousand-year-old eggs, noodles, soybeans, peanuts, candied fruit, and two different types of jiaozi's are all the dishes Janene and I could remember, and there were several more that we just as soon forgot. All of this was washed down with beer and two different kinds of sweet wine. As if this wasn't enough to fill us, we were given oranges and rice pudding dumplings for dessert. The entire banquet was cooked on primitive charcoal burners from the small, third-floor communal kitchen, so along with all the money our hosts expended was the enormous effort and time that went into purchasing, preparing, and cooking this feast as well as cleaning up from the festivities the next day.

Lao Zhou's wife, who quarterbacked the feast, was associated in some way with the Tianjin Academy of Fine Arts, so it was through her and not via our institute, his own dan wei, that Zhou and his family were able to secure housing in an earthquake-damaged metropolis, where accommodations were so dearly sought after. Because of this, the neighbors who trotted in and out throughout the evening were mainly artists, writers, dancers, and performers, and we were fascinated with the bits and pieces of stories they shared during our brief conversations throughout the evening. Lao Zhou had also invited Lao Chen, his cochair, and a couple of other teachers from our institute, so we had a wonderful mix of companions, and naturally, we appreciated their help in trying to polish off the succession of dishes that occupied most of our attention and all of our gastrointestinal systems that evening.

Our kids appeared intermittently throughout the meal, Christine running in and out with about a dozen other young children holding red plastic lanterns lit by candles. And Derick hung out with an older group of boys intent on cannonading the building into smithereens with sizable firecrackers. They started their explosions outdoors, but probably not so much due to the winter cold but because the resulting echoes magnified the sound of the explosions severalfold, the boys began lighting their fireworks indoors, finally working their way to the third-floor hallway where, mercifully, they ran out of ammunition about the same time the floor had filled with the acrid smoke of gunpowder and our ears were about to be punctured. Reflecting on that evening the next day, Janene and I almost laughed at how incongruent such an experience would have been back in the States. After all, there are fire codes, city restrictions, not to mention the ever-present threat of lawsuits in America, any one of which would have prevented or rapidly curtailed the merriment the kids were having in Lao Zhou's apartment complex. But miraculously, no one lost a finger, an eye, or even their hearing that night.

I was a bit younger than Derick when I was a boy in Huaiyuan, and it was not during Spring Festival but one summer day when my two older brothers were home from their boarding school in Shanghai. Partly in Chinese deference to older siblings but largely due to the realization that Jim and Carl were actually interested in playing with me, the sound and smell of firecrackers always take me back to that sultry afternoon on the lawn in front of our house in the late forties. My brothers had a boyish fascination with explosives, and living in China was a male adolescent's dream since fireworks of any size were readily available. One time, they got into considerable trouble at their Shanghai boarding school because of their incendiary interests, but that is a story for them to tell. On that particular day at our home in Huaiyuan, they were interested in discovering how large a firecracker you could hold by your fingertips without seriously damaging any of your appendages. Of course, they did not volunteer to participate directly in this intriguing experiment, but fortunately, they had a little brother who was more than willing to please his older siblings. I was to stand in the middle of the yard with my arm outstretched and hold each firecracker between my thumb and index finger while turning my head and face as far as possible away from the impending blast while simultaneously wrapping my other hand around the exposed ear to minimize the sound of the explosion. My brothers were kind enough to tear away a small piece of the red covering at the end of the firecracker opposite the fuse so that when it exploded, it blew out of my fingers and did not blow them off. I don't recall how many times they lit the fuse and sprinted to the edge of the yard to witness the explosions, but I do remember they were solicitous enough to ask if I was all right and if I could still hear. Except for slightly blackened fingertips, the residual smell of gunpowder, and a distinct ringing in my ears, like my own son so many years later, I survived the incident and still savor the memory of an experience that was equal parts exhilaration and stupidity.

In some ways, our first week or two in Tianjin replicated our schedule in Beijing, and once again, we felt more like tourists than teachers. We visited the Zhou Enlai Middle School, where the much-admired premier gained his early education. Unlike the vast majority of schools around the country, this was designated a key institution and thus was given more funding and recognition and naturally was filled with an unduly large number of pupils whose parents were Party members or bureaucrats. We also were treated to a couple of concerts and to visits to some local factories. In anticipation of the Chinese New Year's festivities, we attended a performance of traditional instruments that was entertaining and informative. What we remembered as much as the music was that some of the female soloists wore dresses, a daring dash of departure from the so-called Mao suits, which at that time appeared to be the national uniform. The concert concluded with a combined orchestra of about a hundred native flutes, reeds, strings, and percussion instruments, and almost in a quaint attempt to link the ancient with the modern, they played a medley of Stephen Foster melodies, ending with "My Old Kentucky Home." The same week, we toured both a carpet and a jade-and-ivory factory and were equally impressed with the incredible craftsmanship displayed by the workers and shocked at their harsh working conditions and pay. Virtually all women, the workers labored long hours at their cold and poorly lighted stations, repeating intricate finger motions with little respite and equally little pay. I'm certain notions such as carpal tunnel syndrome were as foreign to them as union contracts. We visited several similar facilities in other parts of China during our stay, and like so many scenes we witnessed, we left with the same ambivalent feelings of awe and dismay.

Like Beijing and every other city open to foreigners that year, Tianjin had a Friendship Store, which catered exclusively to foreigners and the few privileged cadres who had access to amenities and services that the average Chinese could only dream of. This was the place we visited most often for there we could purchase cookies, candy, toys, gifts, and other commodities that were produced in China specifically for foreign export or for foreign visitors. One of our best buys was a down-filled mountaineering jacket for Janene, who felt the cold more than the rest of us and who would not have survived the bike rides in the dead of winter without the warmth and protection from the wind this superbly made jacket provided. Later in the year, we also bought a small violin for Christine, and neither of these high-end products were available in China except in a large Friendship Store such as ours. The bulk of the merchandise was targeted for tourists, however, so there were shelves of Chinese medicine, embroidery, lacquerware, bronze bowls, cloisonné dishes, scrolls by the hundreds, ink brushes and inkstones especially treasured by Japanese tourists, and ivory chops, which you could have your name carved in Chinese characters on the spot to use as your personally engraved seal. We bought almost none of these items since we were showered with these distinctive native artifacts as gifts throughout the year, but during our early visits to the store, we were disturbed by some of what we saw for sale.

There was an abundance of works of art carved from ivory, and some were small and tasteful, similar to the slim statue of Guanyin, the goddess of mercy, that Janene and I bought on a visit to Taiwan years earlier or the squat replica of Confucius, which my folks purchased in Beijing in the early thirties and had already yellowed with age, but many were huge. Most of the larger objects immediately revealed their origin, for they were long, curved pieces about three to six feet in length, broad at one end, and tapered almost to a point at the other. There was no mistaking that these impressively engraved bridges, village scenes, and encircled chains were carved from a single elephant tusk, and from the score of pieces displayed in our store alone, at least a dozen African elephants had been killed so that their poached tusks could end up in China to be carved and sold to tourists at exorbitant prices. In the Chinese medicine section of the store, there were pills, powders, ointments, and tinctures made of all sorts of animal parts, most of which I was happily ignorant of, but I did identify several that contained rhinoceros horn, and like the ivory pieces, they were telling evidence that a large and endangered African animal had been slaughtered just so people half a world away could use an insignificant part of their body, in this case, for dubious health benefits. The callous disregard for threatened species was not confined to land animals. At about half of the many banquets hosted for us that year, we were served shark's fin soup, a tasty chowder flavored with slivers of cartilaginous dorsal fin from whatever hapless shark happened to have been caught. I'm no epicurean, but to me, the soup would've tasted just as good if the shark fins had been replaced with slivers of any form of seafood. Often the fishermen providing this Chinese delicacy simply slice off the fin and throw the mutilated shark back into the ocean to die, about the most inefficient use of animal food on the planet. The most unsettling sight in the store was an animal pelt that remained in a display case for most of the year until it was finally sold. It was the skin of an adult panda spread out like a bearskin rug, and though I have no idea whether the panda died in a zoo or suffered the same death as its fellow mammals from Africa, I found it brazenly distasteful to turn this rare and universally adored creature into a throw rug. We would've never guessed that, a decade or two later, the Chinese would make infinitely more money off pandas, loaning live ones to foreign zoos at prices that would make a usurer blush.

The children and their education were a major concern of ours during that time of adjustment. The initial invitation extended by the Chinese liaison office in Washington was to me as a faculty member of the University of Pittsburgh, and it was only after they learned that I was married, had a family, and would not be willing to leave them for a year that Janene was also invited and that support for all four of us was approved. The generosity of the Chinese government to invite us as a family proved valuable in many ways, not the least of which was the support and encouragement we were able to provide one another as a family unit during that difficult year. But having two children tag along raised several challenges, and the major one confronting us was their education. We had brought along a suitcase full of books and scholastic materials to help Derick keep up with the curricular demands of his middle school back home and to introduce Christine to materials and activities to prepare her for kindergarten, but we wanted both children to have a direct and formal experience with Chinese schooling. This proved to be relatively easy for our daughter but extremely difficult for our son.

Janene and Christine spent one morning visiting a nursery school that was about a mile from our hotel and that had been recommended to us, and we quickly approved of them and they of us. Because she spoke English (though nary a word of Chinese), she was placed in the most advanced class of six-year-olds. She would stay from 8:00 a.m. to 4:30 p.m. every weekday, and there she and the other children would have lessons in music, dance, art, and math, and be fed a hot meal and take obligatory naps. The courtyard, playground, and rooms were a bit barren and colorless, especially when viewed in the dead of winter, but the white-smocked staff of women seemed cheerful and enthusiastic. We were told it was the best nursery in the city, but we had already suspected that by the very fact that the only little Thai-American in Tianjin was directed there. Our suspicions were reinforced when we saw black sedans picking up and dropping off children, and they were confirmed when we saw from the sign over the gate that it was called the No. 1 Nursery. We were to encounter further evidence of the nursery's status in the days to come. Like any little girl new to a strange country and people, Christine was reluctant to be left at first. One of us would walk her sitting sidesaddle on our bike to the nursery every morning because it was against the traffic code to ride more than one on a bike, and when we kissed her good-bye, it was tough to turn around and cycle off when she cried desperately for us not to leave. She came home sick several times, partly from a wretchedly prolonged cold and partly from familial estrangement. The hardest day was toward the end of the second week when I plopped her down inside the gate to say good-bye, and with tears welling up in her trembling face, she bade farewell with a brave "Look, Daddy, I'm not crying!" Being Thai and bundled up against the cold like all the other Chinese kids, she looked like one of them, and she soon adjusted to her new life and was sometimes even reluctant to leave at the end of the day. The staff was wonderful, so much so that she became the unofficial nursery mascot, and she was sometimes treated with too much attention. Over the Spring Festival holiday, when most kids were home with their families and the staff had little to do, the teachers took her to a hairdresser and, with their own money, paid to have her given a permanent. When we arrived to pick her up, the staff half-sheepishly presented our overly coiffured daughter to us, and though we didn't approve much of the styling, we knew she was the object of more than just our affection.

Derick's education was a much more difficult venture, and negotiating his schooling eventually involved coordination among several dan wei, a special ruling from the Tianjin Revolutionary Committee, and the threat of a worker's strike. As a twelve-year-old, he had been in middle school in the States, but the Chinese education system at that time was basically two-tiered; the majority of kids studied an ordinary and general curriculum, but a small and elite percentage attended specialized "attached" middle schools (*fu zhong*) that fed into institutes or universities that streamed students for a particular specialty. As the only visiting American at the time, Derick was a de facto member of the elite, and because he was talented musically and music education involved less reliance on competence in Chinese, the middle school attached to the Tianjin Music Conservatory seemed to be the most appropriate fit for him. He could study all morning while Janene was teaching her classes at our institute, and then they could both cycle back to the hotel from their respective schools to meet for lunch and an afternoon of homeschooling together. As an experienced and certified middle school teacher back in Pennsylvania, Janene could ensure that even with half a day's curriculum, Derick would not fall behind in his American studies during that year of sojourn in China, and with intensive musical training every morning from superb Chinese teachers, he would greatly enhance his skills in music. Ultimately, these goals were achieved, and Derick returned to the States at the end of the year a well-educated, talented, and mature young man. Ah, but setting all this up was not easy!

Luckily, a week or two after our arrival, the conservatory happened to be giving a concert as part of the examination process for the more advanced students, so we were able to attend this performance and take advantage of an ideal opportunity to meet the teachers and to arrange for the possibility of our son to study there. The concert in and of itself was an illustrative clash of contradictions. Remember that only a few years earlier in China, the goal of all the arts was to serve the revolution and that anything foreign, especially effete Western music, was considered bourgeois and counterrevolutionary. So it was with amazement that we listened to skilled soloists performing classical European and traditional Chinese music on the violin, cello, piano, and indigenous instruments, such as the *er hu* (two-stringed violin). A young soprano gave a stirring rendition of an aria from *Carmen*, and several instructors performed impressively. Considering the difficult era every one of these musicians had just emerged from, their performances were extraordinary. Except for a few occasions when revolutionary music was needed, none of the performers had been able to practice these pieces or perform them publicly during the Cultural Revolution, and most of the teachers had virtually no opportunities to study, practice, or play foreign music for fear of reprisals since they were members of a counterrevolutionary class. Heartened by the opportunities we foresaw for our son's education and thoroughly entertained by the music, the two and a half hours that evening in a cold concert hall sped quickly.

Conversely, the performance by the audience was a noticeable contrast to that of the soloists on stage. We could partially forgive the latecomers who entered when a young woman introduced the concert with a Beethoven piano sonata. They loudly directed one another to various seats while squeezing down the rows and snapping the folded wooden seats down when they finally found a spot to their liking. But the rudeness was not confined to those arriving late for it seemed as if throughout the evening, every other person was engaged in conversation from time to time, and the coughing and clearing of throats grew to be contagious. Others would abruptly exchange seats in the middle of a piece, and all of them at one time or another would laugh at or heckle the announcer or the stagehands in between performances, and clapping was intermittent and sometimes inappropriate. We were quite annoyed considering the quality of musicianship and the appreciation that the performers deserved considering the humiliations they had been subjected to previously, but each soloist performed their memorized piece with pluck, undisturbed by what we thought was boorish behavior. Janene pointed out afterward that every member of the audience had been shaped by years of antibourgeoisie thinking, so they really didn't know how to act appropriately in this their first post–Cultural Revolution concert. Besides, she pointed out, they all seemed to enjoy this rare opportunity to hear good music. We met briefly with some of the teachers afterward, and yes, they appeared eager to have this young American boy study at their institute. Now the fun was about to begin.

In retrospect, there was a simple reason why the selection of and enrollment into our daughter's nursery were effected so seamlessly. The Tianjin Hotel was administered by the municipality of Tianjin as was the No. 1 Nursery, and because we were residents of the hotel, it was easy to gain permission for our daughter to attend the nursery since both places were overseen by the same administrative unit. Not so with the music conservatory. There were two challenges involved with adjudicating the decision to grant Derick permission to attend this school. First was the fact that unlike the nursery, the conservatory was not directly under the control of the municipality but was administered by the Ministry of Education, a completely different fiefdom. There was also the problem that unlike our hotel, the nursery, and the institute where we would be teaching, the conservatory was not on the western and nice side of the river but across the banks in the eastern and more industrial side of town. From this unfortunate piece of geography, an even greater barrier arose to our hopes of having our son secure musical training.

We quickly realized from the first problem that the China we were living in was tightly stratified into vertical institutions. Like skyscrapers crowded together in the heart of a city, each dan wei functioned well as an entity unto itself, but the only formal communication among work units had to be into and out of the gatekeepers that controlled their entrances and through which all intercourse transpired. For millennia, Chinese society had been vertically stratified in a much more natural and personal manner via clans. Thus, being a member of the *Wong* clan endowed you from birth with all the rights and responsibilities of that familiar grouping but, at the same time, blocked you from enjoying similar rights with another clan, say the *Li*. For the *Li*, the other clan would obviously be *wong*. The stratification into clans was exactly why marriage was such an important and elaborate institution in traditional Chinese society, for it trumped the consanguineous membership of the clan with an affinal and social contract between clans that only marriage could sanction. After Liberation in 1949, when both the nation and its culture were reconstructed, the Communists wittingly or not replaced the clan with the work unit, the dan wei, and this new allegiance was especially hammered home with a vengeance during the Cultural Revolution through which every Chinese we met that year had just endured. So for us, the decision about our son's education was simple and personal. We wanted him to attend the conservatory; they wanted him to attend, so what's the big deal? After all, the decision to enroll Christine into the nursery was effortless; what's all the fuss about making a similar decision for Derick?

Patience, negotiation, and flexibility on all sides solved our first problem. Both being educational institutions and sheltered by the same administrative umbrella, the music conservatory and our institute worked out some sort of deal where the former received compensation from the latter, which was responsible for our family benefits, and both parties agreed to allow Derick to study music every morning during our tenure in Tianjin. Although our choice as parents precipitated all of these negotiations, it is worth emphasizing that important decisions like this were not made by the individuals involved, but by the dan wei for whom the individuals worked. *Whew*, we thought, *the problem of our son's Chinese education is solved, and we can now tackle our work as teachers.* But wait! Still remaining was the small matter of the conservatory's location. Except for the Tianjin Music Conservatory, our accommodations, work, shopping, and daily activities were all situated in the western district of the city that once housed all the foreign concessions. As already mentioned, our hotel was situated in the former British section of town, and to get to our institute, which was located in the former French concession, we had to cycle through an area that was formerly German. But because we were located on the west bank of the *Hai He*, getting to and from the conservatory meant that Derick would have to take the ferry across the river every morning and then bike a mile or two through the busy and somewhat seedy industrialized eastern section of the city. We felt that our twelve-year-old could achieve what thousands of other Chinese middle school students were able to accomplish on a daily basis and that undertaking this somewhat rigorous commute was in itself part of his young education.

Again, we were mistakenly looking at the picture through the eyes of individuals as well as the round and alien eyes of American parents, and we did not examine the scene from a more comprehensive and collective perspective. The conservatory and institutes were just two tiny dan wei floating in the much larger sea of the Tianjin municipality that was responsible for every ferry crossing, intersection, and city block that Derick would traverse during his daily commute. Unlike his fellow Chinese adolescents, he was a foreigner, a guest of the Beijing government, and a potential risk in terms of national and international publicity should even the slightest mishap befall him during his daily travels. What if he had a bike accident and broke his leg? What if a gang of bullies not recognizing his white face lost in the bundle of winter clothing beat him up? And what if, most unimaginable of horrors, he should fall off the crowded ferry and drown in the icy river? Mind you, this was ages before the Internet and YouTube; furthermore, the Chinese were not litigious. The driving force behind all of these concerns was a serious sense of responsibility for our welfare coupled with the dictum followed by bureaucrats the world over. You are remembered more for any mistakes made during your watch than for any achievements: higher ups will quickly take responsibility for the latter. So the question came down to whose head would roll if any of the above adverse scenarios were to transpire.

Day after day, Xiao Zhang would report that no progress had been made in securing permission for our son to attend the conservatory, and day after day, Derick and his parents would get more and more restless about his being sequestered in our hotel room, often all by himself. Being more resolute than I, Janene raised the stakes on a Wednesday morning after we had barely started work at the institute, and unable to control her emotions, she implored the leadership to allow our son to cycle to his school. She followed up her plea with a pledge to conduct an American boycott and not show up for work Monday morning unless this matter was resolved. A strike? This was indeed a foreign concept in a worker's paradise, so the idea itself was threatening as well as the heretofore genial American teacher. For a few days, there was an embarrassing and uneasy silence in any contacts we had with our new workplace, but Sunday, Xiao Zhang showed up at the hotel with some welcome news. Both our institute and the conservatory had pleaded our case with the Tianjin Revolutionary Committee (the city council), and like his parents, the two institutions agreed to accept responsibility for the American boy if something untoward happened to him on his way to and from school, but even this overture did not win the city's approval. Perhaps it was the surprise threat of a strike or simply the natural ponderousness of collective decision making, but according to Zhang, after various members of the city council kept passing the buck among themselves, the council member in charge of public security finally agreed to take full responsibility for the matter, and this happy resolution was quickly relayed first to the institutions and then, through Zhang that evening, to us. Our son could only commute after the early morning rush hour had wound down, and he was urged to cycle with "good driving habits" at all times. All parties were relieved that the incident was resolved but perhaps none more than Derick, who learned a great deal that year at the conservatory and also during his bike rides on the streets of Tianjin.

A final footnote demands mention. During our negotiations over this matter, we got to know and appreciate Xiao Zhang a lot better, for he became our intermediary, taking our concerns to Lao Shen and the institute leadership, who passed them on in turn to the appropriate municipal office. I remember in one of our discussions with him, we exclaimed quite impatiently, "We simply want our son to be able to bike back and forth to his school. We'll take complete responsibility if anything happens, so don't worry. This is all so trivial!" I'll never forget his reply because it was one of the most telling comments we have ever heard anyone make about modern China. He looked at us with his usually happy countenance transfigured by the seriousness of what he was about to share. "In China," he intoned, staring intently at both of us, "nothing is trivial." In a word, everything was in the details.

Just as our fair city was the least of the three metropolitan districts, so was our educational institution, the Tianjin Foreign Languages Institute, clearly the lesser of the city's pedagogical establishments. Thankfully, it was not considered among those occupying the lowest tier, but the very fact that it was labeled an institute quickly distinguished it from such lofty places as Tianjin University or the even more exalted Nan Kai University. The latter was a key national institution; ours was but a local doorknob of a place, and you couldn't even find it listed on a detailed map of the metropolitan area. Because we were one of the very first American couples to be invited as official foreign experts to China and because we were active professionally throughout out stay in Tianjin and during our many travels around the country, we were happy to elevate the institute's status by our presence and willingness to sing its praises wherever we went. Years later, when we revisited the city, it was heartening to learn that it is now called the Tianjin Foreign Languages University. Of course, virtually every other tertiary educational institution in the nation now bears this more imposing sobriquet though, like the past, there are still firsts among many equals. We grew to appreciate our modest institution and in retrospect, preferred it to any of the many establishments we saw during our travels.

We quickly learned how to bike to our institute, which was conveniently located only about a mile and a half from our hotel. We'd cycle two short blocks west past the imposing municipality offices, whose steps were almost always crowded with various and ever-changing groups of protesters, and then head southwest, passing part of the old German section and the famous Kiesling's Restaurant and then into the former French quarter along *Ma Chang Dao* (Horse Racecourse Road) to the gates of our institute on the left. The racecourse had disappeared along with the European colonialists decades before, but the horses were still present, plodding on the streets, that is, along with mules and donkeys, pulling carts at a much more pedestrian pace than their colonial predecessors. Gates are important in China, and like so many other entrances that we saw, ours was framed by a pair of red, vertical signs emblazoned with white characters. *Xuexi, xuexi* declared the left side; *Zai xuexi!* proclaimed the right. "Study, study, and study yet again!" Facing you as you wheeled through the gateway was a large, three-storied, European-looking building with arched windows. The first floor was built of stone, and the top two were of light orange brick. The roof was decorated with two triangular peaks at either end and the middle with a dome housing a clock whose hands never moved. This structure was obviously neither designed nor built by the same workers who constructed all the dull rectangular buildings of concrete and brick that covered most of postrevolutionary China, and being the handsomest on campus, it naturally housed the offices for all the administrators.

Like the rest of the city, the campus was crammed with temporary shelters built after the devastating earthquake of 1976, and what little open space remained was dirt with a few leafless trees. With the exception of the front gate, flanked by crimson, the entire scene was colored in gray and dun. Behind the administration building was our office, a nondescript three-story shamble of classrooms and offices with a front door that was half broken, unable to impede the winter wind. Janene and I shared an office on the third floor, and we quickly grew to appreciate its southern exposure that allowed the smog-filtered sunlight to warm it on cloudless days, and as the days started to lengthen, the sun did a much better job of lighting that dark room than the low-wattage bulb dangling on a wire from the ceiling. We moved our desks as close to the window as possible to take advantage of nature's nuclear energy and also because the only radiator was situated there right under the sill. One of our colleagues brought in a newly purchased portable radiant heater that had a three-pronged plug and looked as if it could drain several kilowatts of energy. No one seemed to mind that the office contained only one two-pronged outlet in the wall, which was so delicately wired; even if we had been successful in plugging this mini furnace into the institute's power supply, it could've drained the electrical grid for Northern China. For the rest of the winter, the heater sat there on the floor, a forlorn reminder of what could have been. Temperatures usually hovered below freezing outside and not much above inside our office, and for the first week or so, I would warm my hands on the radiator to take advantage of the trickle of heat that seemed to emanate from this fixture. I finally found out the reason it was tepid was not because of any steam circulating through the system, but due to its proximity to the window, the radiator provided a hint of warmth solely from the radiant energy of the sunlight.

Like so much of China, the campus was a crowded place. Buildings similar to our department's housed dormitories, classrooms, and offices for teachers and cadres, but cluttered in between them were primitive, one-story temporary shelters where most of the teachers and staff lived. Lined between these were bricked walkways, but except for an outdoor basketball court and a few open areas of dirt and trees here and there, it was a crowded village inside a teeming metropolis. At that time of year, not a single leaf, patch of ivy, or blade of grass greened the landscape, and it was not until later, during a surprise visit to a unique enclave in town, did we ever see a lawn in Tianjin. No description of our institute would be complete without mention of the complicated question of whether or not we had a swimming pool.

As a linguist, I was intrigued with the semantic debates we would often have when teaching English to our students or discussing modern China with our friends. Lexical meaning is such a convoluted domain, linguists tend to avoid it like the plague and leave it to higher minds such as philosophers to decipher, but because it is the centerpiece of communication, naturally, we had to tackle it in the classroom and in all our conversations. When students chose a word that happened to be inaccurate or inapt in English due to its connotative meaning, it was often easy to demonstrate that another word was a better target. Thus, when students referred to Disney's most famous character as Mickey Rat, we could successfully convince our class that there was a cuter synonym for this famous rodent. However, the question of whether or not our campus contained a swimming pool introduced us to a much thornier pedagogical challenge. Superficially, it was simply a difference over the denotative meaning of a word, but in actual fact, it was a disagreement over perception. In essence, the problem wasn't linguistic but psychological.

Our students maintained that *Tian Wai*, (the) Tian(jin) Foreign (Language Institute), did indeed have a swimming pool. We insisted that we had combed the campus thoroughly and found nothing that in any manner, shape, or form could be defined as a large container of water constructed for the specific purpose of allowing people to swim. After corroborating that there was no disagreement over the exact definition of this word in either Chinese or English, we challenged our students to show us this alleged facility. Out we marched from the classroom, down three flights of stairs, and over to the back of the campus next to what had previously been a football field but was now blanketed with huts. "There!" They pointed triumphantly at a large rectangular hole in the ground about six feet deep and filled completely with temporary shelters. Except for some mud and a few kettles and pails here and there, there wasn't a drop of water inside this indentation in the campus landscape, and no sunbather, wader, or swimmer was anywhere within eyesight. We tried to contend that this may have been a swimming pool at one point in the (imperialist) past, but there was no way by any interpretation of the lexical item under dispute that this could at that present moment be construed as a swimming pool. "Of course it is. It's just like our football field," they remonstrated as they turned to gesture to the much larger sea of temporary shelters behind us. I was reminded of an ancient Chinese story that foreshadowed modern psychology as well as our little debate over the existence of soccer fields and swimming pools. For a long time, I attributed this fable to the legendary Daoist philosopher, Zhuangzi (389–286 BC), who is probably most celebrated for his reflections on dreams. Having awoken from one in which he was a butterfly, he wondered whether he was a human who dreamt that he was a butterfly or, at that moment, a butterfly dreaming he was a human. It has been pointed out to me that the following story actually comes from a Chan Buddhist tradition several centuries later. Whatever its attribution, it aptly epitomizes our lesson about swimming pools and many other discussions we had in China.

Long ago, two disciples of a master philosopher were watching a banner fluttering in the wind. "Look," said one, "we can see the wind move." "No, you don't," countered the other. "The wind is invisible. What we see moving is the banner, not the wind." "You are wrong," replied the first. "Without the wind, the banner is motionless." "True," the second responded, "but what you actually see moving is the cloth banner, not the invisible wind." After bantering about the banner for some time, they decided to have their teacher resolve the contradiction, so they approached him to end the debate. "Master," began the first disciple, "isn't it true that we see the wind moving." "No, my son," he replied, "it is not the wind that moves." "Aha!" the second was quick to answer, "so I am right. It is the flag that is moving." "And no, my son, you too are mistaken. The banner is not moving." Confused and disappointed, they asked how could they both be wrong. "What is moving," their master replied, "is neither the wind nor the banner but your minds." Zhuangzi (as I would like to claim) was the first cognitive psychologist because he acknowledged that perception is ultimately not the physical vision that is photographed by your eyes, but the mental picture developed by your mind. So the existence of the swimming pool did not pivot on any linguistic definition but on our Weltanschauung or worldview that shaped what we expected or perhaps wanted to see. We tended to view China as a limited place, especially compared to the world we had lived in outside the Middle Kingdom. Our students with a natural sense of pride about their locale saw the campus as a place of opportunity and potential. Were we both right or both wrong. I wish the master had been there.

Pierre, our affable foreign expert colleague from France, related a similar experience with his students in French class. Limited in the teaching materials he had access to like us, he bought some postcards in Beijing and asked his class at the institute to describe what they saw in French, cleverly linking Chinese content matter that the students knew well with their limited knowledge of French. It turned out that they knew the Chinese scenes all too well. He was particularly exasperated when he asked his students to describe a picture of the Summer Palace. There was no problem when they began by describing the pavilion, the willows, and the lake depicted on the postcard, but then they went on to say that you could see that in wintertime people enjoyed ice-skating on the lake. "No," Pierre protested adamantly, "you cannot see any such thing. Tell me only what you can see in the picture." "But people do ice-skate on the lake in winter!" his students responded with equal vehemence. "The lake freezes over every winter. Go to Beijing this December and see for yourself!" Once again, what differed was not what was in front of their eyes but what was confronting their minds. It reminded me what an art teacher told me about an introductory pastel class he taught. "One of the hardest things for a beginner is to draw the tree that is in front of him and not a picture of what he thinks a tree looks like." Whether in America, France, or China, things are not always like the way they look.

One of the first buildings we visited at the institute was the library, where we hoped to find reference books, multiple copies of texts, and other materials to supplement the limited amount of reading we were able to fly in from the States. From its external appearance alone, we got an instant taste of how this facility functioned in post-Cultural Revolution China. Especially during the early years of that tumultuous decade, virtually anything old or foreign was suspect, and the bands of *hong wei bing* (Red Guards) that roved the nation to purge it of anything alien to the gospel of Mao directed undue attention to books. Suspicious reading materials of all kinds were confiscated or destroyed, sometimes with ludicrous results. Being young, unruly, and typically illiterate in other languages, there were instances of Red Guards going so far as to burn the English version of the *Quotations from Chairman Mao Tse-Tung*. As a result of this, librarians defended their domains as best they could in anticipation of the worst or belatedly, after an attack, to prevent any further vandalism. The windows of our library were barred and the entry door thick and well bolted, and we were told that despite several assaults on its premises, the library suffered few losses during that time of ferment. Even though the Cultural Revolution had died off a few years earlier, our librarians still harbored a siege mentality and were loathe to lose even one volume of their precious hoard to the world of barbarian vandals that surrounded their bastion of literacy. As faculty members, we were able to borrow a few books for short periods at a time, but it was always an effort, and quite frankly, there wasn't much of a trove of good reading in the place to begin with. The librarians were horrified to learn that libraries in the States had open stacks, that bevies of books could be lent for weeks at a time, and that, horror of horrors, even students could check out books anytime they wished! "Don't books get lost or stolen?" they asked almost in pity. And they followed this up with, "We haven't lost a single copy in years." Two definitions again: a library is a place where books are borrowed or a place where books are incarcerated.

There was a small, one-story building in the middle of campus that appeared even better fortified than the library, and so thick were its walls and so tiny its windows, it could've easily doubled as a military bunker abandoned decades before by the Japanese Imperial Army. The dirty windows and the dead leaves and dirt swirling around the threshold of its sturdy door enhanced its isolated status, and though we passed this place daily for almost a year, we never saw anyone enter or leave. None of the teachers or students seemed to know anything about it, and its very presence in a city where space and shelter were so prized only heightened the mystery that grew every time we passed by. Later, we were privileged to meet the man who held its key, and he opened more than just that solid door. He lovingly displayed to us the remarkable contents stored inside, and in this process, revealed the presence of one of the world's most renowned paleontologists and theologians who years before had been our predecessor. But that is a story for another chapter. After weeks of dining, touring, and settling in, we were eager to begin our life as teachers.

Tian Wai specialized in the teaching of six foreign languages: English, Japanese, French, German, Spanish, and Russian. There were approximately 160 English majors at our institute and roughly the same number studying the other foreign languages. Given its geographical proximity to Japan and long ties to that island nation, our institute had a strong reputation for Japanese language instruction and had approximately a hundred Japanese majors. When the new academic year began late that summer, our institute enrolled seventy-two new students majoring in English, fifty in Japanese, fourteen in French, and none in the other three languages. Right after the formation of the PRC, Russian was the most commonly taught foreign language, and English wasn't even second, superseded by the then more popular Spanish. After the Cultural Revolution, English once again rose to prominence as a result of Deng Xiaoping's promotion of the Four Modernizations (agriculture, industry, science, and the army). English was the foreign language of choice, and many students majoring in other languages told us that their primary interest was in English. It was not uncommon for students trained in other European languages to upgrade their skills in English and to rely on these linguistic skills to secure attractive jobs once they had graduated. There were no students studying Russian that year although the handful of instructors in that department dutifully reported to work, spending the day making tea and reading *Pravda* (truth) and *Izvestia* (news) as well as any truthful news they could glean from Chinese papers. Janene had a very unusual student in her class who actually wanted to study Russian but wasn't allowed to. Given China's ideological, historical, and geographical bonds with what was then the Union of Soviet Socialist Republics, it was equally ironic and pitiful that not a single student at our institute was being trained in this strategic world language.

Like so many other tertiary level educational institutions in China, Tian Wai hired several native speakers as foreign experts or foreign teachers to teach classes and assist the Chinese faculty in their pedagogical duties. During our work at the institute and over the course of our visits to other educational institutions, we met many of these foreigners, and they represented a checkered mélange of backgrounds. Initially, they tended to be non-Americans and predominantly friends of China, chosen more for their ideological leanings or cultural affinity for things Chinese rather than for their pedagogical experience. Until the autumn of 1979, when more Americans and also more qualified foreign experts started to arrive in significant numbers, we encountered no one nearly as trained or as experienced as we in English language teaching, a sad contrast to the intelligent and highly motivated students that these foreigners were privileged to teach. Here is a representative sample of some of the foreign English teachers I remembered meeting in China during the first six months: an astronomer, a museum curator, a restaurant owner, a law professor, a college dropout, and a former Amtrak clerk. Long gone should be the days when the only qualification to teach a foreign language is the ability to speak the target tongue natively. All swimmers do not great swim coaches make. All pianists are not equally endowed to teach piano. Being a successful painter does not ensure that you can successfully transmit your art to others. Since language acquisition is also an incredibly complex and creative skill and because it is the more demanding if we consider the high level of proficiency among the English majors we were fortunate to teach, it was a pity to see that most of our foreign peers were experts only by virtue of their Chinese title, *wai guo yu zhuan jia* (foreign language expert). Most of them were expert only in the sense of my favorite etymology of that term: the prefix *ex* means a has-been, and the root *spurt* refers to a drip under pressure! I was frank when sharing my views about this matter during several visits to the Foreign Experts Office in Beijing, and I was delighted that when I had the opportunity to fly to the States in the early spring to attend the annual convention of Teachers of English to Speakers of Other Languages (TESOL) in Boston, I helped foster a surge of interest among its members, qualified professionals like Janene and me who took me up on the invitation to consider teaching in China. Upon my return from that brief trip, I visited the Foreign Experts Bureau in Beijing and was happy to deliver to them the applications of ninety-three TESOL teachers, genuine *zhuan jia*, who had jumped at the opportunity to teach in China.

The small foreign staff at Tian Wai was no exception to the generalization about foreign experts just made. They appeared to be well-intentioned and reasonably hardworking, but none of them struck us as exceptional language teachers; compared to most of their Chinese colleagues, they appeared to be singularly undistinguished. There was a Peruvian who taught the few students majoring in Spanish, and he had been in China the longest. His family was one of several who had fled Peru during one of the Rightist military coups in the sixties. A rather taciturn elderly man from Japan was the Japanese expert, and he also lived at the Tianjin Hotel. Also living at our hotel but teaching at Nankai University were two elderly Canadian foreign experts: a Caucasian woman who taught English and a Canadian-Chinese man who taught science. We had no German or Russian foreign experts at our institute, but a young and enthusiastic couple was there teaching French. Besides the two of us, also teaching English at the same time was a young woman from New York City and, later in the year, a middle-aged single mother with her young son from the States. Attempting to speak more out of honesty than conceit, I think it's fair to conclude that due to our professional expertise and previous overseas experience, Janene and I made much more of a contribution to the institute that year than any of our expatriate colleagues.

Like any arbitrarily chosen set of people, the foreign experts we met or heard about that year in China varied in personality and personal behavior, but the lack of cultural sensitivity on the part of many of these aliens and the provincial naiveté of many of their Chinese employers made for a dangerous cross-cultural mix. Take the example of an American, thankfully not from our institute but who came in the early autumn to teach at Nankai University. Young, ignorant of Asian cultures, and recently divorced, she arrived with her son, who was the same age as Derick, and this in itself created some problems. The poor kid was left alone a lot and got into some minor troubles at our hotel and on the street for which our son was sometimes blamed. If this were only the second white-skinned boy you ever saw, it is easy to understand how all American boys looked alike to the Chinese, but Derick resented being blamed for this recently arrived upstart's escapades. But it was the boy's mom who really got into hot water when she fell in love with one of her students at Nankai and planned to marry him, a simple, quick, and cheap procedure in China. Unfortunately, she seemed clueless about how complex, tedious, and calamitous her actions were for the poor student, her Chinese colleagues, and her dan wei. When the affair became public knowledge (and in China this happens at the speed of light), the senior student was expelled, and the teacher who worked most closely with her was severely reprimanded for the American's misbehavior. We rarely met with her, but when I tried to explain to her the impropriety of even dating a student, I was dismayed at her reaction. She seemed to think the Nankai officials were upset because this would be an interracial marriage, and while racism certainly could've been part of the equation, it was the violation of the teacher-to-student covenant that the Chinese rightly viewed as almost sacrilegious. Once more, I was bewildered why a person like this was chosen to teach in China and at a key university no less. Oh well, at least she wasn't as bad as the British foreign expert we heard about who taught at Beijing University and was one of the few experts who actually got fired and sent home. The authorities tolerated his incessant sexual harassment of the females in his classes and his constant attempts to lure students from the nearby girl's dorm into his flat for sex. They also put up with his bouts of drunken behavior on weekends, but when one of these binges led him to throw his small refrigerator out of his upstairs apartment, he also tossed out any chance of staying in China and was sent packing. Abusing women and getting plowed was tolerated; after all, he was a barbarian, but a new fridge cost the dan wei a pretty penny and was expensive to replace.

We hadn't been at Tian Wai long at all when we discovered how the Cultural Revolution, which was so intent on eliminating the traditional Chinese veneration of formal education, in a strange reversal, actually spawned an entire school of extremely bright and highly motivated students. These young scholars were the very ones entrusted to our care. Just three years before our arrival, like almost all other tertiary establishments in the nation, Tian Wai had for all intents and purposes been closed down by the Cultural Revolution, so in 1976, when that national turmoil ended, the class of seniors Janene was fortunate enough to teach was the first cohort to enter the institute. This meant that they were the first students in about a decade to take official entrance exams in order to pursue a university education, and as a result, they were young women and men of exceptional intellectual precocity given that they represented the best and the brightest out of a decade of university-age high school graduates. Because of the gap in years, Janene's class also ranged in age from eighteen to twenty-five. Due to a legacy from the Cultural Revolution, her students also shared something else in common in addition to their academic brilliance; they were all more or less children from families who were *gong nong bing* (workers, peasants, soldiers), the elite class in a classless society. As rigid as a military academy, our institute ranked grade levels and individuals within them in a clear-cut hierarchy. Janene's class was the top group of the '76 class, and since these students were selected from this very first post–Cultural Revolution cohort, they were indeed the crème de la crème. As befitting their lofty status, they got the top floor of the building while the classes of '77, '78, and '79 occupied the second and first floors. Within each grade level, classrooms were divided by academic ranking from number 1 (Janene's class again) on down, and the location of these classrooms also followed the numerical ranking so that the poorest students in the freshman class were placed on the cold north side of the first floor of the building next to the gaping front door and, worst yet, adjoining a reeking bathroom. Rank has its privileges.

Students received instruction six days a week with formal class work occupying the entire morning whereas the afternoons were filled with the obligatory after lunch naps followed by tutorials, special lectures, political meetings, language lab practice, and an occasional film. The curriculum for the English majors consisted of six hours a week of intensive reading with two each for grammar, extensive reading, translation, and listening (in the language lab). They also spent an additional weekly total of six hours studying another foreign language, Chinese, and political philosophy. During their first year, all students had four hours of extra classes devoted to current events and the history of the Chinese Communist Party. The size of the teaching faculty seemed extraordinarily high compared to what we had experienced in Thailand and the United States; there were about 230 faculty members, fewer than two students for every teacher! Teachers also appeared to have the world's lightest teaching load—six contact hours a week or one hour a day.

However, context is everything, and it should be emphasized that our Chinese colleagues faced many constraints that sapped their time and energy: weekly political and pedagogical meetings, a lack of materials, little experience in using English in authentic and communicative situations, a limited supply of multiple copies of textbooks, substandard and often broken audiovisual equipment, personal or family health problems, the pressing daily grind of surviving in a city that was still recovering from the Tangshan earthquake, and certainly not least among these limitations, the residual psychological trauma of what they all had just endured during the Cultural Revolution. In addition to all of this, some teachers were assigned to special projects, such as writing textbooks or compiling dictionaries. We also were struck by the inordinately large number of non-academic staff; they equaled the faculty in number and were comprised mainly of administrative cadres.

Janene's schedule was confined to the morning, so she could return to the hotel at noon to lunch with Derick and teach him his American curriculum in the afternoon. She was given the institute's top class of English majors and met with them five days a week from 8:00 a.m. to 10:00 a.m., covering a syllabus that was somewhat evenly divided between a concentration on English language skills and literature and culture. This opportunity to work closely with a small and consistent band of students forged an abiding friendship among them that Janene found difficult to relinquish when we finally left for the United States at the end of the year. During the second half of the morning, she met with a rotation of three different teaching groups to answer their questions and to discuss matters both personal and pedagogical. These groups consisted of eight young to middle-aged teachers who were responsible for three different grades of English majors, and Janene could read in their eyes and faces a deep appreciation not just for her knowledge as a foreigner and native speaker of English but even more for her professional expertise and personal warmth. During her spare time, she met with Xiao Zhang for Chinese lessons and labored throughout that year to overcome a natural proclivity to use Thai, which she had learned well, and to become more fluent in Mandarin. Truth be told, I was slightly jealous of her schedule for mine was less structured, and because it involved a variety of changing activities, I never was able to bond closely to any group. Accordingly, when we left Tianjin in December, I was saying good-bye to colleagues and acquaintances, but Janene was bidding farewell to an intimate family of friends.

Eighteen students greeted her eagerly every morning, and she developed a quick affection for each one and also for their English, which was exceptionally fluent considering their limited contact with native speakers. Both their speech and writing were peppered with quaint collocations; along with the usual "warmly welcomes" and "you must be tireds" were gems like "my heart leaped with joy," "we were deeply moved," and "that's a tough nut to crack." We soon learned that certain words with neutral connotation to us carried a lot of negative freight in China. One day, Janene lightheartedly called the boy who wanted to study Russian a rascal, and instantly, the class fell silent in stunned and angry astonishment. Only after some coaxing on her part did Janene learn that this term referred to one of the many categories of political criminals created and punished during the Cultural Revolution and certainly was inappropriate to use in jest.

Every classroom had a monitor who served as a captain for that particular team of students. Janene's monitor was a confident and outgoing young woman, pigtailed like most of her young female contemporaries, and surprisingly outspoken. Her monitoring worked both ways: as a facilitator between Janene and the class, like over the rascal incident, and also as a conduit between what transpired in the American teacher's class and the leadership of the institute. It was a challenging dual role, but Xiao Liu was up to the task and overall was of able assistance throughout the challenges Janene faced teaching in a very different pedagogical world from the suburban middle school in Pittsburgh from which she had just traveled.

We both noticed that our students and teaching colleagues had a fascination and facility with English grammar, and this was no surprise in a culture where attention to detail is almost synonymous with education. Learning a language is a complex enterprise that involves a multitude of overlapping skills, and it's no wonder that in every country children take around a decade to master their mother tongues. Learning a new and alien language after that time is an even more daunting task for it often includes literacy skills beyond the ken of an average ten-year-old. No linguist would deny that grammar plays a significant role in foreign language learning, but to overemphasize its role in a curriculum would be as misinformed as it would to devote the bulk of your musical training to playing octaves or the majority of your practice as a discus thrower doing push-ups. During our tenure at the institute, Janene and I tried to redress this pedagogical imbalance in various ways with various degrees of success.

As already mentioned, her students were used to a curriculum that devoted large chunks of class time to what the Chinese called intensive reading or what the French call *expliqué de text*. Considerably less time was allocated to general reading for comprehension, so-called extensive reading. The former was basically a word-by-word analysis and exegesis of a passage during which the class and teacher would painfully dissect each phrase, clause, and sentence as joylessly and meticulously as a group of fifth graders would a worm. A story that began with "Once upon a time," for instance, would elicit a discussion of the difference between *one* and *once*, which could lead to a foray into the etymology of *twice* and *thrice* before returning to the second word of this phrase, which was clearly a compound preposition, etc., etc. With so many nits to pick, it took an understandably long time to troll through the lexico-grammatical mysteries of each sentence, and this is why her class would have spent an entire four-month semester to explicate a slim paperback devoted to the life and accomplishments of Madame Curie. To be fair, this grammar-translation method of teaching English did not differ that much from foreign language teaching in other countries, and in fact, the brief description just given may very well evoke memories from Americans of high school foreign language classes in years gone by.

Fortunately, Janene was married to a language specialist, that rare scholar who delights in contemplating matters of profound communicative relevance such as the difference between gerunds and participles, so she could rely on me for all the intensive reading questions thrown at her throughout the week. It was apparent to both of us that one contribution we were qualified to make as part of our work was to emphasize and amplify our students' skills in extensive reading. The students had textbooks published in China, but irrespective of the dryness of their content and their consistent political slant, they focused mainly on form and structure and minimally on function and meaning. Seeking out any available alternatives, we turned to the institute's library to see if it contained multiple copies of any genre of literature in English that Janene could use for her class. Due to the fortress-under-siege mentality of the place, it was a challenge simply to successfully extract even a single copy of a book, so suffice it to say, she was content to emerge at the end of the day with a copy of a book she felt might work—John Gunther's *Death Be Not Proud*. There wasn't much to choose from, but she was confident that this poignant account of a father's journey with the disease and ultimate death of his young son would cross the cultural divide that separated Americana from her students and would motivate them to read extensively. Finding a book was the easy part, but how to generate multiple copies?

The only duplicating process available to teachers at our institute was an old-fashioned mimeograph machine similar to one we had used when we taught in Bangkok in the mid-sixties, so Janene bravely set out to copy Gunther's entire book for her class. Night after night, she would type out page after page of the book in our hotel room on the portable typewriter we had brought from the States. The legal-size stencils she used were onion-paper thin, and whenever she made a mistake, she was forced to brush a nail polish–like correction fluid on the stencil, blow it dry, and then carefully retype the correction. With the devotion of a mediaeval monk, over several months, she was able to transform the library's single copy into an extensive reading textbook available to every student in her class and to many teachers in addition. In the morning, she would give the stencils from her previous evening's labors to the department secretaries and, after much cajoling on Janene's part, succeeded in wooing them away from their typical morning's activity of reading the *Tianjin Ribao* (*Tianjin Daily*) and running off ink-stained copies for her students.

On the first day that Janene handed out a few pages of Gunther's first chapter for her students to read for their homework, there was a mini Cultural Revolution. The task was absolutely impossible, their American teacher utterly unrealistic, and there was no way on earth that they could fulfill their teacher's excessive demands! After negotiation, first with Xiao Liu and then with the entire class, Janene effected a compromise. At first, they would have to read only one page a night, and she reminded them that this was no *expliqué de text*, so they didn't have to comprehend every word and phrase but simply get the gist of what they had read. Because the students lived together in dorms and could help one another with each day's assignments, collectively and gradually, they discovered they were actually capable of understanding this story. Week by week, Janene was able to increase the number of pages the class could comfortably cover in a day although this added even more work to her stenographic duties every evening. Slowly but surely the transformation occurred. As young Johnny got sicker and sicker and the specter of death drew closer and closer, the students became consumed by the story and not by the individual words on the page, and they were swept into reading extensively. When death came, the students could empathize not just because the author's son was their age but also because death was still close to all of them three years after that devastating Tangshan earthquake. Soon, English was much more than a language of gerunds and participles; like Chinese, it was a way of reading and talking about ultimate concerns. Another transformation was also achieved, for—little by little— the differences between Janene and her students, which appeared so glaring at the beginning of the year, slowly began to diminish during those morning hours together.

Whereas Janene's schedule was well structured, consistent, and focused by and large on teaching the students, my work at Tian Wai was less defined, flexible, and devoted mainly to working with the teachers. I gave many informal talks and lectures to the faculty on topics dealing with linguistics, methodology, and the English language. I worked weekly with a dictionary group that was intent on publishing a comprehensive glossary of English phrases and idioms containing prepositions, and I quickly was enlisted to teach the first group of postgraduate students that would be admitted into the institute's nascent graduate program. Janene and I would bike to work together in the morning, one of us taking a slight detour to drop Christine off at her nursery, and then like my Chinese colleagues, I'd spend the rest of the day at the institute six days a week although I'd rarely spend a full Saturday since those afternoons were often devoted to political meetings, a chore Janene and I were obviously happy to be excused from. Every Saturday, as I'd hop on my bike to cycle home in the early afternoon, it was always amusing to hear my colleagues or students sing out, "Have a nice weekend." Once again, the problem of definitions emerged: aren't weekends longer than forty-two hours?

No sooner had we begun teaching than both of us unwittingly left our Chinese colleagues with the somewhat undeserved impression that we were workaholics. We soon noticed that an important part of the daily schedule and, for some, the highlight of the workday was the afternoon nap. As soon as the noon meal was completed, in their dorms, temporary shelters, classrooms or offices, all of the Tian Wai students, teachers, staff, and cadres collapsed on beds and cots or slumped on tables and desks and rapidly fell into a blissful state of unconsciousness. This nationally prescribed siesta was an hour for the colder months but doubled as soon as the languid days of spring warmed the city. So pervasive was this practice that even the streets seemed less crowded in the early afternoon, and those still peddling to and fro did so at a more leisurely pace. Coming from a culture where five days of work were the norm, it seemed fair to us for the Chinese to throw in a short break each day considering they were used to a six-day workweek, and since neither of us napped at home, we used this hour or two to read and write undisturbed. This innocent behavior on our part impressed our Chinese students, colleagues, and leaders and, as on occasion happens in China, grew legendary. After word got around that we were model workers laboring arduously even through the sacred rest hour to serve the institute, we were bombarded with accolades and were greeted with more "you must be tireds" than ever before. In the long run, we could see several benefits of this tradition. In addition to the salubrious effect of having workers take a rest after their noonday meal and enjoying a short break from the daily grind, adding an hour when almost nothing was done to the daily work schedule helped mitigate the effects of overemployment. With such a huge population, it behooved the leaders of China to deploy an overabundance of workers to ensure that almost everyone had a job, so an hour or two of enforced work stoppage every day indirectly helped balance out the fact that the workforce outnumbered the jobs to which it was assigned. For our part, we were happy to garner the praise of our colleagues and tried to maintain our status as model workers throughout our stay, but when the heat and humidity of summer enveloped the city, it became increasingly difficult for us to avoid joining our compatriots for a little afternoon snooze.

One of the most professionally exciting opportunities I experienced while teaching at the institute was assisting the faculty and leadership to set up an MA program in English language studies and to teach one of the courses for this new degree. In 1979, very few Chinese students had an opportunity to attend a university, and only a miniscule number of those were able to pursue a postgraduate degree (what we would call a graduate degree in the States). At that time, the educational pyramid in China had an exceptionally broad base with roughly 145 million elementary pupils diminishing to approximately half that number in middle and high school. The pyramid rapidly tapered, however, with only about a million and a half studying at the university level and then shrunk to a tiny point with barely thirty thousand doing any type of postgraduate work. As a consequence, at that time, only one elementary child in a hundred continued on to college, and among those few, only one in fifty studied further. To rectify this highly uneven distribution and to encourage science and technology, one of the Four Modernizations, the government persuaded institutions like ours to initiate MA programs. With memories of the anti-intellectualism of the Cultural Revolution hovering so close to the collective consciousness, it took a remarkable mix of courage and discernment on the part of my colleagues to create this new degree, but they were able to do so rapidly and effectively. By late spring, entrance examinations were written and administered, and in a surprisingly short span of time, Tian Wai had an incoming class of about half a dozen MA students with about as many visiting professors auditing our new program. Tellingly, there was only one female participant in that initial class.

Among several courses open to me, I jumped at the opportunity to be the first professor in China ever to teach a course in psycholinguistics, a choice my colleagues were willing to endorse. A subject that examines the ways in which language and speech are windows to the functioning of the human mind and brain may seem too esoteric for graduate students interested in linguistics and English language teaching, particularly considering the time and the place of my class. Still, several factors argued for its inclusion in the new curriculum. In the late seventies, the now established field of second language acquisition was in its infancy and since psycholinguistics covered many aspects of that then nascent subject, it seemed reasonable to introduce an established field with introductory textbooks readily available. While working in Thailand, I started a psycholinguistics course for university students there, so I already had experience teaching and adopting the field to meet the needs of Asian students who were preparing to be English teachers or translators. Finally, knowing that none of the teachers or students at our institute had any background in psychology since it had been banned by the Party for several decades, I felt it was worthwhile to redress this gap in their education by introducing basic terms, concepts, and perspectives in this new course. So we had a course, an instructor, a classroom, and a group of eager graduate students and auditors. All we needed was a textbook.

As soon as it became clear that I'd be teaching this new course, I wrote to a friend back in the States and asked him to order and immediately ship to me twenty copies of Dan Slobin's *Psycholinguistics*, a short, moderately priced, and accessible introduction to the field. Already well aware that much of our mail was censored, I naively thought that books dealing with such trivial, apolitical, and stultifying topics such as the effects of constituent boundaries on immediate memory would have no trouble avoiding the heavy hand of Chinese censorship. I was mistaken. The date for our new MA program to commence came, and the texts still hadn't arrived, so I began our class with a general introduction to the foundations of psychology and linguistics. About two weeks into the course, just about the same time I was running out of introductory material to cover, a box containing *half* my order arrived from the US publisher, Scott, Foresman and Company. The invoice accompanying this package acknowledged my order of twenty copies and indicated that two boxes of ten books each had been airmailed to me on the same date from their Illinois office. The other box never came, and it was only a year later, after our family returned to the States, that I discovered what had happened. Meanwhile, my graduate students and auditors shared our limited supply of ten, one pair to a textbook, and since they were already so experienced in sharing materials, everyone was able to keep up with the reading assignments, and the course continued and was concluded successfully. But what about the odd case of the missing package?

After our return to Pittsburgh, I wrote to Scott, Foresman and Company inquiring about the order I had placed from China the year before. They replied that they had indeed airmailed two boxes of Slobin's text to Tianjin as ordered and paid for, but a few weeks after the publisher posted them, one of the boxes was returned to them. Perplexed and not knowing how to respond, they still had the leftover ten books, and in due course, they sent them to me although by then I had no need of this particular text. Based on my various experiences with Chinese censors during our year in China and from what I would learn about the Party's policy toward psychology, I have a fairly good hunch about what had transpired. The censors at the Tianjin Post Office appeared to be somewhat careless in their duties, so some correspondence seemed to get through to us either unchecked or ignored, and this was obviously the case with the first package of psycholinguistic textbooks. It seems logical to assume that the second box was opened up, and after the censors checked the title of the enclosed texts, they found that it named a forbidden topic, *xin li xue* (psychology). Dutifully, they rewrapped the box, and finding the books quite useless (unlike useful materials such as *Playboy*, which were immediately confiscated), they posted the package back to the publisher in Illinois. Since psychology was banned, so too were any books that talked about this counterrevolutionary topic. During that remarkable year, we were able to witness several noteworthy changes in the Party's policies, and in the fall, I was able to observe firsthand the resurrection of not just psychology but of a much more significant body of belief.

During the first few months of the spring semester, I was assigned to a team that was charged with creating a new type of English-Chinese dictionary. I would huddle together in a small room along with about half a dozen of the more senior teachers in our department, sipping tea and pondering long lists of collocations of English phrases that contained prepositions. The idea for this project was actually quite innovative for it predated by a couple of decades the now popular notion in linguistics that native speakers of all languages are not walking dictionaries with heads filled with individual words listed neatly in alphabetical order. Rather, all of us have immediate access to thousands of fixed or semifixed phrases that form the scaffolding for any utterances we create. This small group of lexicographers at Tian Wai was also clever to restrict their inquiry to phrases containing prepositions because English has a special affinity to use them as the grammatical glue for a huge number of collocations. So once a week, I would help my colleagues by suggesting that, yes, one could be disappointed *in*, disappointed *at*, disappointed *about*, or disappointed *over* something, but, no, one could not be disappointed *of*, disappointed *into*, disappointed *to*, or disappointed *upon* something. Like most linguists, I tried to avoid defending these choices even though my fellow lexicographers would continuously wonder why. When pressed too strenuously or too long, I would come up with examples from Chinese that, like the English phrases we pored over, ultimately defied logic. Despite their inherent interest in details and precision, my peers came to realize that language, like culture, has a "fiddler on the roof" quality in which a rich, complex, and often illogical repertoire of behaviors gets transmitted from generation to generation. To members of that linguistic community, it's simply the way we talk. To auslanders, however, the way they talk is strange or funny or both.

I looked forward to these weekly meetings with the team even though our progress seemed tediously slow, but one morning, I was met with unhappy faces and some distressing news. Somehow, one of our team members found out that another institute in western China had been compiling an identical dictionary, and worse yet, they had completed this project and were about to publish their work! Mind you, China is a huge country, and back then, telecommunication was limited, and contacts between colleagues even in the same profession were rare and tended to be confined by geography. Like my Tian Wai colleagues, I found the news frustrating, and I felt a personal loss as we had all grown closer, sipping tea and mulling over word choices in that small cluster of scholars united by our arcane interest in words. We had talked about these collocations a great deal, but now we were living them; all of us were disappointed in, at, about, and over the dismantling of our little community.

About the same time, our institute was contracted to help train and orient a large group of professors, engineers, doctors, and bureaucrats for an opportunity to study abroad for a one-year stint as visiting scholars in largely English-speaking nations. This ambitious program, which ultimately gave thousands of Chinese a chance to upgrade and update their technical expertise, was evidently a direct consequence of the Party's policy to promote the Four Modernizations, and because our institute was contracted to teach over a hundred candidates from the Tianjin area, the leadership was eager to enlist our expertise. Consequently, on top of our growing responsibilities, we began spending a couple of hours each week trying to improve the limited English skills of a diversely talented and unequally motivated group of mostly middle-aged professionals from widely divergent disciplines with a curriculum that appeared to be designed by morticians. Some, mostly those who crowded into the front row, seemed genuinely engaged, but the large majority seemed disinterested in our attempts to transform water into wine and only displayed signs of life when our class was dismissed. I was reminded of a sign I once saw in a store back in the States. "If you don't believe in the resurrection of the dead," it began, "you should stick around and watch our employees at closing time."

I gave approximately fifty public lectures that year, about half of them in Tianjin and the remainder at various institutes and universities during our travels around China. With few exceptions, they dealt with linguistics or English language teaching, areas of my academic expertise, and though they could not replicate the dynamic and personal experience forged over several months of contact with students in a classroom, they did enlarge my classroom and exponentially increased the number of students I reached. In subsequent years, I would occasionally meet Chinese graduate students or visiting scholars in the States or at international conferences, and in typical Chinese fashion, they would greet me excitedly with, "Professor Scovel, remember me? I was your student in Shanghai!" Because my dan wei was in Tianjin not Shanghai in 1979, I would rapidly attempt to recall the series of itinerant lectures I delivered that year, a task that grew increasingly difficult as time progressed, and then reply with a hesitant, "Oh yes. You must be from East China Normal University." Still not satisfied, my interlocutor would press me with something like, "Of course, remember I asked you a question about the audio-lingual method?" What counted in these exchanges was the fact that even though we had shared only an hour and a half together with scores of other people in a large auditorium several years before, I remained her teacher and she my student. There is something indelible about the student-teacher relationship in China, and I appreciated that this bond could be forged albeit partially, through the many talks I was privileged to deliver.

As a psycholinguist, teacher, parent, and husband, I have always been intrigued by the fact that communication does not just hinge upon what you say or write; it depends much more upon what your listener or reader hears or comprehends. Thus, what intrigued me most during the many public addresses I presented that year was not what I said, for unsurprisingly none of it was new or especially insightful to me. What caught my attention most was what transpired during the discussions and question-and-answer periods that took place after I had spoken. It was here I could hear what the participants heard, understand what they understood, and most importantly of all, learn what they were interested in. A brief recapitulation of one of the talks I gave at Tian Wai serves as a representative example.

Wanting to connect as quickly as possible with my audience, I often chose Chinese proverbs for a title or sprinkled them through my talks as illustrations. The leadership at Tian Wai was happy to trot me out in public in a part to advertise the fact that despite their modest status, our little institute had a real American expert (China-born, no less), and for one of my first lectures, they invited teachers and professors from all over the city, places of lesser or equal status, such as from some of the local high schools and the Tianjin Teachers College, but also from Tianjin University and lofty Nankai. Sharing their interest in linguistic detail but wanting to challenge my audience to look at the larger and ultimate issue of meaning, I chose one of my favorite Chinese apothegms for my title: *jian le zhi ma, diu le xi gua* (in trying to pick up the sesame seeds, you drop the watermelon). In sum, I tried to argue that if linguists and language teachers continued to focus on the specifics of grammar, they would be unable to see the forest for the trees, or to wax biblical, it's misguided to strain at gnats but swallow camels. One theme from modern linguistics that I introduced in this lecture was the idea that there is often a mismatch between what linguists call surface structure from the underlying deep structure of an utterance. For instance, "John is eager to please." is superficially similar to "John is easy to please." However, the deeper meaning differs between these two claims: John does the pleasing in the first sentence but someone else does the pleasing in the second.

Daunted by the large crowd and unwilling to be embarrassed by what could appear to be a silly response, there were few questions raised from the audience right after my talk, but as was often the case, participants were eager to engage me in private discussion once much of the crowd had left. Several young teachers seemed especially keen on talking to me, so I turned my attention to them, ingenuously expecting them to seize upon the major insight that I had just shared. Alas, their interest was solely in how many sesame seeds can dance on the head of a pin. I learned they were a group of high school English teachers, and for some time, they had been long vexed by a grammar question, and now they had this rare chance to find the answer from a native speaker with a PhD in linguistics to boot. Disappointed that their sole concern was in the very topic that I had just devoted ninety minutes deprecating, I reluctantly asked them to continue. Almost unable to contain their excitement, one of them carefully spelled out the problem. "What part of speech is *times,*" he asked, "in the sentence, two times two equals four?" I suddenly realized that more was going on than just a simple grammar test.

Questions and answers are serious business in China, and once the trap is set, there is no recourse to the glib replies that Americans are prone to toss out, such as "Who cares?" or "Whatever!" At once, I realized that I was being drawn into a hidden debate and was expected to come up with a clever compromise. Not being Zhuangzi, I chose a delaying tactic and asked, "Why do you want to know?" They replied somewhat impatiently that their students might ask them about this point, and it might very well be on the entrance examination, so what is the answer? Leaving the natural world of communication for a moment and plunging into the netherworld of grammar, I sympathized with the problem they had given me for both *times* and *equals* are apparently marked with third person singular present tense suffixes, making both words appear as the main verbs of that simple sentence. However, as we all remember from our high school English classes, a simple sentence can contain only one finite verb. They nodded in agreement, and one of them admitted that "it's a tough nut to crack." Not wanting to diminish my "expert" status nor to have them go away unsatisfied, I gave them a solution that the Danish grammarian, Otto Jespersen, came up with decades earlier and told them that maybe *times* wasn't a verb but a noun, so the *-s* suffix marked it as a plural. That is, another way of analyzing this equation is to look at it as "Two, two times equals four" or 2 X 2 = 4. Thus, the contradiction is resolved, and the sentence has only one main verb, *equals*. First, there was a flash of recognition then murmurs of agreement and then expressions of gratitude for helping them untie this grammatical Gordian knot.

Not content to let this teachable moment go by, however, I snatched the opportunity to go back to the main point of the lecture they had just heard and hammer home the importance of meaning. I asked for a piece of paper, and turning the tables on them, I asked them to analyze a sentence for me. Happy to receive so much attention, they watched me as I thought up a simple multiplication problem and printed it neatly down for all of them to see: "47 multiplied by 6 equals 283." Visions of sesame seeds danced in their heads, and their focus centered on *multiplied* with arguments for and against it being a verb, this time in the past tense. The discussion ebbed and flowed over what part of speech it was, and the group was starting to become almost as agitated over this new problem as the one they had originally brought to me. Waiting a few minutes, I then sprang my trap. "Look," I said, perhaps a bit too smugly, "47 times 6 doesn't equal 283. It equals 282!" They paused a minute, a bit nonplused that I had distracted them momentarily from the central task at hand, and then brushing my comment aside, they returned to the intriguing question of the grammatical status of *multiplied*. This was an isolated incident, of course, and one swallow does not a summer make, but I would claim that I learned more than those young teachers did that afternoon, and alas, I don't think they got the message that I had tried so hard to convey.

We were bombarded with questions throughout our stay, a logical consequence of the Chinese propensity for curiosity and our presence as the first American teachers in that city in many decades. These inquiries dealt with all kinds of issues, many of them beyond our expertise, but the funniest one of all came after one of my lectures on applied linguistics, and because it was a public forum, it took an enormous amount of self-control to contain my mirth since any humorous reaction on my part would have unintentionally discredited the questioner. I had just finished one of the many talks I gave that year—this one on the various ways both a learner's mother tongue and her limited knowledge of a second language created an approximation of the latter that was error-filled but creative and moving toward accuracy. Linguists call this transition stage interlanguage. I had an attentive audience of teachers, but the first question floored me. Only the few, the proud, and the brave dared to ask questions in public. For one thing, in a room full of English teachers, you were surrounded by critics waiting to pounce on the slightest mispronunciation, infelicitous word choice, or grammatical blunder. For another, the Cultural Revolution had left a legacy of anxiety about making any public comments for these provided a permanent record that could be used or misinterpreted by anyone at any time in the future as a potential refutation of Mao Zedong thought. That is why most questioners caught me outside after my talks to engage in private, like the young teachers who were so infatuated with finite verbs, and for this reason, I bent over backward to be solicitous to the brave soul who confronted me with the following query. "Thank you for your most interesting lecture, Professor Scovel," he began, "but I want to know how long it takes students in America to get over *intercourse.*" If I had betrayed even the slightest smirk in reaction to his inquiry, he would've been instantly surrounded by laughter and ridicule and later criticized for not knowing that his version of my technical term was a synonym for copulation. But as I've already acknowledged, it was obligatory at those moments to be stoic and courteous, and I bit my tongue as I thought of all the ways I could've responded were I somewhere else. "Well, I don't know about what happens in China, but the typical American male gets over it in about thirty seconds, way too quickly if you ask the average American woman." Instead, I took the high road and replied in kind, "Thank you for your most interesting question. With constant study, opportunity, and motivation, many learners move beyond *interlanguage* and eventually end up successful bilinguals, like all of you." And I gestured to my still-serious audience with a sweep of the hand.

Some of our presentations were a success, however, both from what we said and what our Chinese participants actually heard. The first public lecture we gave at Tian Wai was by far the one I remember best although it was on a topic that was about as far afield from my professional expertise as you could stray. Like many of our Chinese experiences, the opportunity sprang upon us with sudden surprise. On a Sunday evening in late February, Lao Chen appeared at our hotel room for an unexpected visit. Of the many cadres we worked with at the institute, even more than Lao Shen or other members of the wai ban, Lao Chen was our chief administrative contact, and as the year progressed, he became a respected colleague, and our friendship grew to become mutual and genuine. He was the cochair of the English department when we first arrived but was quickly promoted to vice president of the institute, and since he was a Party official, he had the political clout to carry through with any negotiations we made. He was fair in his decisions and honest in expressing his various frustrations with us. A chain-smoker, he had a husky voice and was not in the best of health, and now long after his passing, what sticks in my mind's eye whenever I think of him was his remarkable resemblance to Ho Chi Minh. So when we welcomed him in to the comfort of our hotel that Sunday evening, knowing his status and appreciating his relationship with us, we guessed that this was more than a courtesy call. "And how is your little daughter?" he began, rubbing his hands from the chilly evening bike ride. We assured him she was finally recovering from a bout of conjunctivitis and that, yes, the rest of us were in quite good health. We poured him some tea, offered him some biscuits from the Friendship Store, and chatted politely about Derick's music school, Janene's students, and the formation of the new MA program. The niceties continued for half an hour or so when Lao Chen, not seeming to impose on our time any more, reached for his scarf and acknowledged that it was late and time to leave. As we walked out into the hallway, he stopped with "By the way." Physicians call this a doorknob moment when at the end of somewhat aimless chitchat with a patient, just as you're about to leave, a critical question pops up.

"By the way," Lao Chen began, "did you know that tomorrow is George Washington's birthday?" "No," we readily admitted, and about the last thing to cross our minds back then was the American calendar and the US presidency. "Well," he continued, "I think it would be appropriate if you could give a little talk to some of the students tomorrow about President Washington. After all, after these many years of isolation, our students know very little about America. It's important to strengthen the friendship between our two nations, and this would help."

"We'd be happy to," Janene responded with enthusiasm, and being a history major, she sensed a rare chance to share some

American culture with her students. "Wonderful," rejoined Lao Chen. "Meet me in the Propaganda Hall tomorrow morning at ten. Good night." I walked him downstairs and to his bike and hurried back upstairs to deconstruct his request with Janene.

Knowing the Chinese tendency to understate requests at times in an attempt to be deferential, I translated Lao Chen's invitation into the more matter-of-fact mode of expression that we Americans are more familiar with. "A little talk" translated into a major two-hour lecture, and "some of the students" should be interpreted as several hundred plus as many faculty as they could squeeze into the institute's main auditorium. Like so many invitations, this too came suddenly, so there was no time to lose. We put the kids to bed and culled through the few materials we had brought from the States to glean any piece of information we could uncover about America's first president. Even if we had a week, we probably wouldn't have been able to squeeze much more out of our meager resources. No Internet, no Google, and no library. Fortunately, before we left Pittsburgh, we purchased a 1979 edition of a world almanac, and this became a treasure chest of useful facts for us throughout our stay. Learning that we came from Pittsburgh, for instance, students wanted to know its exact population ("What a small city," they exclaimed in sympathy), the name of its mayor ("Do all American cities have Italian leaders?), and the enrollment at my campus ("What a huge university," they exclaimed in admiration). The almanac had a paragraph on Washington's life and presidency and contained other minutiae about him with which we could pad our talk. Did you know, by the way, that by dying eleven days before Christmas in 1799, he missed seeing a new millennium by a mere two weeks? As a history major, Janene organized all the biographical data and would present this as the historical first half of our lecture. In keeping with the title I chose for our joint presentation, I would continue and conclude the talk with an interpretive explanation of why George Washington was, in our eyes, the most revered of all American presidents.

Fatigued from our late-hour preparations and understandably nervous, we cycled to the institute that morning for our first public presentation. The Propaganda Hall was a dark, unheated auditorium that looked like it had been largely cemented over, yet despite the dull walls and chilly atmosphere, its vaulted ceiling and high-arched windows gave the impression that the hall once served as a chapel. Janene and I were seated with several cadres on a wooden podium facing hundreds of students, faculty members, and outside guests crammed together on folded chairs and dimly lit by the low, slanting winter sun penetrating the dirty windows and dusty air. The Chinese appeared to enjoy these public gatherings, especially since they knew there would be no lengthy expositions of Marxist-Leninist or Mao Zedong thought, and they were anticipating a full two hours of entertainment. After the unpredictable loudspeaker system was turned on and tamed, we and our topic were introduced. "The Scovels will present an address entitled 'George Washington: A Revolutionary Capitalist.'" With much trepidation, Janene began, and date by date, event by event, she elaborated on the life of America's first president. After she had ably filled almost half the time, it was my turn.

I chose the title with a couple of aims in mind. Knowing that the Chinese have an affinity for contradictions and that these underlie several concepts acceptable to the Party, it was natural to contrast *revolutionary*, which in Communist terms has only positive connotations with *capitalist*, which to them represents almost the exact antonym. From our brief foray into early American history the night before, it also struck us that Washington was indeed a person very different from the wealthy Virginians who represented his peers. In contrast to their colonial and royalist leanings, he was willing to join the revolution of workers, peasants, and soldiers and risk his all in the belief that this fragile uprising would swell into a successful victory over the powerful forces of the king. But unlike the Chinese image of a faithful revolutionary, Washington loved his estate (and the slaves that went with it) and his occupation as a gentleman farmer, and he lived most of his life, including the last three years after he left the presidency, as a successful capitalist. Finally, I could not resist the temptation, even so early in our tenure at Tian Wai, to offer an alternative voice to the continuous chorus of praise extolling the virtues of the Party and its leaders' unremitting devotion to the Chinese people. I had seen strong evidence to the contrary growing up in China as a young boy, and already in just our second month living there, it was obvious that all was not well. So what better forum to snipe at the Party than during that cold morning in the Propaganda Hall?

Washington was indeed a great revolutionary general, as Janene had documented. He rallied his beleaguered troops after several defeats from superior forces, and in a slight embellishment of actual events, he took them on a long march to escape enemy capture and led them to ultimate victory and independence from a foreign colonial power. I emphasized that he was also a great political leader and pointed out that his presidency was so popular that, despite his reluctance, he was urged to run for a second term. After eight years, however, he refused to continue, and stepping down from the highest office in the land, he retired from political life completely to live his last few years as a happy and wealthy landlord. Here, I concluded our presentation with my own doorknob message, saving the best and most salient point for last. "Americans remember and honor George Washington for all that he did, but perhaps his greatest accomplishment was stepping down and retiring completely from political life. Unlike some contemporary revolutionary leaders in Asia," I continued, now clearly entering dangerous territory, "Washington relinquished all political power and allowed other great leaders to continue his legacy, men like Thomas Jefferson, John Adams, and James Madison. We can think of how different Washington's legacy is compared to some contemporaries." I continued, and here I began to name names. "Sukarno of Indonesia, for example, fought against the Japanese and led the revolution against Dutch colonial control but stubbornly held on to power until he was deposed by a coup." I went on to mention Ho Chi Minh from nearby Vietnam, and having made my point, I went no further. "Today," I concluded, "one way we honor Washington is through a law that prevents any American president, even a great one, from serving more than eight years. Yes, he was a successful capitalist and landlord, and certainly, he was a fine general and true revolutionary, but above all, he was a great leader because he knew when it was time to step down and let others lead the nation."

We had filled almost two hours with our deliberately slow delivery, and if nothing else, we hoped that most of the audience, whose comprehension of spoken English was limited, gained some confidence in learning that they actually caught the gist of what we were saying. And knowing their fascination with details, we were confident that many of the students and teachers had picked up some new words and fresh collocations to expand their English lexicons. But there were also many in the audience, like Lao Chen, whose proficiency was so good that they could not have missed any major point of our joint presentation, and certainly they were savvy enough to know that I spoke obliquely but disapprovingly of Chairman Mao, whose control over China evaporated only with his death less than three years before. Janene was a bit concerned that I had been too transparent in my conclusion and wondered if our invitation to teach in China would be abruptly withdrawn. After some perfunctory handshakes and compliments from those who shared the podium with us, Lao Chen strode up to us with his feedback. He paused, smiled, and vigorously shook our hands one at a time and thanked us. "Very good," he exclaimed and then added with as close as I ever saw him to winking, "just what I wanted!"

CHAPTER 3

性相紧，习相远

xing xiang jin, xi xiang yuan

Nature brings us together;
customs pull us apart.

In the kaleidoscopic blend of thoughts, emotions, recollections, and impressions that swirl through my mind when I think about that year in China, in the haze of events and experiences, in the maze of people and places, so many memories still endure even now, some thirty years later. Naturally, it is difficult to sift through them and winnow out the coherent and the significant for a book like this. I wanted to avoid a straightforward chronology because this I already had in the copious written records we compiled via our daily journal entries and weekly letters to family and friends back in the States. Besides, our memories of life are less driven by chronology than by salience, a fact that becomes more apparent the older we grow. So here I will focus on events and experiences, recognizing, of course, that ultimately our memories are as holistic as life itself and cannot be easily disassembled into separate categories or be neatly pigeonholed and chronicled for others to understand.

No consideration of our life that year in Tianjin can begin without an appreciation of the devastation wrought by the tragic Tangshan earthquake that struck that area of China two and a half years before our arrival. While the psychological damage had pretty much diminished over that span of time, the physical destruction and its toll on the citizenry was apparent throughout the metropolis. On July 27, 1976, an earthquake of approximately

7.5 on the Richter scale struck Hebei Province, its epicenter very close to Tangshan, a large city about sixty-five miles northeast of Tianjin. Like similar disasters around the globe, well-built structures survived largely intact, but because the majority of buildings were not designed and constructed to withstand large shocks, because of the length of the initial quake, because of the repetition of large aftershocks subsequent to the initial strike, and most of all, because this tremor hit an area inhabited by millions of people, the human devastation was truly awful. To this day, precise figures of the damage are either hidden or unknown, but most estimates are that approximately a quarter of a million people lost their lives that summer day, and overall, the death toll could have hit 650,000. Earthquakes have always been part of Chinese life and historically have been viewed as harbingers of future misfortune. Such was the case that summer, when only a little over a month later, Chairman Mao, modern China's Great Helmsman, passed away. Earlier that same year, Zhou Enlai, Mao's alter ego, and Zhu De, the great military commander, also died, so the earthquake that killed so many ordinary citizens served to punctuate the deaths of the Party's heroic triumvirate.

To put this disaster in perspective, compare it to the 9.0 tremor that struck the coast of Sumatra the day after Christmas in 2004. Even though that quake generated an enormous tsunami that engulfed the shores of Indonesia, Thailand, Burma, Sri Lanka, and even far-off India, there were more casualties from the just first day of the Tangshan quake than from all those devastated nations put together. Granted, there were no cell phones or a World Wide Web back in 1976, but it wasn't the lack of telecommunication systems or media outlets that kept this event hidden from worldview. It was the Party that concealed almost all information about this event—not just from the outside world but from the Chinese people themselves. Naturally, the Party's policy to this day gives new meaning to the phrase "cover the news." Whether it was earthquakes, famines, or floods in the past or, more recently, airplane crashes, AIDS, or avian flu, it does an excellent job of covering bad news. The Party covers it up exceedingly well.

With millions of people homeless and so many structures irreparably damaged, the city was forced to commandeer every possible square foot of space for the construction of temporary shelters. Parks, sidewalks, playgrounds, and yes, even soccer pitches and swimming pools were immediately filled with squatters' huts. Considering that most metropolitan Chinese live in high-rise apartments, a building with a relatively modest footprint could easily house thousands of residents, but now that much of this vertical space was lost, that same number of people was forced to scatter over a wide horizontal surface, cramming Tianjin's teeming populace into an even more crowded space. Except in front of a select number of buildings, such as stores, hotels, and government offices, and along a few major thoroughfares, all sidewalks were turned into unbroken lines of huts, each housing a family. The street immediately behind our hotel, which ran along the river, became an alley flanked on both sides by lines of temporary shelters broken only occasionally by large dumps of garbage.

The shelters themselves were constructed of bricks, door and window frames, and any other remnants from the earthquake its occupants were fortunate enough to salvage. Typically, they had one enclosed room that served as the living and sleeping area and a covered outside kitchen, where food and hot water could be heated on a coal fire. Their dilapidated roofs leaked in the rain and melting snow, and their interiors were frigid in winter and steamy during the humid summers. Water came from the nearest communal spigot, and human waste was disposed of via chamber pots, the street, and public toilets. Every time we walked out to shop, every time we rode our bikes on errands, every time we entered our campus, we passed thousands of our fellow citizens whose lives were confined to these squalid conditions. We lived in two different worlds that year: a twentieth century one of heated, spacious rooms, clean clothes, abundant water (either hot or cold), easily available food of our own choosing, and modern plumbing, but we passed by and sometimes entered a medieval world of shabbily constructed huts, primitive facilities, and constant dirt and squalor. Most of our colleagues at the institute and some of our students lived like this, and it's no wonder that they spent all the time they could in our institute's classrooms and offices, for destitute as these appeared to us, these premises afforded our friends a chance to enjoy the comforts of modernity. How ironic, I thought, that thirty years after Liberation, we still resided like foreign imperialists and our Chinese brethren lived like refugees in their own land!

Unlike Beijing, whose huge Friendship Hotel cradled hundreds of foreign experts and temporary visitors, or other institutions around the country, because of the earthquake and the tight squeeze on housing, Tian Wai had no special apartments set aside for foreign teachers on its campus, and that is why the Tianjin Hotel became our home for the year. In retrospect, it was a fortuitous choice for us because this provided some separation both from work and from most of the other foreign teachers. We could come and go without the common knowledge of everyone in the institute, and more importantly, we could welcome various visitors during the year without them passing the scrutiny of the institute's gateman and, in turn, his administrators. The Chinese had a strong proclivity for herding the foreigners under their care together, and this was annoying to us. To be candid, we did not choose to live an entire year in China to spend most of our free time with Americans, Europeans, and other expatriates. Although we did forge a few friendships with foreigners we met during our stay, just as we had done when we lived in Thailand, we disliked the way most foreigners tended to spend their time together—criticizing their Chinese colleagues and grousing about their places of work and their host society. They also seemed to be overly preoccupied with the scant news they received from their homeland, such as the Three Mile Island nuclear generator accident in Pennsylvania or the Jonestown massacre, both events transpiring back in the States the year we were in China. Granted, we were not above critiquing our situation or searching for newsworthy tidbits from home, but these behaviors seem to quickly magnify whenever expats clustered together. We were fortunate then to be able to live two lives that year: our very public life at Tian Wai and our not completely private life at the hotel or on the road.

We had no radio, and except for a couple of nightly forays into the hotel's makeshift lounge for the staff, which boasted the hotel's only television, we rarely watched any TV. Consequently, part of our family entertainment was gazing at the busy thoroughfare outside our second-story window and observing the life of the people living in the temporary shelters clustered across the street from us. Here was reality TV long before its actual inception. With their community faucet in full view, we saw the inhabitants come and go day and night, drawing water to heat their tea, hauling buckets for laundry and personal hygiene, or to meet, mingle, exchange news, or bicker. It was an ancient village well smack in the midst of a modern metropolis. When the weather warmed, the elderly emerged each morning to practice *tai ji quan* (tai chi), one of them an energetic man who sped through ever accelerating drills with a flashing sword with its red tassels flying. Now and then, before the dawn broke, someone practiced operatic arias in full voice, his identity hidden by the darkness. In the summer, one of the huts directly across from us was able to grow several giant sunflowers, and their bright yellow added a dash of seasonal color to the otherwise drab, perennial shades that darkened that dreary encampment. There we were, living in the former Astor House, and there they were, refugees in the former British rose garden. Again, the contrast between Tianjin's foreign and imperial past seemed to collide with its Republican present: alien versus Chinese, possessor versus dispossessed, color and wealth versus dreariness and poverty.

We ate virtually all our meals in the hotel, and it became readily apparent that the more we adopted this public environment as our home and the more we adapted to the constraints of such an arrangement, the happier our family would be. Since food is both the fuel and the magnet for family functions, naturally our attention was directed toward making mealtime an inexpensive, efficient, and comfortable time for the four of us. Inexpensive because the terms of our eventual contract spelled out that we were responsible for paying for board, and to our surprise and dismay, the lessons about the evils of capitalism of the Cultural Revolution seemed to have evaporated when it came to making a quick buck. Both at our hotel and at many other accommodations, we were initially presented with astronomically high bills and had to negotiate them downward. Efficient because, especially at breakfast, we had a window of about thirty minutes between when the restaurant opened at seven and the time that we had to take off to our institute via Christine's nursery and Derick needed to set out to cross the river to his conservatory. Finally, since the restaurant served as our family kitchen and dining room, despite the few regular guests and the rotation of new ones milling around us, we tried hard to transform this very public space into a comfortable refuge where we could digest a meal and the events of the day in imagined privacy.

An initial and continuing challenge was trying to avoid being overcharged for food at the hotel and in many other places we visited. Normally, we were presented with unreasonably high bills, and because we had to pay for almost all the meals the family ate that year out of our own pocket, we were usually prudent in our choice of menu items and somewhat prudish about accepting outlandish tabs. During lunch one day with Pierre and his wife, Janene learned that, as foreign experts at the institute, we were entitled to a discount on all hotel food, so after negotiation with the staff, we were given the 20 percent discount we should have received for every meal since our arrival in the city a fortnight earlier. Five days later, the discount disappeared from Janene and Derick's lunch, and had we stopped scrutinizing the sea of bills we were given for every meal we ate that year, we would have been continually overcharged. The price of eating is eternal vigilance.

The first month or so of breakfasts was a portent that efficiency might not be an attainable goal. We habitually were the first to enter the dining room in the morning, leaping to our seats at our usual table, the first one on the left, and having already memorized the limited breakfast menu, we would repeat the same choices we had ordered the day before and the day before that and virtually every day since the moment of our arrival weeks earlier. Scrambled eggs, toast, pancakes, coffee for Janene, tea for me, and hot chocolate for the kids. Because almost all our other meals were comprised of Chinese food, breakfast was a time to imitate our American diet. Even though we were typically the only guests in the restaurant at that hour, getting the attention of the nearest fu wu ren took about five minutes. Having them write down the order took another five (not once were we asked, "you'll have the usual today?"). Then it took about another quarter of an hour or so before the food came to the table, leaving the four of us a brief moment to bolt and swill down what we had ordered and a morning's worth of indigestion from our binging.

There was a logical solution to this daily challenge, and we thought we had addressed it in a successful fashion. One evening after our usual leisurely dinner (after all, there was no rush at the end of the day), I called several of the fu wu ren together and explained in my best Chinese that each morning we would be ordering exactly the same menu items. I reiterated our ritual morning choices and reassured them that all they had to do was to go into the kitchen when the restaurant opened and tell the cooks that the *mei guo wai bing* (the American guests) were ordering the same dishes they always did, a fact that we assumed would not be a surprise to the hotel chefs. "*Keyi keyi!*" was the quick reply, and seeing that comprehension and satisfaction was shared all around, we again assumed that "Can do, can do!" confirmed the deal. The next morning, we swept into the dining room at precisely seven thirty and sat down expectantly at our usual table. Spying no visible appreciation of our presence among the statutory fu wu ren, I called out, "Comrades, a little help please!" The taller one with the pigtails hurried over, pencil in hand, waiting for our order. She was one of the previous night's group of "can dos," but our order of scrambled eggs, toast, pancakes, coffee for Janene, tea for me, and hot chocolate for the kids was seemingly news to her. She bustled off to the kitchen with our order, and as sure as death, our hearty breakfast arrived at 7:55 a.m., just in time for another quick gobble and speedy bike ride to work.

Plan B was equally logical but was cleverly (or so we thought) directed at what now looked like the underlying source of all our efforts to encourage the hotel staff to perform more efficiently—motivation! Like Janene's students at the institute, the fu wu ren at the hotel secured their positions via their worker-peasant-soldier family status although, unlike the students, they were neither the sharpest knives in the drawer nor the most highly motivated of workers. Like hundreds of millions of Chinese who worked for the state, they had an "iron rice bowl" (*tie fan wan*). To call them slow-witted or lethargic would be unfair; it was just that they seemed to go out of their way to appear so. How then could we bribe them into action? Money was out of the question largely because there was no tipping, and any exchange of currency outside of sanctioned transactions came too close to being considered a political crime. Finally, we came up with our second solution. We had come to China as English teachers, and though back then there were very few foreign tourists visiting China and fewer still showing up in Tianjin, we knew that the gates to the world were widening each passing year, and in their future, these lucky fu wu ren would be promoted to the most attractive positions thanks to their opportunity to have studied hotel English with us. Management liked our idea enormously as long as we used Chinese-prepared materials, and once we got the okay from the Municipal Office of Hotel Management, we volunteered free classes a couple of afternoons a week. Naturally, having scratched their backs with this overly generous offer, we expected some reciprocal back-scratching, specifically our breakfast order waiting hot and hearty for our seven thirty arrival each workday morning. They and we were disappointed.

The time when we were all free for these special lessons happened to be midafternoon, right after and often interfering with the staff's sacred nap time. Considering their lack of experience with formal education, their apparent inability to foresee the long-range benefits from this sudden disruption of their normally leisurely afternoon schedule, and the weird experience of attending to and attempting to replicate the strange sounds of a barbarian tongue, contrary to our expectations, their motivation was low. Compounding the situation was the fact that we were asked to use material that was pedagogically outdated. Consider these eight phrases that we had to present in a lesson on rebuffing bad behavior.

1. Behave yourself!
2. Mind your manners!
3. Such behavior is not tolerated in China!
4. You are not so friendly!
5. You must be responsible for what you have done.
6. This is your fault. Why didn't you make yourself clear beforehand?
7. Your behavior will harm the friendly relations between our two peoples.
8. We are very sorry for what you have done.

Attendance in these afternoon classes started to dwindle, and having experienced no acceleration in our breakfast service, we agreed to discontinue lessons when the offer was politely tendered. The hotel management, in appreciation of our pedagogical attempts, did treat us to a fine dinner in early May, an unexpected but not the desired benefit of our efforts. When the weather improved and Janene was able to find a limited choice of fruit in stores or on the street, we simplified our breakfast orders and supplemented them with food we had bought, and this mitigated some of the stress in our morning rush to work. As for the fu wu ren, I wonder if their behavior ever changed so that it no longer harmed the friendly relations between our two peoples or, years later, after foreign tourists started to flood China, if they were ever very sorry for what they had done.

Ours was a small, European-style establishment with fewer than a hundred rooms and a dining room that could accommodate about the same number of guests, though it was rarely crowded. There were a few foreign regulars like our family, a Japanese businessman and his wife and baby, and the two Canadians who taught at Nankai University, but initially, there were few outside guests; however, their numbers grew as the year progressed. They comprised a motley group of mostly business people, and because they were about the only visitors from abroad that we chanced to meet in Tianjin, they were a source of interest and news, just as travelers were in ancient times. On rare occasions, we encountered some truly bizarre guests whom we naturally tried to shun, such as the underdressed but oversexed man from Yemen. Notwithstanding the momentary contact we had and the length of time that has passed since those brief meetings, several of these guests stand out in our collective memory.

There was a Swiss businessman and his wife who were as happy to meet our acquaintance at dinner as we theirs and whom we invited up to our room for late-evening tea. She, having special pity on our two children, gave us a few Swiss chocolate candy bars when we bade farewell, and her generosity was both a blessing and a curse. Surely it was the finest confection we ever tasted during that China sojourn, but on the other hand, from then on, the waxy Chinese milk chocolate bars that we could buy at the local Friendship Store no longer were the delicacy that we previously enjoyed, and until the end of our stay, they only served to evoke memories of mouthwatering Toblerones.

Another European guest was a lonely East German who felt compelled to share with us stories about his unhappy life on the wrong side of the Iron Curtain and about his similarly depressing marital relationship. He was desperate for some hard currency to buy his wife's affection back at a duty-free shop at one of the airports on his flight home, but to his disappointment, we were Americans without American currency. The last evening of his stay, he broke out a harmonica in the dinning room and played song after song louder and louder, swaying, tapping, and bouncing to the music.

Another time, we introduced ourselves to two Egyptian businessmen who looked ignored at the far end of the almost empty dining room on that particular evening. After greeting them and welcoming them to our hotel, I made the mistake of starting our conversation by acknowledging that they must have been struck by several similarities between their nation and China given that both were newly independent nations, heavily populated, and boasted a historical legacy few other places on earth could match. They immediately took umbrage to what they perceived as my overly facile generalization and started to catalog the ways Egypt differed from (was superior to) the PRC, ending with the claim that the only two things that prevented their country from becoming one of the developed nations of the globe was water and foreign investment. I couldn't resist pointing out that China (at least in 1979) lacked only the latter. We did not invite them upstairs for tea nor would they have come had I.

One Saturday night, several African students studying at Nankai University cycled over to enjoy a meal at our hotel as a respite from their studies as international students. It was not a particularly busy evening, but our fu wu ren suddenly developed visual agnosia for their particular table and neglected the students' frequent glances and polite calls for attention. The longer he watched this, the more agitated our son became, and finally, unable to bridle his sense of fair play, Derick abruptly leaped out of his chair, grabbed some menus, strode over to the students' table, and distributed them to the pleasantly surprised group. Exposed and embarrassed by a young foreigner's spontaneous action, the fu wu ren suddenly became aware of the Africans' presence and need for service, and ultimately the students were served, albeit much later than anyone else in the room. Unquestionably, there was a contradiction between what Derick and we had just witnessed that evening and the many propaganda pictures, posters, and billboards we saw that year depicting workers representing all the races of the world under the familiar slogan, "Workers of the world unite. You have nothing to lose but your chains!" Alas, the chains of racism seem to bind all of humanity irrespective of ethnicity or ideology.

With diplomatic recognition between the PRC and the USA having just taken place, rarely did we meet any Americans during our stay, and so any chance encounters with our countrymen were inordinately memorable for it gave us the opportunity to glean news directly from our native land. Only a few weeks after our arrival, we met a group of Texans who were on their way home via Beijing, and we were excited at this first chance to chat with some compatriots. There was an even more compelling reason for our excitement. It just so happened that the Pittsburgh Steelers and the Dallas Cowboys were slated to compete in Super Bowl XIII the third week of January that year, and now that the month had nearly ended, we had still received no news about that event. Spotting the Americans entering the dining room and then hearing their accent, we immediately guessed that they were from Texas and assumed they could share with us the results of this epic battle. Without a shortwave radio or a visit to Beijing, where world news was more accessible, it was impossible for us to learn who had won the game. *Tianjin Ribao* carried little international news and nothing about foreign sports. It was difficult and expensive to arrange for an international phone call at that time, so we weren't going to waste money on a simple sporting event. The week before, I had cycled over to the post office and sent our first telegram back to the States, addressing it to the Pittsburgh Steelers, Pittsburgh, Pennsylvania, USA. Embellishing the Chinese fan base slightly, the cable read: FOUR SCOVELS AND EIGHT HUNDRED MILLION CHINESE SEND BEST WISHES FOR A VICTORY! Imagine our excitement then when we chanced upon this opportunity to finally find out how our Steelers performed. Regrettably, the Texans, though happy to meet us, were as much in the dark as we for they were on the way to Beijing from some remote Chinese city and were disappointed that we knew no more than they.

About a week later, Janene received a post card from one of her middle school students, and our anxiety was only heightened when she penned something like, "I bet you were excited about this year's Super Bowl!" Finally, in early February, our closest friends in Pittsburgh sent us a cassette tape of the radio broadcast of that contest, and even though the packet included a note with the final score, Derick and I sweated through the entire broadcast of that exciting game, wondering until the very end whether the Steelers really were able to pull out a 35–31 victory.

Although most of their visits were brief (after all, Tianjin was no Beijing or Shanghai), some guests were forced by business commitments to extend their stay, and the longest-staying resident was the young Japanese businessman who, along with his wife and baby son, had been exiled to Tianjin for four lonely years. Imagine how repugnant this was for a well-educated salaryman from cosmopolitan Tokyo to be incarcerated with his wife and child in an earthquake-ravaged city whose populace harbored a distaste for his race due to the cruelty wreaked by his father's generation during the anti-Japanese war. For the three of them to endure this for a month would be purgatory; to survive all this for four interminable years must have been hell. Knowing a little about how Japanese corporations work, I would guess that his Tianjin assignment was probably an unusually attenuated case of delayed gratification. Having survived his years in the hinterlands of the Greater East Asia Co-prosperity Sphere, this man would most probably be rewarded handsomely with a prime position in the Tokyo office for the rest of his employment with the firm. We had special compassion for his wife, who was trapped for the most part in the hotel day after day, caring for her baby without any support from friends or family and, unlike her husband, would garner no direct reward for her long and lonely sacrifice.

Since his English was limited and my Japanese even more so, it was hard for us to befriend them though try we did. Janene immediately noticed that the Japanese family, like us, sat at the same table and that the older Japanese language instructor at our institute, who was also housed that year at the Tianjin Hotel, almost always chose a table on the opposite side of the restaurant. To Americans, this behavior may have seemed odd, but it was not so remarkable for Japanese. After all, these men worked for completely different organizations, were from different parts of Japan, and differed greatly in age and station. Besides, they had never been formally introduced! Unable to tolerate the situation any longer after one evening meal, Janene motioned to the Japanese businessman and took him by the arm over to the Japanese teacher's table. With obviously exaggerated surprise, the latter rose from his seat to greet for the first time the only other fellow Japanese he had seen for weeks on end. There was bowing, exchanging of each other's *meishi* (business cards) with both hands, and polite and perfunctory expressions of pleasure over this surprise encounter. From then on, thanks to Janene's breaking the ice, our Japanese residents enjoyed a warm relationship throughout their Tianjin tenure.

Undoubtedly the most forlorn among all the guests who visited our hotel that year was a businessman from New York City who stayed for a little over a week while it was still winter and came over brimming with confidence and left as gloomy as the dismal weather that enveloped his stay. We introduced ourselves after he first arrived, and since he was obviously lonely and needed to share his story and because we were the only other English speakers he met each evening, he shared with us his mournful saga of love's labors lost. It seems he worked for a large garment firm in New York, and his boss had been able to secure the necessary permits to contract with a clothing factory in Tianjin to produce men's suits for sale in the Big Apple. When he arrived, this man could barely contain his excitement over the potential commercial success of this enterprise for it married China's infinite ability to produce quality goods with cheap labor to America's passion for expensive clothing, a mathematical equation that would guarantee a rich profit for his boss's company and unbelievable wealth for this lucky businessman. After hearing the opening act of this singular drama, I felt like I was sitting next to strangers who had never seen a performance of *Romeo and Juliet* and hearing them gush over how much they enjoyed a good love story. I then wondered whether or not to spill the beans and tell him that he was not going to like the ending. Our friendly New Yorker's zeal seemed to diminish slightly with each passing day while his after dinner drinking appeared to increase inversely.

Act I. About the third night, he started to lament about still not being able to visit the factory where the alleged mountain of suits already paid for were being produced. "I wasn't able to get there today," he complained, "because the strike is still on." "Strike?" I asked, a bit too incredulously, "there are no strikes in a worker's paradise." He was now frustrated and confused.

Act II. About two nights later, he was truly distressed. By this time, he was thoroughly fed up with his Chinese contact, who spent most of each day taking our new friend to the few sights Tianjin had to offer but never near the alleged factory that was producing his alleged product. The strike mysteriously ended the morning after the businessman had shared with his Chinese counterparts our belief that striking was illegal in China, but abruptly, there seemed to be some other sort of trouble, this time dealing with roadwork to that particular district of the city. Despite the inconvenience and expense it entailed, he made daily calls to his boss back in New York in the hotel's old-fashioned international phone booth, and it became apparent that this poor man was being squeezed both ways. In fact, the better analogy wasn't so much to a Shakespearean tragedy as it was to *Death of a Salesman*. Quite despondent, our sad friend grumbled that his American counterparts simply had no conception of how desperate his situation was. "My boss swore at me and told me to rent a car and drive out there to the factory myself, and he didn't believe me when I told him that there wasn't a single Hertz or Avis in this entire damn city!"

Act III. The last night of his stay, he walked into the dining hall so crushed and disconsolate we avoided eye contact and thought it best to let him initiate dialogue. Sure enough, fueled more by alcohol than by food, he related the sad ending to his saga. Earlier that day, the strike long gone and the roads miraculously and rapidly repaired, he was driven to the factory, where he was warmly welcomed and received like visiting royalty. At last, he was allowed to see the suits his boss had already so handsomely invested in and whose marked-up sales in New York City would transform him into a millionaire. The first floor was devoted to pants, and their sizes and quality were excellent. Our Willie Loman was ecstatic. The second floor produced the vests and the third the jackets, and yes, they too were all well tailored and a cut above anything in that price range back home in the garment district. Alas, however, the three floors seemed to have operated separately, like the three kingdoms of ancient China, and neither the colors nor the materials matched! He was not at all assuaged by his Chinese colleague's suggestion that his company could sell the pants, vest, and jackets as separate items and thus make even more money. By this time, our tough young capitalist from the toughest city in America was crying uncontrollably. It would have been utterly inconceivable to us that evening after hearing this sad soliloquy to believe that some day in the future, we would be living in a world where Chinese-made goods would monopolize virtually every corner of the consumer market in the United States, but it would not have surprised us in the slightest if we learned that in this future world, Chinese businessmen would play their American counterparts like an *er hou*.

It would be a mistake to conclude that our hotel was the center of our private life, for though food and accommodations were the centripetal forces that continually brought us back to this temporary home, our interests were equally centrifugal. We spent an inordinately large amount of time outside and away, both in the city itself and via many trips to other parts of China. Even before winter ended, we would cycle or walk on the snowiest days for shopping trips or simply to get outside, and as the sun edged seasonally higher, these excursions became more frequent. There was a small shopping district two blocks from the hotel, but we initially had trouble finding which store sold what unless one of our colleagues accompanied us. If we were unaccompanied, their directions proved unhelpful. "If you want office supplies, go to the store between the hardware shop and the grocery." During the winter months, when doors and windows were closed from the wind and snow and the poorly lit streets were already dark by the time work was over, it was hard for us to distinguish one place from another. Furthermore, because there were no neon signs or display windows, and the signs that were posted above each shop were in characters unreadable to me due to my limited Chinese literacy, it was challenging for us to recognize the identity of even a single shop. Everything looked the same to us. In contrast, by late spring, we could set out on errands unerringly, and our mental maps of the city grew more detailed and intricate each month, a direct reflection of how much we had acculturated.

The small shops and markets in our section of town could not supply all our needs, however, and since we were only able to bring a limited amount of clothing, we were in special need of warm clothes to stave off the bitter cold outside and the chilly interiors of the nursery, conservatory, and institute. This necessitated a trip downtown to the largest department store, and unlike a Friendship Store, this place was for the locals. Crowds immediately swarmed around us, enjoying the novelty of seeing three white faces and a small Asian one (Christine was often mistaken for being Chinese despite her distinctly Thai visage). They were always curious and fascinated to see at which items these foreign millionaires would fling their unlimited supply of money. Many common household commodities were rationed back then, so despite our foreign status, we too would be unable to purchase clothing without *piao* for cotton, and these were provided to us via our institute's wai ban, enough for a prespecified allotment of so many square meters of cotton for the four of us. Armed with our *piao*, cash, and one of our colleagues to interpret, we plunged into the crowded department store and upstairs to the clothing department.

Word soon spread that the store was going to provide special entertainment on the second floor that morning: four *wai guo bing* of various sizes dressed in strange outfits were about to make some purchases, but of what? We were so quickly encircled that a cop was called up from the street, and throughout our negotiations and purchases, he desperately tried to quell the crowd with a handheld loudspeaker, adding to the cacophony of voices echoing around us and only succeeding in attracting more spectators to the old curiosity shop. We bought thick, dark blue cotton pants and zippered jackets for Janene and Derick, who were unusually chilled by the winter biking, and lighter blue cotton pants and matching "Mao jackets" for Janene and me. We also got some face masks to help protect against the pollution and the frigid cold while biking. Fighting our way over to the counter that sold children's clothes, we purchased red corduroy pants and a mustard-yellow shirt for Christine. The grand total of $65 seemed exceptionally high considering the average wage was between $20 and $30 a month, but unlike the hotel, all prices were final, and there was no bargaining. It was even more of a struggle to fight the scrum down the stairs and back to the sanctuary of the institute car waiting on the street below. The entire experience was much more reminiscent of Shinjuku Station during an evening rush hour in Tokyo than the quiet and elegant ambiance of an American Nordstrom.

We never got accustomed to the crowds that congealed around us almost everywhere we went, and it bothered me that I was bothered since I remember being stared at as a kid growing up in China in an earlier era. Maybe that was it. The jostling swarms of interested bystanders weren't quite as bad as the gawkers who would gaze in almost incredulous attention, sometimes within a few inches of our faces. Like dealing with the cold of winter and the summer humidity, sometimes levity was the about the only effective coping mechanism. After Janene's incident with one of her lenses, I made a trip to the post office to mail the damaged lens back to the States to be polished and returned. Xiao Zhang insisted on accompanying me since mailing packages was much more complicated than posting a simple letter. The requisite crowd assembled around us as soon as the two of us made our way to the counter, and as we described the contents, filled out forms, ever curious, the throng was eager to find out exactly what I was sending. To satisfy the multitude, Xiao Zhang would shout out a running commentary on what was happening up front to the people gathering in the back, and like the policeman's bullhorn in the department store, this only attracted more curiosity seekers. The clerk insisted that nothing could be sent abroad in a simple cardboard box or thick envelope but only in a wooden box, so I purchased one three by three by seven inches in size. Unlike the United States, the Chinese postal and immigration authorities were as interested in controlling what went out of China as what came in, so the clerk had to inspect the contents I was about to post. After he had ascertained that only the lens case, a few cassettes we had recorded for friends and family, and some stuffing had gone into the box, he handed me the top, a small hammer, and some tiny nails. My hammering excited the crowd even more, and by now, everyone was wondering what the foreigner was doing. "It's a mouse coffin," I exclaimed. "I'm sending a Chinese mouse to America." When Zhang relayed this to the assembled audience, there was much laughter although I suspect that some returned home that night to confirm to their families that foreigners are indeed strange. Why on earth would anyone mail a rodent to Mickey Rat's homeland?

Throughout our stay, the Chinese were gracious hosts, and the wai ban at our institute and those attached to all the other institutions we visited that year went out of their way to provide entertainment for us. I realize that contrasting the way we were cared for in China with the way foreign scholars are treated in the United States is a bit like comparing persimmons and pomegranates, but even the most illustrious foreign faculty members attached to American universities for a year are not accorded the hospitality that was lavished on us, ordinary *wai guo zhuan jia* though we were. Starting with our arrival in Beijing and right up to our final departure from Tianjin, we were entertained with movies, plays, concerts, volleyball games, and acrobatic shows, and we were taken to weekend visits to farming communes, ancient monuments, and even oil fields, and to top it off, the institute paid for our transportation almost anywhere in China for our month of summer vacation.

Midweek at the end of January, we were invited to see the Tianjin Acrobats, whose performance was timed to help celebrate the Chinese New Year. The athleticism and artistry of Chinese gymnasts is now world famous thanks to the many international tours various Chinese troupes have taken and also indirectly witnessed via the domination of PRC athletes every four years in Olympic gymnastics, especially the women. There were clowns, contortionists, jugglers, trapeze artists, and a variety of acrobatic acts with stools, chairs, ladders, and other people's heads, arms, and legs that defied both gravity and credulity. A strongman twirled an allegedly 220-pound weight as if it were a toothpick. One group balanced themselves in every position imaginable while riding bikes, and another roller-skated on top of a small table. Our favorite was an act called the "Happy Chef," which featured a guy dressed as a cook who started to spin one plate on a long stick, and once he got that one balancing by itself, he and his sous-chefs added another and then another until he had a line of about twenty twirling platters, all of them winding down and threatening to fall at any moment in time. Their frenzied rushing from one about-to-topple plate to another brought shrieks of delighted laughter from the audience, and their feigned desperation won our appreciation for their skill and showmanship. Xiao Zhang, who often accompanied us on these excursions, let it be known with an overzealous touch of local pride that, truth be told, our Tianjin artists were even better than the more famous Beijing and Shanghai troupes. Even young Derick remembered them in his diary that night with remarkable and uncanny prescience. "If they came to the United States," he recorded, "they would make a mint [with the last word underlined three times]."

Another Chinese New Year's performance was a concert held in the city's indoor stadium. We had heard the Central Orchestra of China perform Tchaikovsky, Mozart, and Dvorak at a concert in Beijing the first week we arrived, and though we took pleasure in a chance to hear some classical music, especially Janene who was a violinist, we were still too tired from our travels to fully appreciate that opportunity. The music in our first Tianjin concert was mostly Chinese and mostly contemporary with a couple of surprises thrown in. There were several soloists who sang patriotic songs about the Yangtze River Bridge and other such achievements with great voices and ardor, and there were many instrumentalists playing both solo and in ensembles: flutes, lutes, violins, and *er hu*'s. The latter was a favorite of Xiao Zhang, who was an English teacher and wai ban employee at our institute by day but a musician at heart and an accomplished flutist in his own right. An older violinist stole the show that night for he was able to turn his instrument into a virtual forest of chirping birds, playing louder and faster until the applause brought his tour of an acoustic aviary to a close. In April, we got a sudden invitation to attend a Thursday-night concert of singers and instrumentalists given by the Beijing Cultural Orchestra, and what stuck out in our memories was one of the last vocalists, who we remembered for what she wore as much as for what she sang. Until we visited Shanghai that summer, except for these concerts, we almost never saw a Chinese woman in a dress. In fact, when some of her female students were visiting Janene in our hotel one day and she showed them one of the few dresses she had brought from the States, they thought it was a nightgown. We had to suppress a giggle when we heard this well-dressed soprano begin to sing, however, for though it had been over three months since the holiday, she sang the well-known Christmas song, "Jingle Bell." Chinese does not mark plurals nor did she in her English rendition.

One time we inadvertently assisted in a dramatic production due to the extraordinary juxtaposition of a train ride, a group of PLA soldiers, San Francisco, Taiwan, and an FBI agent. On rare occasions, we would spend a weekend in Beijing, shopping for necessities unobtainable in Tianjin, visiting the American consulate for English language materials, and giving our kids a chance to play with native-speaking peers for a few hours. On the train ride home from one of these trips, we happened to be seated next to a group of PLA soldiers, immediately attracting their interest and conversely catching Derick's, who had a boyish addiction to uniforms, weapons, and military history. We learned that they too were stationed in Tianjin and were part of a propaganda unit in charge of producing plays. It took me a while to recalibrate my mental dictionary of English to get used to the connotations of certain words that were a frequent part of our daily discourse in China. *Propaganda*, for instance, was closer in meaning to *advertising* or *public relations*, so it was understandable why the People's Liberation Army would want to entertain its troops with material that was both enjoyable and edifying. Learning that we were Americans, they asked if we were from *jiu jin shan* (Old Gold Mountain, San Francisco), another accidental bit of prescience since we lived in Pittsburgh at that time, but a few years after returning from China, we moved to the San Francisco area, which has been our home for decades. They were happy to learn that we had visited this city, for it turned out to be the setting for the play they were writing. The soldiers were happier still to hear that we would be willing to meet with them in Tianjin to answer the many questions they had about the locale and American customs. We agreed on a date, and the following week, the troupe of soldiers trooped upstairs and, with Xiao Zhang's help as an interpreter, peppered us with all sorts of inquiries. As Janene and I and the four khaki-dressed soldiers with their red stars pinned to their caps chatted and laughed together, a strange sense of familiarity crept into my consciousness, a sense of déjà vu that took me back to my childhood.

It was 1950, after my parents had been reassigned to Canton and shortly after Mao had proclaimed the formation of the People's Republic of China. Our city had just been liberated by the Communists a few months earlier. The PLA had set up an antiaircraft battery on the other side of the wall that ran along our backyard, and in the afternoon, when the soldiers manning this station had some free time, they would clamber up and sit on top of the wall. There they would sit, their legs dangling down on our side, and I, barely eleven, along with my younger sister Judy would chat in Mandarin and teach them songs in English. One of their favorites was the following jingle that was especially apt since it made full use of their feet dangling just above our heads. Even more fittingly, it was so repetitious that it was ideal for teaching anyone who had no knowledge of English and most probably had never even heard that strange tongue spoken before. Little did we know that we, two little kids, would one day grow up to teach this language in foreign lands. Here's what we taught the mighty army that had crushed the Nationalist forces and had just conquered us.

> Put your little foot, put your little foot,
> Put your little foot right there.
> Put your little foot, put your little foot,
> Put your little foot right there.
> Do you see my new shoes? Do you see my new shoes?
> Do you see my new shoes? Do you see my new shoes?

Now, so many years later, I was an adult and I and my family were helping another generation of PLA soldiers understand an alien language and culture, and once again, I experienced a flashbulb memory that lit the present with a brief snapshot from my childish past. The plot of the play this troupe was producing was intriguing but ultimately predictable. A young Chinese woman goes to San Francisco to study and meets another foreign student, a young man from Taiwan. They fall in love, and he, sensing a sudden longing to emigrate to the motherland, agrees to accompany her on her return to Mother China. But hold! American FBI agents alerted by the nationalist police back in Taiwan confront our stalwart hero, threatening to jail him on the spot to prevent his defection to Red China. But he, inflamed with equal parts of romantic love and socialist passion, rebuffs them, and love's labor is not lost, and the play ends with the couple setting off to live happily ever after in China.

Questions of all sorts were thrown at us. One of them was, "In America, would students from the People's Republic of China be allowed to meet and mingle with students from the Republic of China (read Taiwan)?" "Yes." "Good, we'll keep this in the plot." Another dealt with the possibility of jail: "Would the FBI place a foreign student in jail if he wanted to leave the United States to live in China?" "No." "Whatever! We're not going to change the plot." From time to time during our conversation, the PLA soldiers briefly tested out certain scenes for our input, and the one that had us all laughing involved the FBI agent. He was supposed to burst onto the scene to confront the young Chinese lovers, threatening the boy from Taiwan with imprisonment. The soldier acting this part said something like "See, I'm from the FBI," showing an imaginary badge on his coat. But instead of grabbing his jacket with his right fist and pulling it open to reveal where an imaginary badge might be pinned inside like a scene from a 1940s Hollywood film, the Chinese soldier daintily pinched the top of his lapel between his thumb and forefinger and turned the narrow strip of clothing over as if a badge had been pinned underneath his lapel. With great amusement, our family took turns demonstrating the correct way a law enforcement officer flashes a hidden badge, and our efforts were rewarded with equal bouts of laughter and appreciation. A month or two later, we were invited to see the play and were impressed with the scenery, costumes, direction, and acting. Some of our suggestions were readily incorporated and some were not, but we smiled satisfactorily toward the end when the brave Chinese lovers were confronted by the evil American FBI agent who burst onto the stage and flashed his badge as boldly and professionally as Eliot Ness. It was great propaganda!

Two of the many events the wai ban arranged for us involved Zhou Enlai: the intelligent, enigmatic, and revered premier and foreign minister of China from the very inception of the People's Republic in 1949. Because of his dynamic personality, political position in the Party, and the fact that he was more of an internationalist in stark contrast to Mao's parochialism, he was viewed more positively by the world outside than the Party chairman, and there are many stories describing his diplomatic charm. One illustrative anecdote comes from Theodore White's *In Search of History*, where the author describes his time in China covering the PLA as a correspondent for *Life* at the beginning of World War II. There was a special feast one night, and Zhou, his associates, and a few foreign journalists were about to enjoy a meal of pork, the quintessential meat of Northern China. Following Chinese custom, the host, Zhou, began to place several slices in the American's bowl with his own chopsticks, serving his guests first, but White protested that he was Jewish and didn't eat pork. Pausing for but a moment, Zhou continued to serve White, explaining that there had been a misunderstanding and that the dish he was serving wasn't pork but Chinese chicken. White concluded the story by admitting he enjoyed Chinese chicken the remainder of his life. One can see that, like Mao, Zhou was a larger-than-life figure, and for some Chinese and certainly for most foreigners, he was more admired than the Great Helmsman.

We were taken to the Zhou Enlai Middle School and spent a few hours seeing where the young Zhou studied and admiring the fine facilities that far surpassed any of the other schools we visited during our China stay. Obviously it was a key institution where children of the elite were privy to attend. Although Zhou died two and a half years before our arrival, the Party was intent on preserving his memory and prolonging the sense of sorrow so many people felt over his death, especially the more educated Chinese. Although Mao's picture was ubiquitous wherever we went in China, at least among the Chinese we worked with, Zhou was the leader most missed. Around the same time we visited his school, we were taken to the institute's Propaganda Hall one evening where, along with most of the student body, we saw a black-and-white film about Zhou Enlai's death and the period of mourning that followed. About half the film consisted of a shot of crowds of mourners circumambulating around Zhou's open coffin guarded by statuesque PLA soldiers. Slowly the mourners shuffled by, almost all of them sobbing uncontrollably, workers, peasants, soldiers, students, men, women, the young, the old, each of them genuinely gripped by grief. Almost on cue, the students in the auditorium around us started to choke up, and soon we were surrounded by as many real mourners as there were virtual ones flickering on the large screen above. The whole experience was so maudlin it almost seemed artificial, and a psychologist might even describe the event as a case of mass sociogenic illness. The entire experience struck us as somewhat surreal. On the one hand, there was no mistaking the sense of genuine admiration both the filmed and the theatre's mourners appeared to have for their fallen leader; on the other, there was no mistaking the manner in which decades of tightly constrained and highly concentrated advertising shaped an overwhelming and virtually identical response among so many different people. It was great propaganda.

What I remembered most about that film was not the weeping and wailing, however. There was something remarkable about Zhou's coffin that was so outstanding that it still remains a vivid memory to this day. Like the funeral of any great national leader, the casket was draped with a flag, but it was not the national emblem, the symbol of the People's Republic of China; it bore the hammer and sickle and was the standard of the Communist Party. I asked some teachers about this the next morning, and they saw nothing odd. "Of course," they replied, "next to Mao, Zhou was the greatest Party leader." I felt as if I was living in another world for, to cite just one counter example, I couldn't imagine President Kennedy's coffin being draped with the flag of the Democratic Party (tastefully not depicting the donkey) were such an emblem even to exist. The memory troubled me throughout our stay. Politics superseded nationalism. In the end, Zhou didn't die as a great Chinese but as a great Communist.

Mao never lived in Tianjin and rarely visited the city; after all, it was neither Beijing nor Shanghai, and as far as I know, no hotel suite in the entire metropolis was ever named after him. He is known to have eaten at one of the restaurants, however, a place famous for *baozi* (stuffed steamed bun), and one time we treated some of the teachers to a lunch there and another time Janene's students. The locals know it as *Gou Bu Li*, a name complicated enough to figure out in Chinese let alone translate into English. It's something like "[Even] Dogs Won't Leave [Them]," a wacky attempt at humor, suggesting that even dogs can't resist their *baozi*, implying that since dogs eat almost everything, they wouldn't refuse a *baozi* from this famous eatery. No, it makes no sense at all, hence the elephant-joke kind of advertising. After once stumbling through an unsuccessful attempt to justify to my Thai students why England's greatest quartet of musicians was called the Beatles, I have come to realize all languages have words with unfathomable etymologies, and so we must simply accept the fact that it was their *baozi*, not their name, that drew both the chairman and our colleagues, students, and us to this establishment for lunch. The waiter directed us to the very table that Mao himself had chosen way back on that historical occasion, and the steamed buns were so plump, tasty, and succulent that not one morsel was left had a wayward dog happened to wander by afterward. We returned to the establishment months later to treat Janene's students to lunch since most of them had rarely eaten at a decent restaurant, and though we were once again privileged to be seated at the very table once graced by the Great Helmsman himself and though the *baozi* were just as delectable, we did not fail to notice that on this occasion, ours was a completely different table from the one selected at our earlier visit. It seems the chairman not only slept around, he ate around as well.

During our seven years living and working in Thailand, we lived through many a military coup, but during our single year in China, war broke out. Oddly, it was not with Taiwan, South Korea, Japan, or any other of the snarling capitalist tigers surrounding the PRC, but with its Communist brother, the Socialist Republic of Vietnam. Although history has sadly demonstrated that our own United States has been far more bellicose than China over the past half century, the People's Republic has had military conflicts with every one of its neighbors at some point over the same period. In all fairness, *war* is too strong a term although it is an accurate description of some of these disputes, but from its 1949 inception, the PRC has battled every one of its contiguous neighbors whether these were heavy skirmishes that involved thousands of deaths, like the border battles with India, the USSR, and Vietnam, or major confrontations like the Korean War or the invasion of Tibet (taking the very un-Chinese view that this province existed as a legitimate independent state).

Logically, it would seem that Vietnam and China would be on the best of terms, especially since the large socialist neighbor to the north fed its little socialist brother to the south all kinds of military supplies throughout its fight for independence from the French and later the American invaders. Just like relations with the USSR, however, once amicable ties took a turn for the worse, ironically, not long after the Americans pulled out of what was then Saigon, and following the formation of the Socialist Republic of Vietnam. The immediate problem may have stemmed from the perceived mistreatment of the large number of Chinese immigrants to Vietnam, who, like their countrymen throughout Southeast Asia, were commercial entrepreneurs and hence were mistrusted by the leaders of the new socialist economy. An underlying and more fundamental issue was Vietnam's centuries-long role as a Chinese vassal state and the ambivalent sentiments Vietnamese harbor toward a civilization that contributed so much to their culture but simultaneously dominated their government and their economy. Think of England and the American colonies two and a half centuries ago for an analogy.

The war lasted about half of April and was much more similar to the 1969 skirmish with the USSR than to the Korean War, but still in terms of fatalities, this affair was an unmitigated disaster for the PLA. The Chinese media was quick and consistent to portray the Vietnamese as the voracious aggressors and the PLA "uncles" as the heroic and victorious forces in this brief conflict. Non-Chinese accounts of this fight generally describe the opposite, that China was the aggressor on the border and lost many more troops to the then battle-seasoned Vietnamese. I was amazed at how, within a fortnight, the PLA propaganda department put together a film and produced enough copies for distribution across the country. In the middle of April, about the time peace was restored to the border, once again we were invited to the institute's theater to view a movie. Unlike the tribute to Zhou, this film was in color and was action packed. There were convoys of supply trucks snaking their way southward through the mountains that separate the two nations; there were courageous PLA uncles leaping out of trenches and charging through enemy fire. There were tanks plowing over barriers and through thick smoke, and there were cannonades of heavy artillery belching death and destruction southward. It all looked very much like a modernized sequel to *All Quiet on the Western Front*. Throughout the film, an announcer shouted out descriptions of each scene as well as political slogans, his voice rising and falling as dramatically as an African-American preacher. At one point, when Chinese troops displayed weapons they had captured from the enemy, his voice went shrill with rage when he pointed out that the munitions depicted were made in the USA and were being turned around by the Vietnamese to kill the very Chinese people who had supported these ungrateful wretches in their war against the American aggressors. Obviously, after sessions like these, we could not return to our classes the next day and use the event as an exercise in critical thinking. "Liwen, can you share with the class one justification Vietnam would have for attacking China?" Or "Xiaoping, what could China have done to have prevented this unfortunate conflict?" It all was very sad, but it made for good theater and even better propaganda.

One advantage of living in a foreign country for a year or more is that you come to appreciate the seasonal changes that transform the life of the people around you. Your memories are then not picture postcards portraying static and unrelated moments in time but are more a dreamy video of dynamic and interrelated natural and national events. Take for example the two major national holidays of the Chinese calendar, the first day of May and October, the birthdays of (as always) first the Party and then the nation. Seasons are counted early in China, so even though the sun was not yet at the solstice and the temperature sometimes chilly, May Day announced the beginning of summer. In the same way, even though the days could be unusually warm, October signaled the advent of winter. On May 1, with schools closed and a midweek holiday to celebrate, the first thing to catch our eyes when we stepped out for a family stroll were the police at our corner. Instead of the dark blue winter uniforms they had been sporting even through some warm April afternoons, they were smartly attired in white, looking like proud Annapolis graduates in their spotless outfits. And on October 1, China's National Day, their now somewhat dirtier uniforms were transformed back into dark blue. Without any calendar, one glimpse of any cop could instantly tell you which of the two six-month seasons the city was in. Unlike the police, the general populace followed the climate, so by the time the summer heat and humidity rolled in, all the long-sleeved dark blues and browns turned into sleeveless whites, and once the autumnal winds whistled in from the north, the dark clothes of winter reappeared. Sensing the importance of these holidays and learning that our academic year would be ending in early July for summer vacation, Janene and I decided to punctuate the calendar with a new and dramatic event. We had now lived long enough in China to appreciate the grim and dreary conditions of the daily life of the people around us, to have learned of the horrors that many of our colleagues or their relatives endured during the immediate past, and to realize that we should respond with some gesture of gratitude for the munificent hospitality that had been showered upon us. China may have already had the Party, but we decided to throw a party, a big one, to celebrate the Fourth of July.

Having controlled the price gouging on our daily meals early in the game and being frugal by nature despite our modest salary (at least compared to our income back home), halfway through our stay we could see that we would be able to leave China at the end of the year with a savings of several thousand dollars. We both felt strongly that we should not leave China with more than we brought, so we tried to spend any discretionary income in China, and while most of it was allocated to dinners, parties, and gifts for our friends, students, and colleagues, we also used much of what was left over at the end of our stay to purchase some beautiful wool carpets and artifacts to take home as permanent reminders of that special year. In sum, our financial strategy was what was gained in Tianjin stayed in Tianjin. We had the gem of an idea and a budget, but the devil was in the details.

The relatively easy part was eliciting the participation of the US consulate in Beijing. Janene had already made several trips to borrow films and teaching materials, and thanks to our acquaintance with Stapleton Roy, who was second-in-command at the embassy only to the newly appointed ambassador, Leonard Woodcock, we had help in high places. We needed a large American flag. No problem. We needed some colorful posters and a bunch of brochures and little knickknacks to distribute to each of the many guests as party favors. Can do. Could we borrow a copy of the film that was made to commemorate the bicentennial celebrations of 1976? Of course. You wouldn't happen to have the sheet music for the "Star Spangled Banner" would you? Sure do. Finally, and this might sound a bit odd, but we need Ambassador Woodcock to tape-record a brief personal greeting to the people of Tianjin to play at our celebration. Why not? Janene returned from her quick weekend visit gleeful from all the loot and favors she had been able to collect.

Recalling Zhang's dictum that nothing is trivial in China and anticipating some bumps in the road to a successful celebration of Independence Day, we decided to start with easy stuff and work upward to the more complicated plans we had dreamed up. Consequently, we began by shopping for the national emblem of the PRC, the bright crimson flag with a big yellow star circled by four little ones supposedly symbolizing the Han majority surrounded by the four largest minorities. We hit both the local shops down the street and the large department stores downtown, but none had Chinese flags for sale. We inquired among our colleagues, and they scratched their heads at our unusual request and murmured something about maybe we needed a permit for such an eccentric purchase. Coming from the States, where it seems that it is everyone's God-given right if not responsibility to fly the American flag from inside churches to the outside of bikini bottoms, we were astounded that civilians could not buy and fly their own national symbol. We worked with the wai ban to get permission, but this was not easy. Even after securing permission to make our purchase, it took some time to select one that would match the size of the American flag we had so readily borrowed from the consulate; obviously, it would not be good form to have the US emblem dwarf its Chinese counterpart nor vice versa. Finally, we succeeded in buying our own *Red Star Over China*, which we still have to this day and have occasionally flown outside our California home for Chinese guests. With only a month to prepare, we began to worry about accomplishing the larger goals we had dreamed up for this party.

By then, thanks to the kids and their forays into every nook inside our establishment, we knew that our hotel had a moderate-sized ballroom that looked as if it had been blocked off and frozen in time since its Victorian heydays. We approached the hotel management for permission to rent this space for a party we planned to host on July 4. The manager stonewalled us for several weeks, initially claiming that the dusty and vacant ballroom was fully booked for the month, but after several meetings in which we let him backpedal from this ludicrous allegation and assured that we would cover all the costs, he relented. With the location and the date confirmed, Janene plunged immediately into selecting appropriate snacks and drinks and ordering and negotiating their costs. But there was also entertainment to be arranged, a projector and screen for the bicentennial film, a mike and speaker system for the many toasts and speeches anticipated, and of course, a piano for the music that we had planned. We asked the management if we could use the hotel's piano; however, at first they denied the very existence of any such instrument on their premises. When taken to the nether regions of the hotel and shown where our kids had found the dusty instrument, they muttered something like, "Oh that piano, but it's not been used for such a long time and doesn't work," implying indirectly that this justified their denial that the piano ever existed in the first place. This was an ironic reversal of the argument about whether or not our institute had a swimming pool. Here the management's argument was the opposite of our students' that a pool is always a pool even if it has no water and is filled with temporary shelters. This wasn't a piano because it wasn't being played! "No problem," we rejoined, "we've already contacted Derick's conservatory and will pay for their piano tuner to come over and get the instrument ready." In the end, not only did we have a piano for our party but after the festivities were over and with the help of a quartet of the strongest fu wu ren, we got permission to haul it upstairs to our sitting room, where it provided family entertainment for the rest of our time in the city.

Food, libations, a venue, decorations, and entertainment were in place, but no political holiday is complete without a politician, and I decided to go to the very top for our invited orator. When the idea of a Fourth of July celebration first crossed our minds, on a whim, I airmailed a blank cassette tape to President Jimmy Carter with a brief note describing our unique situation. Here we were, the first US residents in a city of seven million, hosting the first American Independence party in over half a century, wondering if he could record a brief greeting for our Chinese guests to help foster the friendly relations between our two great nations. How spectacular, I thought, if our Chinese friends, their glasses poised for a toast, could hear the southern twang of the president of the United States himself, greeting them personally at our momentous midsummer gathering. It would be quite literally a Carter to cadre moment! Granted, it was a long shot, and given our experiences with the Chinese censors, my hopes were high but expectations low. Unsurprisingly, I never did get a reply, and chances are, the packet never even got out of China, a free cassette perhaps for some sticky-fingered censor. We did have a viable backup nonetheless, thanks to Janene's trip to Beijing and Ambassador Woodcock's willingness to lend his voice to our cause.

Now came the most delicate part of the entire operation: choosing whom to invite. The modest ballroom and our equally limited budget dictated a list of no more than seventy-five guests, but within that half a year of residency, there were already almost twice that number of people we wished to have in attendance. Protocol and politics forced us to select leading cadres from our institute, Derick's conservatory, Christine's nursery, and the metropolitan government, so there went a dozen or so invites alone. We felt it crucial for Janene's class of young students to experience this tiny episode of history, so there went an additional score of guests to add. Our children's teachers, the colleagues we worked with most closely, a sample of the foreign experts teaching in Tianjin, and a few Chinese friends who came from outside any of the official dan wei represented swelled the list to overflowing. We designed and had printed up a colorful card that invited each guest to an afternoon party celebrating America's Independence Day with food and drink, music and a movie, and promising that a very special mystery celebrity would be in attendance. I added the latter knowing full well the Chinese penchant for curiosity, and many of our colleagues—after receiving an invitation—immediately began pestering me for the identity of this luminary. Lao Jin, the most senior and serious scholar on our faculty and someone who I worked with closely throughout the year, was particularly inquisitive. He leaned on our intimate working ties and promised not to let anyone else know, for he was unable to bridle his overriding inquisitiveness. With some honesty, I fended off all the pestering with the claim that I myself wasn't certain who our invited star was in that I had been holding out hope right up to the last mail call before July 4 that a cassette tape from the White House had managed to speed across the Pacific, elude the Tianjin censors, and end up in my hands in time to be a part of our celebrations.

July 4 turned out to be a long, hot day. Tianjin is on almost exactly the same latitude as Washington, DC, and though its winters are colder because it is not warmed by the Gulf Stream because it sits near the coast, it can be as muggy and unbearable in the summer as our nation's capital. That morning we had to gather at the institute for a group photograph of the visiting scholars class we had been teaching for the semester. Chairs and bleachers were lined up, facing southeast into the blazing midmorning sun, and our photographer squeezed every minute of control he could muster during his brief (but our long) moment in the sun. Because we were semi–big shots, we were posed first, sitting in the front row alone before the school's administrative cadres arrived. Slowly, the photographer directed each row of visiting scholars and teachers to be filled up behind us, an effort that seemed interminable as we squinted directly into the intense sunlight, sweat already dripping from our underarms. Finally, the cadres appeared, and with proud smiles, they joined us a moment before the group photo was snapped. But wait, another picture or two to ensure that everybody was included. We cycled back to the hotel in order to hurry through all the final preparations for the early evening festivities. As fate would have it, the water in the hotel had been turned off all day, and just forty-five minutes before the celebrations were to begin, the water was turned back on, and we were able to take a quick shower and change into our best clothes so that we could appear as cool, clean, and acceptable hosts.

The excitement built as each guest arrived, and despite our best efforts to balance off our duties as hospitable greeters and responsible gatekeepers, several uninvited but unrefusable people showed up at the last minute. With everyone seated, I asked our musicians to open the ceremonies. Derick and Yu *Laoshi* (Teacher), his young trombone teacher, nervously stepped up to their music stands with Xu Laoshi, Derick's brilliant piano teacher, poised as the accompanist. Equally anxious, the two took a deep breath and plunged into a trombone duet of "The Star Spangled Banner" and after a deferential applause, they followed up with "My Country 'Tis of Thee." It was a very emotional moment for Janene and me. Naturally, there was parental pride in watching our twelve-year-old son perform, but there was much more. As we looked up at the two flags pinned to the far wall, listening to our talented son and his teachers, we were overcome with the knowledge that those notes had not rung out for at least fifty years anywhere in that city or the surrounding countryside, and scanning the respectful faces crowding the room, it seemed as if the music was washing away decades of hatred and misunderstanding with each cadence and that by the final crescendo, much of this mistrust had been expunged. Seizing the opportunity to play in front of a captive audience, Derick played two solo pieces on the piano, Yu Laoshi played two short Stephen Foster melodies on the trombone, and Xu Laoshi returned to the piano and whipped off Chopin's Polonaise in A. I couldn't resist a chance to prime our guests' growing curiosity over who the mystery guest might be, so when I introduced Xu Laoshi's piece, I mentioned almost as an aside that Chopin's work was our mystery guest's favorite. After this musical interlude, I announced that in honor of our host nation, Xu Laoshi would play the modern Chinese composition "Revolutionary Concerto." Again, we all listened attentively, mesmerized by the flashing arpeggios of this exciting composition, and again we were enthralled by the way music spoke a communal language, uniting all of us with an eloquence that words rarely capture.

The time had now come for the formal toasts, and Janene bravely began with a welcome she had memorized in Chinese. I had carefully composed one ahead of time, largely so I would remember to say the right things but also to help my interpreter, Lao Jin, prepare an accurate translation ahead of time. Pausing between phrases allowed him to repeat what I had just said in Chinese since most of those assembled either had limited English proficiency or none at all, but the hesitations also added a cadenced dignity to my somewhat overly grandiloquent oratory.

> All of you here tonight have played a role in helping us to adjust to our life and work in Tianjin.
>
> All of you have contributed to the friendship that we have so richly enjoyed.
>
> All of you have helped rebuild the bridge of peace and understanding between our two great nations, China and America.
>
> Teacher, student, administrator, worker—you have all done your part in helping us personally and contributing in a larger measure to the friendship between our two lands.

From each member of our family, we simply but sincerely offer you our deep thanks.

And so on this first American Independence Day since normalization, it is fitting and proper that we congratulate each other on the fact that this bridge of friendship has been built.

Unlike the famous Nanjing Yangtze River Bridge, the bridge that we have helped construct has not been built of steel and concrete, but of hope and aspiration.

But like the mighty Yangtze edifice itself, our new relation stands as a testimony to the dedication and industry of the Chinese and American people.

It is built on the banks of the past; it leaps across the torrents of the present, and it reaches out far, far beyond the distant shores of the future.

My friends, let us celebrate the building of this new bridge tonight—this bridge of peace, friendship, and understanding.

I therefore would like to propose a toast to the bridge makers—to Chairman Hua and Vice Premier Deng, to President Carter and Ambassador Woodcock, and to the great people of China and America. Happy Independence Day!

Speaking on behalf of our institute, Lao Chen responded with some thoughtful remarks, and then on cue, food and drinks were provided by the fu wu ren. The room was darkened and suddenly filled with sweeping panoramas of America, and the guests heard stories of our nation's brief history as we viewed the bicentennial film. At the end of the movie, it was time for more speeches and toasts, and having been careful to invite a distinguished cadre from each of the dan wei responsible for us, for the first time, the party started to drag a little. I saved the best for last, announcing that now that all our Chinese dignitaries had spoken, it was the moment they had all been waiting for, a toast from a distinguished American celebrity. Never letting on that my original aim had been much higher, I invited the Right

Honorable Leonard Woodcock, ambassador plenipotentiary, from the United States of America to have the final word. The ballroom buzzed with excitement as the guests glanced around to see from which door His Excellency would make his dramatic entrance. Even I must admit there was a sense of denouement as I pressed play on our little recorder as our only contact with our mystery luminary was through his voice. But our stock rose considerably when in his prefatory comments, Ambassador Woodcock referred to Janene and me as his good friends and then proceeded to bless our gathering and praise the friendship between our two great nations and peoples. Raising our glasses with resounding and final *ganbei*'s ("Cheers!") we could all drink to that. Each guest met us personally at the door, reluctant to let the evening end and practically shaking our hands off in their gratitude almost as if they were trying to prolong the party as they lingered in their farewells. It was great propaganda, but it was an even greater event. Indeed, it was our proudest moment that year in China.

Surpassing any of the performances we were privileged to be taken to that year, the city streets provided the best entertainment and the most revealing insights into the life of our fellow citizens. As the weather improved and the people shed their heavy winter clothing, we were able to see more of them in both senses of the phrase as we made our daily rounds by bike and foot. Except for trips to the theater, railroad station, or another educational institution when our wai ban furnished a car, we had the open and unobstructed views of our surroundings that only pedestrians or bike riders can command. As a runner, I had an added advantage when I went out on my late-afternoon jaunts of three to six miles, usually up one side of the river and back down the other. Always moving, usually at an even faster pace than the rush-hour cyclists who were packed together, I never attracted a crowd, and because I traveled a considerable distance, usually on backstreets and alleys, I saw scenes rarely viewed on the more fashionable thoroughfares such as Revolutionary Avenue, which ran in front of our hotel.

The variety in the modes and patterns of transportation we witnessed or used during that year were enormous and were partly the result of natural historical progress and partly due to foreign influence. In the early fifties, when China and the USSR were on amicable terms, Soviet cars, trucks, and airplanes represented the greatest advances in post-Liberation transportation. Even when we were there almost three decades later, everywhere there were still vestiges of this Russian influence in the streets and in the air. Volgas and Zhinas still plied the road and Ilyushin-62s and MIG-23s flitted across the skies overhead. But ideological history gradually gave way to economic independence, and again, it is in the realm of mechanized transportation where this was most conspicuous. China's newer economic friendship was with its former enemies, Japan and the United States, thus Toyotas, Isuzus, and Hinos were starting to appear on the ground while Boeings were beginning to replace the Ilyushins in the skies.

The greatest variation was not due to these international connections, however important they may have been to China's modernization, but it came as a consequence of time. Like any developing nation, the PRC is a land where one can see evidence of many periods of history all jumbled together on the streets in front of you. It is this marvelous propinquity of past and present, Neolithic and contemporary, medieval and modern that makes China watching such wonderful theater. Outside the cities, on the country roads and rivers, and in the streets and skies, you can view a panoramic chronicling of human transportation from the discovery of the wheel to the launching of spacecraft. The thoroughfares of this land are a daily reenactment of that history, and along any given road, you'll find this fascinating chronological parade, an evolutionary pilgrimage: pedestrians by the thousands plodding soberly along in the bipedal fashion unique to our species, taking what the Chinese whimsically call the number 11 Bus. Hunchbacked peasant boys, heads bowed to the endless road in front of them, sweating and heaving as they lurch forward, drag overloaded carts with their weary fathers pushing behind. Then there's the discovery of domesticated animal power: parades of horse carts, large wooden vehicles with truck tires fitted underneath, the only modern incongruity in this otherwise medieval spectacle. Powered by mules, horses, or donkeys that wince to the occasional rifle crack of their owners' whips, they march along in evolutionary time. The advent of the machine is announced by the unmistakably boisterous roar of an oncoming internal combustion engine. Chugging into view is the ubiquitous two-wheeled tractor, motoring down the road like a rototiller pulling a four-wheeled hay wagon encumbered with drowsy peasants, its rider steering the angry contraption by its broad handlebars like a proud cowboy at the reins of a surrey. Then comes the thunder of a distant truck, the sturdy olive-drab army vehicle used all over China as the modern workhorse of labor, honking incessantly through the traffic, the mastodon of the roads. Its driver with his dark sunglasses worn day or night is the vainest teamster of them all, gloating in the fact that only he and his brothers, the drivers of cars, buses, and other petroleum-guzzling vehicles, sit on the very top of the food chain of transportation. And weaving in and out of this diverse array of locomotion are the bicycles as plentiful as the dust.

This historical progression is not confined to the road, however. The variation is just as great when one looks at the rivers and skies. In the muddy rivers of northern and central China, in the *Huang He* (Yellow River) and the *Chang Jiang* (Long River or Yangtze), the chronological evolution is replicated. Naked boys swim in summer delight; their sweating parents struggle to propel wooden rafts and gently curved boats with oars, poles, sculls, or hawsers. Motorized barges and muscular tugs strain at lines of floating houseboats like angry mules, and now and then, these are quickly passed by modern passenger ships. If you choose your location carefully, say the *Zhu Jiang* (Pearl River) estuary leading from Canton to Hong Kong, you can spy a Chinese-built hydrofoil skimming the water like a dragonfly, a proud icon of the technological achievements of a twentieth-century industrial nation. Or look carefully at the skies over any large city. Using X-ray vision to pierce the smog cover, you can catch a glimpse of a Chinese-made jet or helicopter, and higher yet, far out in the heavens that have been revered in China for millennia, are satellites designed, built, and launched by the Chinese themselves, propelling them from the dusty footpaths of prehistory into the giddy heights of space-age technology. All of this and more confront the eyes of any visitor, and you find yourself tossing quick glances at your mental clock to check which historical time zone you're in. To your dismay, you find that the hands are spinning so fast that you can't even determine the hour let alone the minute, so you make the best guess you can, say sometime between a few minutes past the Renaissance and a quarter after the 1970s. Yes, the thoroughfares of China are indeed unusual. The peasant boy lugging his heart out, head bowed to the eternal earth, and way above, higher than he will ever dare to dream, a satellite glides effortlessly in the immortal sky like the mandate of heaven.

Our mode of transportation turned out to be the bicycle, and it was an uncommon and generally beneficial experience for our family to spend an entire year biking together. Excluding Christine, who was four and had to ride sidesaddle as Janene or I ferried her around, we all gained the natural benefit of some moderate exercise since we rarely cycled too far or too fast given the two-wheeled masses that filled the streets around us each day. With the exception of the winter snow and subsequent ice, Tianjin was an ideal city for cycling. It was flat and fairly dry, and thanks to the post-Liberation urban deconstruction and reconstruction, there were several broad avenues intersecting the city. At first, there were virtually no bike lanes because cyclists occupied every thoroughfare and took over all the city streets with the primordial rights of a plague of locusts. Naturally, they gave way reluctantly to the few cars and the slow-moving city buses and displayed quicker heed when a truck came barreling down the road, but there was strength in numbers, so even when outweighed and outsped, the bikers acted as if they owned the road. There were no stop signs, but major intersections had traffic lights that cyclists allegedly were supposed to obey; nevertheless, until the beginning of June, Tianjin bicyclists behaved like the wanton days of the Israelites when the Old Testament prophets lamented that "each man was a law unto himself." Because the bikes were so heavy, the streets so crowded, and almost no one had such amenities as swept-down handlebars or gears, we all rode bolt upright exposed to the wind but with a clear view of the peloton ahead, around, and even behind us. Unlike driving a car, this unobstructed view allowed us to spot the subtle changes in body language that the cyclist in front of us was going to make an abrupt stop to readjust his load or the bike to our left was about to suddenly cut in front of us as we approached an intersection. Thank God cell phones had yet not been invented since most commuters used both hands to steer and brake, and their attentions were devoted to the here and now and not focused on someone else on a cell far away.

Like automobiles in America, bicycles played an important role in a family's living patterns, in dictating its social habits, and in displaying its economic success. A family that owned a bike enjoyed a much more flexible lifestyle than one that did not, and if each older member owned one, the advantages were enormous. Father and mother could avoid the long queues at the bus stop and pedal straight to work, either one of them dropping their infant off at the nursery. Grandfather didn't waste an entire morning fighting the bus lines to get across town to the department store, and the teenager could cut the walking time to the factory or school by two-thirds. The bicycle made leisure time just as convenient as well. A new movie in a distant suburb, a Sunday morning at a park on the edge of town, or a quiet tête-à-tête with a lover behind an abandoned warehouse along the river became a reality in the life of the owners of this two-wheeled steed. Bicycles were not simply possessions of convenience; like the car, they could also dominate the life of the owner, especially in terms of expense. It is surprising how costly they were even though no nation made more of them. Despite the enormity of this supply, the demand for them was voracious, and consequently, the price for a new bike was about 180 yuan (c. $113), which worked out to about four or five months salary for the average worker, making a cycle roughly equivalent to a car in the States in terms of comparative value.

Like so many other times during our early weeks of acculturation when it was difficult to distinguish differences, initially all the bikes looked identical, black with two wheels. As our eyes adjusted, we could identify different makes and often stereotype the personalities that pedaled them. A young worker cycling to work on his new Flying Pigeon jingles his rotating bell constantly and weaves in and out among the commuters with the universal incaution of youth. A cadre pumps along slowly on stout but aging legs, his small, black bag with Tianjin stamped in fading white letters dangles from his upscale Red Flag, a Shanghai bike of considerable prestige. And over there is a middle-aged peasant cycling into town on his oversized country bike loaded down with scallions to sell at a convenient street corner. Its wheels are large, sturdy, and brown without the citified pretentiousness of fenders, and its frame is broad and reinforced for heavy loads and boasts no bell or chrome; it is simple and strong like its owner, and it's easy to imagine that vehicle and peasant are one, one robust and durable transporter of goods from the strong brown earth of the countryside dedicated to feeding the unending appetite of the city.

In contrast to the peasant is the rare sight of someone with enough money and connections to whiz around on a fancy velocipede, say the latest model Phoenix. You barely notice its dark green-and-gold frame because your eye is instantly drawn to all the extras that are rarely found on other bikes: two large rearview mirrors on the handlebars flanking a small battery-operated electric horn. No clinking bell for this plutocrat! Then on the front fender, get a load of that headlight wrapped in a plastic bag to prevent rust and dust from tarnishing its all-chrome finish. The top tube of the frame is wrapped tightly in red velvet, and the seat is decorated in matching trim. The rack behind the seat is chrome, not gunmetal black, and yes, it's true, his bike actually has gears, three of them: one for a quick start at traffic lights, another for the loping speed of normal commuting, and a third to outdistance any show-off on a Flying Pigeon audacious enough to drag-race its owner. However, it is the lower portion of the back fender that establishes the owner as a genuine playboy of the roads. The fad that was current at that time dictated that the bottom portion of the rear fender was to be decorated with a leftover beverage can as a kind of custom-built metallic mudguard, so imagine the glory of pedaling a Phoenix whose rear fender was decked out with that then-rare symbol of globalization, a Coca-Cola can! We had innocently hoped during that year in China we would get some respite from the materialism that seemed to consume our homeland, but simply by looking at the bikes that surrounded us each day, the universals of greed, vanity, and avarice were apparent and united us all, capitalist and Communist, American and Chinese, into one universal brotherhood. Still, there were glimpses of human hope on the streets of Tianjin.

Occasionally, you'd catch a most remarkable sight. An older woman slowly pumps into view on a three-wheeled contraption built from what looks like an old rickshaw seat attached to the two rear wheels. You can see she's a paraplegic, her legs immobilized and wrapped in a blanket from the cold wind, her left hand pumping a circular handle driving the rear wheels via a chain-and-cog mechanism gerrymandered from a regular cycle, and her right hand steering the handlebars. She moves slower than all of the other vehicles on the road, and they continually swerve to overtake her. Though she is sometimes slower than many of the pedestrians, if you look very carefully at her unrelenting face, if you observe with keen attention those proud brown eyes, you can catch a magnificent sense of self-reliance. What a gift to be able to transport yourself to work with your own two hands!

The traffic code prohibited riding more than one person per bike, so when within sight of a police kiosk or cycling on a major avenue during the day, most people would dutifully walk their cycles with their passenger seated sidesaddle between their arms. If I were pressed for time when taking Christine to or from her nursery or if I were carrying her a fair distance, I too would quickly hop out of my seat to push her when it looked like a cop was nearby and then swing my leg up and go back to pedaling when the coast was clear. A few parents constructed makeshift sidecars for their infants, but these looked so flimsy we never bothered to inquire about their cost or availability. We often saw the very elderly being wheeled by their adult children, and sometimes the former looked frightfully ill, so the bike was serving as a temporary ambulance. The extremely sick or wounded were laid in the large box between the two back wheels of the tricycles used to ferry goods about town.

Naturally, we were exposed to the elements, a disadvantage during the extremes in weather that were part of the annual cycle of life. Our twin enemies in winter were the wind and snow, and sometimes they attacked simultaneously. A February blizzard, for instance, brought five inches of snow, nothing compared to the bitter Manchurian winters northeast of us but enough to divert us off our bikes and onto the electric buses for our commute to work. The city had no snowplows, so united by a common invader and invigorated by a spirit of community service, people emerged from their shops, shelters, and apartments and attacked the stuff with brooms. Worst of all were a couple of late snowfalls in April when we thought we were done with our winter of discontent. When the snow was fresh and relatively dry, we could cycle gingerly through the stuff, taking extra precaution at every turn, but when it congealed into ice, everyone except the young and foolish would walk their bikes as if they were carrying the ghost of winter sidesaddle between their arms. Janene wore her mountaineering jacket or a long plaid coat, thick gloves, and a fuzzy white hat tied tightly around her face by white tasseled balls, and from her outfit and her tall, upright posture, she stood out like a Mary Poppins among the frozen sea of darkly clad cyclists around her. The days of spring and fall were ideal for biking except for the occasional rainstorms. When it poured, our fellow commuters would roll up their pant legs to their knees, hood themselves with whatever spare plastic they had available, and exchange shoes for flip-flops, then off they would cycle into the downpour albeit a bit more tentatively. In summer, our adversaries were the merciless heat and humidity, and we sought slight respite from both from the artificial breeze created by our moving bikes. Except for a few days after rain or a strong wind when the air was clear, in every week of each of the seasons, we had to cope with the pollution.

We acculturated to most of the changes and exigencies that confronted us that year, but we never were able to tolerate the continual degradation of our atmosphere. Coal was by far the predominant source of energy, and it fueled factories and the heating plants for large buildings as well as the small stoves and tiny cookers for every apartment and temporary shelter. Although China boasts an abundance of the raw material ranging from anthracite to lignite, at least in the north, most of the coal was bituminous, a soft mineral that emits lots of yellowish smoke and black cinders when it is burnt. Factories ran and people cooked all year, so we had a constant and free supply of smog, but it grew luxuriously thick during winter when even more coal was burnt for heating. One day in late March, the sky was so black at midday that we pedaled home through the smog as fast as we could because we were certain a spring thunderstorm was about to cascade upon us. I was reminded of a description of Pittsburgh back in the twenties where the city of steel and industry was so darkened by factory smoke that drivers were forced to use their headlights during the day in order to negotiate the streets. This claim was made with a post–Industrial Revolution sense of pride, an overly arrogant feeling of accomplishment that man was finally able to conquer nature. Imagine that! Factories could turn day into night, and electric-generating plants could transform night into day. There in Tianjin, a half a century later, a similar sentiment lingered fostered by ten-year plans and slogans urging the populace to produce more for the state.

We were somewhat protected whenever we were inside but were at the mercy of our filthy ecosystem whenever we stepped out, and cycling through the polluted air was especially hard on the eyes. Because she wore contacts, Janene's vision was particularly affected, and almost daily, her eyes were scratched, and relief would come only when tears of irritation and aggravation would wash out the grit and temporarily relieve her distress. Among the supplies I purchased during my February trip to attend the TESOL convention in the States was a pair of swim goggles that Janene wore when biking on bad days. Though they helped prevent the dust and cinders from peppering her vision, they had a tendency to steam over, and after a scratched cornea in the late summer precipitated a visit to an ophthalmologist, she replaced her contacts with glasses whenever she rode her bike.

Although we all seemed to catch an inordinate number of upper-respiratory afflictions, especially Christine, whose tropical, Thai genes did not prepare her for the inhospitable climate of Northern China, we were lucky that none of our family came to China with allergies or asthma. A colleague of mine from the University of Pittsburgh, a Chinese language specialist who had longed for a chance to visit the PRC one day, arrived in Beijing in the autumn to begin a stint teaching there; however, his asthma was so aggravated by the smog that he lasted only a month or two, much of the time hospitalized, and was forced to give up his post and dream and return to the clean air of modern Pittsburgh. Speaking of which, two months after returning to our home in the United States, an article in the *Pittsburgh Press* reported that the haze over Beijing contained over 150 microns of particulates per cubic meter, six times the level of pollution considered safe by the US Environmental Protection Agency. When we first began teaching at the institute and started to hear about how many teachers or family members were sick, we first thought that we were surrounded by hypochondriacs who used the slightest cough as an excuse to get out of work. The iron rice bowl did encourage slackers, but once we ourselves started to succumb to the murky atmosphere, we became much more empathetic and realized, while we were forced to inhale the stuff fewer than four hundred days, our friends and colleagues had to breathe it for decades. As the people of Pittsburgh and America had already learned decades earlier, the Chinese were beginning to realize that ultimately, man never conquers nature and what humans send around comes back to plague them.

We rarely cycled at night, but when we did, the streets were transformed. Virtually no bikes had lights, and since the streets were lit intermittently by the dim streetlamps, we would cycle in quiet darkness in and out of temporary circles of light. Intersections were especially dangerous because despite the fact they were lit, the motorized traffic tended to drive with only the parking lights on or none at all (remember this was to save electricity), and while it was easy to survive a bump from another bike, there was all hell to pay if you were blindsided by a truck. I liked the night, however. For one thing, because it was difficult to see, our anonymity was protected, and we drew fewer stares, and no cyclists suddenly started to stalk behind us simply to scrutinize the barbarians in front of them, trying to discover what they were up to. Horses, mules, donkeys, and other livestock were banned from the streets downtown during the day, but at nighttime, you could hear their melodic clopping on any major thoroughfare, and it was fun to cycle next to a mule cart and pedal in cadence to the clippety-clop and hear the whistled breathing of the sturdy animal next to you. One time we were returning home from a late dinner at a friend's house on an especially tranquil night, and we started to pass a pack of donkeys loaded with goods ambling down the middle of the street. Just as I cycled past one of them, he (though maybe it was a she) lifted its head and brayed in full voice. Derick chuckled as he saw me veer in front of him, almost tumbling a sleepy Christine perched on the top tube between my arms.

I never took an official survey, but I had the strong impression that discounting the bicycles, whose colossal numbers would have skewed the statistics to begin with, there were many more human-powered wheels on the roads than motorized ones. There were some changes from my childhood, for I never once saw a rickshaw, those high-wheeled, old-fashioned carriages that were always pulled at a slow trot and were the favored taxis of the rich in every large town in pre-Liberation China. My parents enjoyed this intimate form of transportation their first year in Beijing and their subsequent years in my hometown, Jining. But I also caught scenes taken right out of my boyhood scrapbook of memories. Rarely in the city itself but all around in the countryside, I spotted the Chinese wheelbarrows, which must not have changed in thousands of years and which carried produce, pigs, and people at a slow but persistent pace from village to village. They were made almost entirely of wood and rope with one large wheel placed in the middle of its center of gravity and were pushed and balanced by the strongest man willing and available. The many horse carts both in and out of the city were just like the ones I remember seeing as a boy in the forties, constructed of wood but secured to the axle and inflated wheels taken from a no-longer-used car or truck. Smaller carts usually attached to two bike wheels were pulled by laborers, men and women, their hard hands gripping the two poles extending from their heavy load and their sweating shoulders lunging against the rope used to help distribute the weight. Their carts always seemed to carry the maximum load possible so that they seemed half full when transporting bricks and metal pipes but were towering and top-heavy when crammed with charcoal or crushed cardboard boxes. They were always burdened with weight. These poor human engines had huge hearts swollen from years of tugging at these almost inhuman burdens, and unlike the four-footed laborers, they barely made a sound as they plodded along. A straining and overloaded mule would attract notice and perhaps even a modicum of pity, but these poor souls were almost invisible.

The darkness permitted a type of human trafficking on the streets that was never seen or smelled during daylight hours—the men responsible for filling and removing the honey buckets that carried human waste out of the city under the cover of night. You could smell a honey bucket approaching any time of night even if it were a city block downwind from you, and with that first whiff, I always felt a pang of remorse for the poor slobs condemned to this onerous and filthy duty. They pedaled a kind of tricycle that carried a large tank of galvanized steel between the two back wheels. Once night fell, they would cycle in with empty tanks from the fields that surrounded the city, a one-way distance of many miles. Then at public toilets or at establishments like our hotel, they would fill their tanks with the day's waste of urine and fecal matter that had lain rotting in storage cisterns, and straining under their putrid load, they would slowly pedal out into the night and back to the fields from which they came. Under the morning sun, farmers would spray this nocturnal nectar onto the vegetables to be sold back in the city, and so in an ironic twist, our waste never left us, it simply returned to be eaten another day! Repugnant as the entire enterprise was or even to describe, it characterizes the symbiotic efficiency the Chinese display in being able to feed hundreds of millions of mouths each day. Waste not, want not! Surely Ben Franklin was of Chinese lineage.

The most hilarious street scene we witnessed that year was a result of a sea change in traffic laws that went into effect on June 1. For weeks, posters all over town announced a draconian change in the vehicular code for cyclists. Beginning on the first day of June, they would have to behave exactly like motorized traffic at all intersections and come to a complete stop at a red light and cross or turn only on green. In all fairness to the bike riders, there were at least two factors that made this superficially logical and easy demand difficult to obey. One was that according to legend, during the Cultural Revolution, cyclists in some cities—in a perverse celebration of doing away with capitalistic and foreign traditions—stopped on green and crossed on red. After all, red was the color of happiness and the Party; how could crimson possibly signal stop? I don't know if this revolutionary approach to traffic lights was practiced in Tianjin, but if it was, you could understand the cavalier disrespect toward lights we witnessed when we lived in the city. A second and probably more influential factor was that traffic lights at all the major intersections were controlled by a cop in a kiosk. From his perch he could see any trucks or cadre-carrying cars approaching from any of the cardinal directions, and he was supposed to switch the light so that motorized vehicles entering the intersection would always get a green for go. Like our fellow bikers, we would often be startled to see a green light ahead of us suddenly turn red within the half second we were about to enter the intersection (there was no cautionary yellow). Anxiety levels thus rose anytime we cycled up to an intersection with traffic lights, but because there were so few motor vehicles at that time and since the strength of China was in her masses (a dictum made famous by Mao), all of us basically learned to ignore traffic lights. Such antirevolutionary behavior would have to cease on the very first day of June, the posters announced, and if Deng Xiaoping had come up with a fifth modernization, it might well have been something like the need to obey all traffic signals.

The appointed date came on a Friday, so as we peddled to work carefully stopping at every red light, we caught scenes of organized confusion at every intersection. It was still morning and already the city's constabulary had confiscated hundreds of bicycles from citizens who had broken the new law. "Guo lai, guo lai," the cops kept screaming over their kiosk loudspeakers at the scores of cyclists pedaling through red lights left and right. A month into their white summer uniforms, the police were everywhere, stopping their startled countrymen and piling their bikes on top of the mounting heaps of cycles at each corner. Angry owners crowded around the kiosks, shouting their complaints at the cops who were unmoved by the arguments that they were ignorant of the new law. Until they received a citation and paid a fine, the surprised commuters were unable to retrieve their Flying Pigeons and resume their journeys, but when they did so, they were sadder, poorer, but still not quite wise to what was happening. It took a few days for the cyclists to catch on and for the heaps of Flying Pigeons to regain their wings, but we were surprised that from then on, the citizens of Tianjin began to stop on red and go on green, and it amazed me how adaptable the Chinese could be in certain situations and how quickly some changes could take place. Perhaps this was a harbinger of things to come.

Unlike other Asian cities like Tokyo, Bangkok, and New Delhi, the streets and buildings of Tianjin were uncluttered by advertising, and any banners, posters, or signage were either devoted to public information or political propaganda. Hence our confusion one winter afternoon toward the end of our year of residence when a billboard caught our eyes. It was new and large, looming over one of the major intersections, and instead of the bright red, white, and yellow favored in Party slogans, it had darker colors, fewer Chinese characters, and a name spelled out in large Roman letters: BLUESKI. My first reaction was that this was a poster promoting the political thoughts of a new or unfamiliar Russian Marxist, but then, catching sight of the Chinese character *tian* (heaven or ski), I realized that for the very first time we were looking at English being used in public, and the billboard was something about Blue Ski. Suddenly, it all made sense for the large cylindrical object painted across the bottom of this giant sign was a tube of toothpaste, and what confronted us was a bilingual advertisement for the same. Though I'm sure this was completely unintentional, the branding of this product was infinitely more politically correct than a brand called Darkie that we saw sold (but never advertised) all over China and can still be purchased here and there to this day. You'd think a more appropriate way to market toothpaste would be to call it Whitie, but the picture on the tube of an Al Jolson–type blackened face highlighting sparkling white teeth revealed the provenience of this particular product. Irrespective of the overt racism displayed and regardless of where this infelicitous name came from, it was comforting to see there was now a brand of toothpaste that had a more colorful name and a less colored etymology. Above all, we felt we had witnessed something momentous that afternoon— the first advertisement. Perhaps it was a harbinger of things to come.

Of all the benefits and advantages of cycling during our Tianjin days, by far, the greatest was the freedom it provided. Whenever we needed to be transported by car, train, or plane, there were all kinds of bureaucratic hoops to jump through so that few of our decisions were spontaneous, private, or free. Take Janene's bimonthly trips to Beijing as a straightforward illustration. Superficially, here was prima facie evidence for a quick and easy trip: Beijing was a ninety-minute train ride away, so as was frequently the case, she could leave in the morning, collect teaching materials at the US embassy, get some shopping done, and whisk back home on a late-afternoon train in time to join us for a late dinner that evening. Not so quick because it wasn't that easy!

Step 1. First of all, even though we were invited by and worked for the Chinese government, as foreign residents we were subject to tight travel restrictions unless, of course, we were on bikes. Through Xiao Zhang, a week or two ahead of time, Janene would first have to secure a travel permit that would allow her to go to the capital city and return. Along with the intended date(s) of her travel, she would also give Zhang her US passport, and he in turn would get a letter permitting such a trip from our institute's wai ban.

Step 2. Zhang was now ready to take these papers to the Tianjin Bureau of Public Security (the police), which in turn would produce in a few days a light-green-colored card specifying that a certain Janene Scovel (occupation teacher) was granted permission (number 792288) to travel to and from Beijing on such and such a date.

Step 3. Armed with permission for Janene to make the trip, Zhang would then go to the railway station, showing the clerk the travel permit and Janene's passport, after which he was able to buy a one-way ticket to the capital city. Yes, one-way (see step 5). Returning to the hotel, Zhang would give her the ticket, passport, and permit whereupon Janene would reimburse him for all the costs incurred.

Step 4. On the selected day, our wai ban would send a car to take Janene to the station where she caught an early morning train to Beijing. At the end of the passenger tunnel after her arrival there, she would show the cop guarding the exit her travel permit and American passport and then immediately turn around and reenter the station to purchase a one-way ticket home.

Step 5. The idea of a round-trip ticket seemed mystifying to the Chinese we talked to, and during our travels, we encountered all kinds of hassles because of this one-way or the highway policy, but people provided all kinds of explanations to justify why this foreign concept would not work in the Middle Kingdom. One favorite was, "What if the traveler decides not to return?" The logical antecedent to this question was never considered, "Having purchased a one-way ticket, what if the traveler decides not to go in the first place?" My own explanation was that round-trip tickets were banned because they were literally counterrevolutionary. Having wasted almost an hour of the morning never having left the Beijing station, Janene would then try to get one of the few taxis available to take her to the embassy, return materials collected many weeks earlier, pick up new ones for her students, and then do some shopping at the well-stocked Friendship Store, and if she had time, go out to the Friendship Hotel to visit with friends and possibly even catch a late lunch.

Step 6. Her errands complete, she would return to the Beijing station to catch the train home to Tianjin. On reaching her destination, she would hustle up and then down the stairs arching over the tracks and exit the station, showing her travel permit one last time and, with any luck, find the institute's car waiting to whisk her back to the hotel in time for supper.

In 1979, Thais, Danes, and Argentineans could all cross their nation's international borders more easily than any foreigner or Chinese citizen was able to travel even one hundred miles within the borders of the People's Republic. Travel permits, passports, itineraries, and permission from the wai ban were not needed anytime we wanted to hop on our bikes, and the zephyr that caressed our faces as we pedaled around the city was really the breath of freedom.

Sundays were our only full day off and were often devoted to free and leisurely bike rides around town. On Easter morning after breakfast, we held the ritual Sunday-morning family worship service that we always had in the privacy of our room, and having brought some dye from the States, Janene helped the kids color some hard-boiled eggs obtained from the kitchen. In honor of the day, the two of us decided to take a long ride around the city to see how many church buildings we could find. We knew of at least one, a ramshackle place that we passed on our way to the institute, and though it had no cross, it was obvious from its architecture that it had been a place of worship, probably Anglican since it lay in the former British quarter. Despite Article 46 of the nation's constitution that guaranteed religious freedom, with rare showcase exceptions, there were no houses of worship open in the entire nation at that time, and all of these had been trashed and turned into warehouses, offices, or simply vacant buildings, their spirits sucked completely out of them.

We had heard that there was a French cathedral beyond our institute, so we cycled far into a part of the city we had never visited. Later, I learned the French had built the Cathedral Notre Dame des Victoires over a century earlier in their quarter of the then European-occupied city, and it had been the site of the infamous 1870 Tianjin massacre, which itself was a prelude to the Boxer Rebellion at the turn of that century. However, on this lazy Sunday morning, we were not in search of history but sought only the comfort of seeing a few former houses of worship in a country that denigrated any faith except one directed to the Party. Finally, we reached the former cathedral, its crossless spires still standing furtively above the surrounding apartment buildings. People immediately huddled around us as we dismounted in front of the steps leading up to the boarded-up doors, and confused by the object of our attention, they turned their backs on the church and stared at us, a sad demonstration of what Easter had become under the Communists. The crowd grew, and it was apparent we were providing a bit of entertainment rarely seen in this quarter of the city. The kids, who always edged to the front, called out either *wai guo bin* (foreign guests) or *mei guo bin* (assuming even back then that all white people were American guests). We tried to ignore their friendly staring and name-calling by directing our focus to the once-holy edifice that soared above us.

An old man slowly but forcefully pushed himself into the circle, shoving aside a few of the children at the very front. His wizened face and inquisitive gaze all suggested that he had been witness to a wide sweep of history. He stopped within arm's reach in front of me, staring intensely while his mind seemed to search desperately for a word buried in his past, almost like an Alzheimer's patient at a zoo, recognizing the animal in front of him and desperately trying to dredge up its name. His right hand rose, pointing only a few inches from my face as a spark of recognition suddenly lit up his. "Yang guizi!" he shouted in satisfaction. The kids and the adults around them were momentarily stunned when they heard these words, a four-letter epithet that polite people never uttered in public. But I couldn't suppress a smile as I immediately replied "duile!" (you're right). If I had one yuan for every time I had been called that as a child growing up in China, I would've been richer than any warlord. "Foreign devil" was the default name of any white foreigner in China back in the old days, and by recognizing that I was one of these rarest of creatures, this old stranger was paying me a left-handed compliment of the highest kind for despite our differences, we were linked at that moment to a common past. But in 1979, on the streets of Tianjin, it was neither polite nor politic to use this term in a nation hell-bent on whitewashing its immediate past and sprinting forward into the Four Modernizations. As we pedaled slowly back to our hotel, meandering along the river and then through the downtown area where a former Methodist church lay equally vacant on that sunny morning, we wondered if the Party would ever return to the days where Article 46 would live up to its wording and become an article of faith for Chinese believers. As for the two of us, we were free that morning to believe what we wanted to and cycle wherever our whimsy would carry us. Cycling was more than transportation that year; it was an exercise of freedom.

All in all, hundreds of millions of people commuted to work, transported their kids to school, went shopping, took Sunday drives, and did practically everything that Americans did in automobiles, and they accomplished all of this while burning up a few calories—yet not a single drop of petroleum—all on a simple, two-wheeled machine made from modest amounts of steel and rubber. Add to this the way bikes can crowd into and negotiate tighter spaces than any car and the ease with which thousands can be mushed together in a relatively small parking space. And how many car owners can carry their vehicle up the stairs and park it next to their third-floor office to ensure it doesn't get swiped while they're at work? Throughout that year, Janene and I were incessantly reminded that China was the world's largest nation of cyclists, and we shuddered with dread whenever we contemplated the possibility of its citizens ever owning cars. What a nightmare that would be to see automobiles usurp the place of bikes! Think of the congestion, the loss of daily exercise, the need for millions of tons of concrete and asphalt for new roads, the national dependence on oil, and above all, the increase in environmental degradation and pollution if that were indeed to come to pass! But then we would sigh and smile to ourselves as we pedaled on because we knew, of course, that this would never happen within our lifetime.

Because Derick was just a young boy and not noticeably alien when bundled up against the elements and because his commute to the conservatory carried him across the river and to the wrong side of town, he witnessed an even less-refined view of the streets than we. There was no bridge near our hotel, so he was forced to begin and end his daily jaunts on a small ferry. This involved carrying his bike over a gangplank while jostling crowds of other and usually larger commuters and fighting to stay upright among the mass of passengers. One time, a hood

(Derick's characterization of the young males who had the temerity to wear dark glasses in public) happened to bump his bicycle one too many times into the bike of a large PLA soldier squeezed next to him. With no warning, the soldier decked the younger commuter with one vicious swing of his fist. When the sides were more equal, Derick saw several fights erupt between toughs entering, leaving, or riding the ferry. Although he made friends at the conservatory, as the only American boy in a city of some seven million, he was sometimes the victim of ridicule from other boys, and one gloomy March day, he cycled home steaming with anger because a couple of kids had punched him. It was no accident that our son came down with a harsh cold the next morning and missed two days of school still upset and literally sick over the incident. Culture shock and illness frequented each member of our family throughout the year in direct or subtle ways, but the China sojourn was especially trying for Derick. As a foreign boy going through pubescence, he had emigrated both from his native culture and from his childhood and now was experiencing the emotional and physical challenges as an immigrant into an alien culture and into that strange new life as an adolescent.

Our daughter experienced different challenges as well as opportunities at the nursery she attended. Only four, Christine was much younger, and being Thai, she was not such a conspicuous foreigner as our son. On the same side of the river, her nursery was closer to our hotel and institute, and so her commute was much more convenient, and this easy access was of great benefit throughout our stay because she had persistent colds, respiratory congestion, and conjunctivitis. It took a long time to adjust to being left alone all day at the nursery despite the solicitous care she received, and once more, it was hard to disassociate the mind from the body. How much of her chronic physical affliction was exacerbated by her unease over the new environment in which she was suddenly submersed? After several hospital visits where overmedication seemed to be the prescription du jour, her ailments slowly dissipated along with her culture shock, and she grew to enjoy the highly structured but warm atmosphere of her nursery where, in her parents' opinion, she had become a bit spoiled as the teachers' pet and quasi school mascot.

Janene and I were amazed at how quickly and effectively the Chinese educational system created a tightly routinized and disciplined community right from the earliest days of nursery school. Well over a hundred kids attended six days a week, ranging from toddlers to six-year-olds, and all of them quickly adapted to a tight and busy routine that pretty much followed this schedule that the nursery staff gave us.

7:30–8:30	Entering the kindergarten
8:00–8:30	Breakfast
8:30–9:30	First class
9:30–9:40	A short rest and go to the bathroom
9:40–10:10	Second class
10:10–10:30	Drink, rest, and go to the bathroom
10:30–11:15	Games
11:15–12:00	Wash hands and lunch
12:00–3:00	Nap time
3:00–3:30	Get up and have afternoon tea
3:30–5:15	Games
5:15–6:30	Leaving the kindergarten

Christine had the most trouble adjusting to the lengthy nap time when her Chinese comrades would almost instantly conk out although usually it was not as long as listed above, especially in the colder months when everyone's siesta was abbreviated. It is not evident from the schedule, but a bulk of the children's time was devoted to learning songs and dances, and the reason for this soon became apparent. Occasionally, the kids would be taken outside on little excursions where, hand in hand, they would walk behind their teacher like tiny elephants linked by trunk and tail. Like any nursery, the routine was interrupted by special events, and one time when I went to pick our daughter up, the children were being treated to a puppet show about a peasant rebellion against a landlord. The kids cheered lustily when the play ended with the landlord's wife carrying off the limp body of her husband beaten to death by the peasants.

Obedience, discipline, and perfection were the order of the day, but the white-smocked women who ran the place didn't strike me as overly authoritarian, and as already noted, they seemed exceptionally friendly to our daughter. Often when we cycled up to the gate to pick Christine up, usually earlier than most parents, the place was so quiet we thought it was deserted, and after tiptoeing up the steps and entering her classroom, expecting to catch the kids in a late nap, we would find them all fully awake at their little desks, sitting on their hands and all looking forward at their teacher, dutifully awaiting her next instructions. Another time, Janene found Christine's class of about twenty sitting in a circle around one of their classmates who was entertaining them with a riveting story complete with sound effects, and they all listened attentively even though no teacher happened to be supervising them at that moment. Many times, we could hear amplified music a block before the nursery and would arrive to find tour buses parked outside and see a bunch of bouncing children entertaining an audience of tourists in rows of chairs in the playground. It was then that we realized that the No. 1 Nursery had an important number 2 function, and all the singing and dancing practice was not simply for pedagogical purposes.

After the Nixon-Kissinger negotiations seven years earlier, various American delegations began to visit China in the seventies on exciting but tightly controlled tours, and I had heard direct accounts about some of these excursions from professional colleagues who had taken part. Although I did not follow political developments closely, I had a rather jaundiced reaction to their enthusiastic accounts of model workers, remarkable public health standards, and pink-cheeked children who had wowed them with talented performances at a typical nursery. In a twist of fate, now I was the parent of one of these "Chinese" kids, arriving at a "typical" nursery to take her home from school. The tourists thought it strange that there was a white face standing in the back with the other Chinese parents proudly enjoying their youngsters' performance while I in turn was straining to figure out which of the performers was Christine since all of the kids were heavily made-up and dressed up with big, red ribbons. There she was, the little one with the triangle in the front row or the third one from the left in the circle of weaving dancers. The teachers enjoyed these displays immensely, maybe more than the children, and they would sing along or accompany them on their accordions with gusto. With natural parental pride, we were impressed with how well Christine had memorized the notes and lyrics to various songs and, along with her classmates, could chirp out such classics as "The Peacock" or "I'm Going on the Long March on Horseback." This was all delightful and innocent entertainment, but we harbored a sense of duplicity that our own daughter had been trained to give foreign visitors a somewhat skewed perception of Chinese society.

Those American visitors who had taken the short and tightly orchestrated tours of the PRC in the few years before our arrival often came back with praiseworthy accounts because of the evils they had not seen. Remarkably, during their two-week sojourns, in all their trips on the streets of China, they never saw rats, flies, prostitutes, venereal diseases, poverty, or beggars. Part of the vacuousness of these claims lay in the unreliability of negative evidence. As any novice scientist knows, the absence of evidence is in itself not evidence. During our bike rides, but especially during the solo runs along the backstreets and alleys I took, I saw at least four of the above, and I wasn't even trying to dredge up any dirt. Brief episodic snapshots of people I encountered during my runs still linger: a young girl sitting in the dirt sobbing, a young man leaning against a wall, covering his bowed head with his hands, a blind man negotiating a broken sidewalk with his cane, two deaf bikers deftly signing with one hand as they cycled down the street, some poor wretch lying on his back unconscious, his face covered with vomit, an elderly couple, each gracefully supporting the other as they toddled down the road, a portrait of Chinese gothic. When the weather warmed, Janene and occasionally Derick would also jog the backstreets in the early morning, and they too caught a different sight of the city. No tourists witnessed what we encountered on those runs behind the hotel along the river. Scavengers foraged through the heaps of garbage with small rakes, desperately searching for something of value in those repugnant piles. The disabled poor were especially pitiful. A man hopping on one leg with his arm curled around a stick crutch. Another with no legs at all, swinging his torso and stumps with his arms for legs and his hands for feet, paddling along through the dirt that was far beneath everyone else. A trip to the post office on September 18 is exemplary. Feeling hungry, I stopped to buy a *shao bing* (a fried biscuit) from a vendor outside the post office steps, and seeing two beggars, I bought some extras to share. One was a disheveled teenage girl playing with some wires in the dirt, not barefoot but her shoes were badly torn. The other was a barefoot man dressed in rags, sound asleep on his back in the dirt. When I turned around after making my purchase, the girl was gone, so I carefully laid four biscuits on the sleeper's chest before continuing my errand inside the post office.

We never saw any aggressive panhandling, and in most cases, the begging was just the opposite: their presence, appearance, and their minimal motions and pleas were enough to reveal their desperation. What galled me the most was the same thing I often witnessed as a high school student in India, the proximity of affluence and destitution. One morning, I saw the manager of our hotel and his wife send their son off to school dressed in a clean, white shirt with a red bandana tied around his neck, the emblem of his status as a Young Pioneer. He enjoyed all the amenities our hotel provided, and on this morning, this scion of privilege walked out right past two other Chinese boys about his age, except these two were barefoot, dressed in rags, and were yoked together, pulling a cart loaded with bricks. A classless society indeed! I don't necessarily criticize the Chinese tourist authorities for presenting the best possible image of China to their guests, but I do find fault with the few foreigners who were permitted to travel on very restricted tours in the nineteen seventies and who apparently lost the objective scrutiny they would apply to any other nation. Many of them returned with Pollyanna accounts of a utopian society, a perspective especially infuriating to me when you consider that the China they viewed was still in the grips of the Cultural Revolution, its most ignominious era in modern times.

One day, when arriving to pick up Christine from her nursery, instead of several tour buses, I found a line of black sedans with red flags decorating their front fenders, and from the well-dressed cadres who represented that day's audience, it was apparent that this was a command performance for a visiting big shot. Almost as surprised as I to meet him, a tall, youngish foreigner introduced himself to me at the end of the show and asked what on earth I was doing there. He turned out to be the lord mayor of Melbourne and was visiting Tianjin to consider as a possible sister city. The cadres handling his visit immediately became uncomfortable with this unscheduled and unscripted encounter in English with another *yang guizi*, but with the informal charm that Aussies often demonstrate, the mayor began peppering me with questions as he was firmly steered toward a limo for his next engagement. Giving me his card, he asked his hosts if Janene and I could pay him a visit that evening at his guesthouse, and he was so insistent in his request that they finally acquiesced.

That evening, a car picked us up at the hotel, driving to an area of the former British quarter unfamiliar to us, and as it wheeled through the gates of a large compound, we were astonished to catch sight of something that is common in most parts of the world but was a rare luxury at that time in Northern China. There, lit by twilight and growing on either side of the curved driveway we had just entered, was grass! After months of seeing asphalt streets, concrete sidewalks, stone pavements, and dirt yards bereft of even weeds, the luxurious green lawn spread out in front of us like a magnificent welcome mat. The driveway led past flower beds and hedges up to a large, multistoried building obviously built by former colonial imperialists, and we learned from the mayor, who welcomed us like a temporary prince in a castle, that it had been the British Club but was now owned by the Tianjin branch of the Party. We oohed and aahed over the well-decorated interior and the rich amenities, such as a bar, pool table, tennis court, swimming pool, and even a bowling alley, but our newfound Australian friend insisted we had seen nothing yet and walked us across his gigantic bedroom to a side door that opened into the strangest water closet ever seen either down under or up over. It was a wide, well-tiled room with about a half dozen toilets of every type lined up along one wall from left to right. You could squat Asian style, sit on a Japanese-built Toto commode, or stand using a tall urinal found in any airport bathroom. Strangely, none of these were separated by stalls or panels. The lord mayor told us that President Nixon and Mao's wife, the infamous Jiang Qing, allegedly stayed in this guesthouse, and thus they would have used one or more of the commodes in front of us although presumably not concurrently. We lingered on in the comfort of the clubhouse, sharing stories and perspectives on China over drinks, none of our accounts bearing any resemblance to the reports and viewpoints our Australian dignitary had been hearing throughout his trip from his Party hosts, some of whom were seated right next to us. As we sat there in the opulence of the former British Club, I was overcome with the way in which we were reliving the conclusion of a famous English novel that Janene had wanted her students to read but had quickly discovered that it had been banned in China. There we were, former pigs, toasting each other in what used to be *Animal Farm*, and if anyone outside had been peeking at us through the windows at that very moment, they would have been hard-pressed to distinguish which animals were the foreign imperialists and which were the patriotic members of the Party!

Especially throughout the winter and well into spring, when fruit and vegetables were extremely limited, Janene made many forays into the streets to see if she could augment our daily intake with something other than an occasional carrot or potato and the ubiquitous *bai cai* (bok choy or Chinese cabbage). The local grocery store had slanting mirrors against one wall, giving the impression that its meager winter supply of apples, carrots, and potatoes was actually double in size. Here and anywhere along the street, piles of light-green-and-white bai cai were deposited, so many that if you had them lined up even forty abreast and marched them into the sea, this infinite parade of Chinese cabbage would never end. As the winter waned and the first frost set in, they would grow limper and begin to rot, and the same horse-and-human carts that trucked them into the city for sale now carried them out again to use as fertilizer. In a desperate attempt to balance our intake of rice, noodles, steamed bread, and meat, we ate bai cai boiled, sautéed, soy-sauced, and sweet and sour, and after a few months, we even began dreaming about the stuff. Our institute had several cars, the oldest being a 1960s era Chevy that was green and white with protruding fins over the back two fenders that made it a garish attraction on rides to such places as the train station. What made it even more outlandish, however, was that it must have been refitted for Hong Kong, where traffic drives on the left, so our Tian Wai driver would be perched on the wrong-hand side of the vehicle, hampering his view of the traffic and testing his luck and our faith whenever he swerved into the oncoming traffic to pass an overloaded bus or truck. Naturally, we named this relic the Flying Bai Cai.

Janene would forage for whatever non-cabbage vegetables she could find and maybe some fruit, although the yellow apples grew more wrinkled and distasteful as the winter progressed. Often there would be long lines, a sure sign that a rare commodity was momentarily available. One winter day, she saw a queue at least half a block long; however, the patient shoppers' only reward at the end was carrots and hard candies. Sometimes she would spot a genuine windfall, say a half dozen cucumbers, a few almost-black bananas, a wizened orange or two, or a rare pineapple, but the clerks always hid the good stuff under their counters, and their favorite response to any inquiry was *"Mei you* [no have]," and it took persistence and a few extra yuan to get them to part with any prized produce. Talk about forbidden fruit! We let the hotel do all the purchasing of grains and meat as the kitchen supplied us with plenty of these staples throughout the year, and besides, these commodities were rationed and required coupons, so we would have had difficulty purchasing them outside the hotel anyway even if we so desired.

One of the teachers in a group that Janene met with each week had a serious blood disease that prevented his body from being able to metabolize animal fats, so he was an involuntary vegetarian, an unusually difficult position for anyone in Northern China, where meat is the richest source of caloric intake and where the Chinese word for it (*rou*), when narrowly defined, means pork. Winters were uncommonly taxing for him since about the only food he could eat along with his rice, bread, and noodles was bai cai. His family was originally from Shanghai, where vegetables were much more available year-round, and though it was highly unusual for anyone to secure permission to be transferred from our dull metropolis to China's most cosmopolitan city, he and his wife were finally able to move to Shanghai in the summer not because of his disease but because his aged father was in poor health. Despite the Cultural Revolution, filial piety was alive and well in postrevolutionary China. We tried to help him by sharing anything we could purchase that wasn't cabbage, and this included buying canned vegetables in the Friendship Store when they were available, but his situation helped reframe our concerns over food. We were inconvenienced; he and many others were desperate.

One of our simple pleasures during the sultry days of summer was to buy a *bing guer* (Popsicle) from a street vendor who pedaled them in and peddled them from an insulated box on the back of his bike. It took a bit of daring to try them at first for I remembered my older sister coming down with cholera from sucking on icicles when we were kids living in Anhui Province, and Janene had memories of amoebic dysentery from unclean water in Thailand. Add to this the fact that when pronounced with a falling rather than a high tone, *bing* was the Chinese word for disease. Equally daunting was their color, which looked suspiciously similar to the Hai River that ran near the ice factory that made them, but after none of us died from our first ingestion, we continued to enjoy them, for as tasteless as the Popsicles were, they helped mitigate the oppressive heat. One day toward the end of summer, Derick and I were biking downtown when we saw a large group of people huddled around a *bing guer* salesman. Knowing there must be something good in the middle of that congregation, we cycled over and waited to buy our treat. Looking at the two that I had just purchased, I discovered the novelty that had attracted the crowd's interest. On top of the light-brownish-colored Popsicle was a soybean, the Chinese equivalent of a maraschino cherry on a chocolate sundae. I bit into the hard soybean, and savoring the way its crunchiness added a bit of pizzazz to what had become a routine snack, I turned to Derick with a "Hmm, not bad." Derick looked at me half quizzically and half in pity and replied, "Dad, you've been in China too long."

We escaped cholera, amoebic dysentery, tuberculosis, and the other diseases that surrounded my childhood in China, but none of us avoided illness that year, especially Christine, who spent the first three months trying to fight off upper-respiratory infections, conjunctivitis, and gastrointestinal bugs. Fortunately, our family was luckier than the French teacher's wife and the Spanish teacher's kids; in April, they all came down with another affliction of my boyhood, tapeworms. Propriety prevents me from describing what I witnessed after my father gave Aizu, my boyhood chum, medication to cleanse his bowels of these evil parasites, but I assure you it was not a pretty picture, and I was happy that our own kids were spared during our China residence. We all had colds our second week in Tianjin, and until summer came, rare was the week that one of us had not caught one. With two unconnected bedrooms, our original plan was to have the kids share one and we the other, but Derick would often pound on the wall between the two rooms in the middle of the night, signaling another nocturnal affliction from the children's ward; consequently, we spent at least half the year sleeping separated so that each child could spend the night in solace with an adult. One January night, Christine vomited five times before dawn. A month later, we took her to the children's hospital where she was given treatment including an ampicillin shot for her bronchitis and still persistent conjunctivitis. Injections were popular, partly because patients left with a sense their affliction had been seriously addressed, but the generous dispensation of injections also tended to discourage hypochondria. Our Chinese friends and her nursery school teachers kept insisting that we did not dress Christine warmly enough. We heard this complaint so often I wish we had had a balaclava, fur-lined parka, down trousers, ski boots, and an eiderdown sleeping bag to submerse her in, for even if she had been thus mummified, I'm sure that we would still hear murmurings that we hadn't put enough clothes on her.

These next two paragraphs can be skipped by the faint of heart for they chronicle two particularly loathsome body excretions: spit and snot. Before delving into the appalling details of how the

Chinese dispose of these excreta, some cross-cultural reflection is called for. Until and even after the invention of Kleenex, Americans thought nothing of expelling the mucous out of their noses into a handkerchief and stuffing this filthy and repugnant cloth into their pockets only to pull it out when needed to fill it up with more snot. When thoroughly soiled, handkerchiefs are then washed along with shirts, blouses, and other clothing, the assumption being that everything is made clean rather than that the snot-rag made everything filthy. If this custom doesn't sound disgusting, then there is little hope for the cross-cultural objectivity necessary to view Chinese customs in a fair-minded manner. The pollution and wind-blown dirt of Northern China function as a persistent expectorant, so oral and nasal discharges are probably more frequent than in many other parts of the world. Spitting and blowing the nose go with the territory. Traditionally, the Chinese blow their nose the way it's done in many countries. You close one nostril, usually with your thumb, and tilting your head so you don't hit part of your own body, you expel the mucous with a forced sneeze out of the open nostril, sending the gooey stuff bouncing out on to the ground, leaving you and your clothes as clean as they were before. Although this is technically a more hygienic way to get rid of nasal waste than the American handkerchief, it has certain liabilities, the main one being that pedestrians have one more obstacle to be wary of when striding down the streets.

Spitting, however, is more problematical, and after the nineteenth-century discovery of how infectious diseases could be spread socially, various Chinese regimes have tried to curtail this habit. Like Europe in earlier days, in modern China spittoons are found inside most residences and public buildings, sometimes doubling as chamber pots, but the many slimy spots we saw even inside buildings betrayed the marksmanship or revealed the apathy of the everyday spitter. The only dangerous part of my late-afternoon runs was trying to avoid getting hit by cyclists immediately in front of me who just happened to be clearing their noses or throats when we were both heading into the wind. There were cartoons and signs all over the city decrying the antirevolutionary nature of spitting, but decades of slogans and health campaigns didn't seem to reduce this seemingly inexhaustible flow of saliva. Except when running, it didn't bother me too much when it was done outside, but I never got used to people spitting inside, and one close encounter still sticks with me like a viscous memory. I was walking down the left-hand side of an upstairs hallway in the administration building at our institute and was approaching the stairway when I heard someone coming up the stairs. A moment before we both turned the corner to confront each other, I heard the sonorous sound of snot being cleared from a nasopharyngeal cavity. The voice sounded so deep, and the rumble of discharge to be expelled sounded so large I expected to confront a huge man about to accidentally propel his excreta on me. To my astonishment, I came face-to-face with a fairly short, middle-aged woman, and with a surprised grunt of apology, she managed to miss me and hit the floor where I had just stepped. If the staff of an institute of higher education didn't get the message, then there wasn't much hope for the rest of China that this engrained form of behavior would change any time soon. Even the Party, despite its most ambitious campaigning, could not eradicate spitting, so the only conclusion I could make is that the Chinese people will continue to expectorate nothing less.

The chronic illnesses that beset our family and a health condition she alone had to bear quickly eroded Janene's spirits, and after only a fortnight in Tianjin, in her diary she penned, "We've been here two weeks, and already it seems like two years." Several years earlier, she had developed pernicious anemia, and from that time, I had to give her B12 injections every three weeks, and uncertain about what would be available in China, we brought along about a dozen and a half one-milliliter vials of cyanocobalamin and an equal number of one-milliliter syringes with 0.5 by 15 millimeter needles. We had her physician write a brief letter documenting her medical needs just in case the Chinese authorities might mistake some sort of drug abuse on our part. Her anemic condition thus meant that on top of the ailments the rest of us faced, Janene would feel her energy slowly seep away in three-week increments, weighing her down with the heaviest health burden of all.

In addition to all of this, she had to endure an unexpected affliction. The Tianjin Hotel did have a laundry service, but the prices were so exorbitant they gave new meaning to the idiom "To be taken to the cleaners." The prices led us to imagine that maybe the management flew the dirty clothes to a relative's laundry in San Francisco's Chinatown and then back again to Tianjin, a conceivable supposition given the expense and that it took a week to get clothes done, and that joint ventures with foreign enterprises were just coming into vogue. For most of our dirty clothes, my industrious wife (and a few times her husband) would soak our coal-stained clothes in the bathtub and laboriously wash them by hand with locally purchased detergent. Janene's hands quickly grew raw and cracked, and she had no soothing hand lotion to ameliorate the condition. Even with the rubber gloves that I purchased during my February trip back to the States, her hands remained irritated throughout the year. With reluctance, we grew to accept the pollution as an environmental given, and on windy days, when the air was almost clean, we tended to forget how all-encompassing it was, but one look at the black water in the tub of laundry, that is after Janene had rinsed the clothes a second time, was ample evidence of how pervasive the pollution proved to be.

Sometimes our health problems had a happy ending. In early summer, before the end of the academic year, I developed a head cold that descended into a case of laryngitis transforming my voice into a raspy whisper. Advised to go to the hospital,

I managed to avoid any injections, and time proved the more effective medication than the pills I was given. Since I sounded much worse than I actually felt and since it was important not to miss any classes with the end of the semester approaching, I biked to work, trusting that my students' hearing was better than my voice projection. We were usually provided with a thermos of hot water and a cup with tea leaves in the classrooms, but as soon as my class of potential foreign scholars could tell that I was nearly voiceless, they plopped a dried chrysanthemum into the tea that they had kindly poured for me, assuring me that this folk remedy was ideal for sore throats. I was actually more impressed with the way the flower expanded in the hot water, gradually filling the entire cup, than any effect the remedy had on my condition, but sips of hot beverage helped me get through the morning.

Watching the scholars' faces intent on trying to catch my every whisper, I knew exactly how this episode would pan out for despite the typical American stereotype of Chinese being cold and inscrutable, I found them atypically romantic and very scrutable. I knew that from this day on a legend was born, that of a brave foreign friend of China who stumbled out of his sick bed in the morning and, despite the protests of everyone, courageously biked to school and gallantly stood for hours on end, swallowing the occasional drop of blood that trickled down the back of his wounded pharynx. Thinking only of his beloved students, he heroically managed to lead the most brilliant of classes before collapsing sick and exhausted at the end of the day! The thank-you letter I received from the class a few weeks later wasn't quite this over-the-top, but in forty-seven years of teaching in the United States, Thailand, and other countries around the world, I never received a letter quite so sweet or so solicitous about my health. Different customs do indeed separate us, but kindness and gratitude are universals of human nature that invariably draw us together.

Training Department
Tianjin Foreign Languages Institute
July 3, 1979

Dear Dr. Scovel,

Thank you so much for having given us a series of such interesting and useful English lessons on medical science. As we all know, you have been very busy, and yet you spared us much of your time, showing your great concern for our English study. Your kindness and patience have made us close to each other and encouraged us to talk more in English. Your enthusiasm and earnestness in teaching have deeply impressed us. We well remember once, in spite of our efforts of advising you to take a rest, yet you insisted on giving us a lesson with your sore throat. For this, we could hardly express ourselves but were deeply moved. We really appreciate your warm friendship which will long remain in our memory. Please accept this photo album as a souvenir. May our friendship last forever!

All the best wishes,
Your Students

CHAPTER 4

十年树木，百年树人

shi nian shu mu, bai nian shu ren

It takes only ten years to grow a
tree but a hundred to grow a person.

Though we live in a physical world and are materialists at heart, we are ultimately a social species and are driven by social relationships. Above everything else, we are people people. You can see this in the way our focal attention is immediately riveted to faces whenever we chance to look at photographs, and advertisers have long known that a person's face, particularly an attractive one, will more quickly catch the eye of anyone viewing their product, whether it's a bottle of shampoo or an expensive sports car. Not long ago, if you encountered someone talking out loud as they strolled by you on the street or sat next to you on a bench, you would rightfully conclude that they had one too many screws loose in their head. But nowadays, especially in Chinese cities, it seems that the majority of people are talking the talk as they walk the walk around town albeit with a cell in hand and ear. There seems to be a primal urge to keep in touch with others, and modern technology has fulfilled this social drive so amply that in it is now difficult for us ever to be alone. Consequently, because of this social instinct, whenever I pause to remember that year in China, faces immediately flood my memory, and without them, no site, incident, or event, however impressive, would have survived so indelibly without the image of the person or people who helped create that memory and kept it alive.

Take for example the day we found out what was in a fortress of a structure that we passed every day next to our building at the institute. Smaller but more indomitably built and more impenetrable than even our library, single-storied and square with small, barred windows too high up to peer into, it could have served as a military bunker. It caught our eye from our very first day on campus and immediately created a sense of mystery since we never saw anyone enter or leave its premises. The most information we could extract about it from the students and faculty we queried was that it wasn't part of our institute but belonged to another dan wei. With typical unexpectedness, Xiao Zhang told us on a snowy Friday afternoon that arrangements had been made for us to visit this sepulcher the next day. And so with childish anticipation on that Saturday afternoon, March 24, we waited outside its leaf-and-dirt-filled doorway in the cold, our drab campus gloriously whitewashed with freshly fallen snow. A tiny figure skipped toward us, and we were about to become time travelers first into the origins of our institute and then be plunged so far back into the past that even China's impressive historical legacy would appear like a mere moment in the present.

To say that Huang Weilong was not a typical Chinese would be akin to claiming that the platypus was not a typical mammal. At about four and a half feet, he wasn't much taller than little Christine, and despite his winter clothing, he looked so frail that the March wind could have blown him away. As the curator of the Tianjin Museum of Paleobiology, he held the secrets to our mystery building. With his diminutive stature, wizened face, and fuzzy hair, he resembled a Qing dynasty eunuch who had come to unlock the gates of a secret treasure at the Imperial Palace. But what caught our attention the most and provoked a few impolite childish giggles from our two kids were his incisors; they protruded under his upper lips so prominently that any American orthodontist would have had a field day with both his dentition and bank account. Because of his overbite, he spoke with a hissing lisp that only served to heighten the mysterious journey through time on which he was about to take us. Even more captivating than his appearance, however, was his behavior. He was one of the most animated conversationalists I have ever encountered and was so lively and bouncy and so filled with unbridled enthusiasm for his subject I swear we would have found that afternoon with him just as fascinating had his specialty been soybeans.

After quick greetings were exchanged all around, he immediately launched into an excited soliloquy while fingering for the right key from a sizable ring of alternatives to unlock the iron door, a task made more difficult by the cold and his divided attention. I strained to catch as much as possible from what he said in Chinese, but Zhang, our faithful translator, was working twice as hard as I since simultaneous interpretation is one of the most taxing cognitive tasks the human mind can be asked to perform, and what with his lisp and his rat-a-tat-tat delivery, Huang Laoshi was rapidly driving Zhang's mind into cerebral overload. When asked how a museum of foreign relics built by French Catholics escaped the hands of the Red Guards during the Cultural Revolution, he jumped over to the front door and pounded on the solid iron. "See," he exulted, "it was bolted with an American lock," and he lifted up a Yale padlock of sturdy brass.

We learned that this was a paleontological museum founded and filled by the great French theologian and paleontologist Pierre Teilhard de Chardin while he was conducting expeditions in Northern China in the 1920s and alternatively teaching and writing on this campus when it was a French Jesuit technical school. Our heads were already spinning. Tian Wai was formerly a Catholic school? No wonder the administration building looked so European and that the Propaganda Hall betrayed its origins as a chapel. And Pierre Teilhard de Chardin himself once taught where we were teaching now? But whoa, Huang was already inside and ahead of us and was beginning to describe the fossils on the dusty shelves with uncontained enthusiasm. We were still reeling from all the information he had flooded us with about the recent history of our school, and now he was already pulling us back in time. We leaped instantly into the Cenozoic era, but in a few moments, he was showing us relics from even further back to the Mesozoic. In the space of a few yards and several minutes, we had entered a time warp with exponential speed and hurtled from 1979 to ten, to sixty, and then to eighty million years back in time. "Here's the jaw of a twelve-million-year-old giraffe, and here, and over here," he exclaimed, grabbing specimens almost randomly, "you can see Teilhard's name in Latin where he discovered a new genus or species." With each specimen, he was showing us literally rock-solid evidence that the famous paleontologist had worked here.

Huang took what looked like a partial skull off one shelf and dramatically described how you could see (well, at least how *he* could see) that this particular animal was a prehistoric elephant that once roamed Northern China and foraged for food by uprooting small trees and shrubs from the ground. It was able to do this because it had four tusks, a pair on both sides protruding from its mouth, and he demonstrated by holding the fragment up under his chin and sticking a pair of fingers out at us on either side. As he chattered on and on in an excited staccato, he transformed into a living reincarnation of the beast, and his voice rose higher and higher as he bent his diminutive frame lower and lower to the cold cement floor, bobbing his head side to side as if to entangle some bushes with his toothy protrusions. Mesmerized by this Pied Piper of paleontology, all of us, including Zhang, who was masterfully trying to keep up with his interpreting, slowly bent down with him. Lower and lower we bowed until, abruptly, Huang jerked straight upright, his hands still clasped tightly on either side of his face with the proud look of a creature that had just uprooted a sizeable tree. So brisk was his motion that all of us were taken unawares, and there was a brief but confused melee of knocked heads and staggering bodies. Ever the consummate teacher, Huang remained unperturbed at our Simon-says confusion and stepped back to ask if there were any questions, his eyes eagerly searching each of ours. He was so stimulated by this Jurassic Park encounter that he literally danced a little jig in celebration. I remember watching him in admiration and thinking that this is how a fifty-five-year-old urchin clad in cloth shoes could keep so much warmer than I in my insulated socks and thick Brooks running shoes: he was warmed by his passion for his field.

Abruptly, he began to talk about his early interest in paleontology that, according to his account, sprang from the fact that his given name was Dragon and *dinosaur* in Chinese is *konglong* (fearful dragon). He told how he followed in Teilhard's footsteps, digging for fossils in Northern China and how in August he would travel outside China for the first time in his life to attend an international congress in Sweden. We wondered how he would fare in a faraway land where virtually no one knew Chinese; perhaps a lucky Xiao Hu or Xiao Zhang would be asked to accompany him. I smiled to think of that short-statured Mandarin chatting excitedly in the middle of a circle of towering Nordic colleagues. For such a little fellow, he was truly a giant of a scientist.

The hour and a half went quickly despite the cold and the fact that the children were with us, and after we hurtled eighty million years back into the present and stepped out into the snow and sunlight and after Huang had locked the door, we thanked him for the honor of being the only visitors to that secretive archive of time. It was a fascinating and informative morning for us, but more than the lessons in science he taught us or the revelation that our humble campus had an exalted past, what I remember most vividly is the wizened face and delightful demeanor of a tiny paleontologist who before our very eyes had brought the dead to life.

Jin is a common surname in China, but the three people you are about to meet are anything but common. One spring morning, we cycled up to our building to begin another day of work when we heard the loud voice of a teacher echoing out of an upstairs window. His English was unmistakably Chinese, but it was the first time we heard a strong American accent as the pronunciation model, for all English teachers at that time in China was standard British RP or BBC English. What caused us to perk up our ears most, however, was not the accent of his morning broadcast but the content of his lecture. "The Battle of Midway was the turning point of World War II." How in the hell did any teacher at our institute who was lucky enough to have just survived the purges of the Cultural Revolution know anything about America's participation in the anti-Japanese war? And who in heaven's name would be gutsy enough to use this knowledge to teach his students at the institute in a loud and confident voice, no less? And by the way, where on earth did this guy pick up an American accent? We parked our bikes and made a mental note to find out who our brave and unusual colleague was.

Jin Laoshi was short and wore glasses, a description that characterized at least half of our faculty, but unlike most Chinese whose access to good food was still limited, especially over the winter months, he was almost plump. I recognized his face from lectures I had given and from department meetings, but he lit up at this, our first formal introduction. He was as garrulous as he was articulate and instantaneously began describing the life events that shaped his American English and his knowledge of military history. Like millions of other Chinese children who grew up in the thirties and forties, he suffered directly from the conquest and occupation of his homeland by the Japanese Imperial Army. I forget the exact details, but he had either lost his parents or was homeless when the United States Marines occupied Tianjin in the autumn of 1945 to facilitate the relocation of the tens of thousands of Japanese troops after Japan's surrender. As fate would have it, he was befriended by a group of American soldiers, and from them he acquired food, shelter, and not just all the stuff GIs talked about, like baseball and movies, but the way they spoke as well.

Jin was a walking and talking repository of trivia about American culture in the forties. He had an excellent ear and mind and vacuumed up almost all the information and language the GIs shared with him during that formative period of his young life, and in contrast to the other faculty in our department, he rarely used the hackneyed expressions like "It's a tough nut to crack," but he salted his English with collocations frozen from the past. He talked about "guys, dames, chow, and snafus." Jin was a Chinese Rip van Winkle. He wanted to know if Joe DiMaggio was still playing baseball, Humphrey Bogart still acting, Nelson Eddy still singing, or Rita Hayworth still gracing pinup posters, and we reluctantly informed him that all but the first were long dead.

Over the months that ensued, we got to know Jin better, and the accounts of his more recent life were ultimately much more intriguing to us than the curious explanation of why he was so well acquainted with Americana. During one conversation, we were puzzled by hearing him claim that he was Korean. Korean? Chinese was his mother tongue; he had lived in China his entire life, and his face betrayed no Korean physical features, yet here he had just alleged he wasn't Chinese. He showed us the identity card that all residents of China were obligated to carry, and along with all the other information required, like his name, birth date, address, and dan wei, was his race. There it listed him as *chao xian zu* (Korean minority). Suddenly, it clicked. The common Korean surname Kim is a cognate of *jin*, the Chinese word for gold and also a popular family name in Chinese. In direct contrast to everything, I knew and opposed to all the classificatory criteria I would use, I was staring at a Mister Kim, a man both blessed and cursed with the same surname as the Dear Leader!

The conundrum became untangled as soon as Kim, I mean Jin, started to explain that even though neither his father nor he had been born in Korea, his paternal grandfather or great-grandfather had originally come from the Land of the Morning Calm; hence, according to the Chinese, he could not be considered a member of the Han majority but was a minority, specifically Korean. Despite this ethnolinguistic misclassification, certain benefits accrued with his subordinate status. The Party went to great lengths to please and sometimes appease the some 10 percent of the PRC population that was officially non-Chinese largely because, with almost no exceptions, the minority people lived along the borders surrounding China and thus formed a human great wall, buffering the country from the barbarian world outside the Middle Kingdom. In many ways, because of bilingual schooling, representation in the National People's Congress, or permission to have many children, the Party's policies toward minorities were more exemplary than the treatment many nations have had toward their native peoples. Take America for example. One of the mixed blessings Kim enjoyed was that, due to some arbitrary decree by the bureaucrats in charge of decisions like these, it was deemed that, since it was a well-known fact that Koreans ate more rice than Chinese, *chao xian zu* were allowed a double ration of rice coupons each month. Bellies are bellies, and rice is rice, so I have no idea why Kim and his misclassified compatriots were singled out for this favor. Nevertheless, with his extra portions of grain, he was able to eat more than his Han colleagues yet, at the same time, was continually exposed as different from them in a distinctly undeserving manner. And so it came to be that our conversations with the Korean Jin were not only amusing in terms of our shared but disparate knowledge about recent American culture, but they helped us to become more aware of how ancient Chinese values about ancestry and race were still very much embedded in the postrevolutionary society in which we lived.

We first met the second Jin not at our institute but at a sports meet. Typical of the wai ban's penchant for providing spontaneous entertainment for us, as I was about to bike back to the hotel on a February Thursday, Zhang announced that our family was invited to see a volleyball tournament that same evening, so after a quick meal, he met the four of us in the Flying Bai Cai, and off we went to the municipal sports hall to watch our local ladies defend their court against a visiting team from Shandong. Because the opponents were from my native province, I was ambivalent about whether to cheer for them or the Tianjin team, and in the end, my ambivalence was rewarded in that the visitors won, but the locals had made them fight for every game. The results should have surprised no one in the crowd as, among other things, Shandong is famous for tall women and men, and it is no accident that the province produces more than its share of soldiers and athletes. Yet once again, what made that event memorable was neither the results nor the event itself, but the people sitting right behind us, specifically one person. Even if you could not detect their provincial accent, you could tell from their spirited cheering each time one of the visiting players spiked the ball down the throats of our undermanned local team that the fans behind us were from Shandong. Unable to let the evening pass without letting them know that the *wai guo bi* sitting in front of them was a native son, I turned and introduced myself, and for the rest of the match, my attention was split between the court in front and below us and my new acquaintances behind and above me. They were also teachers from Shandong University and were in Tianjin for some conference and, like us, had a chance to catch the game. The more we chatted, the more my concentration focused on a well-bundled individual sitting in their midst, for he was different in some indefinable way.

The lighting was not good, and toward the top of the auditorium where we were sitting, the air had thickened with cigarette smoke, and craning my head back every time we conversed prevented me from getting a long, hard look at him, but this Jin Laoshi, when I finally caught his name, was paler and pudgier than all the others in the Shandong entourage, and like Huang, the paleontologist, one feature of his physiognomy distinguished him instantly from the crowd. He had an uncommonly large nose, but unlike a Roman one, this was flattened into his face, giving him the appearance of a retired pugilist. Jin, the Nose, spoke the colloquial Shandong dialect like the others, but despite the ease and fluency of his speech, he spoke with a nonnative disregard for tones. The next day, when some of this group came to visit us at the institute, I was finally able to see him in the clear light of day, and it was apparent that, like Jin, the Korean, my fresh acquaintance was not Chinese. You did not need the National Institute of Minority's classification system to figure out that he was foreign-born. His original name was Sam Ginsbourg, a Russian Jew with a life story worthy of a book. Indeed, two years after this first of several fortuitous meetings with him, *My First Sixty Years in China* was published by New World Press in Beijing.

You can read the whole 373 pages of his autobiography, but here's a one-minute synopsis of his remarkable life. He was born in Siberia, but like so many Russian Jewish families fleeing the Bolshevik Revolution, his parents moved to Harbin in northeastern China, which was then very much a Russian city. After a short residence back in the newly formed Union of Soviet Socialist Republics in the icy city of Vladivostok, the family moved to Shanghai, a haven for Russian refugees until Liberation. Unlike most other Europeans living in China at that time, Sam did not flee the Communist insurgency during China's civil war and anti-Japanese conflict, and in 1947, he eventually joined the revolution and adopted the PRC as his homeland. He married a Chinese woman, raised two daughters and a son, and eventually secured a position teaching English at Shandong University. Like countless millions of Chinese, he was buffeted by the ever-changing political winds that billowed across the nation after Liberation, and despite his unswerving allegiance to the Party, he survived all kinds of deprivations.

I met Sam several times that year during visits to Shandong and even agreed to edit parts of the lengthy manuscript he was working on that eventually emerged as his published autobiography. Throughout our year in China, we were continually reminded of foreigners like Sam who caught the revolutionary spirit, supported the Party, and chose to live in China for a few years or more, but in Sam's case, it was virtually an entire lifetime. Except for Edgar Snow, the American journalist who published *Red Star Over China* the year before I was born, I had never heard of any of these people, these great friends of China: Rewi Alley, Norman Betheune, David and Isabel Crook, or Agnes Smedley; however, these were household names among all English-speaking Chinese. I had several misgivings about the manner in which these figures were lionized, but it is unfortunate that Sam Ginsbourg was a virtual unknown despite his fascinating life history and his enduring commitment to the people and the Party. As far as I know, Sam gained little notoriety even after the publication of his autobiography, but I doubt if this caused him much regret. He struck me as modest and pragmatic. The epilogue, which concludes his lengthy book, begins this way:

> The other day, I met an American, an associate professor, working temporarily in our country. He had read my book in manuscript and was eager to have a talk with its "legendary" author, as he insisted on styling me. I'll not go into what kind of an American he was, nor what his attitude toward me personally, toward China was. I'll just discuss the questions, direct and indirect, pertinent and impertinent, which he was pleased to fire at me.
>
> —Sam Ginsbourg, *My First Sixty Years in China*, p. 367.

Sam concludes this final chapter by recounting his recollections of conversations with the curious American as a framework from which he justified his ideology and his unwavering confidence in the Party. My views were very different from his despite the fact that our formative years were shaped by China although, to be sure, he had five times my life history among the Chinese. I can't be sure that it was I who was the curious American Lao Jin described to conclude the story of his extraordinary life, but I am certain that the chance meeting at a volleyball tournament on a winter night in Tianjin gave me an opportunity to appreciate China and the revolution from a very different and challenging perspective.

The third of the three Jins was neither Korean nor Russian, and like every "true" Chinese living in the PRC with variations of that surname, Jin Di was Han through and through. Of all the colleagues and all the people I spent time with that year, he was the one with whom I worked most intimately and with whom I forged the closest relationship. Having said this, it was difficult for me to claim him as a good friend. So bright was his intellect, so intense his curiosity, so assiduous his passion for scholarship, I always looked at him first as my mentor, and because he was somewhat older than I, in my mind he was and will remain always Lao Jin. He spoke beautiful RP, revealing the opportunity he had once gained to study in England with a concentration in phonetics, and with his thin-rimmed glasses and serious demeanor, had he been dressed in a tweed jacket, tie, and slacks instead of the rumpled, blue cottons that we all wore during the winter months, he could have easily passed as a Chinese version of an Oxbridge don. Who knows, this may have been an opportunity that had been open to him when he was in the UK had he, like many other Chinese intellectuals, chosen to stay on and not return home to serve the motherland. He had a quick smile and could be personable and make small talk when the occasion demanded, but most of our conversations revolved around his fascination with language, especially translation. He had worked with several foreign experts over the years both in Tianjin and Beijing, but I sensed our collegiality was especially close because of my training and interest in linguistics and because of the cultural sensitivity I had due to my early Chinese heritage.

Because he was in charge of the dictionary group, initially I worked with him daily as our team mulled over which prepositional collocations were acceptable in English and how they would be translated into Chinese. I abruptly learned that my native speaking status and PhD in theoretical linguistics were no match for Jin's intellect. At first I was amused and then somewhat annoyed at his propensity to correct my English. Yes, a nonnative speaker who had spent only a year or two in England had the temerity to suggest that on occasion, the illustrious graduate of the world-renowned program in linguistics at the University of Michigan used incorrect grammar or misused certain words! I'll never forget the first time this happened.

Lao Jin stopped me almost in midsentence to inform me that *continuously* and *continually* were not synonyms, and I can't remember which word he claimed I was misusing, but he pointed out that the former referred to uninterrupted actions whereas the latter should only be used with intermittent actions. Much to my chagrin, the English language dictionaries the group used seemed to support his overly meticulous distinction, but they also allowed me some wiggle room. This and several later verbal skirmishes demonstrated that he, not I, was the resident English lexicographer, but they also illustrated different views about language that underlay the way Chinese teachers looked at words and the manner I did. To my prescriptive colleagues, different words, different phrases, or different grammatical constructions always denoted different meanings. Although I would hold that this claim is largely true, there are exceptions, and at times, contrasting language structures can still carry the same thought. Philosophers like Kierkegaard have written voluminously about topics like this, but in 1979, neither Lao Jin nor I had time to argue philosophy; we had dictionaries to compile and students to teach. Nonetheless, from that initial scuffle on, and I choose my words carefully here, he and I would have disagreements over English usage *continually*.

It is a ready testament to the many obstacles that prevent perfect mastery of a language learned later in life and not an indictment on Lao Jin's impressive command of English that he could go on and on *continuously* about the subtlest facets of word choice or grammar, but now and then goof up in the simplest of ways. I'm not talking about pronunciation for, as already mentioned, he spoke the Queen's English fluently albeit with a slight accent, a natural constraint for anyone who has not acquired the language from birth. A perfect example of a linguistic faux pas he made was to mix up his *she's* and *he's*. As I have already pointed out, Chinese uses only one pronoun, *ta*, to refer to the third person, so naturally, there's interference from the mother tongue and the proclivity to confuse the two words in English when in Chinese there's only one. None of this research seems to shed light on the differences between the way Chinese and English use these pronouns however. Anyway, unlike most of the un-Chinese-like usages in English that create problems for the Chinese, *he* and *she* seem fiendishly difficult for them to master, and this was true even of Lao Jin. When talking about his children, for example, I sometimes had to remember he was talking about his son when "she" was the offspring in Inner Mongolia or remember it was one of his two daughters when "he" was the student about to attend university in Beijing. Again, I'm not criticizing Jin's command of English, which was superb, but the fact remains that certain structures in English were so challenging that even an ubergrammarian like him occasionally slipped up. I am proud to say that I never seized on these infelicities to stop him in midsentence with a correction, though the urge was *continuously* present.

Jin lived in a temporary shelter on campus within a stone's throw of the foreign languages building, and he, his wife and daughters, and all his scholarly possessions were crammed into that makeshift hut. In the fall, when the weather was still warm enough for us to sit just outside the temporary shelter that served as his family's tiny home, he invited us over for lunch. Typical of Chinese hospitality where the hosts are expected to overfeed and the guests are required to overeat, we were given a feast: several dishes of pork, two of chicken, a large fish, innumerable vegetable dishes, roasted peanuts and walnuts, a surprisingly tasty special plate of kidneys, drinks galore, all followed by the specialty we had requested, *jiaozi* (steamed dumplings). All of this was cooked by Jin's wife and daughters in a tiny kitchen on two natural gas burners! As we ate, we tried to ignore the sound of a rat rustling in the makeshift straw roof that had been repaired here and there with old newspapers. Waving off a fly hovering above our plates, Lao Jin asked if his home would be considered a slum in America, and he was quick enough to read my equivocating reply about how matters like that are really relative as an unequivocating affirmative. Having confronted conditions such as this during my childhood in China and India, I had grown somewhat hardened to the contrasts between abject poverty and unabashed wealth, but experiences like this affected Janene profoundly, who was too empathetic to forget what she had seen after we returned to live our American life of enormous prosperity.

After the meal, Jin showed off some of the furniture squeezed into the tight confines of his house that he himself had made having learned carpentry as a trade during part of his exile from Tianjin and academia during the Cultural Revolution. As a farewell gift when we left at the end of the year, he presented me with a small box he had made containing a traditional Chinese chop and a small bowl of waxy, red ink. The box was so well constructed that even now, thirty years later, the ink is still moist enough for me to stamp the seal in bright crimson. I was saddened to see him and his family live that way. It seemed like such a gross contrast to have this fine intellect and productive professor confined to a hovel with his family when so many of the cadres connected to our institute lived in well-lit, heated apartments with running water and modern plumbing.

Not all our conversations centered on linguistics, language pedagogy, and translation, and usually there was a mutually beneficial exchange of information between us whenever we discussed Chinese history or world events. Again, I was sometimes surprised at gaps in his otherwise broad acumen. Lao Jin loved literature, and despite having lived for decades in a world sealed for the most part from access to foreign writings, his grasp of the English canon far exceeded mine. Still, there were inconsistencies in his knowledge. One time we were discussing foreign friends of China, and Jin was taken aback when I made an offhand comment about even Edgar Snow being an unknown in the United States, except among China watchers. At first, he thought I was joking since he tended to be serious whereas I often interposed our conversations with humor. He was flabbergasted when I told him that Snow was such a minor literary figure that if you asked any group of educated Americans to list the top one hundred American writers, his name would never appear. It was true, I equivocated, that those with an interest in contemporary Chinese history would recognize him, but the majority of readers, like I, had never read *Red Star Over China*. Jin found my claim unbelievable; conversely, I found his incredulity astounding. It was one of innumerable examples we encountered during that year that demonstrated how tightly the Party could circumscribe the knowledge that an ordinary Chinese had access to, and even such an extraordinary man as Lao Jin was tethered by this constraint.

Aside from his linguistic prowess and sharp intellect, Lao Jin exhibited an intractable and resolute drive that at times could border on stubbornness, but which overall helped shape his success. Most academics were quickly and very often literally beaten into submission by the Red Guards during the Cultural Revolution, but it is impossible for me to imagine Lao Jin being subjugated by anyone. I can see him wearing down his opponents during hours and hours of meetings and interrogations with the sheer strength of his will, countering their accusations in his sometimes shrill voice with endless arguments and a never-ending list of objections. I can see them finally giving up on any hope of rehabilitating this obdurate old man and leaving him alone in disgust to continue with his carpentry as the only residual form of punishment. While we were there, he fell and fractured his foot, but he walked around on it for over a week before relenting to seeing a doctor and getting a cast. This same seeming-unlimited zeal drove Jin in his academic work at the institute, and because this was his passion and what he was trained to do, he was a prolific carpenter of language and crafted articles and translations with ceaseless energy.

Toward the end of our stay, I gave him several books that I had brought with me and, after returning to the States, helped secure funding for him, so he was eventually able to further his study of translation in America. Ultimately, like many Chinese visiting scholars, he became an expatriate, making his home abroad in the world of English speakers and pursuing his primary passion. Not too long ago, he completed his life's work, the Chinese translation of James Joyce's *Ulysses*. Who could have guessed, least of all Lao Jin himself, that a Chinese teacher of English humiliated and exiled to the countryside by his own people and government would some day achieve an intellectual feat of mind-boggling proportions, translating a twisting narrative about a day in the life of an Irish Jew in far-off Dublin, a story filled with complex allusions to Irish culture of several generations back, and a novel written with sentences so long and discourse so impenetrable that even I could not wade through more than the first few pages. Yet here he took every syllable of that tome and translated it into Chinese, a language that is about as far from English phonologically, lexically, and grammatically as Tianjin is from Dublin. That Lao Jin was able to accomplish this discloses beyond all measure his creativity, brilliant intellect, bilingual talent, exquisite attention to detail, and his remarkable perseverance. I was fortunate to have him as a colleague, a mentor, and yes, even a friend.

Despite everything the Party had laudably attempted to encourage gender equality in China over thirty years of rule and despite all the rather superficial propaganda purportedly demonstrating that women were the equal of men in the modern haven that it had socially engineered, like so many other aspects of the society we observed around us, this claim was fraught with contradictions. Take Mao's famous observation that "men are the sky and women the earth," a clever melding of the ancient Chinese cosmological concept of *tian di* (the symbiotic harmony between heaven and earth) with the very un-Confucian concept that women are just as important as men. Like yin and yang, it takes two to make a circle. You don't have to be a Freudian psychologist to instantly figure out who gets put down and ends up at the bottom of this relationship, and from our observations, women enjoyed more opportunities and a higher status in a capitalistic nation like Thailand than they did in socialist China. Throughout our stay in Tianjin and during our visits to many other cities and institutions, I was the one welcomed, introduced, honored, thanked, and the person with whom all details were negotiated. Janene was an add-on usually lumped together with the two kids as if she were family baggage that had come along for the ride, yet she had the same foreign expert status as I. Because I was China-born, spoke the language, and because at that time I had a doctorate while she was still in the process of pursuing one, it is natural to assume that I would attract more attention and deference than Janene, but even early on, we could see that our respective genders played a major role in this inequality. This is best demonstrated during the few times Janene played the violin in public. On each of these occasions, our Chinese host first turned to me and thanked me for Janene's performance. As you can readily guess, never once did anyone ever turn to my wife after any of my public lectures to thank her for sharing her husband with them. As my parents learned in language school in Beijing almost half a century before, the husband sings, and the wife follows. There should be no surprise then that this chapter about the people who stood out in our lives that year is filled with stories about men, and while about a third of our students and colleagues were women, they did not play nearly as prominent a part in our lives as their dominant and dominating male counterparts.

Sun Laoshi stood out from both our male and female colleagues, and though we never worked directly with her, we rapidly developed an easy friendship and enjoyed intermittent conversations together throughout our tenure in China. About our age, she was attractive even in the drab outfits that all of us wore, and she spoke beautiful English in a deep and resonant voice. She allegedly was born and raised abroad, somewhere in Southeast Asia, and this may have accounted for her foreign language fluency. It was apparent she had been a confidante of several of the foreign experts who had preceded us at the institute, for she talked about the Australian or the Canadian so easily that I can imagine that not long after our departure, she would be relating stories about the American couple to future generations of expat teachers. When the weather warmed and the early chill of suspicion institutions harbored toward foreigners began to thaw, she, like many of our colleagues, was able to reciprocate the hospitality we extended at our hotel and invited us to her home for an evening meal. At every one of these occasions, we implored our hosts to keep it as simple as possible, and in this case as in every other, our friends would insist on putting on the dog, not literally, by the way, since we never once encountered dogmeat in China. Besides, exotic cuisine tended to be eschewed in the north and chewed more to the south.

Because this was an unofficial gathering and not endorsed by our wai ban, we didn't leave directly from our hotel but rendezvoused at a neutral site, the Friendship Hotel, which fortunately, for our purposes that evening, was welcoming a swarm of Japanese tourists, so we were relatively inconspicuous. Unlike Lao Jin, who was her senior in both age and academic expertise, Sun got to live in an apartment building; accordingly, she was either fortunate not to have her original dwelling damaged by the earthquake or was better connected politically than he. She lived in a basement apartment that was damper and gloomier than any of the dank domiciles we had already visited, and at first, Derick thought it was a bomb shelter. The walls were painted yellow and white, the only tint of cheerfulness in an otherwise dour atmosphere. At the door, she introduced us to the three members of her family. Her husband, who was also an academic, seemed sweet but not as bright as his wife. Despite his labored English, he was soon to leave, having been chosen as a visiting scholar to Canada, an award his sharper and more deserving wife should have garnered. Second was her mother-in-law, who lived with them following a long-standing Chinese tradition. Last and definitely least was her teenage son, who, on that evening in any case, appeared lonely and unwanted. Irrespective of the crowded living conditions that one would expect anywhere in metropolitan China, the living arrangements were the oddest we ever encountered. Sun slept alone in the best bed and largest room; her husband shared a smaller room with his mother, a custom that followed no Chinese tradition I had ever heard of, and the lonely son got the kitchen, which doubled as the open stairwell to the rest of the apartment building above. Like most of the flats we saw, her family had to share an upstairs bathroom with other tenants in the building, and they in turn got to share the kitchen sink below. Perhaps her poor kitchen-dwelling son wasn't that lonely after all.

We squeezed two on a side around their family table, and once more we were struck by the liberality of our Chinese friends. Sometimes deprivation spawns a generosity that surprises. I don't recall any specifics about the meal or our conversation that night, but in addition to the atypical family dynamics, there was something about Sun that appeared quite alien to any of the expectations I held based on my experiences with Chinese people. The closest descriptor I can come up with is that she struck me as somewhat bohemian. Even now, that characterization jars mightily in my mind as bohemian and Chinese do not seem to collocate, especially when framed by the society I knew back then in 1979.

Like so many of our English-teaching colleagues, she had a love of literature and art and was aesthetic in her approach to language in contrast to my mechanistic bias as a linguist. But beyond this love of art lay a sometimes countercultural approach she took during our conversations, and we were taken aback at times by the refreshing frankness she displayed when discussing the issues of the day. Even during private conversations, most Chinese we talked to gave predictable and stock responses that did not stray too far from the Party line, but Sun was different. Whenever the Cultural Revolution was raised as a topic of conversation, which was done frequently by our Chinese friends, the blame fell inexorably on the Gang of Four (Wang Hongwen, Yao Wenyuan, Zhang Chunqiao, and Mao's wife, Jiang Qing). However, Sun would begin with an obligatory mention of the gang but go on to implicate a broad range of people, going so far as to laying some of the guilt at the feet of the Great Helmsman himself, a daring display of audacity at that time. We were never sure if these remarks were a sincere expression of her innermost thoughts to be shared with trusted foreigners or whether they were made more to entertain us with avant-garde gossip. If it were the latter, then my perception that she was bohemian was justified for saying things simply to get a rise out of an interlocutor or to push people's buttons was definitely uncharacteristic behavior in China. People like Sun helped caution me about making glib generalizations about women and about the Chinese.

Just from her name alone, you could tell straight away that Jennie Xue was a different sort of woman from Sun, and by the end of the year, after we got to know her better, we could appreciate the depth of that difference. Unlike the Japanese, for example, Chinese like Jennie, who have learned English or have had extensive contacts with English speakers, follow a long tradition of adopting English given names. Quite the reverse is true with Japanese in similar positions although Japan has had continuous and extensive contacts with Europeans and Americans for 160 years. I have had many Japanese students and friends, and I can't recall ever knowing a Mary Tejima or a Sammy Yamamura, and though English first names disappeared during the Cultural Revolution and were rare when we resided in China, they were common in earlier periods and are prolific today. Again, if one takes the Whorfian view that differences between languages reveal corresponding dissimilarities in how native speakers view the world, one would readily assume that China has been much more open to foreign influence than insular Japan. Not true! From the midnineteenth century on, by almost any measure, Japan has absorbed many more ideas, technology, vocabulary, and popular culture from America and Europe than has China over that same time span, so do not be deceived by superficial similarities. English names are as easy to slip on as jeans, and a Chinese who bears both is usually as different from an American as their respective genetic histories.

Jennie was a generation older than either Sun or us, and as a middle school teacher, she attended several of my public lectures on linguistics and language teaching at the institute. We were first introduced to her by an elderly Chinese-American teacher of Chinese from the University of Pittsburgh who, by that autumn, had been reassigned to Beijing as part of a growing contingent of American visiting scholars, and because Professor Yang had lived in China before Liberation, he knew Jennie and a few others of her generation because they once worshipped together in the same Christian community. Especially because of our common faith, she soon became one of the Chinese outside our dan wei we enjoyed seeing, and at that time when political constraints were loosening, we learned that she had remained a member of the small congregation of Christians that was hoping to reopen one of the former churches in the city. We were delighted to accept her invitation to come to her home to make jiaozi for an evening meal.

The spiritual leader of Jennie's group of Christians was Pastor Liu Qingfen, an incredible individual in his own right, and because he had already visited us at our hotel and knew where Jennie lived, he volunteered to direct us to our jiaozi party that autumnal evening. Unlike most of the other times we were invited to people's homes, the authorities had not approved this soiree, but unlike our visit to Sun's home, there were several aspects of this engagement that made it politically sensitive. Jennie was from another dan wei; we were meeting as a group of individuals, not as a family. Finally, what we all had in common was our religious faith, a common denominator the party at that time found exceptionally divisive. So we sensed both excitement and apprehension as the date arrived for our surreptitious meeting. It was already dark when Pastor Liu met us, and because this was the first time we were gathering with a group of Chinese Christians, we were more than unusually excited. The sad events of the Cultural Revolution and the fact that people of any faith were still prevented from worshipping publicly belied the constitutional guarantee of freedom of religion, and the experience that night evoked thoughts of the persecution of the early Christian congregations during Roman rule. Jennie lived a couple of floors up in a decrepit set of flats that had somehow survived the earthquake, and with no outdoor lighting, we groped up a dirty, narrow stairwell that also served as a storage way for the tenants. Fittingly, Pastor Liu led the way with a small flashlight, and following his light, we reached the door to an upper room that was flung open to welcome us.

We ate many jiaozis that year in China, most of them in our hotel because they were a favorite of every member of the family, and equally important, they were the only menu item that appeared in our bowls within about a quarter of an hour after we had ordered them from our friendly but still lethargic fu wu ren in the dining room. Soon after our arrival in Tianjin, when the hotel was all but deserted over the Spring Festival holidays, we sat in the kitchen with some of the cooks and helped them make jiaozis, so we knew firsthand what was in them and where they came from, and for me, who nurtured many happy memories of jiaozi-making and even happier ones of eating them as a child, these occasions were a cheerful reminder of my Chinese heritage. In our many excursions around China that year, we met and ate jiaozi of all types: vegetarian, stuffed with plump shrimp, traditional pork-filled ones, succulent and heavily infused with garlic, and untraditional dumplings wrapped in thin skins made of egg batter. None of these gastronomic encounters ever compared with the jiaozi party we enjoyed that night at Jennie's, however. I certainly wouldn't assert that those were the most delicious dumplings we ever ate in China, but the collective experience itself stood out. As we spooned the prepared stuffing on to circular doilies of dough and pinched these together, each in our own individualistic manner, we listened to Jennie and her friends talk about the grim hardships they had endured because of their faith. The stories continued as we watched the jiaozis roll in the boiling pot on top of the coal burner and smelled the moist, doughy aroma as they cooked firm, and we continued to listen as we managed to capture the slippery creatures of our creation with chopsticks, dip them into the small bowls of vinegar and soy sauce that dotted the table, and slurp as many of them as our stomachs and propriety would allow.

Long after we had cycled home and decades later, even to this day, the entire evening remains an experiential gestalt, the poorly lit and humble upper room, the stories of faith and survival, the contented and smiling faces of Pastor Liu and Jennie, and the steaming jiaozis suffusing the air with their particular incense along with the obligatory hot tea that we sipped throughout the evening. It was not a meal but a service of Holy Communion. At the end of our stay, Jennie penned a lovely farewell letter to us in exquisitely handwritten English. Among other things, she expressed her thanks for "your whole hearted devotion to your work, your service to Chinese education, your contribution to the building of the friendly relations between America and China. These certainly will be a force to the progress and peace of mankind. You are going back with high praises and deep love of the Tianjin people." Kind words indeed, but whatever their surnames, it is the Jennie Xies of China who should be thanked and praised for their devotion to their countrymen and for their abiding faith in the face of persecution.

Liu Peichu was one of Janene's students, so she was younger by far than either Sun or Jennie, but with them, she forms a trio of three generations of Chinese women. How fascinating it would have been to have put the three together one Sunday afternoon and get them talking about and contrasting their experiences, their attitudes, and their perspectives regarding the role of women in contemporary China. We were not savvy enough to come up with this idea that year, but come to think of it, I doubt if it would have worked. The three were unacquainted with one another and came from different stations, so Janene and I were the only connection and a foreign and temporary one at best. Furthermore, in those days, our Chinese friends were usually uncomfortable talking about personal matters if other Chinese were within earshot, so though this idea could probably be pursued today, back then, it was no more than a thought experiment.

Xiao Liu was Janene's class monitor, and if you remember from a previous chapter, this position was a definite honor but also a difficult role to assume. The easy part was being captain of the team, leading the students in any of their routines and representing their collective voice to Janene when they needed to be heard. The hard part was that she also had to report to the department cadres about anything they deemed of interest, and this sometimes meant she had to report on her teacher. Like it or not, Liu was the open mike in Janene's classroom. She was the most outgoing student in the class, man or woman, and with her pigtails, active demeanor, and a gift for bluster, she struck me as a bit of a tomboy. She must have had a clean political slate to have been chosen for this position, but her strong and outgoing personality certainly played a part in the selection. When all is said and done, she was a wonderful help to Janene and, like all the other members of that remarkable class, became an extended member of our family that year.

The Japanese have a saying that has a strong Confucian flavor, "The nail that sticks out gets hammered down," and this apothegm definitely characterized the survival strategy of the Chinese during the Cultural Revolution and was still an accurate characterization of Chinese behavior while we were there. Given the Confucian hierarchy of old over young, master over pupil, and man over woman, most of the female students in our institute lay low. Liu stood up and out! Throughout both semesters, Janene had trouble getting any of her female students to answer questions or initiate activities in class, and they were even reluctant to sit in the front row; Liu was the exception. The most salient illustration of her spunkiness was in the late spring when the students decided to honor Janene on the American, not Chinese, holiday of Mother's Day by arranging to take our family to the water park for a Sunday picnic. Being class monitor, Liu allocated duties, and one of Janene's top students, Yang Bing, took the initiative and made most of the arrangements for the big event. All went well until the actual day arrived when we were unexpectedly delayed because of Liu.

Some of the students met us at the hotel quite early that morning to beat the Sunday crowds and accompanied us on the 94 Bus to our destination. There we met almost all of the other members of the class who had biked to the park directly from the institute, but there was no sign of a few other students and Liu, who, as class leader, had the tickets. Tens of minutes ticked by, and being a warm Sunday, the weekend for most Chinese workers, families were streaming into the gates behind us as we watched impatiently outside. Finally, Liu and her fellow students popped out one of the buses that came by periodically to add to the crowds streaming through the gates. She was fuming, and her quick smile had disappeared, replaced by a face redder more from fury than from the morning warmth and the crowded bus, and if her pigtails were physical appendages rather than hair, I'm certain they would've been bristling upright in her rage. Leaving the institute late and cycling too fast and too carelessly through an intersection, she and her companions were called over to the police kiosk by a cop looking for Sunday-morning speeders. According to Liu, the cop was utterly disrespectful, was unimpressed that she had a good excuse for running the red light, was unmoved by her argument that everyone else did it (which was true, for this was early May before a June 1 sea change in traffic laws), and most egregious of all, was not at all persuaded by her charge that she was a university student and thus should be treated with respect. The last card she played was a particularly inept choice since students were viewed by most of the populace as a pampered and supercilious elite, and cops the world over do not take well to the "do you know who I am?" defense. Surprisingly (to Liu), the policeman showed no sympathy but seemed to grow more and more aggravated the more she blustered. Anger ultimately led to tears of remorse, but the cop remained indifferent. Following public security protocol, her bike was confiscated, and only after paying a fine the next day would she be able to retrieve it, and she and her classmates were forced to wait for a bus to bring them to us at the park. I didn't know whether to be amazed at her courage or at her brazenness. Not only did she disregard all the Confucian expectations about the role of women when dealing with older men in authority, she flaunted the universal code of behavior whenever a civilian of any age, position, or gender is stopped by a policemen: be polite and contrite.

A bit late, we entered the park and still had a lovely time, and with more than twenty children celebrating her Mother's Day Sunday, Janene basked in the well-deserved adulation. It seemed as if all of Tianjin had also decided to commemorate the day for crowds constantly jostled us, except when we were on our rental boat, floating in one of the man-made lakes. As for Liu, she gradually cooled down and seemed proud that her efforts and those of her fellow students' were so appreciated. Not all nails got hammered down, and it was a privilege for us to know a young woman who stood up tall and was as strong as tempered steel, and like Churchill's England, Liu not only survived but endured.

Among all the many people we met, it might seem strange to single out for recognition a person who was neither a friend nor an acquaintance; in fact, we never met him at all. Nevertheless, he deserves mention simply because his name spoke volumes about the sociocultural milieu in which we lived. At the end of every month, we would line up with all the other teachers in the institute outside the bursar's office on the ground floor of the administration building to receive our monthly stipend. Back then, the payroll office issued no checks, and naturally, there were no automatic deposits made by computer. Instead, when we reached the head of the queue, the cadre in charge would find our name in a heavy ledger, look up our apportionment, and count out our pay in renminbi (Chinese currency). For Americans who tend to be open about everything except their salary, it was a bit embarrassing for us to have our remittance become public knowledge, particularly when I was paid 600 renminbi a month (392 dollars). This was roughly ten times what a starting teacher made. It exceeded Vice President Chen's salary, and according to the Foreign Experts Bureau in Beijing, it was more than what cabinet ministers were paid, and here I wasn't even a member of the Party! Needless to say, this grand sum was a pittance compared to my salary back home in the States, but we were in China, so the only fair comparison was with our Chinese colleagues. We were at the top end of the salary scale, but we were not entirely alone.

Every time we picked up our monthly remuneration, we went through a little routine that once again demonstrated that the whirlwinds of the Cultural Revolution that had just preceded us had not blown away all vestiges of traditional culture. Brushes and ink have always been the primary instruments of art and literature in China, and by ink, I mean the jet-black stuff that you grind out and moisten on an inkstone. The first time I got paid, the institute's cashier pointed to my name in the ledger (next to which was the amount of my monthly salary for all to see) and told me to sign on the corresponding blank. She gave me an angry look and a quick "*Buxing* [not acceptable]" when I whipped out a ballpoint pen and pointed instead to the fountain pen lying next to the ledger. For anything official and important, real ink was obligatory, and to use anything else would have been akin to have having signed your real name as Mickey Mouse. There was an art to writing your signature, and only the right stuff would suffice.

I found out, first from Lao Jin and then from others, that the most senior member of the English department was a renowned grammarian who was allegedly busy working on a book. Given my training and professional interests, I logically wanted to meet him so we could discuss our mutual interests in English linguistics, but whenever I broached this possibility, I was given a rather vague answer, something about him being ensconced at home. Month after month went by without the most famous member of our department ever making an appearance, and I began to doubt his existence. Perhaps long ago there actually was such a renowned scholar, a Chinese counterpart or contemporary of Tielhard de Chardin, whose spirit was still with us, and it was his ephemeral presence that my colleagues were actually referring to. But no, this now infamous professor was alive and well for I learned that he was lucky enough to get about the same monthly stipend as I. One payday, I actually got to meet him. Well, sort of. I had queued up along with the other teachers, and everyone was chatting happily as we anticipated the wad of cash we would receive to balance off another four weeks of drained finances when one of my colleagues grabbed my arm and said, "Look, quick, there he is!" The cashier had just opened up her window, and there at the head of our line with his back to us was a gray-haired man who was quick to receive his pay and even quicker to disappear around the corner, ostensibly to get back to work on his never seen and never published scholarship. That was as close as I ever got to meeting the institute's most illustrious and most overpaid professor, and I never even got to glimpse his face, but I did get to learn his name. "Oh, him," the teacher standing next to me said, "that's Mr. End-of-the-Month!"

Looking back on 1979, it is astonishing to recall how many friendships were forged and to reflect on the number of faces that fill my memory, and all this is a testimony to the intensity of our life that year. My early Chinese heritage, the uniqueness of our situation in Tianjin, the impact of the major events that had just transpired, and above all the hardships that our family and, much more, the Chinese people endured, all served to create opportunities to transform complete strangers into friends, a transformation that would have consumed a decade of experiences at most other places or at any other time. Like the inside of a crucible above a Bunsen burner, the catalytic heat of those intense moments created tight and lasting bonds that probably would have never melded under more benign conditions. And so it is difficult to choose which faces to portray, which people to describe, and when to curtail what could become an endless chapter of mini biographies. We were close to a considerable number of people, and a few of them have continued as intimates now more than three decades later. I have chosen to conclude this chapter by describing a man both Janene and I knew well and who we deeply admired, and since he has passed away, I do not feel uncomfortable writing about him in public in a personal way. Inevitably, memories of him are intertwined with noteworthy aspects of Chinese culture as well as significant personal events in our life; therefore, there is much more to the story about to enfold than a simple biography.

Like most of the people I met who weren't attached to either our dan wei or those representing the schools our two children attended, I first became acquainted with Wang Zhanmei after one of my public lectures at our institute. Actually, I initially confused him with another Wang since I was introduced to them both at the same time and they were both tall, spoke good English, and came from the same place, the Tianjin Teachers College down the road from us. Psychologists claim that it's easy to mix up two new words if they're similar and are taught simultaneously, and like the many people who have trouble distinguishing between *stalactite* and *stalagmite*, at first, I confused the two Wangs. Because his was the more effusive personality and because he shared a keen interest in methodology with Janene and me, he quickly became the right Wang, so to speak, and by the time we left, he and his family were among our very closest friends. Tall and animated, were it not for his thick glasses, he could have been mistaken for a basketball player, a sport that was immensely popular in China long before the arrival of Yao Ming on the NBA stage in America. As bright or brighter than the other academics we met, he was more affable and easygoing than the others and, despite poor dentition, displayed a broad and quick smile. His wife, Cai Liwen, was equally sharp and just as kind to us and, in an unusual reversal of gender roles, held the more prestigious position as a teacher at Nankai University. It was a toss up whether the Tianjin Teachers College or our Foreign Language Institute ranked higher in academic prestige, but both institutions paid obeisance to Nankai, which people viewed as the apogee of higher education in our city. He had two teenage sons, the youngest about Derick's age, who, like virtually all Chinese children we met, displayed a commitment to schooling found infrequently among American teenagers. Like kids the world over, had the boys been left to their own predilections, I'm sure they would have likely been as academically indifferent as their counterparts on the other side of the Pacific, but unlike the States, this was not an option. Chinese parents, especially those involved with education, would have considered it child endangerment if they did not constantly hold their sons' noses to the scholastic grindstone.

As I got to know Wang Laoshi better, I also grew more interested in his institute, for if the Four Modernizations were to be achieved as a national goal, English language teaching definitely needed to be upgraded, for already the world was becoming more globalized, and it was clear that English was both a fuel and a lubricant for this globalization. Following this premise, in order to ensure that English would be taught more effectively, it was necessary to improve the way in which future language teachers would be trained. With plenty of experience in teaching English in a foreign country already and with a professional interest in methodology, it was natural that I wanted to visit the Teachers College and Wang turned out to be most supportive of this venture.

It was still relatively early in our stay, so the political atmosphere was not as open as it was later on in the autumn, and the invisible but well-fortified walls among various dan wei were still very much present as we had already witnessed in trying to get permission for Derick to attend the music conservatory. Unlike securing permission for our kids to attend their respective schools, however, there was an added layer to penetrate because of the barriers that separated Tian Wai and me from the Teachers College and Wang. From my perspective, our institutes were equal and collegial counterparts, both sharing a common mission to train students and teachers to teach English, a language that would one day infatuate the nation, but from the perspective of our administration, the Teachers College was a step down in academic status. Naturally, my institute understandably but selfishly demanded the true measure of my devotion, but because of this perceived difference in status, they also felt that if I, their foreign star, was seen gallivanting with a lesser dan wei, Tian Wai's reputation would be somehow sullied. I was theirs but not to share. I counterargued that I was hired and ultimately paid for by the Foreign Experts Bureau in Beijing and thus had a national as well as a local commitment, and I also stressed how I acknowledged my appreciation of Tian Wai at every public forum I attended away from the institute, thus enhancing the very status they so coveted. Thankfully, the Tian Wai authorities granted me permission to visit Wang's home institution and, over time, many other universities around China as well. In hindsight, Janene and I were lucky to have worked in a Chinese institute that was progressive for its time, and once again, Lao Chen and some of the other cadres are to be commended for their open-mindedness.

At about the same time Wang Laoshi and I were getting to know each other better, he and Janene also started to develop a friendship because he was intrigued with her growing interest in pursuing research on the history of English language teaching as a window to political change in modern China. As a mark of his intellectual inquisitiveness, his courage, and ultimately his friendship, he began cycling over to our hotel in the evening, and in the warm comfort and security of our sitting room, he would share story after story about the ways in which recent events had affected education in China, peppering these accounts with vivid anecdotes about how both he and his students were directly influenced by the vagaries of political change. One incident he recounted is still fresh. In the early sixties, during the Party's Great Leap Forward, the nation was in desperate need of steel, having not yet developed the huge industry that it deploys today, and so rural communes as well as city schools were encouraged to produce this then precious metal. Lacking iron ore, metallurgical engineers, Bessemer furnaces, and all the other necessities for such a major operation, his school dutifully took up this quixotic task, cancelled classes, and encouraged teachers and students alike to round up every piece of scrap iron they could lay their hands on. Tables, chairs, gates, and the like were ripped apart and thrown into a makeshift furnace fired by their institute's limited supply of coal and wood, but alas, none of this resulted in one shiny ingot of steel since, for one thing, they were unable to generate enough heat to smelt even a paper clip. Wang related this story with great skill and a tragicomic sense of what can truly be called irony. But as he went on to describe the pervasive hunger that he and his fellow students experienced and the way their afternoon nap times were extended to husband their limited energy, we appreciated his honesty and the manner in which he portrayed a very human and universal condition. Crying and laughter are but two faces of the same experience, or as a neurologist I read once observed, humans are the only animal that laughs and weeps, for they are the only animal that is struck by the difference between what things are and what they might have been. This single anecdote that he related about just one tiny corner of a giant nation is illustrative. It is estimated that twenty million Chinese died of starvation during the so-called Great Leap Forward.

Wang's resume is typical of the more senior colleagues we worked with at Tian Wai and elsewhere, and the details of his early life come partly from my notes and recollections but largely from his son, who kindly provided me with the most relevant information. Zhanmei's father studied and practiced law long before Liberation, and because the Nationalists controlled the government at that time, he was classified by the Party after the Communist takeover as a historical antirevolutionary. It was also rumored that Wang's father was friendly with someone who had collaborated with the Japanese during their occupation of China. Whatever the reasons, unlike contemporary antirevolutionaries, whose perceived sins were committed after Liberation, the older Wang wasn't thrown into jail but was never able to secure a job from then on.

According to long-standing Chinese tradition, your father and his lineage dictate in large part your own identity; it is difficult, if not impossible, to escape from your ancestral past, specifically your paternalistic past. A classic illustration of this is the concept of *lao jia* (ancestral home). Rather than name the city or province a person was actually born in when asked where he came from, Chinese tend to cite their father's birthplace. Both of Wang's sons were born in Tianjin, for instance, but their official *lao jia* was Shanghai, the actual birthplace of their father and grandfather, and it is not uncommon for a daughter or son to name as their home a city or province they have never been to. The Party has followed this same tradition in the insidious way it classifies individuals politically, and because Wang's father had an unclean political past, Wang Laoshi was haunted by his paternal specter his entire life. The words of Ezekiel over two and a half millennia earlier express this inequity perfectly, "The fathers have eaten sour grapes, and the children's teeth are set on edge." The Red Guards pasted up a poster criticizing Wang in front of his apartment during the Cultural Revolution that put this ancient observation in cruder and more contemporary terms. "If the father is a reactionary, the son is a son of a bitch!"

Wang grew up in Shanghai and, like me, had childhood memories of both the anti-Japanese conflict, the civil war with the Nationalists, and the Liberation. He moved to Tianjin as a university student, studying English language and literature at

Nankai University, and graduated among the top of his class at the end of the Great Leap Forward. Branded with the stigma of his father's supposedly antirevolutionary past, he was not offered a teaching post at Nankai, breaking the accepted practice in China of offering top ranking graduates a faculty position, and instead was given a job at the lowly Tianjin Teachers College. Like almost every academic during the Cultural Revolution, Wang was sent to the countryside to be "reeducated" and was also subjected to demotion and vilification for almost a decade before finally getting his position and academic rank restored just the year before we met him. And again, like most English teachers we met, he nurtured a love for literature and translation though not to the passionate and stratospheric level of Lao Jin; still, he had published translations of Agatha Christie, Robert Frost, and D.H. Lawrence.

After we returned to the United States, I tried hard to support the quest of a few of our Chinese friends to win acceptance and a scholarship to a graduate program in America so they could further their academic careers and also serve as a bridge between the world's most populous nation and its richest upon their return to their homeland. As evidenced by the class Janene and I taught at Tian Wai to prepare a cohort of visiting scholars to go abroad, every educational institution in China was teeming with teachers of every age and in every discipline raring to grasp any opportunity to study in a foreign university, especially an American institution. Two years after our return to the States, I was able to secure a position and partial funding for Wang Laoshi to pursue graduate studies in the Faculty of Education at the University of Pittsburgh, but unfortunately for Wang, he was unable to gain matching funds from his dan wei or the Ministry of Education or, more significantly, permission to leave, and he never got an opportunity to visit the United States. In another exception to the overall gender bias of the nation, probably partially due to the prestige of her dan wei (Nankai University), his wife did win a scholarship to the University of Minnesota and studied in the States while Wang stayed home to take care of the two boys and continue with his work at the Teachers College. He eventually got permission and support to study in New Zealand for a brief period, but he never was able to go to America even after his son had emigrated there.

I saw Wang Laoshi for the last time in 1984. Because I was already committed to a teaching stint in southwestern China that summer, I responded to his invitation to go on to Tianjin to speak at an international linguistics conference he and the other Wang had organized at the Teachers College, quite an academic coup for them considering that going to China was still the rage in the United States and their humble institution had managed to pull this off ahead of more well-known universities. Little did I know when I agreed to attend that I would come close to not ever seeing him again, or anyone else for that matter!

My talks down in the hot, muggy Southwest went smoothly, and stifling as the summer weather was, I was fortunate to be located in a distant and quiet suburb of Chongqing, a sprawling and smoggy metropolis known as one of the four summer furnaces of China. When my work there concluded, I went to the Chongqing Airport to catch a morning flight to Beijing, where Wang Laoshi would be waiting to accompany me by train to Tianjin, where I could shower, catch a good night's rest, and be fresh the next morning for the opening session of the conference he and his colleagues had so fastidiously arranged. At that time, the Civil Aviation Administration of China (CAAC) was the national carrier both for international and domestic travel, and I rarely encountered anything but third-class experiences with them, a tale for another day, so my expectation for the impending flight was considerably lower than their cruising altitude. I was pleasantly surprised, however, when we boarded and took off on time, and as I looked down at the smoggy countryside of Sichuan Province from my starboard window, I remember feeling relaxed and content and started to daydream about seeing Wang again.

The plane had just leveled off when there was a muffled bang in the back of the cabin that precipitated considerable commotion, and though there seemed to be no discernable change in the plane's flight path, I was greatly alarmed to see the pilot burst from the door of the cockpit and stride to the rear of the plane with an agitated face. Pilots were close to gods in those days, and like the emperor in imperial China, you almost felt compelled to avert your eyes from their majestic presence, so the fact that he chose to mingle with the hoi polloi in the back was a bad sign indeed. He strode back to the cockpit even more agitated, and a moment after he had regained control of the plane, we banked downward very rapidly in a tight spiral, the circular motion pinning us safely to our seats since seat belts were often treated like neckties at that time, a nuisance worn only on formal occasions. The only announcement that the captain gave was after we had stopped our downward spiraling and had leveled off and resumed a normal flight pattern, and his remark was abrupt and pithy. "We are returning to Chongqing" was the only thing he said. The only other non-Chinese on that flight was a small delegation of foreign geologists returning from a rare trip to Tibet, and they broke out into a cacophony of questions, interjections, complaints, and shouting, especially since they didn't understand the pilot's terse announcement in Chinese. We landed smoothly (by CAAC standards), and the Chinese passengers applauded in relief, and as we stepped out of the plane to walk down the steps to the tarmac, I, like all the others lined up in front of me, looked back at the tail where a small hole had blown open on the portside of the fuselage. Later, from the scuttlebutt I heard among the Chinese passengers, it seems that the ground crew servicing the plane there in Chongqing had failed to secure the exterior door to the sewage tank in the plane's tail, and once we had reached altitude, the door and parts of the fuselage were blown off by the pressure in the cabin. The pilot's perilously quick descent saved us from the disastrously sudden loss of cabin pressure, so one man's folly was saved by another's quick thinking.

Following customary CAAC procedure, no one was told anything initially, but after about an hour or two, all the passengers were assembled in the airport's waiting room and notified that a new plane was being sent from Beijing to pick us up and take us to our destination, and in the meantime, we would be served a free hot lunch kindness of CAAC. This elicited more questions, interjections, complaints, and shouting from the international delegation of rock scientists, and one of them, a gentleman from Turkey (and thankfully not a fellow American) became apoplectic. He had never seen such poor service in his life; were it possible, he would have sued the airline for all manners of evil, and there was no way in hell he would ever set foot in a CAAC airplane again, least of all consider flying with them to Beijing that same day. Because of his anger and the fact that both he and the airline representatives were communicating in a second language, I stepped in to help translate and to spell out an alternative offer the Chinese carrier finally provided. After much negotiation, CAAC arranged to put him on a train that evening for Beijing, but they warned him that instead of a few hours, it would take him about two days to reach the capital city. I marveled at how quickly the airlines was able to promise a trip with a completely separate dan wei, but given that at that time CAAC was the demigod of transportation, the mortal railways had no choice but to acquiesce to any divine edicts. The Turk was finally sent off in a taxi for the railway station, still fuming like a smoldering volcano over the injustices perpetrated on him personally, on his lofty scientific profession, and on his nation, but by this time, the other geologists had grown dormant and, like the rest of us, awaited the backup flight to Beijing.

I sat at a table with some other Chinese passengers to enjoy the free lunch, and like most people flying those days, they all appeared to be cadres with a few military types thrown in. Because of my limited Chinese, I couldn't follow the conversation completely, but naturally, it focused on our collective near-death experience with a clear contrast between the seasoned fliers and the novice air travelers. The former, like me, were scared witless while the latter seemed to be amused as if they had just gotten off a roller coaster at a county fair. Lucky for them they were too naïve to realize that passenger planes should not wheel and dive like jet fighters. But the conversation then grew far more intriguing when the subject of the black box emerged as the center of our colloquy. As you would expect, I thought my fellow travelers were talking about the crash-proof container of instruments that proves invaluable to air safety specialists after an air accident, but what was fascinating was that the conversation actually revolved around a Chinese urban legend created from a misunderstanding of this term.

Though I had trouble following the give-and-take, it became apparent that my tablemates believed that the black box was a small, fireproof container with a slot on top like a miniature ballot box carried on all flights. If a CAAC plane were in danger of crashing, the stewardess would hurriedly pass the box around the cabin, allowing each passenger to write a quick note to a loved one and pop it into the security of this container. Thanks to this last-minute service, their notes would survive the ensuing disaster, and grieving family and friends would find some solace in the loving messages written so hastily by their dearly departed. Once I understood the gist of the discourse, I was too fascinated with what happened next to try to persuade my interlocutors that they were completely off the mark. One by one, they began to volunteer whom they would write their final words to and what they would hurriedly pen. Parents, wives (my tablemates were all men), and sons prevailed as recipients, and there were genuine expressions of love and remorse. Finally, they all looked at me with somber faces, and though they were already aware of my imperfect Chinese, they wondered what an American guest would choose to write. "If I had to write a letter like this," I began, "I would address it to our comrades at CAAC." And then I would write, "Once again, I must complain about your execrable service." For the first time that afternoon, we broke out in laughter.

The flight from Beijing arrived at dusk tardier than expected (no surprise there), but we took off immediately and landed in Beijing late at night about ten hours behind schedule, but faithful Wang Laoshi was waiting for me in the crowd after I cleared security, and it was a delight and a relief to see the face of a friend after that long day's journey into night. Because we had obviously missed the last train to Tianjin, we were trapped in the capital city, so Wang arranged for a cab to the International Friendship Guesthouse. It was well after midnight when we arrived at the locked gates, and it took time for the gateman to let us in and to find someone who could arrange for accommodations. Because I was a foreigner, an American, and white, a room was available for me in the flats for foreign experts where we stayed when our family first arrived in Beijing five and a half years earlier, but it seemed that there was no room for Wang in the Chinese accommodations. Never losing his temper despite the strain of that long day and the discriminatory treatment he faced, Wang tried to negotiate a room for both of us, and I buttressed his argument with an offer to pay the cost of a full night's stay despite the late hour. Exhausted and unable to get around the restriction that an American and a Chinese could not share a room, we finally won permission to doze off on some wooden chairs in the waiting room of the Chinese dorm if we would leave by six and not tell anyone that we had violated protocol. We each grabbed two wooden chairs, pivoting them to face each other, and on these makeshift beds, we caught a few hours of restless repose before getting up at sunrise and catching a cab for the railway station and the first train to Tianjin. We arrived back in my old city about an hour before the opening ceremony for the conference, and I remember taking the quickest shave and shower I've ever managed before rushing to the auditorium in time to be introduced.

The conference went well, and the following two days were a delightful though sleep-deprived mix of professional and personal sharing highlighted by a dinner at Wang's home with his wife and sons, and at the end of the conference, he saw me to the train station to say good-bye before I returned to Beijing and my flight home. His long and faithful wait for me at the airport a few days earlier, his anguish and embarrassment when we were forced to bivouac at the International Friendship Guesthouse, and his solicitous attempts to be the best host possible during the Tianjin conference demonstrated a friendship that I did not deserve but which I was privileged to enjoy. With that still broad smile, he shook my hand vigorously before I got on the train, and because there was still a chance he would win a scholarship abroad, we both expressed the hope that we'd be meeting in the States the next time. The train pulled quickly out of the station, and with his tall stature, it was easy to spot him waving good-bye among the others. Wang always stood out among the rest.

He remained active at his college for many years, perhaps too active considering his high blood pressure and heart problems, and on October 30, 1999, while speaking at a meeting of city educators, he suddenly dropped dead of a heart attack. I wonder if all those years living under the stain and pain of his ancestral past finally caught up with him, for what he really died of was a broken heart.

CHAPTER 5

读万卷书，不无行万里路

du wan juan shu, bu wu xing wan li lu

Reading ten thousand books cannot
compare with traveling ten thousand *li*.

The homing instinct is intense in many animals but not quite so powerful in humans. Take my mother for example, who grew up in a small working-class family along the Hudson River in upstate New York and who nurtured aspirations for greater things. While she was completing her nurse's training in nearby Syracuse, she met my father, who was a resident in the same hospital, and they fell in love. My father shared with her his childhood calling to become a medical missionary to China, so were they to marry, she would have to leave the Hudson Valley and her family forever and join him in a new life halfway around the world. This challenge would have been a turnoff for most American young women in the late twenties whose roots were grounded in that area of the country, but my mother instantly embraced both him and the opportunity and thus began the unfolding of my own life narrative. My older siblings have always joked that my parents' betrothal was one made in heaven because my mother couldn't get out of Mechanicville fast enough. In this sense, I am not my mother's son in that I had always wanted to return to China to visit the places where I grew up. Naturally, I was not Chinese by race or family tradition, and certainly Shandong was not my *lao jia* since, according to Chinese reckoning, this would've been upstate New York, where my father was born. But my longing to return some day was genuine, a hunger for memory. When we were first notified back in Pittsburgh that we had an invitation to teach in China, my sole personal enticement was that desire to visit the places I remembered so well from my childhood.

It didn't take much time for us to realize after our arrival how restrictive China was for foreign travelers and how unrealistic my aspirations had been to return to my childhood homes. True, Nixon, Kissinger, and ping-pong diplomacy had helped open the doors to American visitors a few years earlier, but foreign guests not only saw just a few selected cities and sites, they also hit the same nurseries, factories, communes, and Friendship Stores within those locales. In 1979 and for several years after, the Shandong town I was born and raised in and the Anhui village where I lived after the end of World War II were, like 99 percent of the country, off limits to any foreign visitors. Imagine my disappointment then when we realized shortly after settling in that any travel we planned to undertake would be to the same spots all tourists and visiting dignitaries had seen. Imagine growing up in Grover's Corners, New Hampshire, and leaving America as a twelve-year-old but one day finally securing a rare chance to return to the States some thirty years later and longing to visit the place where you grew up. Then you were told the bad news that you'd be unable to go anywhere near "Our Town." The good news, however, would be that you could go sightseeing in San Francisco, spend a day in Disneyland, visit the Gateway Arch in Saint Louis, tour all of Washington, and end up with a shopping spree in Manhattan. Now wouldn't that just sate your lifelong desire to return home one day? Imagine my frustration.

We had been in Tianjin barely a fortnight when we became aware that our days of sightseeing, welcoming feasts, and waiting would be further attenuated by China's major holiday, which was just around the corner, and that our teaching work would not begin until *chunjie* (Spring Festival or Chinese New Year's) had been amply celebrated. With no work commitments for at least another week, what a perfect opportunity to visit my birthplace, only three hundred miles to the south by train. We would pay for the entire trip ourselves, and with practically the entire nation shut down for at least a week, we would miss no obligations to our dan wei or any other commitments in Tianjin. Spring Festival began on the last Sunday in January, and we had just finished breakfast when a delegation of the leading cadres of our institute arrived to extend their official greetings. Except for Lao Chen and Lao Zhou, cochairs of our department, we didn't recognize any of them and for good reason; they seemed to materialize only at perfunctory banquets a few times a year or, in this case, obligatory public appearances. The apparent top dog among these fat cats was a plump old man who talked in a whisper and had a passing resemblance to Marlon Brando's portrayal of Don Corleone. When asked which of the twelve astrological beasts would animate the new year, there was complete agreement that we were leaving the year of the horse, but there was some confusion over whether we were entering the year of the rabbit or the ram, with consensus finally and correctly resting on the latter. We appreciated the holiday recognition the leading cadres had paid, but it made us realize that if we were to attempt a visit to Shandong during the holidays, we had better mobilize quickly. It was Epiphany Sunday, celebrating the arrival of the wise men from the East, and on the TV news that evening watched by the hotel staff, there was great fanfare over Deng Xiaoping's departure for a state visit to the United States. At the moment, I did not realize how his journey would open the door for my attempt to return to my childhood home. In some ways, we were both following a star: he, a very wise man from the West (to be geographically accurate), and I, no wise man but definitely a visitor from the East.

New, naïve, and innocent, I did not anticipate all the challenges that went into arranging for simple trips in China let alone attempts to secure a visit to places officially closed to visitors, and had I been as cognizant of these difficulties as I was later on, I would have immediately started petitioning the authorities for permission to go to my hometown the morning of our very first day in Beijing. I also did not apprehend the political contrasts among the various areas of China and how the three major municipalities, Beijing, Shanghai, and Tianjin, were relatively liberal in their interpretation of Party edicts whereas certain provinces, especially Shandong, were relatively conservative. A universal theme in all countries is the dissimilarity between city slickers and country bumpkins that tends to be framed, as the choice of words indicates, by the former more than by the latter. In China, Shanghai is the archetypical residence of smart, sophisticated, liberal, and not-completely-trustworthy people whereas Shandong is known as the home of dim-witted, stolid, conservative salt-of-the-earth types, and given that it is the second most populous province in the nation, it produces more than its share of peasants, workers, soldiers, and athletes. Like all national narratives, there are glaring exceptions to this easy generalization. Confucius himself was a native of Shandong and was born not far from my own birthplace, but humans seem to thrive on having someone to ridicule, so these regional perceptions have remained even in a supposedly egalitarian state that is ruled by a party that has extolled the virtues of country bumpkins and criticized the petty bourgeoisie.

In sum, I was ignorant of the number of obstacles facing our innocent goal of using the holidays to return to my native home. It took time to secure permission to travel even to cities open to foreigners. As already illustrated by our forays to Beijing, we had to secure permission both to leave our city of residence (Tianjin) and to be allowed into our city of destination (in this case, Jining). Further, my hometown had been closed to all foreign visitors for thirty years. To compound our problems, it was located in a conservative province where the wheels of government inched more slowly than in our city of Tianjin. Additionally, though not as many Chinese traveled during Spring Festival as they do now, trains were packed, so it was difficult to book tickets. Finally, as Xiao Zhang had so wisely reminded us, nothing was trivial in China, so our decision to leave the city and travel to a strange destination in another province was not taken lightly by our wai ban. But here is where Deng Xiaoping came to our rescue.

Our initial petition for the family to travel down to Jining during the break was summarily rejected by our wai ban. "Foreigners are forbidden to enter that district. Why don't you go to Beijing instead. It's closer and much more attractive." I responded first by playing my roots card, embellishing my heritage slightly, and blurring the distinction between birthplace (*faxiangdi*) and ancestral home (*laojia*) and then playing my filial piety card, claiming quite truthfully that I had promised my aged parents back in America that I would travel to their former home to pay my respects and to honor the heritage they had given me. One never knows what moves authorities to make decisions behind the closed doors of bureaucracy, but my guess is that the final argument I made encouraged the Foreign Affairs Bureaus in both Tianjin and Shandong to let us visit the heretofore forbidden city. My ultimate contention went something like this.

> Every day the news is filled with accounts of Deng's historic visit to the United States, and on the evening TV broadcasts, we see him dining with President Carter in the White House, visiting a car factory in Detroit, or donning a cowboy hat during a visit to Texas. So excited are the Americans about this new friendship with the Chinese people that every city is happy to welcome Premier Deng. In the same spirit, is it too much to ask that in this blossoming of friendship between our two great nations you grant permission for me, Shandong born and raised, to return to my *laojia* and share this visit with my parents when I return to the States?

Two days later, Xiao Zhang came to our hotel to report that despite great difficulties, permission had been granted for us to go to Jinan, the provincial capital and a city officially open to foreigners, but as for my hometown of Jining, we would have to wait until we arrived in Jinan to see if the Shandong authorities would be swayed by all my pleas to visit my birthplace.

We packed, picked up sandwiches and hard-boiled eggs from the kitchen and, accompanied by Zhang, our companion on almost all our trips out of town, caught the ten thirty morning train for Jinan, the capital of Shandong and one of the few cities in the province that was open to foreigners. The train rolled through miles of dusty plains, and the lifestyle of the peasants along the way seemed frozen in time when compared to the rapidly changing cities. Before leaving Pittsburgh, I asked a Chinese geographer what the topography of that area of the country was like. "Flat," he replied with a horizontal sweep of his outstretched palm, "nothing but flat." When the train made its first Shandong stop early that afternoon at Dezhou, a city on the provincial border, we purchased some roasted chicken at the station from our window and savored a country welcome. About two hours later, we crossed China's second largest river, the Huang (Yellow) and rolled into Jinan, the large provincial capital, where we would spend a day and two nights before leaving for Jining farther south. Though large and polluted like any other Chinese metropolis, the streets appeared a tad less crowded. The trees and bushes along the streets gave verdant hints of spring, and at one park, we even saw grass. Even our ordinary guesthouse appeared warmer that winter evening. Sightseeing is a mandatory activity in China not a leisurely option, but by then, we had learned to be more proactive in selecting and justifying the tour schedule. After paying brief and obligatory homage to popular local sites, like the Baotu Springs and Daming Lake, the following morning, we headed for the places that I had chosen due to their significance in my family's history. First of these was the Shandong Medical

College with its pre-Liberation architecture of matching brick buildings and tiled Chinese roofs. In a former incarnation it was known as Cheeloo Medical School, built by the American Presbyterian mission that had sponsored my parents' work in China. I asked which building housed the department of obstetrics and then pointed to the second floor where my older brother and older sister were born, and I found myself strangely stirred by seeing for the first time a small part of the world that was once the entire world to my family.

Next, we paid visits first to Shandong Teachers College and then set out across the city to the eastern suburbs where Shandong University was located. I have no childhood memories of Jinan though my parents had overnighted there on their way to other places I can recall, summer vacations halfway up Mount Tai (*Tai Shan*) or at the expansive beaches of Qingdao, but as we drove toward the university, familiar sights appeared like old photographs from a dusty family album. Street vendors were selling candied crab apples on bamboo skewers, their bright vermilion catching the low winter sun, the only visual cheer among the dark grays, browns, and blues that filled the streets. Farther along, I saw another vendor offering steamed sweet potatoes, and I had to stop our car. Naturally, a crowd immediately surrounded us, and the vendor seemed uneasy over the sudden attention he had attracted. I ordered several, sharing them with our family, Xiao Zhang and our two carloads of cadres and drivers. I broke mine open to enjoy the steaming orange treat while the others were more reticent. Our accompanying cadres, obviously city slickers, protested that sweet potatoes invariably gave you indigestion and warned us about eating such provincial fare. We did suffer upset stomachs and gastrointestinal problems off and on throughout our China sojourn but certainly not that week. Strange that such a simple pleasure from my youth would carry over to midlife and make me halt our caravan in the middle of a street in Jinan and just as strange that I can vividly recall that moment when we stopped for Shandong sweet potatoes decades later as an old man. But it is not so strange that the most enduring memories in the sweep of life are not just what we once saw and heard but are also the smells and tastes we remember from our childhood.

As we entered the eastern suburbs and were approaching the main entrance to the university, an unusual sight suddenly materialized in front of us, completely unexpected and out of place. Twin spires stretched heavenward above the monotonous rows of apartments and ramshackle homes, and as we rounded a corner, there smack in front of us was a gothic cathedral, unmistakable despite the broken windows, chipped cornices, and dust-drenched façade. Two red stars replaced crosses that had once topped the towers, and like so many former houses of worship, this one seemed to be used as a warehouse. Our Shandong hosts thought it was once a German cathedral, and this sounded plausible since the port city of Qingdao at the tip of the Shandong Peninsula to the east of us was transformed into a German city at the turn of the century, but like most European colonialists, Germany extended its influence well into the province beyond its coastal concession and had done so in Shandong by building an east-west railroad. Our route bypassed the church, and as we neared the campus, I turned back and could still see the two spires stretching high above all the other buildings like two thin arms lifted in supplication.

Our meeting at Shandong University was so hospitable and the interest and friendship expressed seemed so genuine that later that spring and again in midautumn, I made return visits to give a few lectures and to follow up on contacts made during this brief initial visit. Being their first American academic and Shandong-born on top of that, I was a natural attraction to the faculty, but more than anything, it was the remarkable leadership of the university's president that made that first meeting so amiable, and that paved the way for my later returns. Wu Fuhan was Harvard educated as a young scholar and chose to return to

China after Liberation, a decision many idealistic Chinese made at the end of World War II and one that did not go unpunished by the Party. Like all the other returnees during the Cultural Revolution, President Wu was criticized, ridiculed, and punished as a suspected stooge of the Americans. What other possible reason could he have proffered for choosing to return to a life of sacrifice and unpredictability in his motherland if it weren't for nefarious reasons? Although not inarticulate by any means, Wu was the most laconic conversationalist I ever met, and you learned quickly to accept a slight smile, a nod, or a turn of the head as an extensive reply to any comments or questions you made. In contrast to Jin Di, whose unrelenting volubility must have eventually drove off his Red Guard tormenters, President Wu's muteness gave his persecutors almost nothing to criticize. He was the perfect exemplar of the sage observation that God gave us two ears but only one mouth for a reason.

Like all the other places we visited that year, invariably we were treated to a multicourse banquet where we were gorged with more dishes than we desired or could consume. One delight for me at this particular feast, however, was to hear our university colleagues converse in the provincial vernacular. Unlike many other parts of China, especially the south, the Shandong dialect is similar to Mandarin but different enough to create misunderstandings, and the locals told several humorous anecdotes about big shots from Beijing coming to Jinan and misunderstanding the natives. The appearance of a large dish of fish as one of our courses prompted our guests to relate this story. It seemed that some Beijing cadres were in town and were hosted at a banquet similar to ours. One of them turned to his Shandong host and, after commenting on the deliciousness of the fish, asked in Chinese, "Is it from the ocean or the river?" His host completely confused him when he replied in the local dialect, "This one is black!" The joke turns on the fact that Shandong folk pronounce *hai* the Mandarin word for ocean as *hei*, which turns out to be the word for black. Our fish was neither black nor from the sea but a delicious freshwater species steamed in herbs and tender to taste but, like every other course, was a meal in itself. Steeped to the gills ourselves with friendships firmed and contacts established, we headed back to our guesthouse and some splendid news. The provincial wai ban granted us permission to visit my hometown for two days, and armed with the proper papers, Zhang immediately left for the train station to purchase tickets for our family. We had trouble sleeping that night not really because of excitement over the forthcoming adventure but since we were given only two small beds for the four of us. Like the night before, Janene and I took turns rotating half the night on half a bed and half the night fully on the floor.

Our morning train left Jinan heading due south on the same tracks that connect Beijing with Shanghai, and soon we passed Tai Shan, China's most historic mountain, a Scovel family summer retreat in the old days and a summer destination for our family during the holidays later on. After about three hours, we got off at Yanzhou and, leaving the main line, boarded train 116 on the short spur southwest that led to my hometown. By the end of that same year, this spur would be extended westward to connect with another major north-south route facilitating Jining's transformation from a dead-end city to one interconnected with the rest of the country and reflecting its evolution to metropolitan status. The half-hour ride from Yanzhou seemed to take us further back in time. There were almost no motorized vehicles along the roads, and animal and human power predominated, and like so many other trips we've taken, it was as if every kilometer we traveled also carried us back a year, so by the time we pulled into the station, we had left 1979 entirely and stepped out of the train carriage into the early forties.

Because it was closed to all foreigners, Jining had no official accommodations for us, and there was no wai ban to take charge of our small party, so help had to be brought in from Qufu, the birthplace of Confucius, many miles to the east. We were met by a group of local Party cadres and Lao Long, the wai ban from Qufu who had been chosen to help us tour a city he had never visited. Long would serve as our go-between, stage manager, and crowd control officer for our stay. Tall, placid, but friendly, his height proved to be of immediate help. As we left the tracks and started to emerge from the station, it was instantly obvious that word had spread around town that aliens were landing in their isolated district. Enveloping us, Long, and our welcoming entourage was a crowd that surrounded the station and all the streets leading to it. "Hey, kids," I shouted to Derick and Christine, "you always wondered what it would be like to be rock stars." An awaiting minivan was about a hundred yards in front of us, only its white roof visible in the sea of people like a life raft floating in the ocean. We were jostled, pushed, and shoved toward our vehicle with Long desperately trying to part the sea of people submersing us, but not being Moses, he was quickly separated from us and was carried downstream as we and a few of the local cadres—who were able to elicit a modicum of respect from the masses—continued to swim upstream toward the minivan. We finally reached it, managed to open the doors, and hustled inside, and the driver inched forward, leaning on his feeble horn while cursing either the crowds or this particular assignment. We looked back at Long, now trapped behind us with just his head sticking out above the throng, and since his arms were pinned helplessly at his sides, he could only vigorously twist his head as if to say, "Get out of here. I'll join up with you later." Eventually the streets started to clear, and we circled around the old center of town through newer suburbs to the west, and this half appeared to have expanded into several square miles of broad streets, factories, and apartment buildings. Somewhere in this newer expanse, we pulled into the compound of the municipal Party guesthouse that would serve as our hotel. Once the center of their attention had disappeared, the crowd dissipated, and Long showed up later relieved that he had not lost his foreign tourists and his job his first hour in Jining.

We ate a huge lunch but paid for it dearly. Remember, this journey was one we initiated, so the entire trip was on us. Never having had foreign guests before and filthy rich American capitalists at that, the manager of the guesthouse was in the same quandary any human hotelier would be in when suddenly forced to accommodate a family of Martians on their first visit to earth. It was indeed a sizable meal, much more substantial than we wanted or could ingest, but seriously, $1,000 just for lunch? With Xiao Zhang and Lao Long's help, we negotiated a much more reasonable price for our room and board, one that I suspected was considerably more generous than what any visiting Party cadres doled out but was closer to earth than the stratospheric guesstimates the manager first came up with. Lunch was to be followed by the obligatory nap time; after all, our hosts predictably observed "You must be tired!" We weren't, and we were not going to waste the precious few hours we had available taking a snooze, so Janene and I made a few strolls around the small courtyard and then headed to the gate where the gateman protested that it was dangerous outside and besides, "You must be tired!" Seeing that his protestations were more perfunctory than mandatory, I quoted a Chinese proverb as we eased by him: *fan hou bai bu zou, neng dao jiushijiu* [stroll a hundred steps after a meal and you'll live to be ninety-nine]. Who could argue with that? We walked as far as the officials would let us, and with another large crowd congealing, we were turned around and urged to hasten back to the seclusion of the guesthouse.

Fed and rested, Long and the cadres were ready to take us on a mandatory tour of the town's two most famous sites: a unique Song pagoda made of iron and the Poet's Pavilion. Though I have faint childhood memories of other places in Shandong, I have absolutely no memories of Jining and remembered being surprised that there were any spots there worth touring at all.

The first site had been a temple with the famed pagoda squeezed in one corner, but the whole area was dominated by modernity. Like practically every other place in China, a large, red sign stood at the entrance, *wei ren min fu* wu (Serve the People), clearly not a vestige from the Song dynasty. A three-story middle school overshadowed the pagoda, and immediately upon our arrival, its outside walkways were crammed with students who had just been handed the ultimate "get out of school" pass, a chance to glimpse the first non-Chinese they had ever seen. Relatively small and slender, the pagoda was indeed made entirely of iron. Each symmetrical and tapering story was capped by a traditional roof, and following traditional architecture, it rose nine stories high. Despite being about a thousand years old, it did not appear the worse for wear, and neither it nor the small temple nearby seemed to have been damaged in the Cultural Revolution, a stark contrast to Qufu about eighty miles to the east. There, Red Guards poured in from Beijing and other major cities to rip apart anything they could find in Confucius's hometown; however, this charming pagoda had been spared since Jining was home to nobodies.

The poet's pavilion was physically less impressive, but it meant much more to me because of the way I believe it affected my mother's life. Coming from a working-class family and with only a high school diploma and a nursing certificate, my mother was ostensibly less educated than my father, but she always had an ear for language and an eye for a good story. Early on in their life together in Jining in the late thirties, she developed an interest in poetry that slowly grew from avocation to vocation. When we arrived at the pavilion and learned about its history, it struck me that this was the spot that spawned my mother's career as a poet. Certainly, her early poems and most of her later ones disclose a definite Chinese influence. They are short and describe natural scenes with strong symbolic overtones like a scroll painted with words instead of ink. We were told that this pavilion was where one of China's greatest poets, Li Bai, sat, drank, and composed when he made a foray to the north long ago, reaching Jining by the Grand Canal, the railroad of the past. One of his lines inscribed there commemorating his residence was, "The wind from the south makes me homesick, but when I get to this place, my homesickness vanishes." Among the many poems my mother published, one of her earliest was a favorite written when she still lived in Jining. She uses a different romanization for his name, but this tribute is clearly to Li Bai, and I would like to imagine that my mother penned this verse while enjoying the quiet sanctuary of the pavilion, away from the war, poverty, and daily pressures that surrounded her life in Jining.

To Li Po, Poet
Myra Scovel

Yellow the willow by your mountain pool.
one golden leaf following your skiff
as you painted brush strokes for these words
twelve hundred years ago.
"Shall goodwill ever be secure?
I watch the long road
of the River of Stars."

Grieved at the uselessness of war,
prey to the whims of the court,
you were exiled to this quiet water.
some say that you embraced the moon in it
and died.

Twelve hundred years, Li Po!
"Shall goodwill ever be secure?"
If it be true that you were drowned
in the silver of your sorrows,
you rose with the lotus, immortality,
dripping from your shoulders.

I, too, must watch, Li Po,
head raised to the long road
of the River of Stars.

We had asked the local cadres to see if they could find anyone among the city's elderly population who remembered the Scovel family, and we were promised one visitor that evening after dinner. It was dusk when we returned to the guesthouse, and still full from lunch and now wary of the bill that would be charged for dinner, we ate lightly and quickly despite being offered yet another sizable feast. As promised, a stranger was brought to the guesthouse, a stooped old man limped in with a cane, his head craning upward to catch a glimpse of us. His hand rose half pointing half in greeting, and in what I first thought was Chinese, he called out, "Jimmee? Carlu?" I realized he was naming my two older brothers. "Tommy," I responded, "Tommy, Si Dehua [my Chinese name]." With the four of us, Long, Zhang, and all the local cadres, the small room was crowded with bodies and anticipation. "I am Lao Li," he announced to us all, slowly becoming aware that he would be the centerpiece of the gathering, and immediately he was given a seat in front of us in the middle of the room. He apologized for forgetting the English he once knew and for his failing memory. "You see," he went on, shaking his cane feebly with one hand, "I had a stroke a while ago and have difficulty walking and talking." We were impressed enough that a man in his eighties could manage so well at the end of the day and under such unusual circumstances, and as he started to spin story after story about my parents, he became more animated and garrulous, and whatever neurological damage that had allegedly affected his use of language before seemed to disappear miraculously, for not only did his Chinese speed up but he started to intersperse it with phrases in English. The climax of the whole evening came when he recounted the famous incident when my father was shot by a Japanese soldier in early June 1938. My siblings and I (and Janene as well) had heard this story many times, and my mother included it in the book she wrote about our life in China, but up to that moment, I always felt that the entire account was a little bit too large for life and had grown to legendary status over time. After all, my father never talked much about it and was a bit reluctant to show off the scar the bullet had left in his side, and my mother was always ready to admit that the singular mark of a great storyteller is not to let the truth get in the way of the narrative, so now I was about to get the real account from an impartial outside source, someone who had never even heard of *The Chinese Ginger Jars*, my mother's first and most famous publication.

As one of the workers at the hospital, Lao Li happened to be standing nearby as a witness to everything that had transpired. My father was at the gate bidding some visitors farewell when a drunken soldier staggered up to him and started talking to him belligerently in Japanese. Although the Japanese Imperial Army occupied Shandong at that time, this was well before any altercations with the United States, and my father flew an American flag over the hospital compound, implying that it was off limits to any occupying forces, and thus there was an explicit agreement between the Presbyterian mission and the Japanese that the hospital was a sanctuary for the Chinese and, of course, for our family. Japanese officials had put up a sign in kanji and hiragana to the effect that the compound was off limits to army personnel, but obviously, this soldier, clearly in a drunken stupor was not about to follow protocol. Despite the language barrier and the soldier's intoxication, my father knew that the intruder's sole interest was finding the nurses' quarters.

At a moment when the soldier's eyes and attention were diverted, Lao Li and the gateman helped my father wrestle the rifle with its fixed bayonet from the soldier's grasp, but unfortunately, a second soldier arrived and, though not drunk, insisted that the rifle be returned to its owner. The second Japanese inexplicably left, and now my father had to face the rearmed, infuriated, and still drunken gunman, literally an explosive combination. Fully into the narrative and having captured every eye in the room, Li stood up, and using his cane as a rifle, he shouted at an imaginary Dr. Scovel in front of him to start walking and then suddenly raised his cane and fired with a loud bang! We all winced, knowing that the point-blank shot could not miss. Indeed, it struck my father in the back, propelling him face first onto the ground. Li then described how the soldier discharged the spent shell and tried to cock his gun, demonstrating with his right hand as if he were operating the bolt-action. "And then he stood above Dr. Scovel like this," Li continued dramatically, demonstrating by pointing his cane down at the head of an imaginary prostrate and helpless victim and pulling an invisible trigger. "But the gun jammed," Li went on as even I at that instant expected to hear another bang! "As the drunk soldier struggled to unjam his rifle, the gateman and I jumped on him, seized his gun, and dragged him out into the street before leaping back into the compound and locking the gate. Dr. Scovel staggered into the hospital, and the staff rushed to help him." Li looked up at all of us, clearly pleased with our rapt interest and slightly amazed that he was able to perform so well. The hour was late, and his best story was over, so it was time to bid farewell. We thanked him for coming to see us and walked him out to the gate reluctantly for we knew we would never meet again. "Be sure to remember me to your dear parents," he said with a final wave, and then he disappeared into the darkness.

Having paid homage to pagodas and poets the day before, it was time to see the place I had waited my entire life to visit, the house I was born and cradled in. After breakfast, we were taken to the hospital compound where my father spent so many years caring for a never-ending stream of needy patients. When my parents arrived at this mission station in 1931, it was funded, built, and owned by the American Presbyterian Board of Foreign Missions and was called the Bachman Hunter Hospital.

Forty-eight years later, we arrived at the campus of the Jining District People's Hospital, a less personalized but also a clearly less imperialistic-sounding title for this place of healing. Now greatly expanded and serving the surrounding countryside as well as the city itself, only one corner of the original main building remained standing with its curved tile roof still arching slightly upward into the gray February sky. We were taken upstairs in one of the new buildings for the obligatory tea and welcome briefing. I couldn't help but notice that instead of the cross of Jesus, on the wall hung pictures of the omnipresent Mao and his designated replacement as chair of the Party, Hua Guofeng. An older man who turned out to be the medical director greeted us with an introduction to the hospital. I was impressed that he did not begin with the usual platitudes contrasting pre-Liberation purgatory with post-Liberation paradise, nor did he gloss over the fact that this place was once served by foreigners. In an almost mechanical manner, the director described how his institution had been expanded from serving a city of two hundred thousand to meeting the needs of a surrounding district of five million inhabitants and how they now had a large outpatient clinic, four hundred inpatient beds, a new radiology department, and so on. Then he made an abrupt transition, "But you are here because of your father and mother." Acknowledging that he did not grow up in Jining and, like all of the others present, never knew my parents, he went on to pay a kind tribute to their legacy, a somewhat bold expression of affection and courage that was unusual for a cadre in his position and at that time and place.

The tea and briefing completed; the director took us downstairs for a tour of the facilities. After quickly viewing the new buildings, he led us through the ever-present swarm of onlookers to the only surviving remnant of the old hospital, and stopping by one of the downstairs windows, he told us that he had been told that before the anti-Japan war, Dr. Si Fulai used to dispense medicine to lines of outpatients from that window.

In Chinese, the syllable *si* sounds like the first syllable of *Scovel*, and my father's given name in Chinese was *fu lai*, which had absolutely no resemblance to *Frederick* but was aptly chosen nonetheless for it meant happiness comes. We were touched by the way in which our hosts were sensitive to our deeply personal reasons for visiting this particular institution given the fact that virtually no one present was old enough to remember my parents, and more importantly, decades of propaganda, reeducation, and very different and legitimate national views of history had reconstructed how these current residents of the city viewed the past. Additionally, every individual we encountered in Jining had been directly affected by the Cultural Revolution, so the interest they shared in our roots trip was remarkable, doubly so considering we were the first foreigners they had encountered. Once again, I couldn't help wondering if a vestige of the culture of yore had survived all the Communist campaigns against the olds, and our Jining hosts supported and admired my filial piety. Honor thy father and thy mother is an enduring commandment in China.

We crossed the street to the former Scovel homestead, the only mission building in the former compound still intact. Viewed across the dirt yard from the entrance gate, it looked exactly like the pictures my parents took almost fifty years earlier, and in keeping with the sense of time travel that pervaded these trips, I almost expected two-year-old Tommy to come tripping out of the front door and down the steps from the arched stone porch. When asked what the building was now used for, we were told that it housed the school of nursing, a choice that pleased my mother when I shared our Jining journey with my parents back in the States since her main work at the hospital was with the nursing staff. We went inside and meandered around the downstairs rooms, which had all been turned into offices. Upstairs, we saw the room that once served as the family's schoolhouse where my mother taught each of us an American curriculum every morning, using materials mailed annually in an oil barrel from the Calvert School in Baltimore. I wish my older siblings were with me at that moment for they would've recalled myriad memories of the childhood we shared together, and because we were interned in this house immediately after Pearl Harbor by Japanese soldiers, many of those remembrances were cemented and sealed by our solitary confinement. I was born in the corner room downstairs toward the back of this very house and spent the first four years of my life in this place, but with no recollection of my time here, no visceral emotions stirred inside me, yet there was a warm satisfaction about having come full cycle, literally circling the globe from birth to middle age and ending up in exactly the same spot where I first set out on the voyage of life. Time and space were one.

People usually display an immediate incredulity whenever I tell them that I was born and raised in China, and when they inquire how this happened, I generally give two glib answers. The first is that since one-sixth of the world's population is born there, would it not be the norm to be China-born and bred? The second retort I offer is that that's where my mother happened to be. However, the latter reply is actually quite profound, for if my father had not felt called to be a missionary as a boy and if my mother had decided to stay in upstate New York and had not joined him on a slow boat to China, my life would have been profoundly different had I a life at all. So even though I had no conscious memory of this room, this house, and this town, it was a sacred place for me at that moment, and this is a memory I will always hold and treasure.

Our very limited and precious time in Jining was almost over, so we returned to the guesthouse to select out, pay for, and wrap up some scrolls and mementos we had ordered the day before as gifts for our families back in the States. We also sat down for a final round of price negotiation with the manager of the guesthouse who was reluctant to let us go without extorting all the lucre he could extract for every grain of rice and square inch of bedding we had cost him. But even this did not diminish the pleasure and excitement of our brief stay, and after bidding good-bye to Lao Long, our hosts, and waving farewell to the crowds of people still swarming around the station, we boarded the evening train for the main line and then north to Tianjin. We spent the first few hours of that trip back in animated recapitulation of the previous two days, and so excited was he one would think that Xiao Zhang himself had just seen his old homestead. Finally fatigue caught up with us, and as the train rolled northward through the winter night, the memories of this most extraordinary of homecomings slowly slipped from consciousness into restless dreams.

About a month later, a reporter from the *Tianjin Daily* showed up at the institute to interview me about our trip to Jining. With Zhang's help as an able interpreter and also as an enthusiastic raconteur, this journalist spent several hours writing copious notes recording the details of our journey, and about a month afterward, a feature story with my picture was published in the Sunday paper, bringing instant but temporary notoriety to our family. Because translation was one of the skills my teacher-training class was working on that semester, I had them write up the English translation of the newspaper story and, after editing it slightly, mailed it to my parents and siblings in the States. The Chinese title (with apologies to Thomas Hardy) was "The Return of the American Native," and overall, I was impressed with the reporter's accuracy and attention to details, only a few of which he missed. There were two major discrepancies between the newspaper story and my interview with the reporter, however, but in retrospect, neither contrast should have surprised me.

First, my frequent mention of my parents' being Christian missionaries and that the hospital was a mission institution was completely ignored. The way the newspaper account spun it, Dr. Si was an individual American who served the people but, in this story, served no other master. The second discrepancy was the theme of change, something I don't recall reporting on during our interview; after all, if I had no childhood memories of Jining, how could it have changed from my perspective? In the interview, I described how my brothers had drawn me a map of our mission compound and a rough draft of the city, and whereas I mentioned how useful this diagram was for me, the newspaper account stressed how the map was completely out of date and had me exclaiming, "Can this be Jining? Ah, my birthplace, how you've changed!" Change was important to the reporter and also to Zhang, and this should not have been surprising for the Party has promoted this theme in many different ways. Visitors to the PRC are given copies of *China Reconstructs*, an English language magazine that lists all the positive transformations that have been effected since 1949. They are also told the same little pun by their English-speaking guides who point to the construction derricks that prick the skyline of every city, and then they remind their guests that the national bird of China is the crane.

Of course, we took several pictures of our Jining visit, and two of these (shown with an old one taken by my father) did indeed indicate how Jining had been transformed but not exactly in a way that fit the newspaper narrative or the theme the Party constantly emphasizes. I found these snapshots so insightful that we ended up using them in the many slide shows and talks we gave on China after returning to Pittsburgh, for they captured in a thousand words the essence of modern China. I would begin with a picture taken behind our old home. In the old days, except for the chimney and a large building housing a flour mill, there were only one- or two-story houses as far as the eye could see, but in my 1979 snapshot of the same scene, Jining had been truly reconstructed: the same view was swept by row after row of multistory apartment buildings towering over the much larger city. So yes, looking in this direction, my, how you've changed! But wait. The second slide in the trio we would show was not mine but an old Kodachrome my father took in the 1930s, looking in the exact opposite direction across the street from our house in Jining toward the hospital compound facing our gate, and despite its age, the colors are still fresh in this picture. The wall and gate are there along with the old hospital building with its upturned roof, and a cyclist and some pedestrians are caught by the camera in the narrow street in the foreground.

The third slide completes the chronological picture. Again, it was taken during our 1979 Jining homecoming, and I snapped it from the same spot my father used for the photo he shot some forty-five years earlier. Amazingly, the two slides look almost like duplicates, for the huge new district hospital buildings are just out of sight in this third picture, and the scene seems to have been frozen in time. The walls, the gate, the hospital building that is shown, and even the street scene appear to be untouched by the years. Only if you look more carefully, you can see that in my 1979 picture that there is a telephone pole and electrical wires that do not appear in the slide my father took decades earlier. These three views summarized our China experience more succinctly and accurately than any lengthy tome could express. Has China changed since it became the People's Republic in 1949? Obviously! So has Yemen, Hungary, Mexico, and every other spot on earth, of course. Nonetheless, especially looking back on the decades since Liberation, it could be argued that China has changed much more than almost any other nation, and my first slide of a Jining horizon swallowed by apartment buildings gave hints at how even back then China was reconstructing and transforming radically. Has China changed? Not at all if we compare the second pair of slides where the Jining my parents saw every morning did not look any different from the Jining we saw from that same perspective in 1979. The Chinese like contradictions, but the authorities would not appreciate the one depicted in our pictures of Jining— everything and nothing has changed. *Plus ça change, plus c'est la même chose.*

Culling through all the papers, photographs, and materials I have kept about that year in China and mulling over the many memories I have of that experience, I forgot how much traveling we were able to accomplish considering the trouble it took to secure travel permits for any trips we initiated, whether it was a one-day visit to nearby Beijing or a multiday journey to Shandong province. As a matter of fact, not all of our attempts to visit other parts of China were successful. Looking forward to our summer break when we would have several weeks of vacation in August, I started to explore the possibility of giving some lectures in Lhasa with the Foreign Experts Bureau central office in Beijing. Having attended high school in the Himalayan foothills in India on the other side of that mountainous southern Great Wall of China and having been enamored with the British Everest expeditions as a boy, I have always loved mountains and mountaineering. Though I harbored no illusions of securing permission to make a quick trip to the northern slopes of Mount Everest, I had always wanted to visit what the Chinese call *Xi Zang Zi Zhi Qu* (The Tibet Autonomous Region). Unlike the request to visit Jining and other sites that year, my appeal was denied, but this was the only time we were turned down, and on the whole, we accomplished an inordinate amount of travel during our stay and saw a great deal of the country and its people. Besides the longer trips we initiated and arranged, like the Jining visit or ones taken over the August holidays and in December on our way out of China, our institute set up several weekend visits to nearby sites, and depending on the journey and destination, these were forays we sometimes enjoyed and at other times barely endured. The trip that Janene and the kids took one spring weekend is representative, for it ended up a little of both.

Over a weekend in early April, I returned to Shandong University to deliver a few lectures and to strengthen the ties with President Wu and the faculty that I had made during our first visit a few months earlier. While I was south during this short sojourn, Janene and the kids went north on an overnight trip to visit some distant historical sites, a tour arranged and paid for by our institute's wai ban. Since I was not a party to this adventure, I rely on Janene's account of the trip she included in one of our weekly letters to the States as a record of this event.

What we had hoped to be an exciting trip and weekend turned out at first to be a nightmare. I should have known by the weather for we woke up to a dark, gray world of rain, and it never stopped no matter how far north we drove through endless plains and then into winding mountains on a one lane road. The rain made visibility almost nil because mud covered our windows like a giant Hershey bar. One village after another no better than the last, over dirt roads, fording streams, hairpin curve after hairpin curve—everyone sick, a couple throwing up, and once we almost slid off the road. After a couple of pit stops and an hour for lunch, after nine and a half hours our bus finally pulled into this god-forsaken hotel—filthy rooms, no heat, dirty sheets, and a kapok mattress with a pillow of seeds, and I won't dare describe the bathroom. We slept with our clothes on for two reasons—to keep warm and because it was cleaner! The kids and I hardly touched the rotten supper, but Derick had a good time running around with Willy, the Peruvian boy. [Several other foreign faculty members and some eastern European workers from the city were also on this trip.] It was fascinating to see the countryside—the harsh landscape with no green and the mountains and clouds that looked like scenes from a Chinese scroll. In general, the farmers' homes are very poor—some of brick but the rest mud and thatch with white paper for windows and almost no glass. A well here and there, an outhouse—such simple lives, such nothingness.

We woke up to another gray morning, but the sun began to shine mid-afternoon. After a lousy breakfast of nuts, rice gruel, and one slice of bread, we toured the Qing dynasty Summer Palace in Cheng De, Hebei province. We walked for miles around the dirt terrain and bare foliage of the palace grounds and lake, which altogether is eight times larger than the Imperial Palace in Beijing and three times larger than the Beijing Summer Palace. Christine and Derick both did very well going so far by foot. After a somewhat better lunch and a one-hour rest, we visited two Mahayanan Buddhist temples, built in 1770 and 1780 in honor of the Emperor's sixtieth and seventieth birthdays. Everything we saw today was in bad repair, but at least none of the Buddha images and artifacts were destroyed during the Cultural Revolution. Our guide claimed that the local residents take great pride in these monuments and threatened the Red Guards so strongly that no damage was done to them. Our guide knew almost nothing about Buddhism, so I was able to explain a lot about the religion and how it is practiced in Thailand. At 5:00, the bus took us back to our hotel tired and exhausted for another tasteless meal we could barely eat. At 7:15, we were taken to the local Beijing Opera production of "The White Snake" but I was already so tired I couldn't fully enjoy the performance and had to pinch myself to stay awake—it lasted almost three hours with no intermission. Because I missed several days of Chinese lessons, Xiao Zhang decided to teach me before I finally went to bed at 11:30.

On Sunday morning, after a short night and another Chinese breakfast—this time of cold vegetables and meat with peanuts, we started out again to see the Bu Ning Temple, which I thought to be the best of all. Built in the 1750's, it had examples of four national architectural styles and languages: Han Chinese, Tibetan, Mongolian, and Manchurian. There was an impressive twenty-two meter high standing wooden Buddha with one hundred arms that had an eye in each palm. It was exquisite! We returned to the hotel for an early lunch and started home before noon for another nine and a half hour return trip, another long, bumpy ride back over the mountains and through the hairpin turns on a dirt road. The ride back was initially fascinating because we had good weather for a couple of hours and this time we could clearly see the countryside and the poverty of the peasants still living in a previous era. The poverty and filth are incredible. They live in small mud houses, grinding their corn on millstones and own very few animals. The peasants work the land every day of the year but do not own it; it belongs to the state, but each has a vegetable plot next to their house for their own consumption. All water has to be carried to their homes from a well, and due to the scarcity of fuel wood and coal, straw is used for warmth and cooking. The scenes reminded me of a motion picture version of "The Man with the Hoe." Zhang pointed out that none were starving, they all have a roof over their heads, and there is no war, so they are better off now than before. At 2:30, we were suddenly hit by a huge dust storm that clogged the air and visibility went back down to almost zero. We were choking inside the bus, but I felt most sorry for all those peasants who were trapped outside in a sea of dust. Long after sunset, we reached Tianjin where Tom was waiting for us, having just returned from his Shandong visit. I spent several hours over the tub hand washing all our filthy laundry. What a great trip! It was so educational, so shocking, and it affected every nerve in my body, and my heart cried out for the agony and misery of all the people we saw.

—Janene Scovel, family letter written April 9, 1979.

Apart from this trip and a few that Janene made to Beijing, we traveled together on all our other journeys, both great and small. The institute's wai ban sponsored several other excursions for us and the other foreign experts: for example, to two model peasant communes in June or, later in July, to the gigantic Da Gang oil fields on the barren coastal flats south of Tianjin. But like our marvelous venture to Jining, the greatest trips were the ones we initiated and planned, and with these, it was not the journey but the destination that mattered. The destination that our institute's wai ban had chosen for the official July vacation trip for all of the some dozen foreign experts and their families was Xishuangbanna Daizu Zizhizhou. This polysyllabic mouthful of a place-name was undecipherable to our foreign colleagues, but Janene and I instantly recognized it as the Chinese transliteration of the Thai name for the area bordering Northern Thailand, Laos, and Southern China: the Land of Twelve Thousand Rice Fields. As part of the contractual arrangements for all the foreign experts working in China, the individual wai ban, in concert with the Bureau of Foreign Experts in Beijing, arranged and paid for three weeks of summer holidays for all foreign experts, and the usual destination chosen, at least for all the foreigners in the frigid and colorless north, was this polysyllabic place at the southern tip of Yunnan Province bordering Laos and Thailand to the south, a tropical paradise of exotic fruits, colorfully dressed tribal minorities, and warmth and sunshine beyond measure. What more could they ask for? A vacation in Shangri-la.

Regrettably, we did ask for more. Unlike our foreign colleagues, we had other plans, and like our petition to visit Jining over the Spring Festival break, once again the Scovels approached the institute's wai ban with a bizarre and iconoclastic proposal that defied Chinese conventional wisdom. Lao Shen, the head of the office and the man who greeted us so warmly in Beijing at the start of the year, by this time must have undoubtedly been eagerly anticipating our eventual departure at year's end because of all our unconventional requests. As for Xiao Zhang, who was our constant go-between, he must have grown tired of being pulled by both sides in the tug-of-war between the wai ban's "our way or the highway" policy and my "okay, but how about *this* highway" response. Naturally, Janene and I harbored some interest in the officially chosen vacation site in Yunnan, for it would have brought us close to Thailand and a culture and people we loved. Furthermore, piqued by my chat with Thai minorities during our first week in Beijing, I would've enjoyed the opportunity to visit the Southeast Asian tribal minorities in that region, having studied their languages while a doctoral student at the University of Michigan. But it was our very familiarity with that area and those people that prompted us to use our precious time in China more prudently. Buoyed by the inspiring visit to Jining, I saw our summer vacation time as the only opportunity to visit the other places in China I had lived in as a child, sites that no wai ban would have chosen and places that few, if any, foreigners would had any interest in seeing. Once again, there was negotiation back and forth and ultimately when Xiao Zhang eagerly agreed to accompany us as the institute's representative and also when it appeared that the cost of the destinations we had chosen would not exceed the expenses incurred if our family had been shipped all the way to the southern tip of the country with all the other foreign experts, Lao Shen and his colleagues generously acquiesced, and Zhang began the lengthy business of securing permissions and purchasing tickets for our family's most excellent summer vacation.

We spent so many hours poring over plans for our summer break that it ended up as meticulously designed as a military campaign. We had two objectives, professional and personal. The former was in response to an invitation to spend almost two weeks in Qingdao, the former German port city near the eastern tip of the Shandong Peninsula. There we were asked to teach an intensive class of English teachers. Through my earlier contacts with Shandong University and other institutions, the Shandong Association of English Teachers organized this summer seminar and invited us to be their first American instructors. Although this assignment would turn more than half of our vacation time into a veritable busman's holiday, it made our petition to travel independently more palatable to our institute's wai ban because we had an official request to spend the summer in Shandong. I spent part of one summer at the beach in Qingdao as a two-year-old, so technically, it was one of my childhood haunts. However, the major personal attraction we had for spending nearly a fortnight there was that Qingdao had been and still was a popular summer vacation site, and if Deng Xiaoping and other Party fat cats enjoyed some of the languid days of August at this coastal resort, why shouldn't we? With Qingdao as the strategic centerpiece of our summer campaign, we now had to make the tactical decisions about how to use our time before and after the teachers' seminar and where to go on our way there and back. After studying a map and checking up on travel permits, we decided to go south to Shanghai to visit China's most modern metropolis and from there take an overnight ship back north to Qingdao and then, after our teaching assignment was completed, return home to Tianjin by train via Weifang, the site of the Japanese civilian detention center where my family was interned during World War II. On our way to Shanghai, we would stop off at two places that were important to me as a child: Tai Shan, the pilgrimage peak in Shandong, and the village of Huaiyuan in Anhui Province. Strategies and tactics completed, rail tickets and travel permits secured, suitcases packed, and teaching materials prepared, along with Xiao Zhang, our fellow traveler and adopted family member, we boarded a night train just before midnight on July 16 that would carry us south and into well-planned excursions and unexpected escapades.

At a little over five thousand feet, Tai Shan (the Exalted Mountain) is dwarfed by the towering peaks that protect the southern and western borders of China, but it dominates the center of Shandong Province and, because of this, has long dominated Chinese history. Quasi-historical records that document its religious importance go way back into the earliest years of the Shang dynasty over four thousand years ago. Like Mount Sinai in the Old Testament or the mythical Mount Meru of South and Southeast Asian civilizations, Tai Shan is venerated as a holy place of pilgrimage and prayer. For dynasty after dynasty, Chinese emperors would be carried here first to rest and pray at the temple at Tai An, the delightful town at its western base, and then be carried up the five miles of some seven thousand stone steps to worship again at the temple on the top and to view the sunrise the next morning. More faithful and devoted than their rulers, millions of pilgrims, mostly old women, have made the journey on foot often to pray for a grandson so that their heritage would outlive their already frail bodies. For several summers, my parents took us as children to a small covey of cottages owned by the mission halfway up the massif to escape the summer heat and to afford us a chance to play in mountain streams and cavort among the rocky slopes.

I can never think of Tai Shan without musing about another Mount Meru, hundreds of miles due east, far past the Yellow Sea, beyond Korea, and almost across the other side of the island of Honshu to the magnificent volcanic cone of a much higher peak, Fujisan (Mount Fuji). In the mid 1930s, my father climbed this mountain to watch the sunrise from its peak while my parents were temporarily delayed in Japan on their way back to Shandong after their first furlough in the States. Years after our stay in China, Derick scaled Fuji as a college student, and shortly after that, I made it three generations of family climbers when I made the pilgrimage with a Japanese friend. It was during my own slow ascent up the slopes of Fuji Yama that I began to wholly apprehend the association between this most beautiful symbol of Japan and the mountain of my Shandong childhood far to the west.

Though full and marvelous, the history of Japan is only about half that of China, and like most of the cultures bordering the Middle Kingdom, its culture has been heavily Sinicized. Take for instance the very name of this island chain, *nihon* (or *nippon*) in Japanese or *riben* in Chinese. Both use the same written characters (kanji and hanzi respectively), and both refer to the nation of Japan, but they literally mean origin of the sun or, more poetically, the land of the rising sun. But stop to think about that for a moment. If you are Japanese inhabiting a group of islands east of both Korea and China, the Land of the Rising Sun could only refer to California, the nearest landfall east of you. However, if you are Chinese dwelling in a land far to the west of this archipelago, then the ancient Chinese name for Japan fits, for that is the direction from which the sun also rises. Now couple with this the fact that for nearly two millennia before Japan had a written history, pilgrims were making their way up the tallest mountain in Shandong to watch the sunrise, it is logical to conclude that the long-standing Japanese tradition of catching the rising sun on the top of Mount Fuji must have been carried over to the island nation along with many other aspects of early Chinese civilization. Both of my claims would be ever so neatly coupled were it possible to catch a glimpse of Japan, the Land of the Rising Sun, squinting eastward from the top of Tai Shan. However, even without the thick pollution of industrialization, the curvature of the earth prevents one from being able to see the end of the Shandong Peninsula let alone the Yellow Sea and points beyond. In sum, I find Mount Tai a special place both personally and cosmologically. It was the place where my love of mountains was nurtured as a child, and it is a mountainous symbol that ties two great Asian nations together. And on top of it all, it links heaven and earth.

After a restless sleep in our private railroad compartment, we got up at five forty-five in the morning and hurriedly dressed and dragged our suitcases to the carriage door, ready to detrain quickly since Tai An was just a short whistle-stop on the train's southward journey. We were taken to a quiet guesthouse near the large temple where centuries before, emperors worshipped and made sacrifices in preparation for their pilgrimage to the mountain's summit; although unlike them and my grandmother, we would not be carried up in a sedan chair, but climb up on our own two feet. I knew Janene and I, along with Derick and Xiao Zhang, could make the day's ascent with little effort, but we were all concerned about four-year-old Christine, who could barely step up on to the first of the reputed seven thousand steps facing us, but because our pace was leisurely, with a little help from us now and then, all four of us completed the ascent by early afternoon. Destinations may have been important to us, but climbing Tai Shan is really all about the journey. Given its history of veneration, summiting this peak is more like ambling up a vertical museum than trekking up a mountain. Years later, on one of our return trips to China, we were dismayed to see that a road had been built about a third of the way up to a cable car that then sped tourists to the summit ridge. The sacred has now been profaned by modernity.

It was already warm by the time we started up, and at the lower slopes, we trudged past small villages with black goats and pigs napping in the dirt, past teahouses beckoning with refreshment, past incessant rows of arches, past once colorful pavilions, and past giant stone slabs filled with various styles of calligraphy. Given Tai Shan's historical legacy, it seemed as if every nook and cranny had been imaginatively named. We stopped to rest at a small cascade, but it was more than that: it was the Black Dragon's Mouth Waterfall. We were far from being alone. Groups of teenage students, clusters of cadres in white short-sleeved shirts, occasional families, burdened coolies, and faith-filled grandmothers were all part of our grand procession snaking slowly upward, but it was the latter two that gained our attention and sympathy. The young men who bore the burden of carrying produce to the summit seemed twinned to their loads whether they were alone, in pairs, or in quartets. Individual bearers represented the greatest number, and in traditional Chinese manner, they carried their load on a bouncing bamboo pole balanced on their shoulders, the weight distributed evenly between two baskets at either end so that, in effect, they were ambulatory scales. Less frequent were two coolies with a heavier load strapped between them as if the scales were suddenly reversed so that the fulcrum was the load and the two humans were now being weighed between it. Occasionally, however, we saw four men groaning under an enormous burden, such as a fifty-pound barrel of fuel oil. In this case, each end of a huge pole was fixed to a smaller perpendicular pole with a laborer shouldering each end of that and thus double yoked like a quartet of human oxen, barrels of fuel oil, refrigerators, furniture, and other modern necessities were slowly borne to the top just as emperors once were. All of these coolies were young men bronzed by the sun, singlets sweating from the heat and sandaled feet deeply callused by all the climbs, and like their charcoal-carrying counterparts in the foothills of India, their overburdened and enlarged hearts prevented them from enjoying the luxury of longevity. Freed at last from their burdens as they descended from the mountaintop, they sprang lithely down the same steps, chatting and singing, trying to forget that there would be a tomorrow.

Equally memorable among our fellow climbers were the grandmothers, short, stocky women with leathered hands and faces, most of whom I took to be octogenarians. As we passed them, they greeted us with toothless smiles and would exclaim surprise at seeing foreigners on this their sacred path. Although they carried at most a small bag of possessions strapped to their backs, their burdens were heavier by far than any borne by the men. Alas, they were old enough to have been young girls when foot-binding was still in fashion, so unlike all the rest of us, they were tottering up the mountain on the crippled stumps that supposedly made them more beautiful. Like Christine, they had to stretch upward to navigate each step, but unlike her, they had to push their full body weight off a tiny foot whose sole comprised of toes crushed and broken under to make the appendage daintier and more diminutive. Each carried a walking stick for balance and partial propulsion, and without this, the eventual descent down the staircase of steps on their tiny stumps would have been impossible. For millennia, grandmothers like them made this pilgrimage, but because foot-binding was a somewhat recent cruelty, most of their predecessors had only age and infirmity to restrict their journey. Why were they there? A question they likely asked of us as well. At the temple near the summit, there is an altar dedicated to barren women, and thus the reason these aged pilgrims make the climb was to pray to the fertility gods for their infertile daughters or daughters-in-law to bear them a son—not a child, needless to say, but a son. Once they reach this temple, they burn incense, perform the necessary incantations, add coins to the alms bucket, and toss a few stones to the ground or place them in tree branches, and only then can they collapse and rest up for the descent the next morning back to their earthly homes. Like pilgrims worldwide, they suffer the journey in silence to seek a higher cause. God bless these women for they are more than pilgrims; they are martyrs to their culture.

Reaching the Middle Gate to Heaven, we looked around for remnants of the former missionary bungalows, but they, like their foreign owners, had long disappeared. Derick forged on ahead of us, and as we ascended the final steep staircase that led to the South Gate of Heaven and the summit ridge, we could hear him lustily cheering our final effort. We had a late lunch and a brief rest at the large inn built to house many of the visitors, and then we toured the Azure Cloud Temple. Perhaps because of its topographical isolation from the rest of the country, this was the first place where we observed some semblance of public worship. And the beautifully carved deities inside the temple and the astrological animals decorating the eaves outside appeared to have emerged untouched by the Cultural Revolution. The smell of incense, the sound of faint chanting, and the sight of the devoted grannies in prayer effused a sense of peace and inner strength that was absent from the life below us and seemed to be nurtured by the mountain itself.

At sunset, the manager of the inn took us out on a promontory aptly named the Terrace for Viewing Shandong Province. Bundled from the now chilly evening air in thick military coats that were part of the overnight package, we sipped tea, which the manager brought us in the ever-reliable Chinese thermoses, and watched the stars come out above and the lights of Tai An come on far beneath us. "Even Confucius himself was not served hot tea on the summit when he visited so long ago," he remarked. Hungry as we were, it was difficult to eat much. Obviously, the cost of food was high given the altitude to which it had been transported, but unfortunately, its flavor was inversely proportional to its price. We clambered into our squalid bunks, which, like our great coats, had been used unchanged the night before by other guests just as new ones the coming evening would sleep on our bedding. With so many other pilgrims packed around us, we felt like sailors trying to catch a few winks cramped into the forward torpedo room of a submarine. We finally fell into a deep sleep just before being awakened at 4:10 a.m. Like Mount Fuji, one climbs Tai Shan not to reach the summit but to catch the sunrise, and since it was midsummer, we had twenty minutes to bundle back up in our army coats and find a viewing spot outside before the sun emerged. As darkness eased into early dawn, we could see that there were hundreds of visitors surrounding us, many of them having climbed all night and bivouacking for an hour or two before the sunrise. Our companions graded the event a C+, complaining there were a tad too many clouds and that the horizon was invisible, but because we had appreciated the good weather and sensed the presence of the divine, we were more generous with our evaluation. The trip down was relatively rapid and unmemorable except for our quadriceps that remembered the jolting descent for at least three days afterward. We had time to tour the temple and the emperor's summer palace at Tai An in the afternoon and admired the harmonious and peaceful gardens, grounds, and architecture, and the way they mirrored down on earth the heavenly spirit we sensed on the summit. An evening train took us south again out of Shandong to Bengpu, the first city in neighboring Anhui Province. Except for the mountain resorts at the southern end of this province, none of it was open to foreigners at that time, so we had to yet again secure special permission to be allowed into this area of China. "It's a poor farming area," we were told. "Why would you want to go there?"

Our actual destination was Huaiyuan, a village about twelve miles to the west of Bengpu at the fork of the Huai and Guo rivers and my family home for two and a half years. Far smaller than Jining, Huaiyuan had no accommodations even for Chinese visitors, so we were put up in a Bengpu hotel for two nights and taken back and forth by cars to another of my childhood homes. When I was a boy, there was no motor road, or had there been one, it had been obliterated by years of war and flooding, so goods and people were ferried by boat along the Huai River, and occasionally, I remember my father, who loved to hike, even walking the distance. Bengpu was on the rail line and had electricity, motor vehicles, and large buildings, but back in my day, Hauiyuan had none of these and was a quiet, backwater hamlet. In fact, the only vehicle I can ever remember seeing there was a jeep driven by a United Nations Relief and Rehabilitation Association official who managed to negotiate the footpath along the river in the dry season. My father returned to China alone in the autumn of 1945 immediately after VJ Day, and after over a year of visiting and assessing all the missionary medical facilities he could get to, many only on foot, he determined that the Presbyterian mission hospital in little Huaiyuan was in greater need of staffing than his former institution in Jining. A year later, my mother brought all six of us plus my grandmother to join him, and this is why I have two and a half years of mostly happy memories of this unpretentious place.

We left Bengpu in two cars the next morning, heading west on a well-maintained road paralleling the Huai for a few miles before crossing it on a newly built dam. We then continued west past Huaiyuan and the fork of the two rivers, crossing the Guo on another new bridge and circling back into town. All along the way, we saw fields green with wheat, corn, sorghum, and soybeans fed by the luxurious abundance the two rivers provided. Just as we observed in other rural areas, people seemed to replace motors and animals and were the beasts of burden. One man was straining forward almost parallel to the ground, grabbing the handles of his two-wheeled cart and straining at the harness that tethered him to a load of six stone slabs. When we entered the village, my overall impression was similar to the one that struck me in Jining, only this time I had several vivid memories of the old days to contrast with what lay before us. Like Jining, the town had expanded greatly and was filled with multistory stores and apartments, but once you got into the center, the streets narrowed down, the buildings diminished in size, and stone walls and masonry predominated, and except for the telephone poles and electric wires overhead, you were suddenly back in the 1940s. Our car barely squeezed through an alley that I remember as the main street of the village. Unlike the modern roads that were paved with macadam or concrete, this was made up of broad, rectangular slabs of stone in the middle flanked by cobblestones that served as sidewalks, but the entire thoroughfare was not more than fifteen feet wide. Passing the now walled-up old gate to the hospital, our cars edged through a newer but still narrow gate into the compound of what used to be Hope Hospital. We were told that Hope had left Huaiyuan some twenty years earlier and had been moved to Bengpu so none of the original or current medical staff were there. The facilities were first transformed into a school of water conservation but were now a school for electricians, and it was the principal of this institution that met us and showed us all around the old missionary compound. We began with the obligatory greeting, briefing, and tea. However, since it was summer, the bevy of girls waiting on us brought in ten watermelons equally divided between yellow and red to go with our tea. By the time we were ready to begin our tour, the jungle telegraph had spread the word that aliens had landed, so like our tour of Jining several months earlier, we were constantly the center of crowds and attention. There seemed to be a disproportionate number of poorly dressed children and babies milling around among the masses, and from their runny noses and open skin sores, you could immediately see that this rural area was much poorer than our home city of Tianjin.

It is typical that children inhabit a world that is larger than life, and this is partly because of their diminutive stature but perhaps even more because of their creative minds that tend to exaggerate events and magnify every object. Thus I remember our two-story stone house in Huaiyuan as a palatial building with large, arched windows and which contained cavernous rooms with high ceilings and was surrounded by an expansive patio overlooking a lawn the size of a football field. But when confronting our former home with the eyes of that same child now thirty years older, I was completely confused for I honestly believed we had been taken to the wrong compound. For some inexplicable reason, the front yard had shrunk, the patio cut in two, and the mansion was now a humble two-story building dwarfed by surrounding trees. In fact, it was hard to catch any views of our former compound because of the forest of onlookers that occupied the grounds and surrounded our family. But no, this was indeed my childhood home. We walked around to the backyard, and there was the charming moon gate, and up the steps further back the former servants' quarters. And there was the old well where the cook would lower perishable food in a screened box to keep it cool on hot summer days such as this one. But the ultimate confirmation that I was home again came when Xiao Zhang, whom I had filled with stories of my childhood on the train ride southward, shot his finger at an outline in the ground and exclaimed, "There it is! Remember?" Sure enough, once we cleared the spectators away, there were the remnants of a shallow, figure-eight-shaped pool where I used to play with toy boats all summer long and the details of which I had described so carefully to Zhang that, for a moment, he appeared to have forgotten that it was I, not him, who grew up in this place and enjoyed this spot as a watery summer playground. We went inside where we had a bit more privacy, but even without people milling around and crowding out a sense of perspective, the rooms looked smaller than the home of my childhood. The house now served as an apartment for a half dozen families, and not wanting to disturb their privacy and seeing how run-down the place had become, we did not linger long. Like our home in Jining, I was surprised to find it still standing given that older buildings in China are rapidly replaced by the ubiquitous apartment buildings that house urban dwellers.

Through the moon gate stood my grandmother's small house and next to it the former chapel, its distinctive latticework sliding panels still visible. A faculty member now lives in the house, and the chapel is a nursery. In the back of this compound and through yet another moon gate was at one time a poet's garden with a duckweed-filled pond and a small *tingzi* (pavilion) that had been a favorite refuge for both my grandmother and her daughter-in-law. These had long disappeared, and the whole plot was overgrown with bushes and weeds. It was here that a young man surnamed Chen was pulled from the crowd and introduced to us as the grandson of my grandmother's former cook. He seemed genuinely touched to meet us, and his eyes teared up when we said an early good-bye, for he had to attend a family funeral that evening. I had no recollection whatsoever of his family but had vivid ones of our cook's son for Aizu and I spent many hours playing and sometimes fighting together. Chen's memory of me was as vague as mine about him, but we both appreciated the opportunity for grandson to reunite with grandson. I had dearly hoped that we would meet Aizu here in Huaiyuan so we could recapture a few of our childhood days together over a beer and I could once again apologize for nearly strangling him in a fury over some silly incident he had precipitated of which I have absolutely no recall. His father, Hu Shifu (master chef Hu) had most likely died years earlier, but despite my pressing our hosts for information about his son, nothing turned up, and I was left with only speculations about what happened to him. No news at all is as about as disquieting as the very worst.

Except for the trip back to Bengpu to spend the night in a hotel, we spent all of two days in Huaiyuan. We visited Milk White Springs, a delightful retreat built into the slopes of West Mountain and with its whitewashed walls and multileveled, tiled terraces, it was far more attractive than from what I remember as a boy. The natural spring is famed for enhancing the flavor of tea, so naturally we were favored with a local cup at the highest terrace, which kept us distant from the swarms of mostly young children who had accompanied us from the village. I'm no epicurean, so tea is tea to me, and whenever asked to savor a different kind of beverage, I'm reminded of one of Lin Yutang's charming Chinese fables. It seems a country bumpkin (perhaps from Shandong) was invited to visit the big city by his sophisticated uncle (maybe a place like Suzhou), and right away, the uncle insisted that his nephew try a cup of the local tea that was renowned beyond measure for its exquisite bouquet. Excitedly, he poured the steaming brew into a porcelain cup and asked his rural relative to take a sip. This his nephew did noisily, the Chinese habit of letting your host know you appreciate his hospitality. "Well?" asked the uncle, almost unable to contain his curiosity. "What did you like best: the smoothness of the liquid, the delicate color, the piquant flavor?" "Hmm," replied the nephew, "there are actually two things I liked." "Yes, yes!" the uncle rejoined, urging him on. "Well," answered the country boy, "it was hot, and it was wet!"

West Mountain was a simple stroll up from Milk White Springs, but East Mountain across the river demanded a half day climb and picnic lunch on top, just as we did in our family getaways in the late forties. Because the slopes had been stripped of trees after centuries of deforestation, we had clear views of the village, the surrounding farmlands, and the junction of the two rivers. As we reached the summit and its ramshackle temple, a robed and elderly man, who may have been a Taoist priest, stepped out of time to greet us, his arms held at chest length in front of him, open right hand clasping his left fist in traditional greeting. Lao Li claimed to have remembered our family treks to East Mountain more than three decades earlier and referred to Janene as *tai tai* (madam), the prerevolutionary title of respect for married women. Like Tai Shan, it was if mountain summits were tiny, anachronistic ecosystems that had escaped most of the revolutionary changes that had transformed the culture down below and had preserved parts of the past that were more familiar to me than the society in which we were immersed that year. That evening, the Party's general secretary of the Huaiyuan District graciously hosted a farewell dinner for us, a tradition of hospitality that remained immutable throughout the many historical changes that had swept that landscape. I had hoped we could take a riverboat for our final farewell journey back to Bengpu to replicate the Scovel family's departure from Huaiyuan in August 1948. I can remember the boat pulling away from the dock crowded with hospital staff and friends whom we would never see again as we left for Bengpu and a perilous flight in a C-47 south to Canton, where my father had been reassigned to practice and teach medicine. As the boat left the shore, a group of Christian friends sang in Chinese, "God be with you till we meet again." However, the new road and dam replaced the river transportation, and thus we had a vehicular, unromantic, and irreligious departure. I did look back at the lights of that once dark town as they slipped behind the low hills overcome with a sense of contentment, satisfied that I had this once-in-a-lifetime chance to return to a place I had loved and knowing I would never need to return.

We were all relieved to leave Bengpu for Shanghai the next morning for it was a dismal place in the middle of nowhere and had none of the charm of Huaiyuan or any of the cachet of our next destination. The steamy weather seemed to protract the long day's journey southward. Now well into the Yangtze River watershed, we passed mile after kilometer of farmlands with wheat fields now giving way to rice and the distinctive hexagonal hats with their pointed tops of Shandong farmers replaced by the circular, domed hats worn by peasants in the South. We crossed the Yangtze on the celebrated Nanjing Bridge that was lauded as a monument to China's expertise in engineering and construction. Just as the Mississippi is America's greatest waterway and divides the nation in two, the Yangtze has served as China's major irrigation system and transportation artery for millennia. But more than this, it also demarcates north from south, lands that differ far more significantly in language, food, and culture than America's East and West or Union and Confederate.

Shanghai surprised us even though we anticipated the best. I remember landing there in 1946 after a trans-Pacific voyage in a troopship when my mother brought our family back to China after the war to reunite with my father, who had already returned a year before. It was big, bustling, exciting, filled with amenities, and undeniably, unquestionably, and indubitably foreign. Unlike Beijing, Nanjing, or Xian, all former capitals dripping with Chinese history, until the European imperialists came along and transformed what had been a sleepy fishing hamlet, Shanghai had no fame, fortune, or foreigners. To me, Shanghai is as much China as Disneyland is America, but who would not want to visit either place? Because I had offered to give some lectures at their institution, we were met by representatives of the Shanghai Teachers University, our host during our three-day stay. As we were driven to their guesthouse, we ogled the streets, buildings, and pedestrians with amazement. Our room was air-conditioned, the bedding spotless, the coffee hot, and the meals tasty. Imagine that! Storefronts were actually discernable and well decorated, the roads clean, the bicycle traffic orderly, the crowds well dressed, and here and there were strips of grass—who would've guessed a Chinese city going green! During our drive from the station, Derick abruptly shouted for our attention, pointing to a woman wearing, of all things, a skirt, and upon closer scrutiny, we noticed many of the women passing by with their hair cut short, and some even had perms. Nanjing Road wasn't Fifth Avenue nor Shanghai Hong Kong, but we had the strong impression that we were no longer foreigners and instead had been teleported into a foreign land.

In between my lectures, we were given tours of museums, a shipyard, the Yu Gardens, and taken to a movie and an evening walk along the Bund, the waterfront skirting the old British quarters where the city's most prominent buildings stood as monumental dowagers to the city's seedy and colonial past. Our hosts treated us to some of the local delicacies: a cold lunch, a Shanghai summer specialty (not so good): *mazi qiu* (sesame seed balls / doughnuts) purchased from a street vendor. Hmm, yummy! My two older brothers attended and graduated from Shanghai American School, where many missionary kids were boarded and educated, and I was able to locate the old campus in the former French quarter. Now it housed offices for the navy, and because of the high wall surrounding the place, I could only catch sight of the roofs. With our driver's permission, I climbed on top of our car and, standing on its roof, snapped a few pictures for a better view of their old school, and by the time I had clambered down, the guards at the nearby gate were there to question me. Throughout our stay, we were frequently reminded not to take pictures of certain strategic sites: bridges, airports, military bases, and now added to that list, former schools for the children of missionaries.

Our hosts from the Teachers Training University assured them that I was an innocent and clueless American teacher incapable of even the most rudimentary form of espionage, and the episode ended quickly with smiles and handshakes. After my final lecture on our third day, we packed up and boarded the Rong Shin (New Glory), a small, ocean-going vessel, at 4:00 p.m. and, leaving the busy Huang Pu River traffic, entered the huge mouth of the Yangtze River, turning east then due north for an overnight voyage to Qingdao, where we would continue our busman's holiday at the Shandong Teachers Association Summer Seminar.

When planning our trip back in Tianjin after we settled on a southern loop through Tai Shan and Huaiyuan to Shanghai, we realized that there was an opportunity to return north by ship to Qingdao rather than simply reversing the long train trip southward already traversed to reach Shanghai. Remember that all tickets were one-way, so there were no specially reduced round-trip train fares, and attracted by the romance of a night at sea, we convinced our institute's wai ban to allow us to take a road less traveled by and complete this part of our return leg by ship. This seemed to be an expedient decision for it ended up cheaper and faster than the circuitous train route all the way north back up to Jinan and then due east to almost the tip of the Shandong Peninsula. In effect, the railroad had to travel two legs of a triangle whereas the ship negotiated only the hypotenuse: it was two if by land but only one if by sea. In retrospect, however, this choice did not turn out to be romantic at all.

Our vessel was only half aptly named for though it was new, only a year old, with peeling paint, ripped up floor mats, and a dirty cabin, it was far from glorious. In the early evening, as the ship emerged from the shelter of land, it began to hit rather heavy seas, and the kids enjoyed dodging the waves breaking over our bow. All the meals were served in a small dining room downstairs, and with the deference continually paid us as foreign guests, we were given the first sitting but tried to eat quickly when we saw the long queue of fellow passengers stretching from our table and circling the deck upstairs. We paid extra for the cabin and the privacy we assumed it would afford, but with no other entertainment for our fellow passengers down below, they came up on deck to stare at us in our well-lit room through the surrounding portholes with groups around each window as if they were individual TV sets. We managed to curtail their view with paper and Scotch Tape, but we were unable to curtain off the constantly blaring loudspeaker that disgorged free and scratchy music from the moment we embarked. About as merciless as the pollution, the air in China was also filled with amplified sound from the cop at the kiosk beneath our hotel window to the martial music and strident announcements reverberating on and off throughout the day at our institute. In fields or factories, on trains or streets, silence is to be avoided at all costs and news broadcasts, martial music, midmorning calisthenics, or simply the squeal of feedback from a nearby microphone deafen the ear and deaden the soul. Stuffing the loudspeaker with tissue paper dampened the sound only by a decibel or two, so with a Swiss Army jackknife, I went for the kill and managed to unscrew the offending speaker from our cabin wall and temporarily disarm it so we could catch some sleep. Though the food did not improve at breakfast, the morning seas were calmer, and all of us gathered at the bow as we approached Qingdao. The footprint of German occupation was clearly visible from a distance: red, tiled roofs along the shore, unobscured by concrete apartment houses or hotels, and there on a hill behind these was a twin-towered cathedral similar to the one we drove past on our way to Shandong University. If history is little more than geography in motion, it was clear how the sea-going imperialists of the nineteenth century so easily captured the port cities of China, coming up from the south behind the Great Wall that was built to exclude the northern barbarians and attacking the exposed underbelly of Middle Kingdom. But on this morning, we came in peace as invited guests on a Chinese vessel. We looked forward to a fun-filled ten days but didn't realize how funny this time would be.

Shanghai surprised us with delights far above any expectation. Qingdao disappointed in exactly reverse fashion. We anticipated a restful balance between morning seminars with the English teachers at the summer institute to which we had been invited and relaxing afternoons and evenings, visiting friends, frolicking in clean ocean waters, and enjoying some good food and beer, relics of the German occupation. But the quaint Bavarian architecture we viewed from afar as our ship approached was in reality a superficial impression, and both the city and its political atmosphere proved unappetizing. To begin with, Qingdao was already terribly overcrowded with a downtown population of a million and a half and with four million in the surrounding district. A visit to the former cathedral was symbolic. Of course, it was an empty tomb of a once proud edifice, the crosses knocked off its twin towers, and only a cross carved in the stone lintel above its dusty door marked its Christian heritage. Worst of all, the city seemed to effuse a Cultural Revolution mentality as if it were years behind Tianjin and a full decade behind Shanghai in progress. We were constantly fighting red tape in securing permission to visit friends or public places, and our hotel seemed to consider us more under house arrest than as paying guests attempting to enjoy a seaside holiday.

One of the additional attractions of spending the largest chunk of our summer holiday in Qingdao was that it was the home of Xu Laoshi, our son's piano instructor. Because he was doing such a fine job as Derick's master teacher and because he was the first Christian with whom we had close contact, he had become a close friend, and when we learned he would spend August in Qingdao with his parents and would be reunited with his wife there after a year of separation, we looked forward to meeting his family and to cultivating our friendship. Though not involved directly with the Shandong Teachers Association, which was our official host, Xu and his father greeted us at the dock and accompanied us to our accommodations for the next fortnight. Our experience at the hotel was an omen of what we would face our entire stay. Outwardly attractive, towering eleven stories, painted in soft pastels, and with two hundred rooms overlooking a broad expanse of beach, it was too new to house any bugs, but as we would find out shortly, it was so new that not all the bugs had been worked out. The town's reactionary mentality was immediately apparent as soon as we entered the hotel gates. If you were not a registered guest, you needed a permission slip to enter the hotel grounds. Throughout our stay, time and again, I had to go to the front gate and sign friends in to allow them to meet us inside or, conversely, to sign them out so they could exit the gate for home. One night, I had to get out of bed, dress, and go down to the front gate to meet a friend who had visited us earlier in the evening. He had brought us a gift in a cardboard box but inadvertently walked off with the cover of the box. Realizing his mistake, he returned to the hotel to leave the cover for us, but this was no trivial matter. He had been "arrested" by the gateman and not allowed to return home until I came out, picked up the cardboard box top, and signed a permission slip for him to leave the hotel grounds and return home.

When we checked in, we found out that we were the very first guests, so perhaps to fill at least 1 percent of the two hundred rooms, the management tried to place us in two rooms since there were four of us. Because we were footing the bill as technically this was our vacation, we finally convinced them to crowd an extra bed into a single room, and shortly after, we were unpacking on the eighth floor, overlooking the beach and bay below from what appeared to be the tallest building in that huge city. Signs of just-completed construction were everywhere: there was an internal telephone system but no line to the outside, the furniture and doorframes had just been freshly varnished, the smell of damp cement and paint perfumed the hallways, and not all the windows had glass or screens. With the warm and moist ocean climate of August, the freshly varnished and unseasoned wood had swollen doors and drawers tightly, so we had to wrestle to get our clothes into the dresser and grapple to open windows and doors. Xiao Zhang and one of the fu wu ren on our floor came in to help us with some of the stickier furniture, and while all six of us were crowded inside, struggling with the gummy drawers, the afternoon ocean breeze suddenly gusted through the open windows and, catching the open door to the hallway, slammed it shut with a terrifying bang. The fu wu ren grabbed the doorknob and pulled with no success. Zhang grabbed the doorknob and pulled without success. I grabbed the doorknob, and the fu wu ren and Zhang grabbed me, and all three of us strained at the wretched door until I feared the knob would come flying off and the three of us would be sent sprawling backward into Janene and the kids, now doubled over in laughter. The fresh varnish, the unseasoned wood of the door and its frame, and the moist sea air had sealed us forever into our beachfront sarcophagus. Zhang grabbed our phone and called down to the front desk for reinforcements. Soon we heard the padding of footsteps down the hall and shouts from the free world outside our door not to worry, that help had arrived. We stepped away from the unruly door, and with a "Yo, heave, ho," our two rescuers on the outside hurled their shoulders into the offending barrier and, bursting it open, came hurtling into our now very overcrowded room. After the laughter subsided, the hotel staff were quick to reassure us that there would be no more problems in the future. "By the time winter comes, the weather is cooler and drier, and the wood will have seasoned. Then you'll have no trouble opening and closing the door!" By now, fully convinced that we would not stay even an hour more than our allotted ten days, we spent the rest of our residence wedging the door open slightly with a slipper even at night so we wouldn't get trapped again.

The next trial was the elevator. We had no concern over its safety for it was made in Shanghai and was obviously a cut above even the ones manufactured in our native Tianjin, so it ostensibly was good to the last drop. It was fully automated, but as yet another illustration of overemployment, it always had an operator day and night. Like the preautomated days of yore, this one never stopped flush with whatever floor it opened on, so the elevator floor was always an inch or two too high or too low; however, unlike the olden days when an operator could make up the difference between the gap by manipulating a handle inside, there was always a gap when the doors opened, tripping the naïve and unwary passengers who let forth a variety of interjections as they jerked, stumbled, and lurched in and out. Occasionally, the doors jammed and had to be pried open manually from the outside, possibly by the same two hotel staff that had rescued us from our room. On further thought, using a full-time operator wasn't overemployment at all; it was an absolute necessity! But funniest of all was the way you called for the elevator.

The fu wu ren seemed even more lethargic than the staff back at the Tianjin Hotel, although to be fair, since they had never served any guests, they were probably more ignorant than indolent. Like all hotels in China, each floor had at least one worker in the hall 24-7, making sure that guests had instant service and also that none of them went anywhere without a following pair of eyes, but our fu wu ren failed in both these duties. Most of the time, the person for our floor was slumped semiconsciously in one of the overstuffed chairs in the hall and had to be roused whatever the time of day. When awakened, he was a cheery soul and never failed to call us comrades in English even when there was only one of us. Requesting his services was necessary when we finally figured out how the call buttons worked for the elevator. At first we were mystified why our lift never arrived even after we had pressed the button several times, never noticing that the hotel staff snoozing nearby was actually a vital cog in this gerrymandered system of telecommunication. Tired of the delay and needing the exercise anyway, we initially took the eight flights of stairs down to the lobby, but strangely, we never experienced any trouble whenever we returned up to our room. Like any other establishment anywhere else in China, Asia, or Mother Earth, you would push a small button next to the elevator door for a lift. But what transpired next made the hotel in Qingdao unique among all establishments anywhere else in the universe. It took us one or two trips to decipher the system, and believe it or not, here's how it went. The elevator buttons remained unconnected to anything else. Remember, this hotel was new, very new! The fu wu ren for your floor would see you pressing the button, and then he would pick up the hall phone and call downstairs to the lobby, and the staff down there would shout out to the elevator operator to go upstairs to the eighth floor to pick up some guests. After a few minutes, the elevator would arrive and take us downstairs. Sometimes when trying to return to our room, it seemed as if the lift had gotten lost on one of the upper floors, and tired of waiting in the lobby, we would all trudge upstairs back to our room. This was a necessity on Saturday nights, when the elevator operator somehow was able to get her friends and family members past the otherwise impervious front gate to see the luxurious interior of Qingdao's newest building and especially to enjoy the rides up to the top floor. The elevator was so packed with these excited sightseers that we reluctantly resorted to the stairs. Our life in this hotel, like the lives of our fellow Chinese, definitely had its ups and downs.

We quickly adjusted to our half-holiday routine. Every morning, while the kids were having fun with some Chinese friends at the beach, strolling out to the end of the jetty that protruded into the bay, or visiting the unhappy sea creatures trapped in the dilapidated aquarium, Janene and I would go to the Oceanography Institute, which hosted the summer seminar, to give lectures and consult with teachers. It may seem odd that a scientific institution would be responsible for a conference on English teaching, but every single establishment of higher education in China had an English Department, and even back then, English language skills were considered crucial to attaining the Four Modernizations. After the political turmoil of the preceding decade, the fifty or so English teachers who were able to attend from various places throughout the province were delighted at this opportunity to grow professionally, and Sam Ginsbourg (the Russian Jin) and his colleagues at Shandong University did a commendable job organizing the schedule and encouraging us to interact with the participants as much as possible. Besides the attraction of working with native speakers of English and true foreign experts in pedagogy and linguistics, the participants were happy to indulge in the summer pleasures that Qingdao afforded, and my guess is that for most of them, this was their first visit to this resort city.

We had most afternoons and evenings free, and besides spending time with the kids at the beach ourselves and going on various tours, we were able to have meals with friends at our hotel or in their homes once we had jumped through all the bureaucratic hoops to secure permission for such gatherings. Qingdao is one of China's largest naval stations and is also a summer resort for the Party bigwigs from Beijing, and this only made obtaining permissions for visits and travel more difficult for us. Early one morning, Janene was running north along the beach and was stopped by a couple of tough guys who made it clear that she could no longer proceed. We walked back later that day to the same point on the road and noticed a sign in Chinese, Japanese, and English that read, "Out of bounds for foreigners without special permits." Beyond, almost out of eyesight, we could see neat bungalows and a clean, almost deserted beach that I found out later belonged to the Party and thus was off limits to ordinary Chinese and foreigners. I discovered later that missionaries used to rent some of these bungalows, so the Scovel family most probably stayed there one summer long ago, and that was the same beach where I played when I was a two-year-old toddler. Like the former British Club in Tianjin that was the exclusive domain of the Party, here too we had the ruling elite appropriate the best real estate for themselves, and these Orwellian reframings of history prompted me to wonder how much China had really changed since Liberation.

Among all the tours we were taken on in China, surely the dullest was a trip arranged for us to see a factory that manufactured furniture. It was almost impossible for us to refuse the hospitality that various wai ban offered us, partly in polite deference to our Chinese hosts, whether they were back home in Tianjin or here in another city, but largely because we knew that they had booked and paid for these excursions although in this case, not being carpenters or cabinet makers, we saw little entertainment in this outing. About halfway through the tour, as the manager was walking us from room to room, he casually mentioned that his factory had made all the furniture for our hotel, even the doors and doorframes. We finally reached the last room and were asked if we had any final questions. "Yes," I responded intemperately, "could we see the room where you jam all the drawers and doors?" With complete seriousness he replied, "No, we don't have such a room. Do they have those in American factories?" In contrast, among all the tours we were taken on in China, surely one of the most impressive was an afternoon drive out of town to a carpet factory that same week. Unlike most briefings, the manager avoided any political mumbo jumbo when introducing his work unit to us, and we learned later that most of their orders came from California, England, and Japan. Like the Tianjin carpet factory we toured in January, all of their products were 100 percent wool, handwoven by mostly young women who had the dexterity, stamina, and perseverance to endure such intensely tedious work. The finished products in the display room were absolutely incredible, an impressive testimony to the artistic creativity and skill of China's culture and people. One huge landscape scene looked exactly like a color photograph, and until you viewed it up close, the mountain stream looked realistic enough to flow right off the wall and onto the floor. Nothing produced in America could begin to compare with this handmade masterpiece.

Long before ever arriving in Qingdao, we had hoped to visit the brewery and see how they made the most famous beer in China, a moist legacy of German culture. As another illustration of the trials we encountered securing approval when we expressed a desire to see or do anything outside of our hotel or the teachers' seminar, we were continually put off by a series of lame excuses. One day toward the end of our stay, after we made yet another request, we were told that we would be able to see the local wine and spirits factory but not the renowned brewery. The excuse this time was lamer than usual. We were told that the day before, a group of Australian tourists (reputedly well-known for their excessive thirst for malt beverages) had gotten drunk on the free drinks provided them and had damaged the assembly line. Although we had been in China long enough to have learned to willingly suspend our disbelief, we didn't buy this explanation for a second although we did admire the discipline of the local cadre who related this fairy story to us without coming close to cracking a smile or suppressing a giggle. Off the four of us went on a tour of the wine and spirits factory, which was slightly more interesting than the furniture manufacturing plant, especially when we came to the end where the assembly line of glass bottles were fed into a machine that capped them. Just before or at the exact moment we stepped into the room, there was some sort of malfunction in the capping mechanism, and instead of delicately placing and pinching a metal cap on each bottle, the antirevolutionary apparatus started plunging into the tops of the bottles, snapping off their necks and scattering shards of glass and splattering sweet red wine all over the floor. As we were immediately urged to step into the gift shop, the obligatory conclusion to any institutional visit in China, I turned to Janene and suggested that now we knew what the hapless Australians were blamed for.

Recall that Derick's piano teacher and our close friend, Xu Laoshi, was also in Qingdao on a rare visit to his wife and his own family, and it was through him that we learned that there would be a music concert in the city auditorium and that he had arranged for us to attend. More than that, he would be performing himself, and even more than that, he had told the authorities that the Scovel family would be willing to participate, an American version of the Von Trapp family, immortalized in *The Sound of Music.* We immediately demurred, suggesting that Derick might be willing to play a piece as Xu's proud pupil, but Derick's parents were in no way, shape, or form going to participate. Regrettably, it seems that that train had already left the station and that Xu's contacts who ran the summer music concert had already been quick to advertise the news that for the very first time, they had been able to book an American family to perform at their concert hall. Janene was always the family musician, having grown up playing the violin and having performed many times both in the States and Thailand. Conversely, though I can sing on pitch and plunk out a tune or two on the piano, by no stretch of the imagination would anyone ever choose me to perform onstage. Probably because she had such excellent musical standards, Janene was more reluctant than I to being dragooned into performing, whereas I with no artistic sensibilities whatsoever saw it as a nothing-to-lose opportunity. "After all," I pointed out to her, "we'll be leaving in a day or two and will never see these people again." Adamantly adhering to her aesthetic values, Janene refused to play the violin unless I was onstage with her, so we effected a compromise and agreed to be on the program along with Xu and Derick. Fortunately, we had brought one of our Rodgers and Hammerstein songbooks with us, and it had piano accompaniments so primitively arranged that even I could finger peck my way through them. Janene borrowed a violin, and we practiced together a few times, and in keeping with *The Sound of Music* theme, we chose "Eidelweiss" and then "America the Beautiful" as a patriotic number for our command performance. The concert actually turned out to be a variety show and was held in the Youth Palace, a dusty, old auditorium that held about eight hundred people, maybe more since all the seats were taken and people stood crowded together on the sides and at the back. It was a long program involving well-costumed dancers, soloists playing traditional instruments, magic acts, singers, acrobats twirling balls and umbrellas, and so on. Although there was no intermission, there were so many interruptions to fix the screeching amplification system that it was almost ten o'clock when Xu and his American friends appeared. Xu and Derick both played some spirited pieces on the piano, and the overheated audience was warm with their applause. Despite the fact Janene and I insisted on going first on the program, our temporary impresario had arranged to save us for last, so with the prestige of Rodgers and Hammerstein and the United States of America resting on our nervous fingertips, we got up and played "Eidelweiss" and "America" more beautifully than any American musicians had ever done before on Chinese soil—well, at least on that summer's night in Qingdao. Proving that they possessed more enthusiasm than musical taste, the house accorded us several rounds of applause, assuming we had an encore, but we had already overstayed our welcome and hurried offstage, never to return again.

Our last day was anticlimactic and only accelerated our desire to leave. We were tired of the bland and greasy food at the hotel that grew less palatable after we had tasted the magnificent home-cooked meals by Xu's family or other friends. We had already become weary of the games with the elevator and sticky drawers, and the fu wu ren seemed to have grown even more disinterested in serving the people with each passing day. In addition, someone misappropriated my bathing suit (I'll avoid saying *stole* since to steal from a foreigner was a political crime). The dark clouds billowing in from the sea after breakfast bore with them a torrential rain that cleared the air but soiled the beach. All the gullies, streams, and drainpipes from the city appeared to lead to the sea, so when we took the kids down to the beach in the afternoon for a final swim after the weather had cleared, the sand and water were littered with plastic bags, watermelon rinds, bai cai, and other unattractive refuse that made us wonder how clean the water had really been all those previous days of swimming and crab hunting. In the afternoon, the teachers' seminar closed with a tea party and farewell speeches, and like every other similar occasion we attended in China, we were showered with kind words and generous gifts. The genuine expressions of gratitude and appreciation from the participants far outweighed the efforts we had extended.

The next morning, as we were checking out, the hotel staff accused us of stealing one of their red plastic combs. Two had been allocated to our room, and now there was only one. I tried to negotiate a prisoner exchange (an unequal one in my eyes, I might add): my red bathing suit for their red comb. Negotiations went nowhere as they knew we had a train to catch, so we dug through our suitcase and found their precious merchandise, and we left for the station with an even worse opinion of the establishment. Had I the time, I would've sat the hotel staff down for the English lesson we used back in Tianjin on rebuffing bad behavior. Recall this was the lesson in the Chinese textbook we had been given that taught the fu wu ren English phrases to use with unruly foreigners, but in my imaginary lesson to the Qingdao staff, the tables were turned, and I would be doing the rebuffing. "Such behavior is not tolerated in China! You are not so friendly! You must be responsible for what you have done!" And the clincher, "Your behavior will harm the friendly relations between our two peoples!" Our annoyance was mitigated by the warm send off at the railroad station where Xu's family and members of the summer seminar bade us a kind farewell. As we headed westward toward Weifang, our last stop before returning home to Tianjin, my thoughts, in concert, turned away from Qingdao and the present moment and back to the farthest reaches of my past, to my very first memory of life.

By the time I was born, the Japanese Imperial Army already controlled the Shandong Peninsula, and though this curtailed my parents' medical work with the Chinese in some ways, it only indirectly affected our family life since we were United States citizens. All this changed abruptly on Monday, December 8, 1941; it was still Sunday morning, a day earlier back in the States. An officer and two soldiers came to our home, and we were told we were now enemy combatants and would be placed under house arrest. A year and a half later, after the Japanese had set up a detainment center in Weifang to house the hundreds of Allied civilians who were living in Northern China, on March 19, 1943, my parents and their five children were packed on a train and shipped to Weifang to be imprisoned along with approximately two thousand other internees. I have no memories of this wretched moment, but one of my older brothers can recall the overwhelming grief of leaving their home forever, sobbing as he hugged our dog good-bye. My mother remembered embracing our beloved amah, Zhang Dasao, who tried to come with us but was torn from my mother's arms by a soldier. My mother looked back one last time to see Zhang Dasao sitting in the middle of the road, her hands clasping her face as she rocked back and forth, wailing in abject grief. My parents told me how they walked from their house to the train station, carrying suitcases with only their most necessary possessions for the ordeal ahead. The Japanese had lined the streets with the local inhabitants so that the Chinese could watch this sorry parade of former white imperialists march off in ignominy and witness the birth of a new Asia, freed from the darkness of Euro-American colonialism to bask in the light of a rising sun.

I was already four at the time but have no vestigial recollections of Jining or of that sad departure; however, I do have several memories of the Weifang internment camp, and if we all nurture a hunger for childhood memories, fittingly, my earliest childhood memories are of hunger. Three scenes remain with me like still-life portraits hanging in permanent display in the museum of my mind. The very first is inside one of the two kitchens that the prisoners used to prepare and cook their daily meals in. My mother has taken her turn in the kitchen and is stirring a giant pot of bai cai, gristle, and bread, a stew that was served as a weekly staple. The steam from this mixture rises up and is caught by a beam of sunlight that comes from an opening in the roof above. I can remember nothing else—what my mother was wearing, anyone else being present, the smell of the brew bubbling in the caldron—just my mother, the steam, and the ray of sun shining above this otherwise drab scene. The second memory is more dramatic. A Japanese guard, who may have longed for his own four-year-old son back home, befriends me and, disobeying orders, takes me outside the barbwire fence to his quarters where he lets me play with his bolt-action rifle and, before returning me to camp, gives me an apple, a rare treat under those conditions. I can remember the crowd of prisoners at the gate, waiting to greet me, my parents in the middle, clearly distraught that I had gone missing and both angry and relieved, reaching out anxiously to embrace me. I remember seeing all those waiting faces and fixating on only one thought: they all want my precious apple! The third scene was the same day, but now it is evening. We have eaten supper, and now back in the small two-room cabin that is our prison home, my father takes out his pocketknife and miraculously divides my apple into seven equal pieces so that each member of us gets a treat. I am so amazed that I forget my earlier selfishness and eat my share in quiet family communion.

Enduring as these pictures are in my mind, they are the only memories I have of our incarceration.

As an adult, I have often talked about our China experiences with my brothers and sisters, especially after Janene and I returned to the States, and I became aware of two ways in which my age and my experiences as a child intertwined and shaped my unique memories of China when compared to my siblings'. Unlike my older sister and especially my two older brothers who were twelve and fourteen, at four years of age, I was far too young to process or remember the horrors of war and encampment. They were cognitively and socially mature enough to ponder questions that were far beyond my little mind and to remember incidents I too may have witnessed but was not old enough to imprint. Conversely, unlike my two-year-old sister and my yet unborn littlest sister, I was old enough to harbor a few memories of China during that era and, of course, a multitude of them after my parents returned to work in Huaiyuan and later in Canton. One by one, my older siblings went off to the States, leaving me as the oldest child and the one with memories bridging both the Japanese occupation and the civil war and the subsequent Communist liberation. In a few minutes, our train would arrive in Weifang, and now I would be the first prisoner to return to the site of that camp, but to our surprise, the goal of our visit was a surprise to everyone there.

An attractive medium-sized city in the middle of the Shandong Peninsula, Weifang sits halfway by rail between Qingdao on the coast and Jinan, the large provincial capital in the west, which we had already visited. It is known for handicrafts, especially paper cuts, kites, and other gift items, but when we arranged for permission for this, our final summer vacation stop, the authorities were surprised that we expressed little interest in these local products but instead wanted to visit the No. 2 Middle School, not even the No. 1 but the No. 2. Isolated from the Yellow River, the sea, and the major north-south trunk line, Weifang is halfway to nowhere and retained a quaint, undeveloped charm. It had few high-rises, its streets were dusty and narrow, and almost next to our guesthouse was a traditional garden with a pond, koi, and a pagoda. After dinner, we were taken to a theater for a three-hour performance of Chinese opera, and in contrast to our air-conditioned minivan, the crowded auditorium seemed like a steam bath that August evening. Because of the strained nasality of the heroine's voice and the migraine-inducing clanging of cymbals, these operas normally seemed interminable, especially for our two kids. Like European opera, the Chinese form is definitely an acquired taste. However, on that muggy night, somehow things were different, and the performance was so colorful and well acted that even Christine remained alert throughout, and we were amazed that the actors with beads of sweat dripping through their thick makeup and over their heavy costumes did not succumb to heat exhaustion, especially during the battle scenes. The next day, we were unable to avoid being taken for a command tour of the handicrafts factory and, of course, their gift shop, but the highlight for us and the unambiguous goal of our sojourn in Weifang was the site of the former World War II civilian detention center also known as the No. 2 Middle School.

In a bit of ironic whimsy during the war, the Japanese turned the grounds of a former Presbyterian mission school and hospital into the famous Weifang civilian internment center, and so it was here that my family and other Presbyterian missionaries were incarcerated along with many other Allied civilians. Before Pearl Harbor, my parents had visited the mission station and had stayed in one of the missionary homes that the Japanese guards had commandeered as their living quarters. As an added quirk of history, one of these houses was the home of Henry Luce, who was born and raised in China like me although a full generation earlier, and while Japanese soldiers were occupying his former home, he, as founder and editor of *Life* and *Time*, was patriotically publishing stories and pictures supporting the American war effort in the fight against imperial Japan in Asia. At the end of the Pacific War and after Liberation, with both the Japanese and missionaries sent packing, the Weifang authorities took over the former mission institution and transformed it into the No. 2 Middle School. So there we were in Weifang, strange guests indeed for we had no interest in their main tourist attraction, and as they were soon to discover, as educators and thus ostensibly interested in visiting one of the city's finer secondary institutions, neither were we really interested in how their students were being educated. What did capture our attention was something that had happened long before any of their children had even been born.

The old mission station and former internment camp was now divided into two institutions, a school and a hospital. Because it was August, the school was not yet in session, so the administration went out of its way to accommodate our visit by rounding up several teachers and preparing a couple of classrooms for us to observe, and this resulted in some awkward moments. No one that we met remembered or was willing to openly acknowledge that this had been the site of a foreign internment camp, so at least from our hosts' perspective, as teachers, our sole interest in visiting their institution was pedagogical. This resulted in a constant bifurcation of our itinerary. Our hosts would direct us to a new building and show off their science lab where a couple of teachers were about to demonstrate an experiment for us, but we, on the other hand, would pay the briefest and most perfunctory of compliments before urging our hosts to take us to that old dormitory over here or to take some pictures of those rows of houses over there. Of enormous help to us was *Shandong Compound*, a marvelous book written by Langdon Gilkey, one of the former prisoners, which contained a detailed hand-drawn map of the camp. Gradually, as we progressed through the campus, constantly examining Gilkey's work and snapping pictures left and right, the motivation for our visit became clear, but again, there was no public recognition on the part of the school or hospital authorities that they knew or cared about this particular episode during the anti-Japan war. In fact, except for a cursory remark by the director of the hospital, no one mentioned that American missionaries had built both institutions.

As one might expect, many former structures had been replaced with new ones so that the compound seemed to have more buildings than in the past, but one of the two camp kitchens remained, and the two-story dormitory where single women were housed was still standing along with row after row of small houses; one of which had served as a refuge for the Scovel family. While we were upstairs in the dorm building, looking down on the campus, Janene made a telling observation. At its fullest, the camp once held about two thousand prisoners, Yanks, Brits, Aussies, priests, prostitutes, athletes, and academics, all crammed into that relatively small piece of real estate. While conversing with our hosts, she learned that along with the old buildings, which now housed teachers and their families and some boarding students, new classrooms and living quarters had been added, and altogether, the campus that spread out beneath us now housed about three thousand people! Having seen several of the overcrowded cities all over China, it suddenly struck us that Beijing, Tianjin, Shanghai, and every other metropolis we had visited were in effect concentration camps, where in terms of space and confinement, our fellow Chinese were no better off than my family and the other foreign prisoners confined here some thirty-six years earlier.

At five forty that afternoon, our train pulled out of Weifang to take us home after three weeks on the road. We slept fitfully as the train carried us in darkness first westward then northward, and at four in the morning, we arrived back in Tianjin disheveled and heavy eyed but brimming with memories. They say a great vacation is when you can't wait for it to begin but when it's about to conclude, you can't wait for it to end. In her diary, Janene exclaimed, "Oh, how good it felt to be home!"

CHAPTER 6

温故知新

wen gu zhi xin

To understand the present,
first review the past.

Accepting the contention that history is essentially geography in motion, any appreciation of the culture and politics of modern China begins with an understanding of the physical and political geography of the country. Since I am writing as a Chinese-born American, I'm especially intrigued by the comparisons and contrasts between these two great nations. Grab any world atlas and you are struck at first by their topographical similarities. They are almost exactly the same size with the Middle Kingdom's 3,694,959 square miles of land mass only a few percentage points larger than the 3,537,455 that makes up all fifty states. Both countries have towering mountains, barren deserts, great plains, and two large rivers. Superimpose a map of one country on top of the other and they are again quite similar: both are rectangular with roughly equivalent north-south and east-west boundaries. The bulk of China sits about five degrees lower in latitude than America, but both can be considered temperate at least in terms of climate. The east coasts of both nations tend to fan out more than the western borders, and this is especially true of China so that its southernmost province (the island of Hainan) is farther south than Florida and its northernmost province, Heilongjiang, reaches farther north than Maine. However, since Hawaii, like Hainan, sits south of the Tropic of Cancer and Alaska stretches far north of Heilongjiang, both countries average out to approximately the same location in latitude, and because of this, in their eastern and midsections, they share almost identical weather patterns. Palm trees sway, orange trees blossom, and beaches fill with tourists in both Hainan and Florida. Winters in Heilongjiang and neighboring provinces are like winters in Maine or Minnesota, freezing the blood of any southern visitors and merely causing the blood to sing for the locals. Because it was the same latitude, Shandong, where I grew up, produces crops similar to Missouri or Kentucky: corn, wheat, tobacco, soybeans, and the like. Northeastern China (Manchuria), because of ready access to natural power, like its counterpart New England, has been the industrial heartland of the People's Republic, and this is why that region was so coveted by the Japanese invaders during the previous century. Having made these comparisons, there are several stark contrasts between the United States and the PRC that cry out for attention.

China has no Pacific Ocean. Well, of course, this is a bald lie for the Taiping Yang (its Chinese name) fronts and dominates the entire east coast, so to put it more accurately, America is flanked by two great oceans but China only by one. The consequences of having no western ocean are enormous. To begin with, the United States has always had two great walls to protect its flanks, natural barriers far more effective and impervious than the famous Great Wall. China's wild west bordered the Soviet Union, but after the dissolution of the USSR, it now has Russia and five -istans along with India sharing its border from north to south with no giant ocean to wall them off. Instead of the Pacific bathing the coves and beaches of our western states, imagine Russia, Korea, Japan, China, and Vietnam one quick step by land across from Alaska, Washington, Oregon, California, and Hawaii. High mountains and deserts help demarcate boundaries and deter enemy intentions, but no geographical barrier is more effective than the world's largest ocean, and for this reason, America is both defined and blessed by having both a left and a right coast.

The Pacific not only protects America's western shores, much more significantly, it bathes the western states with the lifeblood of every human civilization: water. Without the Pacific, California would not be the fruit and vegetable garden of America; without the Pacific, the Northwest would be without timber or waterpower, and without the Pacific, there would be no runoff into the Colorado to sustain monstrous metropolises like Los Angeles, Las Vegas, and Phoenix. Because of its western ocean, for centuries Americans have been able to respond to the call to follow the setting sun, and its population center has long ago moved west of the Mississippi River. Contrast all of this with China. If we draw a north-south line down the Middle Kingdom's middle running from the cities of Lanzhou in the north, Chengdu in the center, and Kunming in the south, well over ninety percent of the population lives to the right or east of this line. To the left and west, there is simply not enough water, and the non-Chinese minorities who have lived there and the Han population that has been shipped out there to balance them off have limited resources, resources so limited that China will never have a populous western province that will come close to equaling the population of California. One of the simplest ways to demonstrate the consequences of this geographical disparity between the two nations is to imagine the following. Suppose the United States had this same geographical constraint and that everything west of the Mississippi was essentially mountains and deserts so that almost the entire population of the United States was forced to reside in the eastern half of the continent. Now replace that population of roughly 300 million souls with China's 1.3 billion. This is the China of today: more than a billion people live in an area that contains only 150 million Americans, all the land east of the Mississippi! Americans may feel that they have many things to be thankful for, but I'm guessing that few of us ever express gratitude for the Pacific Ocean.

There is another major way in which geology and geography have carved out a contrast between the two countries. As already acknowledged, both nations have two great rivers, but China's twins run from west to east, America's from north to south, and unlike the Yellow and the Yangtze, the Missouri empties into the Mississippi, making it the nation's single greatest waterway. Once again, we witness how geography helps sculpt out the history of a nation. Large rivers have always served as both carriers and barriers. Because of the former, they attract people like magnets for they provide life-giving water for crops, they carry and deposit rich soil for abundant harvests, and in the days before good roads and motorized transportation, they were the only highways (as during my childhood days back in Huaiyuan). They also flood from time to time, and in both America and China, the rivers of life have also brought death and destruction although, because of their greater population and longer history, China's rivers have wreaked far greater havoc than the Missouri and Mississippi. Yet their magnetic ability to sustain and enhance life has drawn people back again and again.

Rivers also serve as barriers and only recently has man been able to bridge the geographical divides they have sliced into the landscape. The great river systems of the United States have created an east-west schism where historically and culturally, the colonial America of the east coast migrated ever westward to form the continental country we recognize today that comprises the fifty united states. America's history is comparatively short and sweet compared to China's, so the east-west divide has not created separate cultures, but as I've already alluded to in previous chapters, the Yellow and especially the Yangtze have sliced China into two nations in several ways. Northerners eat wheat and pork, speak dialects of Mandarin, and tend to be tall and conservative. Southerners are rice eaters and are more eclectic in their choice of food and speak in tongues that are alien to the Mandarin ear. Southerners tend to be shorter and more open-minded. The North has given China her soldiers and emperors; the South has provided the nation with businessmen and intellectuals (except for Confucius, who grew up a neighbor of mine in Shandong albeit over two thousand years before I was born). In contrast to the east-west migration pattern of the United States, the Han, who represent the ethnolinguistic majority who we call the Chinese people, have migrated ever southward over the millennia, assimilating, conquering, or pushing out those who are not Han. Ironically, China's north-south divide is evident even among the Chinese emigrants to the United States.

Except recently, Chinese-Americans almost all came from the South, the land of adventuresome people, and a plurality of these immigrants stem from one small district southwest of Canton. These southerners have brought their culture with them, and you can even spot them by the way they spell their names in English. I never saw a Wong until I came to America; northerners (and the official pinyin romanization) spell this the most common family name, Wang. These immigrants also speak a dialect of Cantonese I can't understand, and they eat strange foods I never heard of until I came to the United States, stuff like dim sum. During Chinese New Year, my American friends greet me with "Gung Hay Fat Choy" and expect a smile of recognition and for me to reply in kind. To this day, I'm uncertain what this Cantonese phrase means; I only know it sounds nothing like *xin nian kuai le* (happy new year) in Mandarin, the language of the North and now the standard tongue for all Chinese. To my great chagrin, the first few times I ate in a Chinese restaurant with American friends, I didn't know what to order for much of the food I knew and loved wasn't on the menu, and the waiter couldn't understand a word of my Mandarin. My American friends were unconvinced by my argument that the contrast between northern and southern Chinese cultures was as vast as that between, say, France and Spain. And so geography has created China and divided her.

What then has united this fragmented land into a mighty and modern nation?

Historians and anthropologists can probably cite several factors that have pulled this huge population of disparate people together over time to create the China that we know today, but as a linguist, naturally I will argue that language was the major centripetal force that helped forge first an empire and then a nation. This might sound contradictory to the claim I have just made in the previous paragraph where I pointed out that many so-called dialects of Chinese are mutually unintelligible. If people from Lisbon, Paris, Rome, and Bucharest cannot understand one another in face-to-face communication and if we insist on claiming these people all speak different languages, since people from Beijing, Shanghai, Canton, and Taipei similarly can't share intelligible conversations, how can I claim one language unites them? Put in another way, if Portuguese, French, Italian, and Romanian are different languages, why are Mandarin, Wu, Yue, and Southern Min only dialects? We call the former the Romance languages but refer to the latter as Chinese dialects.

To begin with, let's not worry about the difference between these two linguistic terms for at best they represent a continuum of language varieties from those that are extremely similar (American English and Canadian English) to those that are extraordinarily different (Japanese and Swahili). I used to tell my students the difference between a dialect and a language is that the latter has its own army and navy. What unites the Chinese varieties I have just listed but doesn't help unify the European examples is a common writing system, specifically a common writing system that does not rely on an alphabet. Although the Romance languages share many cognates that are transparent even though different spelling systems are employed, being literate in French does not come close to making you literate in Portuguese, Italian, and Romanian. This is because, by and large, the alphabetic writing system of each of these tongues is based on how words are pronounced although we could forgive anyone learning the language of Napoleon if they claimed this was definitely not true of French, which has a spelling system about as perverse as English. With very few exceptions, however, speakers of any variety of Chinese can communicate perfectly through writing since their orthography is not based on the correspondence between letters and sounds, but between symbols and words. It's as if their entire writing system is identical to the way Arabic numerals are used around the world. The number 4 can be pronounced "four," "vier," "char," or "shi," and despite their different sounds and divergent writing systems, English, German, Hindi, and Japanese speakers all immediately recognize what this symbol stands for. Imagine then all the words of Chinese written with symbols just like Arabic numbers and you can start to understand how this marvelous system of writing served to unify millions and millions of people who speak in different tongues. Like the Pentecost experience recorded in the book of Acts, from early times, Chinese characters unified and mobilized a group of people who would eventually leave an indelible mark on human history. A writing system that was first etched on oracle bones long ago in prehistory emerged to unite a group of people in a way that geography never could.

A common writing system based on meaning and not on pronunciation is only one explanation for a unified Chinese people, however. Another major force is the philosophy founded by my fellow Shandong countryman and master teacher, Kongzi, known to all English speakers as Confucius. He lived during a legendary time in world history when great spiritual leaders seemed to have thrived (c. 552–479 BC), during the Zhou dynasty according to the Chinese calendar. In early October, we managed a final family trip to Shandong, this time to Confucius's birthplace, Qufu, a small town about forty miles northeast of Jining, where I grew up two and a half millennia later. It was the weekend of Derick's birthday, and we thought a little wisdom of the Sage might rub off on him if he were there to celebrate turning thirteen. Actually, he was suffering from the flu, but even he enjoyed the visit, and the Master's acumen must have worked its magic for Derick has emerged many years later into a wise young man. We took this final family trip on our own without Xiao Zhang's able assistance and with relatively few hassles in securing travel permits and train tickets, and all this was a mark of how trust was slowly growing and doors were inching open. Change was visible in the autumn air: the railroad stations were freshly painted, geraniums were planted in the flowerpots along the platforms, the train attendants were more affable, and the car we rode in was new, clean, and almost spiffy.

The town of Qufu is about fifteen miles from the nearest rail station, and as we were driven to our destination, we saw the same rural scenes we had witnessed on our earlier trip to Jining. As we entered the large gate with parts of the old city wall still standing on either side, we felt as if we had left the twentieth century and were traveling into the era when Confucianism dominated China's culture. At our guesthouse, we bumped into Lao Long, the guide who had gone to Jining from this town to help us negotiate the hordes of people who surrounded us on that memorable visit to my native place. We also met the seventy-sixth indirect descendent of Confucius himself and were told that his direct counterpart had fled to another province just before Liberation (translation: he was a member of the Nationalist party and now lived in Taiwan). We visited the three temples built in the Sage's honor and were amazed to see that the original colors had been restored and maintained. The columns, eaves, frames, and lintels were bright with light green, turquoise, vermilion, gold, orange, and lapis lazuli blue. In particular, we enjoyed the little forest that had been preserved and allegedly been planted by Confucius's disciples shortly after his death. As we walked among the large copse of trees lit by shafts of soft autumnal sunlight, we saw butterflies, heard birds singing, and smelled the clean scent of cedar and pine. We had entered a completely different universe.

We knew that during the campaign against the olds promulgated during the Cultural Revolution, Confucianism had been at the center of this criticism, and at our institute, we had seen a propaganda film extolling the zeal of Beijing University students who, during that time of unrest, came down to Qufu and destroyed as many historical artifacts as they could as a literal attempt to smash Confucianism. Fortunately, the locals, many of whom were descendants of the Kong family, were able to protect many of these treasured historical sites, but evidence of the students' vandalism was apparent everywhere. Sadly, the huge stone that supposedly marked Confucius's grave had been toppled and broken in two; now it stood upright again but with a white cement bandage holding its irregular pieces together. The footprint of the previous violence was apparent everywhere we went in China in 1979, but it was less evident in Qufu than in most other places, and even back then, one had a sense that the Cultural Revolution was a brief and embarrassing blemish on Chinese history, and after 2,500 years, the ideas of the Great Master had not only survived, they had endured to shape the years to come.

Being neither a Sinologist nor a student of Confucianism, my knowledge of the Sage's teachings has been acquired directly through a little reading but mostly indirectly by experiencing and observing how Confucianism has shaped Chinese society as well as its neighbors to the east. Learning is an important virtue, and were it ever to be labeled a religion, Confucianism is at most a humanistic faith, for there is the strong belief that good and proper behavior is and should be learned and that both inner and communal peace comes from wisdom. Propriety, humaneness, ritual, and virtue should be the lifelong goals of all educated men (remember, males have ruled China). Above all doctrines is the concept of harmony (*he*), and this is most clearly manifested in a series of hierarchical relationships. If there is harmony between father and son, then there is peace in the home; if there is harmony between townspeople and their magistrate, then there is peace in the village; if there is harmony between citizens and the emperor, there is peace in the nation. Then and only then can there be harmony between heaven and earth.

Although coming from a different and sometimes competing tradition, Daoism also values this hierarchical and holistic harmony that is so fundamental to Confucianism. Laozi, the purported founder of the way (the literal meaning of *dao*) was supposedly born about a generation before Confucius and allegedly came out of the womb with snow-white hair and the features of an eighty-year-old, thus the world's wisest baby!

Confucianism is not unique to China, for over a millennium it spread into Korean and Japanese culture so pervasively that ideas such as obedience to authority both familial and civil or preserving harmonious relationships both at home and at work are followed even more intently by China's neighbors than by people in the modern homeland. During the Cultural Revolution, when the PRC was doing almost everything possible to eliminate the scourge of past beliefs, practices, and culture, Confucian scholars and disciples in Taiwan, Korea, and Japan were the only true keepers of the faith and remain to this day on the forefront of Confucian studies. As yet another illustration of the incongruous turn of events that can suddenly transpire in modern China, the same party that unleashed wave upon wave of Red Guards to obliterate any vestiges of Confucianism is the same party that today extols Confucian harmony as a uniquely Chinese philosophy that should be followed in part because it contrasts with such alien concepts as Western democracy. And the same party that urged the masses assembled in Tiananmen Square to burn the Sage's teachings a generation ago is the same party that suddenly erected a giant bronze statue of the now rehabilitated Master in that very same square. Today, China sponsors more than three hundred Confucian institutes around the globe. Except for these one-hundred-and-eighty-degree political vacillations over the last fifty or so years, which in the Chinese calendar is a mere instant in time, along with a shared writing system, Confucianism has been the social glue that has held families, villages, districts, and provinces together and has given the emperor the Mandate of Heaven to control and even expand an empire for well over two thousand years.

With its emphasis on wisdom and social harmony, Confucianism has also left Chinese culture imbued with a veneration of learning, and Chinese families value education with an esteem that few other societies can match. I've already cited examples of what psychologists call field independence, the focus on the particular rather than the general, and this specific emphasis is an essential aspect of Chinese education from nursery school up. Take the teaching of art as just one illustration. Along with rehearsing skits, dances, and songs for the tourists visiting her nursery, little Christine also participated in educational activities found in any preschool around the world: learning new vocabulary, practicing how to read and spell simple words, and acquiring basic skills in the visual arts. One day in late spring, I was able to observe one of her art classes at the nursery, where each child was asked to color in a design for the outline of a jacket using crayons. As in any class, the youngsters varied in their artistic abilities, but all tried hard to follow their teacher's instructions and stay assiduously within the lines, but after viewing all the sketches, their teacher and I then noticed one striking difference between our daughter's jacket and all the others being colored in the room. It had a head! On top of the jacket the kids were instructed to color, Christine had added a circular face with a pudgy nose, two eyes, a wide smile, and rosy cheeks just like the rouge-smeared faces of the kids whenever they performed for a visiting troupe of tourists. The teacher saw the head as a distraction, not part of the assignment, and rightly observed that

Christine had not colored the jacket completely and urged her to finish the assignment. I wouldn't go so far as to criticize the nursery for promoting decapitation or dehumanizing art, but the message was clear: don't draw or think outside the box.

Art classes with Derick further illustrated this trend. Because his morning hours at the Tianjin Conservatory were devoted solely to piano and trombone and because Janene worked with him in the afternoons on his American curriculum, we didn't want our son to leave China without some formal introduction to Chinese culture. Through our contacts at the conservatory, we arranged for a teacher of traditional Chinese painting to come to the hotel for a few hours each week to teach Derick. Our son's Chinese was minimal and the teacher's English nonexistent, but like music instruction, the teaching of painting is mostly observing and imitating, so Derick was able to follow along quite quickly. Whether it's mathematics, engineering, music, or art, you tend to begin with the fundamentals, and this was certainly true in this case, but it seemed like Derick's art teacher was interested only in the fundamentals. A long time was spent in how to hold the body and arms by relying on your *qi* (the inner breath, spirit, or force as in "May the force be with you"). More time was spent on holding the brush vertically, cupped in a firm but relaxed right hand. Watching this evoked memories of a few calligraphy lessons I had as a young boy where my nemesis was being forced to hold the brush in my right hand. When I objected that I was left-handed, my Chinese instructor looked at me with a mixture of pity and disbelief and then continued right on with his tutelage as if I had complained about a hangnail. Finally, after learning how to grind just enough black ink powder, to mix it with just enough water, and to dab just the right amount onto the brush, Derick began to trace flower stems, leaves, and eventually flower blossoms. We would've had to stay another year before he would've been able to begin sketching birds.

It would be easy to criticize such instruction as obsessively detailed rote learning and complain that it stifled creativity, but I cite these examples with just the opposite intent. This rigorous early training in field independence creates keen eyes and ears that attend to every detail and ultimately crafts hands and fingers that can eventually produce unbelievably beautiful paintings, cloisonné, and carvings in jade and ivory. It is the same training that today also successfully educates a generation of engineers, computer scientists, and medical researchers. Having said this, as anyone who witnessed the opening and closing spectacles of the 2008 Beijing Olympics can attest, no one can deny that the Chinese cannot think outside the box or protest that they lack creativity. But their strength is as old as the Master himself. Confucius is in the details!

Chinese history is as well documented as it is lengthy, so the foundations of the modern nation we identify today are deeper, broader, and vaster than that of any nation on earth. I would go further and make the following claim. If we chronicle human events by millennia, not centuries, no people on the face of this planet have dominated and contributed to human civilization more than the Chinese. The Egyptians, Greeks, Romans, Arabs, Spanish, Dutch, French, English, and Americans have all had their day, even their centuries, but their empires have waxed and waned like the moon and pale in comparison to the solar brilliance of Chinese civilization over the past four thousand years. The domestication of pigs, pottery wheels, a logographic writing system, silk, carved ivory and jade, the crossbow, glazed pottery, the seismograph, inoculation against smallpox, antimalarial drugs, paper, the use of coal, gunpowder, the compass, the abacus, cloisonné, and so on were all discovered, created, and employed by the Chinese while others had their day and ceased to be. From this broader perspective of time, the Chinese have indeed suffered setbacks to their sovereignty, but in the vast view of history, these have been relatively momentary aberrations. Take the European domination of China's coastal cities and capital from the middle of the nineteenth century to the middle of the last one, but then look at China today. Who dominates the global market? Who has massive investments in land, industries, and banks around the world? Who is today's supreme economic power? The Greater East Asia Co-Prosperity Sphere that was Japan's dream seventy years ago has finally become a reality, but it is China who rules the Asian marketplace and in a manner never dreamed of by the Japanese imperialists of the past, and China dominates the markets of mighty Europe and America as well.

This rich history and incredible continuity have imbued the Chinese with an enormous confidence in their heritage. Surprisingly, this legacy has not left them with a sense of hubris or entitlement, and Confucianism has always promoted humility over trash-talking and self-effacement over self-aggrandizement. Hard work trumps loud words. Still, this confidence in who they are and where they come from has left its mark. Americans may navel-gaze and wallow in self-doubt about who they are, where they came from, and where they are going, but these are questions I've never heard voiced among my Chinese friends. Given their magnificent historical heritage, it's no wonder that the Chinese call themselves Zhong Guo, the Middle Nation. They have been in the middle of human history since the beginning of time, and based on the evidence from the past four thousand years, they will maintain this position in the millennia to come. So along with a common orthography and a Confucian philosophy, a rich and continuous history has also cemented the Chinese people together into one cohesive society.

Although these and other centripetal forces have played a powerful role in holding China together, there have been several times when the nation has threatened to spin out of control, scattering its people apart and fragmenting the Middle Kingdom into tiny peripheral bits. The Communists have long claimed to be the revolutionary party, but China's greatest revolution took place a century before Mao Zedong came to power. For almost twenty years, from 1845 to 1864, China was torn in two by a civil war that killed at least twenty million people and was ended only with the help of European forces whom the Qing government had invited to intervene. The leader and fomenter of this bloody revolution was a person very much like the Great Helmsan. Like Mao, Hong Xiuquan was born of unpretentious heritage in the South, radicalized by Western thought, was a cunning military strategist who took several great marches in order to fight another day, and was charismatic and self-promoting enough to become a cult figure. And like the Communist leader who followed him a century later, he wanted to form an egalitarian people's republic and snatch the Mandate of Heaven from his nationalist enemies. The similarities should not obscure several stark differences between the two revolutions, however. Whereas Mao was influenced by the secular writings of Karl Marx, Hong's egalitarianism came from his reputed conversion to Christianity, and the latter's messianic ambitions were so deep that he actually believed he was a reincarnation of Jesus's younger brother! Following a dynastic line of many emperors, Mao chose Beijing for his capital whereas, unable to unseat the reigning Qing emperor, Hong ruled for a time from the southern capital of Nanjing. Although a few European soldiers of fortune joined forces with the Taiping revolutionaries, the civil war ended only with the military help of Europeans whom the Qing invited to quell Hong's forces. As a consequence, once invited into the Chinese henhouse, the European foxes were loath to leave, leading to almost a century of foreign domination. Despite these colonial incursions, China's greatest revolution did not succeed nor did it destroy the long legacy of a united people, and it indirectly set the stage for the eventual success of Mao and his party a hundred years later. But enough of history; back to geography.

All of us carry mental maps of our surroundings whether they are pictures of the layout of our kitchen, our daily route to work, or how to get over the river and through the woods to Grandmother's house. But along with these individual representations of the space around us are the maps that we have collectively acquired through formal education, and these mental images of our world reveal a great deal about us as a people. In the United States, I still see them around occasionally on the walls of offices or in older books, but they have been replaced by a geographically more accurate view of the continents that now stands as the picture of the world most Americans are used to seeing. I'm referring here to the older world map Americans used to rely on that had North and South America smack in the middle with Europe, Africa, and the Middle East on the right-hand side, and since Eurasia was sliced in two, China, Japan, Southeast Asia, and most of the USSR was on the left. According to this representation of the globe, the United States was the middle kingdom, and appropriately enough, the Communists in China, Russia, North Korea, and Vietnam were clearly far to our left. One of the many problems with this worldview, however, was that Southeast Asia was sliced away from India so that the former was on the left of the map and the latter way over on the right. To me it appeared bizarre and unfair to claim that India, where I attended high school, was almost entirely all the way around the world from Thailand, where my wife and I lived when we were first married. The modern maps of China and its neighbors are far more telling, and like a common writing system, Confucianism and a mighty history have served to bind the Chinese people together in a common view of the universe.

I have always loved maps, so I came to China armed with several we had acquired in the States in preparation for our year in the PRC, and after arriving, I purchased many Chinese maps of cities and provinces as well as those of the nation and the larger world outside. One of the most helpful references in writing this book has been my well-used 1977 edition of *Zhonghua Renmin Gongheguo Fen Sheng Dituji* (*The People's Republic of China Atlas*).

In this day and age, when trip finders and GPS-linked navigation systems have usurped the role of conventional maps, a traditional atlas might seem a bit anachronistic to employ as a useful source of information. I would contend, however, that my faithful atlas can tell you more about the Chinese worldview than any one of the multitude of contemporary books that attempt to describe how the Chinese view the world around them. Let's start with the provinces. They are all colorfully and accurately depicted with large, two-page maps provided for each with a massive index of towns and cities in the back conveniently listing each name in both Chinese characters and pinyin romanization. There is a large area in Western China that, like a few other divisions, is not called a province but an autonomous region. Just as no American would think that New Mexico was not part of the United States but a slice of Mexico, no Chinese (well, no Han Chinese) would dream of considering Xizang Zizhiqu (the Tibet Autonomous Region) as a separate nation.

Way over on the eastern side of China is another interesting province that happens to be a separate nation as far as most of the rest of the world is concerned. This is the province of Taiwan. According to my Chinese atlas, this province does not differ in any way from the other regions that comprise the People's Republic, and there is not the slightest hint that after the Nationalists lost the civil war to the Communists in 1949, this island that once was called Formosa has been home to the Republic of China. When Janene and I were about to leave Pittsburgh for our work in Tianjin, we instructed all our American friends to be sure to carefully address all letters to the People's Republic of China and not just China and certainly not Republic of China or their correspondence would surely end up on this island province / nation. Back then, it seemed ludicrous to me that for most Americans, China could be either Taiwan or the mainland, and often people would ask just that. "When you say China, do you mean Taiwan or the mainland?" To me, this kind of geographical misrepresentation is just as if someone told you they were about to travel to the United States and you would respond, "How nice. Do you mean Hawaii or the mainland?" Now, decades later, China is China, and Taiwan is Taiwan on all non-Chinese mental maps except during the Olympics and other awkward times when China's richest province is forced to be named after its largest city and called Chinese Taipei or some other queer solecism. With more than two generations of Chinese raised and educated with one very clearly delineated national picture, it is just as hard for most Chinese to think of Tibet or Taiwan as free and independent constituencies as it would be for Americans to believe that Hawaii and New Mexico are not a legitimate part of the United States.

Chinese cartographers also have unusual ways of demarcating international borders and labeling other parts of the world, and these boundaries and nomenclature invariably serve the Party's goal of promulgating a common and singular worldview among the populace. To begin with, take Hong Kong. In 1979, this modern metropolis was still a British colony, one of the last appendages of the Victorian Empire upon which the sun never set, and it would be another eighteen years before the Chinese would regain sovereignty over this small southern strip of the mainland. On all my 1979 Chinese maps, it is hard to find Xianggang (Fragrant Harbor) although it is there in tiny letters, identifying it as a town and not a city despite the fact that millions of people crowd together in that diminutive colony. Guangzhou (Canton), the first Chinese city to the north, is identified with such large, bold, and dark letters that using print as an indication of population status, one would assume that Hong Kong was an insignificant little hamlet hugging the Chinese coast. If you look carefully, you can see a dotted line surrounding this area indicating a border, but there is no acknowledgement that this is British territory, and the only hint that this real estate belongs to another country is that *Hong Kong* is printed in miniscule letters under the Chinese name on some, but not all, maps of the PRC. But creative cartography extends far beyond the borders of China. Take Korea. On all world maps back then as well as any Chinese ones that included their northeastern neighbor, Korea is one contiguous country whose capital is Pyongyang. Seoul, which is much more populous, appears as a town in the southern portion of the Democratic People's Republic. Also, there is no Israel, and in its place is a country called Palestine, but it is a nation without a capital.

One could argue that every country has the right to define its own borders and label its constituent parts any way it wishes, but we have already seen some discrepancies between the manner in which the PRC identifies its borders and names its provinces and the way almost all other nations look at these demarcations. These discrepancies increase dramatically, however, when we examine the way the Chinese depict the rest of the world. Take any Chinese map of China and you will see something quite amazing. It can be a giant chart, filling an entire wall, or one found in a book like in my trusty Chinese atlas, or it can be as tiny as a map of the nation depicted on a postage stamp. In every one, at first blush, the nation's borders seem unremarkably typical, separating the motherland from Korea, Russia, and Mongolia in the north; the -istans in the west; and India, Nepal, Burma, Laos, and Vietnam in the southwest. But wait a minute. When we get to what everyone calls the South China Sea, the southernmost border suddenly plunges downward a good twelve hundred miles, skirting Vietnam on the left and the Philippines on the right all the way down to the northern coast of Borneo. In fact, from the way the Chinese draw their southern border, it looks like if unwary swimmers left the warm beaches of Brunei or northern Malaysia, they could be immediately arrested by the Chinese navy for entering the country without a visa! I like to compare this bit of geographical gerrymandering by transposing the same measurements to the United States.

Imagine every American schoolchild being introduced to a national map whose southern borders swooped down from the Gulf of Mexico and Florida to the very beaches of Venezuela, claiming all the territory encompassed between the Mexican coast in the west and the Bahamas in the east. Naturally, there would be loud and justifiable cries of Yankee imperialism from the entire world community, but for one delicious moment, think of all the oil we could claim were we able to pull off such a preposterous trick! This is the primary motivation why the People's Republic of China believes it owns the South China Sea, the new Persian Gulf. Besides the territory itself and its ocean of seafood, there are vast tapped and untapped oil reserves in this area, and this is why all the contiguous nations currently bicker over who owns what. Every islet and rock in this huge expanse of sea is in contention, and even Japan has joined Taiwan (the nation, not the province), the Philippines, Malaysia, and Vietnam in squabbling over this watery real estate. But for the over one billion people educated by Chinese maps of the world, there is no question that just like Tibet and Taiwan, these southern waters have always been and will continue to remain part of the motherland.

My preoccupation with maps and geography might appear to be excessive, and I've already admitted that this has been a personal predilection of mine. Nevertheless, as an illustration of their importance in understanding the Chinese psyche (acknowledging that there are really over a billion of them), let me cite a contemporary illustration of how our mental maps mold our perceptions of international incidents. It was April Fool's Day 2001 when Americans learned that one of their spy planes, which routinely flew missions near the coast of China, was involved in an accident with a Chinese Air Force plane about seventy miles south of Hainan Island. The details of this incident are now pretty much cut and dried. The American EP-3E ARIES II, a four-engined turboprop heavily loaded with surveillance gear and a crew of twenty-four, collided with a Chinese J-8 fighter jet and, despite heavy damage, was skillfully piloted to an emergency landing on Hainan, where the plane and crew were sequestered by Chinese authorities. The J-8 piloted by Lieutenant Commander Wang Wei did not fare as well and plunged into the ocean, taking with it the life of its Chinese pilot. Both the American plane and its crew were released ten days later after the United States issued a letter of two sorries, regretting the death of Commander Wang and regretting entering Chinese airspace and landing at a Chinese airport without permission. There was subsequent posturing between the US and the PRC as to whether the Americans apologized or merely expressed regret, but in brief, this was the entire incident. But like any good narrative, there is more to the story.

Two years earlier, American fighter-bombers under NATO command had mistakenly hit the PRC embassy in Belgrade, killing several of the Chinese staff, so simply from a historical perspective, here was one more example of military aggression by the United States in its quest for hegemonic domination of world affairs. No one likes people loitering around their homes even if they happen to remain on public property, so in addition to blatant acts like the unfortunate Belgrade bombing, no Chinese enjoys the fact that US planes, ships, and satellites stalk them on a daily basis albeit legally and in international sea or airspace. In consequence, the slow-burning fuse of nationalist indignation was already smoldering. But what really infuriated the Chinese in 2001 are the two events for which they demanded the Americans to apologize. According to the Chinese version of the story, the old, heavily laden, propeller-driven airplane flown by the United States Air Force veered at a wide angle toward Wang's J-8, striking it and causing it to crash into the ocean. In the Chinese media, their Internet, the public protests on the streets, and in conversations private citizens had with foreigners, there was virtual unanimity of belief in this account. There was barely any expression of doubt about a Chinese fighter jet that was capable of doubling the sound barrier suddenly becoming a defenseless target of a ramming attempt by what for all purposes was an overloaded, propeller-driven cargo plane. No one asked why an American pilot would risk his own life and that of his two dozen crew members even if it were possible for him to have pulled off this aeronautical feat of legerdemain. Few in China had any access to the official account by the American crew that the EP-3E was flying on automatic pilot at the time and had been closely buzzed by Commander Wang's J-8 in the past as it was, alas, too closely this time. We are all prisoners of our national and cultural heritages, and we all too frequently divide the world into us versus them, but here is one of several cases where even educated Chinese are willing to buy a cockamamie story that defies credulity simply because it fits the "barbarians at the gates" narrative that they have been spoon-fed since childhood. But there is more than just propaganda or competing political views, there is the role of geography.

If we buy the United States Air Force account that their spy plane was in international waters, a good seventy miles south of Hainan Island, China's southernmost landmass, let's look at the American claim from a Chinese perspective. Recall that on all of their maps of the motherland, the southern border of the PRC extends 1,200 miles south of Hainan, all the way to the island of Borneo. Again, to make my point, let me transpose this point of view to a map of America. Supposing a Chinese surveillance plane made routine flights well into American airspace— not seventy miles south of Key West, not seventy miles south of Miami but, say, a thousand miles farther north, say, around Philadelphia. How charitable would we be about this incursion, especially if it involved the death of one of our military pilots? I realize I'm comparing ketchup with soy sauce here in terms of this particular geographical analogy, but my major point is that what the rest of the world might consider international waters is to the Chinese a real and legitimate part of China, an unseen wall that surrounds Southern China just as the Great Wall once marked its northern frontier.

Geography, history, language, Confucianism have all melded together in a marvelous alchemy to create a people and a Weltanschauung unique to human history, but there is one remaining force that bears mention if we are to understand modern China completely. That, of course, is the Party. One of the places we were taken to see during our summer trip to Shanghai was a beautifully preserved house in the former French quarter, the alleged site of the first meeting of the Chinese Communist Party (CCP) in 1921. Within that small and secret enclave of dissidents was a twenty-eight-year-old revolutionary from Hunan named Mao Zedong, but he played a minor role in the formation of what would some day become the single most powerful political organization on earth and was absent from that first meeting. Instead, an anonymous Russian advisor helped shape a predominantly Leninist interpretation of Marx's original philosophy that has left its mark on the CCP until this day. The young man from Hunan quickly ascended through the leadership ranks of the still weak and initially clandestine party and rapidly developed a talent for grassroots organization, a skill in interpreting opaque theory into effective practice, and above all, a ruthless and cunning ability to manipulate people and events for self-aggrandizement. Mao and his followers emerged as Chiang's and the Nationalists' major competitors, so even before Japan began its encroachment into Manchuria in 1931, China was caught in another civil war less than a century after the Taiping Rebellion. So bitter and deadly was this conflict between Chiang's Nationalist forces and Mao's Communists that initially, both sides virtually ignored the Japanese invasion although posturing all the while that they were doing the opposite. Instead, they devoted most of their energy in trying to exterminate their fellow Chinese opponents. Moreover, neither party was shy about enlisting help from the omnipresent warlords who ruled huge chunks of China like dictators of medieval fiefdoms and who vacillated in their allegiance and were driven by power, not politics. In addition, both sides engaged in massive executions and the use of tortures so deviant and abhorrent that just reading their descriptions alone makes you want to vomit. With Chiang's initially superior forces, the Nationalists forced the Communists into a long series of retreats in 1934–1935 that grew into the legendary Long March immortalized in later years by the Party. These more accurately named protracted withdrawals from Chiang's Nationalist forces is enshrined as a painful but shining moment in the Party's hagiography of the Great Helmsman, but in reality, this arduous journey had more to do with Mao's eventually successful but mutinous attempts to captain the ship of state than to steer it to safety.

As the decades progressed, most of the Party leadership, like Chairman Mao and Premier Zhou, was dominated by veterans of this expedition, and because the young PLA lived to fight another day, this epic retreat forged their wills and tempered their bodies and prepared the Communists for their eventual victory over the hated KMT (*kuo min dang* or the Nationalist Party). In no small measure, their success was also due to the support of Stalin, who, like Mao, had a propensity to play everybody against one another. Thanks to decades of Party propaganda, the Long March is to the Chinese what Exodus is to the Jews, and Mao endured as the Chinese Moses with Zhou Enlai serving at times as his Aaron. A few years later, after Chiang was temporarily kidnapped and held hostage by PLA soldiers in Xian, the two antagonistic sides reluctantly and haphazardly collaborated in a united Chinese front against the Japanese invaders only to turn against each other in 1945 as soon as the foreigners were defeated, only this time, the Communist forces were much larger, better armed, and more seasoned. Within four years, Mao's army and party had crushed the Nationalists; Chiang and his minions were sent packing to the island province / nation of Taiwan, and Mao proudly proclaimed the founding of the People's Republic of China on October 1, 1949. It was the first time in a century that the Chinese had regained full dominion over their own land. The barbarians had at last been defeated once and for all.

Although the Communists did not have complete control of China on that historic day, like the Fourth of July in the United States, *jie fang ri* (the day of liberation) is celebrated as the beginning of a new era. But what exactly were the Chinese liberated from? I've heard this question asked somewhat facetiously in the past by Americans, most of whom are unsympathetic toward Communism. Well, for one thing, given all the trees that have been planted, all the dams that have been constructed, all the roads and rail lines that have been built (including the almost impossible feat of engineering a line all the way to Lhasa), and all the telecommunication systems that now instantly link any part of China with any other (but most importantly with Beijing), certainly the Communists have liberated the country from the fetters of geography. I may be stretching the term slightly, but I would also contend that the Chinese people were liberated from the languages of the past. Due to the May Fourth Movement of 1919 led mostly by students and intellectuals, the very formal Mandarin of public discourse had already been replaced by a more informal vernacular, but when the Communists gained control thirty years later, they attempted to make the standard tongue more egalitarian and the written form more accessible. Literacy rates increased enormously, thanks in large part to the decision to simplify many of the most frequently used characters. Although non-Han minorities were allowed to teach in their mother tongue in primary school, all children in China were schooled in Mandarin, which, along with the rapid increase in literacy rates, united the population for the first time in a common spoken tongue and liberated them from the Tower of Babel that had divided the Chinese people linguistically. One could say that, thanks to the Communists, the dialects were liberated by Marx's dialectic.

Thirdly, most dramatically during the Cultural Revolution but very consciously and consistently, the Party liberated China from its historical past. Not the great achievements, of course, for these stand as a rightful national legacy, but the closer the historical record approaches modern times, the more it has been whitewashed, airbrushed, and doctored up so that the story of the Chinese people has become a narrative written by the Party. The retelling of history naturally included a reinterpretation of Confucianism. For decades, the Sage and his teachings were vilified as feudal and reactionary, one of the olds that was worthy of elimination, a backward thesis that was contradicted by the antithesis of Mao Zedong thought. In an exquisite piece of incongruity demonstrating once again the Party's ability to rewrite the history books, in this new millennium, Chinese leaders are promoting Confucian ideals, especially harmony, which they now promulgate as a uniquely Chinese virtue. Finally, it is possible to argue that once the Communists took over, the people were liberated from a slavish attention to detail. Facts, specifics, and particulars are only important if they serve the Party line, and as we have already seen, by the very fact that details are relatively insignificant compared to the big picture, it is permissible to manipulate them. From 1949 (and even before), the Party has produced a catalogue of prevarications that include national records of massive scope, such as the tedious and predictable five-year plans, down to personal stories that would make even the most flamboyant publicist cringe, such as Mao's record-setting swim in the Yangtze at the age of seventy-two. All in all, *jie fang ri* was a momentous date in Chinese history, and I was lucky enough to be there when it all happened.

Looking back on my adolescence, I realize now how fortunate I was to have lived in China during much of this revolutionary period, to have witnessed firsthand the Communist liberation of a war-torn country raped by the Japanese Imperial Army and ravaged by internecine warfare with the Nationalist, and to have seen with my own eyes the birth of the world's most populous and arguably most powerful nation. I was even more fortunate that, unlike the hundreds of millions of Chinese who were fellow spectators with me during this tortuous time, because of my white skin, I was able to escape the decades of propaganda, conflict, famine, and in some cases, genocide that followed, and I grew up enjoying the inalienable rights of life, liberty, and the pursuit of happiness. I was equally blessed to have been educated in India and the United States and to have lived for many years in Thailand, and this multicultural experience has given me a more global perspective from which to view my motherland. In sum, I am what anthropologists might call a participant observer: a disinterested but certainly not uninterested eyewitness to modern Chinese history. Because I was present during the War of Liberation and witnessed the formation of the new People's Republic and, just as significantly, because I was old enough to remember many of the events that transpired during those turbulent days, I ask you now to go back with me in time to thirty years before Janene and I were invited to teach in Tianjin and observe the events that helped created the China we became acquainted with in 1979 and that ultimately shaped the China we know today over sixty years later.

Even though I was barely into my first decade of life at the time, I can remember many of the events surrounding Liberation almost as vividly as I can recall what transpired last week. In August 1948, our family flew south from Huaiyuan to Canton (Guangzhou) where my father was reassigned to practice medicine at the local mission hospital and to begin teaching medicine at what was then called Lingnam University. With my family, my frail grandmother, and as many of our belongings as we could stuff into a C-47, our plane barely cleared the trees, ringing the makeshift wheat field of a runway, stopping at Hanzhou to refuel, and then continuing south to Canton. The crew let my older brother sit behind them in the navigator's seat, and I began the flight along with him up front, but after a bouncy hour or two, I was so airsick that I was forced to crawl over the luggage and retreat to the comfort of my family sitting in the aft. At evening, we descended in a slow circle past White Cloud Mountain and landed in Canton, our new and final home in China. Less than a year later, the winds of revolution that seemed to constantly stalk us would gust down from the north and envelop my family and all of China in a turbulent storm of change that would create a new heaven and a new earth.

Of all the places I lived in China, the compound of Hackett Medical Center on the western outskirts of Canton was by far the most luxurious. We shared a spacious two-story duplex with a Chinese doctor's family. It had electricity that miraculously worked most of the time. It had ceiling fans, a fireplace, screened windows, outdoor verandas on both floors, and tiled gutter pipes, which I occasionally used to climb down from my upstairs bedroom when no one was watching. Our home looked out on a tennis court and a huge lawn ringed with tropical trees and potted flowers. Across the lawn was the large hospital, affording instant access day or night for my diligent father.

Upstairs in the back over the kitchen and cook's quarters was a room my mother used as our schoolhouse. I spent a few days in a Chinese school back north in Huaiyuan, but my literacy skills were so poor and, more importantly, my parents wanted to make certain that we had an education in English, so she was our teacher. My three older siblings attended Shanghai American School when they finished their elementary homeschooling, but the younger half of our Scovel clan didn't leave home for high school until after our family had been reassigned to India. Except for furloughs in the States, my mother provided primary and elementary education for all six of her children, using material from the Calvert School in Baltimore that was sent to her once a year in a fifty-gallon missionary barrel. It is a remarkable testimony to her skills as a teacher that all six of us ultimately received a university education, and half of us continued on and garnered postgraduate degrees. She left us this legacy despite the fact that she herself never went to college, and because of her other commitments she taught us only half a day in the morning. Sometimes, my lessons took place outside the schoolroom.

Ai Yang, our cook and only servant, was missing. I don't recall for how long and under what circumstances, but it was not a serious incident for the matter lasted only a day or two. What does remain etched in my memory, however, was an event that took place the afternoon of the day we received the news. I accompanied my mother to the shopping district among the back alleys near our home where our cook bought much of our food and where we hoped to gain news about her from one of the shopkeepers, but nobody had seen her that day. It was early evening when we headed back for home, and my mother was mulling over possibilities out loud, half to herself and half to me. "You don't have to worry, Mom," I remember trying to console her, "she's just a Chinese." I had spoken in jest for even as a young boy I liked to toy and tease with words. She stopped dead in her tracks and turned to me in fury. "Don't you ever say things like that again, Tommy!" she scowled at me, and when I cringed and cried in protest that I was only kidding, this seemed to fuel her anger even more, and right there in the middle of the alley, she whacked me hard on my behind as she repeated her first admonition. Tears came to my eyes, partly from the shock of the sudden change in her temperament, partly from the humiliation of being spanked out there for all to see, and partly from the childish perception that I was unjustly punished because, after all, I was only fooling. It was the only time I ever remember being struck by either parent, and the lesson was learned quickly and well. God created all of us equal, no fooling.

It may sound a bit incongruous to head south to escape the warmth of summer, but during our first two years in Canton, we did exactly this, taking a family vacation in Hong Kong for a few weeks in midsummer. The mission owned a cluster of cabins on the top of Lantao Island, and shrouded often by morning mist or rain clouds and soaring above the rest of the colony at nearly three thousand feet, this spot afforded us a cool retreat from Canton's sticky heat. I learned to swim in the mountain stream that had been blocked up to create a little swimming pool, but I nearly drowned in my initial attempts the first summer. Fortunately, one of the adults spotted me going down a third time and alertly pulled me out of the water. Her quick actions saved my life, and taking into account the manner in which our swimming hole had been constructed, I can state without exaggeration that a missionary rescued me from the dammed. My sisters and I reveled in the camp camaraderie, the adventure of exploring new trails, and the quiet, peaceful freshness of the mountain, an invigorating contrast to our crowded city life. But getting there was as much fun for me as the destination itself. We took an overnight riverboat from Canton to Hong Kong and then a ferry over to Lantao, and because the Pearl River delta was reputedly infested with pirates who often mounted night raids on the river traffic, there was a great deal of suspense as we embarked from the safety of the city. Sandbags lined the railings of our vessel, and each male passenger was given a rifle before departure. As we started to pull away from shore, I could hardly contain my excitement over the possibility of being attacked in the middle of the night and witnessing the thrill of a firefight from the deck outside our cabin. Heightening the suspense even further, a group of young Brits had come down to see some of their friends off, and well lubricated with alcohol, they began to sing as we pulled away from the shore.

> Oh they built the ship Titanic to sail the ocean blue,
> And they said it was the ship the water would ne'er get through.
> It was on its maiden trip when an iceberg struck the ship.
> It was sad when the great ship went down.

Sound travels far over water, and we were already well away from the dock when our revelers joyfully belted out the chorus.

> Oh, it was sad; oh it was sad!
> It was sad when the great ship went down to the bottom
> of the—
> Husbands and wives, little children lost their lives;
> It was sad when the great ship went down.

Rather than terrifying me with the threat of an early demise, the singing only added to the romantic atmosphere, and I was reluctant to climb into my bunk for fear I would miss even a minute of the impending attack. The morning sun was already spilling through our port window when I awoke after sleeping through another disappointing and unremarkable passage south.

Our one-room schoolhouse in Canton overlooked a canal, and more than once, my two younger sisters and I were drawn away from our desks to peer down at the water traffic beneath us. As Dragon Boat Festival drew near, we would huddle at the window at the first sound of drums and cymbals and gaze in fascination as competing teams of boats paddled furiously by. A year or so later, I was to witness much more somber scenes. Unlike Jining and Huaiyuan, Canton was a large modern metropolis with a huge contingent of foreigners living on Shamian Island, which we would visit once a week when, following my father's lead, we'd march across town to worship in English at an Anglican church. On weekends, we would hire a small boat and picnic on board as the boatman poled down the canal and then sculled us out on the river, and there we'd relax together, just the five of us, my parents, two sisters, and me, enjoying the quiet coolness of still waters. Almost every afternoon, I would play with my Chinese friends, and we spent hours together flying kites, playing Ping-Pong, or engaging in long games of war using wooden rifles that the hospital carpenter had cut for us from spare wood and painted black. My hours of play were usually prematurely curtailed by my mother calling me in for dinner, and reluctantly, I would emerge from battle amidst the overgrown foliage at one edge of the compound and trudge home sweaty and dirty to end another glorious episode of play. It was indeed the best of times.

The first sign that all this would not last came in early December. My father was an only child, so way back in 1932, barely into my parent's first long tour of duty in China, he was devastated to receive a telegram from the States bearing the news of his father's fatal heart attack. Partly influenced by a sense of filial piety that he had already absorbed from his newly adopted homeland, my father arranged for my grandmother to join us as an integral part of our China family, first in Jining and then Huaiyuan. She was a well-educated lady with the morals and carriage of a Victorian aristocrat, and despite the amenities and reverence my parents attempted to offer, it must have been exceptionally difficult for her to spend the final years of her life in a country so distant and different from the life of privilege she had enjoyed in America. I remember spending time by her bedside in Huaiyuan and later in Canton, for by then the effects of Parkinson's disease and age had exacted their toll. On the day she died, I can recollect failing to console my always stoic and upbeat father, who, buried by grief, sat crying in his small sanctuary of a study by the stairwell. A day or two later, we all dressed up in our Sunday best and attended the memorial service at the church on Shamian and afterward boarded a riverboat that bore us and my grandmother's coffin downstream several miles, landing at the small British graveyard on the left bank. There we left her, cocooned in her casket and covered with fresh dirt, and even though I was only nine, I was old enough to sense a portent that things would change, that my idyllic childhood in China would not last forever.

For a while, our family life proceeded at the same pleasant pace. Unlike the cheerless winters in Jining and Huaiyuan, where the icy floors and frigid water of our home served more effectively than any alarm clock, the climate was much warmer in the south, and the crimson poinsettias outside our house were at their largest and most brilliant in January. It was 1949, and in that same month, I reached the first decade of life. Much more monumentally, the year of the ox would soon welcome in a new China, a People's Republic that would demand the spirit of the ox from each of its citizens: fortitude, steadfastness, and unrelenting endurance. Later in the year, in a strange and prescient reversal of play imitating life, the innocent afternoon war games with my Chinese playmates turned real with men replacing boys and howitzers taking the place of wooden rifles. By midautumn, the sounds of artillery barrages to the north of us grew louder and more common, and at night, my sisters and I could often see explosive flashes from our vantage point on the upstairs veranda outside our bedrooms. One day in particular stands out with episodic clarity. I was standing outside, talking with a member of the hospital staff on a sunny October afternoon with one foot resting on a stone bench that separated the lawn in front of me and the cement tennis courts to my back. Suddenly, I felt the stone tremble slightly, and I immediately thought it was a small earthquake as tremors slight and sometimes large were not uncommon in China. About a second or so later, I heard a loud boom to my left, and both of us jerked our heads in that direction, toward the center of the city, and a moment later, a large, white cloud trailed across the sky like a giant copy of the white kites my friends and I loved to fly. The next day, we learned that Nationalist troops had blown up the Haizhu Bridge, the only direct link between the center of the city and Canton's suburbs to the south. Since that was where Lingnam University was located, my father's long trips to the medical school now required the use of a ferry over the Pearl River. Mao had already proclaimed the establishment of the People's Republic on the first of that month, and this desperate last-minute piece of sabotage by the KMT proved the city would fall at any moment.

While Mao and most of the Party leadership were busy consolidating forces and founding a new nation in Beijing, one of his most trusted associates, General Lin Biao, was leading the PLA on their rapid and concluding campaign in the South with Canton targeted as the final prize. Not surprisingly, Lin's loyalty and military achievements were eventually reinterpreted as a direct threat to Mao's leadership, and after becoming persona non grata to the Party, twenty-two years after he liberated the south for the newborn nation, Lin Biao was killed in a mysterious air crash. But back then, the Party was unified in its intent to defeat the Nationalists, and the assault on Canton was swift and relentless. A few nights after the bridge was sabotaged, my sisters and I were treated to the closest and loudest display of pyrotechnics yet as the retreating Nationalists blew up their entire remaining munition dumps in a grand succession of explosions. Our neighborhood was unusually quiet the next morning, and our parents, still in bed, called us kids into their bedroom. It was one of those hushed and tense moments in the life of a family when ominous news was about to be broached. My mother tried to console us and, in a controlled and calm voice, reported that the fighting was over and that the Communists had taken over the city during the night. I remember feeling instantly relieved that my parents weren't delivering more serious news, like they had suddenly learned that the rumor was indeed true that I actually did hang my sisters' dolls from the ceiling fan and had turned it on to its fastest revolution. My parents were a bit surprised to find that the fall of Canton was no surprise to us for they may not have known we had been nightly spectators to the fighting all along, nor may they have quite realized we were too young to comprehend the consequences of what had just transpired.

A few days later, it was Sunday morning, and as was our custom, we dressed up and walked the two miles through town to Shamian to attend church. Having lived through warlords, the Japanese occupation, internment camp, socioeconomic upheaval, and the vicissitudes of the civil war, my parents were fueled by a trusting faith and a pervasive pragmatism that made them approach this Sunday morning as no different from all the others. Shamian was an oval-shaped island about a half a mile in width and separated from the city proper by a narrow canal on its northern side. Thus geographically distinct from Chinese Canton, it housed the city's largest foreign enclave: consulates, businesses, banks, and many handsome homes. A few rich Chinese lived there too, but it was basically a white ghetto inhabited mostly by Brits who had already made major inroads from Hong Kong for well over a century. I remember my mother taking me there one weekday to visit an English friend of hers, and while they talked over afternoon tea in a house more palatial than I recall ever seeing, I was mesmerized by our hostess's two shepherd dogs who were so large and furry their eyes were hidden in a mound of white fluff. They reminded me of two enormous marshmallows. But on this first Sunday morning after Liberation, the imperialists were no longer in control, especially of Shamian, for a contingent of Lin's army had sailed down a northern tributary of the Pearl and, circling around the city, had unloaded squads of PLA soldiers on the southern side of the island. As we reached the island and turned to head southward to cross one of the short, curved bridges, I was astonished to see row upon row of real soldiers brushing by us as they marched smartly across in the opposite direction. I was amazed! Here at last was the invisible enemy I had heard so much about and whose siege I had witnessed for weeks from our upstairs veranda. They seemed so young and confident, almost lighthearted as they trudged by. Each had a real rifle, and on their backs, each carried a pack on which was tied an extra pair of sneakers and around which was wrapped a blanket roll curled around the pack like an inverted U. Following my parents lead, we greeted them in Mandarin, and most of them appeared delighted that the first foreign devils they were to encounter proved to be so amiable. Perhaps they too were amazed. It is fitting that one of the first sections of Canton to be liberated by the Chinese was Shamian, the last vestige of Victoria's empire in the Middle Kingdom. Gone forever were the rich imperialists and their magnificent pets.

Like time-lapse photography, my memory of events have accelerated them through time, but it seemed to me that ordinary street life in Canton changed rapidly after Liberation. During the final months of the civil war, the city was dirty and unkempt. Because of severe gasoline shortages, Canton ran on fumes quite literally. The buses all had large metal canisters of burning charcoal strapped to their backs that fed the engine up front with a meager stream of combustible gas. Fortunately, most of the city was flat, so the crowded buses could wheeze weakly through the streets, discharging black billows of foul-smelling exhaust. There were scenes far more perverse, however. I remember a shopping trip with my mother a few blocks from our home when she seemed singularly intent on directing my attention sideways toward the dull shop fronts to our right, but glancing up, I saw the body of a man who had hanged himself dangling from the second-story sign post of the store we were just passing. Neither of us commented on what we had just seen, and like the one or two times I saw bodies floating in the river during our occasional family weekend outings, there was an unspoken pact of silence where pretence served as a protection from grim truths. Suicides were common in China during times of political upheaval, but at least they were rare and sporadic, unlike the deaths I would witness later. In contrast to all this and seemingly very soon after Liberation, the city suddenly appeared cleaner. The buses switched back to their preferred diet of gasoline and were refurbished and repainted. People displayed a fresh interest in cleaning the sidewalks and gutters in front of their shops, and for the first time in my young life, I saw water trucks spraying the streets to wash away the grit and to dampen what had once been dusty thoroughfares. Chinese who remember those first few years after Liberation can attest to much more substantive illustrations of positive social change, and from the personal accounts our Chinese friends shared with us in 1979 about the good old days, it appeared as if there were genuine feelings of optimism, patriotism, and unanimity of purpose that pervaded the new society. For the first time in the lives of that generation, there were tangible manifestations of change that augured hope for the years to come. Granted, compared to the previous few decades, any measure of peace and stability would have been welcomed, but my own miniature memories of the time confirm the historical records of so many Chinese and suggest that China was at last truly liberated from the shackles of the past and that she would now enjoy a new zeitgeist of promise and potential.

During the first few weeks after the Nationalists had been sent packing, the hospital filled with wounded patients, some civilians but mostly PLA soldiers, either casualties of the recent fighting or diseased from the long march south. Most of them were young men from the northern provinces, predominantly from my native province of Shandong, so there was instant rapport between them and my parents. Despite their racial and ideological contrasts, the Communist troops and the American missionaries shared much in common: both were interlopers from the North, both spoke a dialect of Mandarin, the soon to be national tongue, and both talked nostalgically of the northern cuisine, especially the simple staples, jiaozis, steamed bread, and wheat noodles. Later on, when my parents were subjected to long sessions of interrogation by the military authorities, they were interviewed directly in Mandarin and did not have to rely on a Cantonese-Mandarin interpreter, and this gained them a modicum of empathy and simultaneously helped them to avoid the risk of their replies being distorted. Much to my boyish delight, a contingent of PLA soldiers set up an antiaircraft battery just on the other side of the wall that separated our house and the hospital compound from the rest of the city, and after school, my sister Judy and I enjoyed many afternoons chatting with them from our side yard as a dozen or so of our supposed enemies sat on the wall facing us. I've already related the account about how we tried to teach them English through children's songs. Linguists would characterize our language teaching as an unprincipled mélange of methodologies, everything from grammar translation to the total physical response; however, had the two of us somehow projected our efforts to teach English fifty years into the future, we would've made a ton of money given China's current thirst for the world's global language. Our lessons did not last long, more due to the ephemeral nature of childhood interests than to an increase in political tension, and soon we had little direct contact with any representatives of the Communists until later when they paid frequent visits to our house.

Although the wall shielded the soldiers and their activities from our vision and us from theirs, we could follow much of their daily life from the sounds emanating daily over the wall, just as in village life in China, the various cries and chants outside on the street announced the passing by of someone selling candied crab apples or the whirling of a small hand drum advertised someone buying trash. Especially in the evenings, loud conversations, singing, and accordion playing would carry over into our yard, and I can imagine that in one way or another, many of these sounds conveyed a longing for home. One weekend morning, there was the noise of an unusual commotion followed by a sudden and horrendous shrieking that I recognized instantly. From the pounding of footsteps, the shouts in Chinese, and the heavy grunting, I could tell the soldiers had gotten a pig and were trying to capture it as it sprinted for life around the yard on the other side of the wall. Suddenly, the pounding and grunting stopped, and then there was a terrifying high-pitched scream from the pig as the men plunged a large metal hook deep into its throat and began to drag the dying animal through the dirt, blood spurting everywhere. I had witnessed this scene in Huaiyuan years back and could follow these gory events in my mind's eye even though my only sensory input were the diverse noises echoing over the wall. Mercifully, the shrieking stopped, and the morning air returned to relative quiet as only the soldiers' conversations could be heard as they began to butcher the carcass and prepare for an extraordinary feast for the coming evening. Gruesome as this little scene may sound, it pales in comparison to the inhuman acts of torture that soldiers wearing Japanese, Nationalist, and PLA uniforms perpetrated on millions of Chinese citizens during that dark era of history. To say that men sometimes act like animals is not only totally inaccurate, it does injustice to this earth's nonhuman population. Once more, Orwell's final image in *Animal Farm* comes to mind. By far the most monstrous insult one could hurl at the pigs who had eventually gotten control over the other farm animals is that now they had become human.

Though driven out of Canton and the entire mainland as well, the Nationalists were frantically launching rearguard attacks from Hainan Island to the south. Simultaneously, they were retreating to Taiwan to ensconce themselves as rulers in exile of what they would deem the Republic of China. Limited in resources after years of battle with the Communists and Japanese, they had no heavy bombers so their periodic aerial bombardments of our city used a variety of smaller planes. Bringing me much preadolescent excitement, these attacks took place near our home since the hospital compound was situated near the city's western railroad yards. The air raid siren would begin wailing almost concurrently with the attack, and if I was lucky enough to be outside and far enough from the house not to hear my mother's frantic screams to sprint home for cover, I got to observe the aerial battle for a few pulse-pounding minutes. From the heavens above, the KMT plane would circle in for the kill, and on the earth below, the soldiers manning the antiaircraft battery would madly wheel their cannon around, frantically trying to line up their sights on the lumbering intruder. *Pow, pow, pow!* The cannon bursts shattered the air and reverberated off every wall. Seconds later, puffs of ack-ack would explode several hundred yards behind the plane. There would be furious shouting from the cannon crew. The gun would slowly spin around in an attempt to catch up with its target, and there would be more sharp blasts. Suddenly, there were new sounds: the dull reverberations of bombs exploding in the vicinity of the railroad.

During one attack, I was again playing outside, and a single intruder suddenly swooped across the sky so close to us it almost seemed as if its target was our hospital. It was a C-47, the same type of American cargo plane that ferried us to Canton a little over a year before, but in this case, it was carrying far more pernicious baggage; the KMT were using it as a makeshift bomber. It banked slightly with its cargo door wide open as it thundered by, and standing in its doorway with arms spread grasping each side, one of its occupants was blocking a bomb with his legs. My mother was screaming at me with unusual vehemence from the limited shelter of our house, and I sprinted toward her more in terror than obedience. Seconds later, the bomb exploded across the wall a few hundred feet behind me, and I remember the whoosh of air from its concussion that seemed to speed me even more rapidly across the veranda and into the arms of my terrified mother at the door. We learned later that this particular bombardment missed the railway yards by a wide margin and hit a school instead, and because it was a weekday, several children were instantly killed.

No part of the city was safe from the Nationalists' haphazard but dangerous air raids, and even Shamian was hit occasionally. One Sunday morning, when we were still allowed to attend services, we arrived to find that another poorly aimed bomb had exploded near the church, demolishing the windows on one wall and scattering pieces of shrapnel inside and out. I collected as many fragments as I could, carefully trying not to cut my fingers on their jagged edges and marveling at the colorful rainbows etched by the fiery force of the bomb's explosion. On the advice of my parents, who were much more alert than I in spotting potential dangers, I emptied my pockets reluctantly, thwarting ambitions of taking the shrapnel to America one day as a proud trophy of my military exploits. But no shard of shrapnel could compare to the prize I found later along the canal during a weekend of foraging.

I used to mount solitary forays outside the hospital compound where the canal behind our house connected with the larger one that led to the river. One Saturday morning, while meandering around the mudflats by the canals, I saw a small piece of metal protruding from the mud like the dorsal fin of a shark. After digging around it with some bamboo, I was elated to discover I had struck the mother lode of all my boyish martial ambitions— an unexploded bomb! I had instant visions of taking it home, cleaning off its rusty surface, and eventually transporting it to America on our next family furlough to display to every kid I met. How green they would turn with envy! What glory I would accrue, the only boy in America who owned a real bomb! Lest you think how stupid I was or what an idiot I had been, I had enough sense to take the precaution of examining the nose of the missile very carefully. It was coated with mud and rust, and I assumed it was left over from the war with Japan for it obviously was not one of the recent munitions hurled by the Nationalists. With the logic and confidence only a ten-year-old could muster, I surmised that if it had not exploded for lo these many years and if it was so rusty and encrusted with muck, it must have been harmless. After finally unearthing it from its miry grave, I grabbed its fins and started dragging it home. Sliding it along the mud next to the canal was easy, but when I got to the road that led to the gates of the hospital, my task grew considerably more difficult for steel against asphalt created much more friction.

Nevertheless, spurred by thoughts of the future glory this trophy would accrue, I continued pulling my reluctant booty up to and through the hospital gates, not quite aware of the consternation I was creating. I was already inside the compound and had reached the circular driveway beyond the gates when Mr. Wong, in charge of buildings and grounds, confronted me. It was only then that I noticed everyone had fled to the safety of the nearest building and that only he and I were standing there alone in the noon sunshine. He was far bigger than I, and since he was also the carpenter who had armed my Chinese friends and me with our wooden rifles, I paid him undue deference. With his right hand stretched out toward me, he approached steadily, constantly reassuring me that no one was going to steal my newfound treasure and that everything would be all right if we just remained calm. I vaguely recall him taking the bomb away from me and shedding tears that afternoon back home, more from the loss of my cherished discovery than from the castigations of my parents. It was about then that the warfare, bombing, and political changes that had already tormented my parents' lives and work started to have an effect on me, and young and innocent as I was, I began to realize that life was turning rapidly for the worse.

By far the worst and most terrible recollection I have of life in Canton after Liberation came unexpectedly not from encounters with bombs and air raids but during an otherwise normal day at school. I've already mentioned that our second-floor schoolroom overlooked a canal, and since the hospital compound bordered the outskirts of the city, on the other side of the canal lay fields and farmhouses extending to the river beyond. One morning, as my sisters and I were semi-intent on our Calvert courses in the schoolroom, we heard a commotion outside too faint to come directly from the traffic along the canal. Happy to muster any excuse to interrupt my studies, I jumped over to the back window and looked out at the fields. There lay several rows of freshly dug trenches too deep for any crops and strangely lined by people with blindfolds and their arms tied behind their backs, kneeling on the fresh dirt in neat lines almost as if they were a living produce about to be planted. There were shouts here and there from men standing behind them waving pistols in their hands. A moment later, they began walking down the line of victims, placing their pistols in the base of each bowed head, firing their weapons, and then, almost gently, pushing the bodies forward till they teetered then fell into the open pit in front of them. Because of the distance, I could hear the crack of the pistol a split second after it was fired almost as if it were the sound of each victim tumbling into the communal grave. I can't remember when I asked my parents for an explanation, but it was surely that same day, perhaps over dinner when my father was home and could help my mother stumble through an interpretation of horrors that challenge translation. I was told that the victims were landlords, innocent people who didn't deserve to die, and that was about it. For a child like me, it was an event better secreted into the quiet recesses of memory than mollified and cheapened by facile explanation. As I look back now with the eyes of a father and grandfather, that day must have been one of several unspeakably difficult times for my parents. What can you say to a son who has seen something you wish he had never witnessed even after you have passed away and he is no longer a boy? How do you comfort a son who is still too young to recognize the stark barriers between life and play? And why would you even try to explain to your child the evil that men do when its very malevolence defies explanation?

Looking back at that time, some thirty years before Janene and I were invited to teach in the new China, it might seem odd that I was unscarred by these close encounters with the horrors of war. Nowadays, children in America would be surrounded by grief counselors and showered with all kinds of pity were they to experience what I had seen as a ten-year-old boy. On reflection, however, it is not so surprising that those memories remain drained of strong emotion, at least for me, and that, except for the mass execution, they linger even now as innocent childish escapades. To begin with, neither I nor my family nor any of my Chinese friends nor anyone I can recall even indirectly connected with our family was ever hurt during that extended period of conflict. Death and injury came to the unknown faces around us; grief, loss, and tragedy were distant and anonymous to me even though they surrounded us at every quarter. Secondly, as an American family, we were in many ways protected from serious harm. My parents were not sympathetic toward either party during the civil war and, in fact, expressed dislike in almost equal proportions for what Generalissimo Chiang and Chairman Mao had done to the Chinese people to whom they had dedicated their medical work. Further, as terrible as it may sound, during those decades of unspeakable violence, there was no strong prohibition against killing Chinese citizens. Tens of millions had been killed in the decades preceding my birth, and tens of millions more would die in the decades following. Killing whites or even attempting to kill them was a serious offense that almost always led to dire consequences. Consider the Boxer Rebellion of 1900 or consider what happened to the drunken Japanese soldier who shot my father. His Japanese commander had him executed in front of his regiment within twenty-four hours. Finally, one does not need to study Piaget to recognize that ten-year-old boys are among the most immature members of our species! Anyone who finds never-ending humor in farts can be forgiven from appreciating the blinding terror of bombs or the inestimable magnitude of war.

During our last year or so in Canton, my memory of events and chronology rapidly began to kaleidoscope together, but I do recall an abrupt change in the political climate after the Chinese entered the Korean conflict. On November 26, 1950, General Peng Dehuai led masses of PLA soldiers across the North Korean border and plunged the United Nations forces into rapid retreat, and my family and I were suddenly no longer viewed as individuals or even American friends of China but only as enemies of the people. While my Chinese friends still played with me, our Ping-Pong games were no longer personal duels but a replication of the battles between the PLA and American forces. On several Saturday shopping trips, we would frequently encounter the huge parades that had been organized with drums, cymbals, innumerable posters, and large cartoons depicting Uncle Sam in various cowardly poses, cowering as a paper tiger or about to be crushed afoot by a giant PLA soldier like an inopportune bug. These demonstrations reached their peak during Hate America Week, which took place in late July, an opportune time since student marchers were on summer holiday. Once we caught the attention of the protesters as they marched by when they spotted our Caucasian faces among the spectators. Quick to defuse a potentially awkward situation, my mother told my sisters and me to wave. "They think we're Russians," she cleverly explained, and her ruse seemed to have worked seeing that the marchers instantly smiled, waved back, and gave a few thumbs-ups. The Party churned out a constant stream of insidious anti-American propaganda, most of it general broadsides, but some of it extremely personal. How could my parents explain to friends and colleagues that American planes couldn't have possibly bombed schools in Beijing let alone any Chinese city that far from the Korean conflict? Then again, with absolutely no access to alternative news sources, how could they be so confident that these events hadn't transpired? About the last time I played with my once friendly Chinese companions, they confounded me with a baffling story about my real mother being dead or living back in America and the woman in our house not being married to my father. Again, it must have been enormously painful for my parents to listen to my innocent account of this confusing encounter and to try to untangle this web of deception, especially since this was no accidental misunderstanding or childish misinterpretation but a rumor planted among my playmates ultimately to fester in our household.

Almost ten years to the day after Pearl Harbor prompted our family's house arrest and eventual incarceration by the Japanese, the Chinese entry into the Korean conflict triggered our house arrest in Canton. Excluding Saturday mornings and brief visits to the hospital next door by my father, our family was confined to our house, and with the exception of a few faithful Chinese friends, we were isolated from the rest of society, living on a familiar but lonely island as political pariahs. For over a score of years, my parents' medical skills had been greatly valued, and their genuine affection for the Chinese people had been sincerely appreciated; however, now politics trumped both professional and personal considerations. Ironically, about a half a year earlier, the provincial branch of the Party had selected my father as one of fourteen citizens of the month for Guangdong, the province in which Canton is located. He was the only foreigner to win such acclaim and was chosen for this award because he had given blood to a poor woman who had lost her leg in one of the bombing raids and thus was one of his patients at the mission hospital. Because he had O negative blood and was almost always in good health, my father donated blood in several emergency cases throughout his tenure in China, but he did so surreptitiously, for most Chinese would be horrified to think that they had been injected with blood from a foreign devil, and this was even before anti-American propaganda had been ratcheted up to a feverish pitch. He was somewhat embarrassed at being singled out but genuinely amused by the fact that during his many years of medical service in China, his recipients included at least one landlord and even a Nationalist soldier. In just a few months, ideology ran thicker than blood, and this sudden contrast between veneration and calumny dripped with irony.

Days of routine and boredom were punctuated now and then by random visits by the police. My father and mother were frequently interrogated at home, usually after the three of us were upstairs in bed and oblivious to my parents' distress below, but I do recall several evenings when our house was searched. No warrants or appeals to a just cause were ever needed in view of the contention that these raids were purportedly a matter of national security. The stories varied each time, but one I remember was the claim that our neighbors had witnessed a parachute drop on our roof the night before, and the police had come to search our house once more, this time for arms that had most probably been sent to us via the alleged air delivery package the previous evening by the Central Intelligence Service (newly formed from the Office of Strategic Services). I was never frightened by these visitations and, on the contrary, found them exciting whenever they took place. After all, almost any change during our home confinement was welcome, and a chance to find real guns ferreted away under our very noses was an adventure too good to miss. I remember showing our night visitors the closet under the stairs behind my father's desk just in case they might overlook this potential hiding spot or that I might miss the chance of finding a US Army–issue .45. Once again, I was almost clueless about the ramifications of what was happening to our family. On the one hand, even with today's military technology, it would be virtually impossible to guide a cargo of arms via parachute in the middle of the night so that it would land safely on the slanted, tiled roof of a house in the middle of a foreign city. Furthermore, athletic as my father was, I doubt if he could've crawled out over the eaves that jutted over the veranda to retrieve this heavy cargo and safely haul it back into the house to squirrel away. On the other hand, why would anyone try to perpetrate such a plot? Were my father's hospital colleagues or medical students involved in some wacky attempt to recapitulate the Taiping Rebellion and overthrow the PLA with a handful of pistols? Once more, how hard it must have been for my father and mother to endure these outrageous accusations and, on that particular evening, to watch their son almost gleefully participating in the fruitless but humiliating harassment.

Every Saturday morning, my father was allowed to walk downtown to the central police station to register a weekly request for an exit visa granting us permission to leave China. From childhood, he had nurtured the dream to become a medical missionary to China, and he and my mother had twice made the decision to endure an unknown and dangerous future by remaining in their adopted country, first after the Japanese invasion of northern China and then this recent choice of staying on after the Communist victory in the south. Now, the decision was reversed. Stripped of any future opportunity to pursue their Christian service and humiliated by the personal and ad hominem attacks that were part of the larger anti-American campaign, they were not only begging to leave, they were indirectly calling into question their lifelong call. During the Saturday morning visits to the police station, my father would alternate taking my mother, my sisters, or me on these trips without much objection from the authorities, and because we traveled a different way each time, they became family excursions. Thus we were able to gain some exercise and attenuate our morning of freedom by an hour or two depending on the circuitous route taken. Except for the variations in our journey to and from the police station, the routine was always the same. My father would patiently fill out the necessary forms for an exit visa for the week ahead, and after a few questions concerning his application, he would be told that our request from the previous week had been denied.

It is impossible to fathom what goes on at the heart of a bureaucracy, assuming, of course, it has a heart, but there was no logical reason to justify why the Party continued holding us as hostages. There was no ransom to be collected, no propaganda points to be won. Moreover, because our family was only confined to house arrest and not jailed, like several single missionaries, it was implied that my parents had committed no serious crimes.

Just as in the case of our incarceration under the Japanese, it was also natural to assume that captors are more merciful when women and children are involved. Maybe all this logic trickled slowly down through the chain of bureaucracy or perhaps it was the approach of Spring Festival, but on a Saturday morning in mid-January 1951, we were abruptly granted permission to leave China.

There were a few harried days of deciding what to take and what to leave behind, interrupted now and then by farewells from a few Chinese friends who braved the criticism and came to our house to bid my parents *yi lu ping an* (along the road, peace). Just as they had done a decade earlier during the Japanese occupation, my father and mother were forced to walk out on a houseful of furniture, clothes, books, dishes, silverware, and all kinds of personal possessions, from the silly stuff you find rightfully shoved into the back of closets to family heirlooms and personal treasures whose provenance alone were of inestimable value. Some had been wisely shipped to Hong Kong after my parents began to suspect the worst, but like the children of Israel fleeing in the night, we had to leave most of these possessions behind and were each allowed to take only one suitcase of possessions. After hours of triage, our family left the house with four bags stuffed mostly with clothes but also containing a few treasured books, toys, and mementos, belongings that were specifically chosen not to attract the undue suspicion or covetousness of the authorities at the border. We had no pets at that time, but I treasured a toy boat that I was forced to abandon. One day, close to either Christmas or my birthday, I was sick in bed, and I must have been quite ill for my parents surprised me with an early present. It was a beautifully constructed motorboat, white with a red hull and powered by a battery-operated electric motor that drove a brass propeller. It was the best toy I ever owned, but it was far too bulky to take with us, and like the rest of my family, I too was forced to leave behind more than just memories.

Ai Yang, our faithful cook, friend, and extended member of the family, was allowed to leave with us. All her close relatives had already fled south to Hong Kong, so as a single woman, she was fortunate to be able to sever ties with the new republic and accompany us as a fellow refugee. On Wednesday morning, January 24, 1951, we were taken to the central railroad station on the north side of town, not too far from White Cloud Mountain and the airfield where we had landed in happier times two and a half years earlier. I had just turned twelve. There our papers were carefully checked, our suitcases thoroughly examined, and each of us was taken one at a time behind a screen where we were stripped to our underwear and searched for any hidden contraband. I learned much later that my father had a few small pieces of gold that he tied to a string and hid in his underpants to escape detection. Before, we had always left China by ship, and even our summer vacations on Lantao Island in Hong Kong were leisurely overnight trips by riverboat, so the train ride south to the British colony was unromantic and brief. The five of us disembarked with all the Chinese passengers and trudged forward toward the head of the train, carrying our heavy suitcases, my father and Ai Yang doubling their load to help out my two little sisters, who clutched their prized dolls and followed, like me, in confused silence. Passing the wheezing steam engine up front, we reached the bridge, where there was one last check of our papers by the soldiers on guard. Greeting us ahead was the supposed promised land, a new world, and an uncertain life. Behind lay our family home for more than twenty years. I felt a great longing for I knew I would never see China again.

CHAPTER 7

为人民服务
wei renmin fu wu!
Serve the people!

Contemporary China is a great nation, a global colossus, a modern superpower, and deservedly yearns for its rightful role on center stage in all aspects of human endeavor although in several arenas, it is embarrassed about being left still waiting in the wings. Take the annual accolades accorded for the greatest achievements in science, literature, economics, and world leadership for example. The very day I am writing this, the Nobel Peace Prize was awarded to Liu Xiaobo, the first Chinese ever to receive this honor, not to mention only the second citizen of the People's Republic at that time ever to win a Nobel laureate in any field. Naturally, all of China would rejoice at this news, and the Party would ensure that every media outlet available would trumpet this singular accomplishment. The barbarians have finally given the motherland its long overdue recognition, and they have partially rectified their past errors of tossing this award to a long and unworthy list of American presidents, bestowing it on Liu, a fifty-four-year-old social and literary critic from Beijing. Alas, in the Kafkaesque world of Communist China, Liu's chair of honor at Oslo remained empty, and for the first time in the history of this prize, neither the winner nor a family member was allowed to be present at the award ceremony. Liu was incarcerated back home in Beijing, serving out the beginning of an eleven-year sentence for inciting subversion. His major crimes were supporting the 1989 protest that led to the Tiananmen incident and more recently, in 2008, for writing a manifesto challenging the Party's political monopoly. The Chinese government reaction to the Nobel laureate was surly and swift. Liu's wife was kept under house arrest and cut off from any outside contact, and China leaned heavily on other nations to boycott the Oslo ceremonies as an act of solidarity, pressure that was partially successful. Predictably, China, Iran, Russia, and Sudan were happy to yank their ambassadorial presence from the event, but even nations like Saudi Arabia and the Philippines joined the boycott, reflecting China's global clout. In a self-serving act of incongruous pretentiousness, the Party simultaneously declared it would create China's own prize for peace to compete with the rest of the world, naming it after Confucius and instantly according this first one to Lien Chan, a Taiwanese politician from the Nationalist Party. This reaction is so preposterous it takes a moment to deconstruct the absurdity of this response.

Back in 1979, during our visit to Confucius's hometown, the temples and tombstones that had been vandalized by the Red Guards were just starting to be restored, but Confucianism was still regarded as one of the stinking olds denigrated by the Party. Back then there was no entry for *Confucius* in the dictionary, as if he had been airbrushed out of twenty-five centuries of Chinese culture. Back then, Communist China was celebrating the thirtieth anniversary of its successful defeat of the Nationalist Party that had fled to the nation/province of Taiwan to rule the island (quite ruthlessly, I might add). Back then, nightly TV entertainment, especially on the army channel, was dominated by war movies where brave PLA "uncles" ultimately defeated the nefarious KMT "bandits" led by the satanic dictator Chiang Kai-shek. Now, in 2010, as an immediate response to the Nobel Prize being granted to a Chinese citizen who had dared to challenge the authority of the Party, the PRC government suddenly created a Chinese prize named in honor of the very sage they had spent decades castigating and awarded it to a Taiwanese official who represented the bitter enemy whom they had ultimately defeated only after bloody decades of civil war. Call it hubris, chutzpah, or just unmitigated gall, but here once again is another illustration of the contrast between China, a modern superpower and Napoleon's slumbering giant now fully awake, and a nation led by a Party ruled by global pygmies!

Contradictions abound in all societies, and history is replete with leaders who have waffled, refrained from telling the whole truth, prevaricated, or simply and unabashedly lied outright, so the difference between the people who took over China when I was a boy and created a new society and contemporary nations like Japan, Thailand, and the United States is not categorical but one of degree. But to what degree? To understand contemporary China, certainly it is imperative to appreciate something about its geography, history, language, culture, and people as I argued in the previous chapter, but even a copious understanding of these is not enough. To understand modern China, one needs to understand the Party, and especially Mao Zedong, the man from Hunan whose words and actions molded the government of today and the man who supplanted Confucius himself in the minds of the Chinese people. And to understand the nation Mao created, it is also important to understand the era in which it was born.

Like a large number of Americans, Janene and I grew up and lived in a world dominated by the Cold War. In the summer of 1962, right after our marriage, I worked the night shift in a large baking factory that produced survival crackers under a contract with the US government, a job I found less than desirable despite the relatively handsome wage garnered. I did not enjoy shoveling tons of heavy dough into a vat that fed on to a conveyer belt that moved inexorably throughout the night, caring not one whit how fatigued I was as the dark hours rolled tediously by. Most of all, I did not enjoy coming home exhausted at seven thirty in the morning just in time to kiss Janene off for her daytime job and having to leave her after supper to return to my unhappy factory and relentless conveyer belt. During that time, when Kennedy was president and the Cuban missile crisis loomed large, many public buildings were ominously marked as bomb shelters, and the fear of a nuclear war was genuine. The Kroger baking factory in Columbus, Ohio, had a contract to produce a nutritious biscuit packaged in khaki-colored tins that were destined to be stored in these bomb shelters as emergency food for all those sequestered. Fed by a kind of outlandish Dr. Strangelove thinking, the idea was that those Americans who were safely sheltered from any nuclear strikes by Soviet missiles would be able to survive on our crackers until the dust settled and the radiation dissipated, and then and only then, they could emerge from the shelters to resume their enjoyment of life, liberty, and the pursuit of happiness. During my first week at the factory, I tried one of my own creations and found that the crackers had the taste and consistency of particleboard. The running joke among my fellow workers was that death by radiation would be more merciful and less painful than the agony ensuing from months of subsistence on the fruits of our labor that summer.

Life during the Cold War did not differ much from life today, but the fear of an apocalypse was real, as my factory job can attest, and during those decades, Americans tended to view Communism as a giant international conglomeration of like-minded evil empires united in policy, politics, purpose, and practice on obliterating every God-fearing democracy on earth. An iconic image capturing this viewpoint was that of Nikita Krushchev's bombastic display during his 1959 visit to the United Nations in New York City when he removed one of his shoes and pounded it on the table with the ominous threat "We will bury you!" Later, after the histrionics subsided, Krushchev supposedly claimed he wanted to bury capitalism, not the United States, but given the linkage between the two, this did little to mollify our fears. But like all simplistic and dualistic views about world events, this one ignored the ways in which Communism changed over time within each nation and, more importantly, in China's case, the manner in which it contrasted substantially among the nations that were members of Comintern (Communists International).

Mao's life and rise to power have been thoroughly documented both by Chinese and non-Chinese authors and historians, though no biography of his has been written so chillingly and meticulously as the volume compiled by the Chinese and British coauthors Jung Chang and Jon Halliday, whose *Mao: The Unknown Story* leaves no stone unturned or unhurled. Except for Sun Yat-sen, the story of twentieth century China is essentially a narrative of the competition between Chiang Kai-shek and Mao, with Mao the eventual winner both over Chiang's Nationalists in the civil war and, just as significantly, over all his rivals within the Party. Sun was the leader of the republican revolution against the emperor in the early part of the previous century, the founder of the Nationalist Party, and a compromiser who was willing to embrace both American ideals and Soviet assistance. Sun's ability to meld competing ideologies is amply exemplified by his three principles, which anchored the political foundation of the KMT: anti-imperialistic nationalism, democracy, and socialism. During my brief tenure as a student in a Chinese school in Huaiyuan, like all the other boys, I wore a black uniform with the red, blue, and yellow sun Nationalist badge pinned to the front of my cap, and every morning, along with the other uniformed students, I would sing the Nationalist anthem, which began, "*san min zhu yi* [the three principles]." Though Chiang took over from Sun upon his mentor's death in 1925, both he and the KMT eventually became Mao and the Party's despised enemy, but Sun remained quasi-venerated after Liberation, and one could almost make the claim that the three principles lauded in the Nationalist anthem remains a paean for the Communists except that they sing the praises of only the first and the last principle. Democracy is no longer singled out for adulation.

After our family left China in 1951 and had furloughed in the United States, my parents were reassigned to northern India, where I attended a marvelous boarding school in the Himalayan foothills. Though I was only starting high school and quite innocent and immature, I remember two questions people asked me when they discovered that this strange American boy knew as much about China as he did about his alleged American homeland. How did India differ from China was one recurring inquiry, and I recall replying that it was much more colorful than the land I grew up in. However, this query made me wonder which system would win out in the end, democracy or totalitarianism? Both Asian nations were geographically immense and diverse, both contained huge basically agrarian populations, and both were relatively poor, so it seemed that here was an ideal sociopolitical experiment on the grandest scale. Sixty years later, it is still difficult to stake any claims about which system has won out, but maybe we could say both given that the Chinese dragon and the Indian tiger stalk the jungle of global commerce as kings of the forest. The other question pressed upon me back then concerned my thoughts about Chiang Kai-shek and Mao Zedong. I had barely become a teenager, had been separated from China for about two years, and was remarkably ignorant of history and politics, so my reply was incredibly simple and superficial. Basically, I claimed from the little I knew that both men caused many Chinese to die, both wanted to control China, and both were consumed with power. Today, I would have called them megalomaniacs. The only difference I could see between them, I continued, was that one was thin and always well dressed and the other was fat and wore dumpy clothes.

When Janene and I first arrived in Beijing, in matters regarding Chinese politics, we were truly innocents abroad. Of course, I came flooded with memories of my childhood, but due to my high school experience in India, any international interests I had in college tended to be directed toward the Asian subcontinent, and as I gradually became drawn to studying linguistics, except for linguistic analyses of Chinese, I never took any courses related to the politics or history of East Asia. As the title of my MA thesis attests, a linguist can dissect the body of a language with surgical precision while never considering the culture, art, and politics that constitute the flesh and blood for all who speak that language as their mother tongue. The title of my master's research reveals the antiseptic approach I took: "A Distinctive Feature Analysis of the Phonemic Segments of Mandarin." After our first stint in graduate school, Janene and I went off to teach in Thailand for seven delightful years, and we immersed ourselves in the language, culture, and history of that colorful nation, and that is where both our children were born and where many dear friends reside. My life in China faded into the dim past, and Thailand became the land of personal enchantment and professional expertise. When it was time to pursue my doctoral research, although I did toss in some Chinese examples, my PhD dissertation was devoted to an analysis of Thai, so even my Chinese language skills had fallen by the wayside. In addition to all of this, I have never been very interested in politics and prefer muddled fence-sitting to polemical mud-slinging, and though never sympathetic toward Communism, I had been open-minded enough to have subscribed to a Soviet English language magazine in college and to have posed as a Communist atheist when once asked to speak on this topic to a church youth group. In brief, when we arrived in Beijing on that freezing evening in early January 1979, I was relatively ill-prepared for what we were about to see, hear, and face.

Although Janene and I were citizens of the Cold War and held conventional American views about Communism, we had moved well beyond viewing all Communists as faceless enemies. During my last summer in graduate school at the University of Michigan, I helped teach a group of visiting Soviet teachers, and we entertained them in our small apartment one evening. We also had a chance to visit them back in their homes in various cities in the USSR on our way back to Thailand. The tight restrictions on the lives of these Soviet teachers as well as on ours as Americans touring their nation demonstrated to us, however, that the contrasts between political systems were indeed genuine, so on our Beijing arrival, we did not expect to be greeted by a nation of Chinese Americans. Janene in particular had trepidations about developing friendships with Party members, and because fewer than 5 percent of the populace had joined the CCP at that time and though we correctly assumed that Lao Chen and other leading cadres were members, until we got to know them better, we didn't know which, if any, of our colleagues were official fellow travelers. Judging from their daily behavior and our day-to-day conversations, it was actually difficult to conclude who was or was not an official Communist, and it was a bit like trying to surmise who among your acquaintances in America was gay, vegetarian, Democrat, or Christian without specific evidence. Xiao Zhang, our loyal assistant and friend, was applying for Party membership at the time, and from him, we could see that it was not easy to get accepted. Only one out of every ten applicants made it. A clean past was obligatory, but you also had to possess the virtues of a Boy Scout and a Puritan and be moral, honest, hardworking, and dedicated to serving the people. Party members eschewed parties but loved meetings. Every Saturday morning was devoted to perusing the directives handed down from the central committee, poring over the voluminous material detailing Mao Zedong thought, and debating the niceties of Marxist-Leninism. No Friday night binges or *Animal House* antics for members of the CCP, yet for many Chinese, young and old, to be among the chosen was a lifelong goal for membership brought economic, political, professional, and social privileges to the fortunate few and for their families as well.

Wang Zhanmei, our close friend at the Tianjin Teachers College, was not as fortunate as Xiao Zhang and most of the others we knew because despite his open-minded intellectualism, he pursued Party membership for many years for just the same reasons as most other Chinese, but because of his dark past, he was not successful until late in life. His son, who was accepted long before his father, observed that Party membership was dangled in front of Wang like a carrot on a stick, and he was constantly reminded, "You're making progress. We have noticed, but you're not there yet. Keep working hard." It was a personal triumph for him when he finally was accepted, and this allowed him to win both respect and academic influence.

The first evidence of how pervasively the Party dominated the nation was displayed in the portraits that dominated the landscape during our initial stay in Beijing, throughout our tenure in Tianjin, and wherever we went in our travels around the country. Mao's mature and solemn face stared down at us from the central squares of every city and from inside virtually every office we visited, decorating the classrooms where we taught, adorning the stores where we shopped, and hanging in the homes where we were invited for meals. Mao was everywhere, an omniscient and somber presence, who seemed to follow us with his eyes wherever we went. Paralleling his gradual rise in the Party from the twenties to his total grip on the entire nation by 1949, admiration turned to veneration and had now been transformed completely into adoration. Second only to Mao and usually twinned with him on the walls of most of the aforementioned establishments was the then current party chairman Hua Guofeng. Third at least in terms of frequency of appearance were the portraits of several other Communist leaders revered and promoted by the Party, whose giant visages flanked those of Mao and Hua in all the city squares. You would guess that these would be other great Chinese heroes of the CCP, men who led the PLA in the early and later battles with the KMT, faithful cadres who had endured the Long March, and above all, devoted followers and supporters of Mao, famous contemporary Chinese leaders like Zhou Enlai,

Liu Xiaoqi, and the two stalwart generals, Peng Dehuai and Zhu De. But no, although Zhou's portrait could be spotted here and there, especially in people's homes, I never saw pictures of any of them as prominently displayed as the white faces of former Soviet leaders. Take the central square in Tianjin for example. Huge portraits framed in red of Mao and Hua naturally took center stage, but flanking them on either side were Stalin, Lenin, Marx, and Engels. Why was it that, except for the Great Helmsman and his successor, foreign faces and Russian names superseded all Chinese in the Party's pantheon of immortals? Even more perplexing to me was why Stalin's face and name was so conspicuously displayed and proclaimed. By that time, Stalin's decades-long reign of terror over his own people was common knowledge around the world, not excepting the Soviet Union itself, where Nikita Krushchev, the Man of Steel's successor, denounced his predecessor soon after gaining power in the mid-1950s and set the USSR on a course of de-Stalinization. Actually, I was more than perplexed; I was embarrassed. To cite an illustration from the same political era, how inconceivable it is to imagine that the Italians, who were once Fascist allies with Nazi Germany, would have portraits of Adolf Hitler hanging in every public square in Italy in 1979 and would praise the Führer's writings, like *Mein Kampf*, as worthy of study!

There are only two possible explanations I can come up with for the prominence given to the Russians over the Chinese. Mao was dead, and Hua was party chair and Mao's heir, so naturally, his was the face of power when we were residing there. The Great Helmsman always gripped the wheel of state with unflinching power and was jealous of any other Party members who were a threat to his captaincy. From his earliest days in the Party, he was clever at squelching any possible mutinies: *tu si gou peng* (kill the hounds for food once the hares are bagged), meaning eliminate trusted aides when they have outlived their usefulness. Stalin and his ilk were icons of Communism, and though Mao constantly quarreled with his Soviet counterparts, they did not pose a direct threat to his leadership, but it was unacceptable to have Zhou's portrait or, worse, Peng Dehuai's face emblazoned publicly in every city square even though they would be appropriately placed beneath Mao's own visage. The second was the insight that came when we viewed the film of Zhou Enlai's funeral and saw the long line of sobbing mourners parading around his flag-draped coffin. The flag, you might recall, was that of the Party's, not the Chinese national emblem. So too the great Soviet patriarchs of the Party dominated the public's view in China. Communism always trumped nationalism, and the message was clear: your ultimate allegiance is to the Party, not to your motherland.

Mao had been dead for slightly over two years when we arrived in China, but his presence was very much alive and evident everywhere and not simply in the ubiquitous portraits. He quickly appeared among the pages of the teaching materials that Chinese students used at every level to learn English. The first phrase in English presented in several primers I saw to introduce the language to elementary students was "Hail Chairman Mao!" As someone trained and experienced in teaching English as a foreign language, I thought that, irrespective of the potential political glory expounded by these first three words, pedagogically, this was simply not an appropriate way to begin an English lesson. In terms of methodology, one could attack the use of this phrase from almost any angle. Grammarians well steeped in Latin might recognize this as the vocative case, an arcane piece of syntax useful only to scholars of classical languages and a linguistic category utterly and mercifully irrelevant to English. Lexically, it is difficult to see why anyone learning English anywhere, anytime, and in any context, including Chinese elementary schools in 1979, would want to acquire as their very first syllable in this strange foreign language the word for "hail." First of all, in terms of usage, the noun form referring to frozen, pellet-sized precipitation is much more common than the verb. Second, even when used as a verb, the primary meaning is to summon and collocates very strongly with cabs and taxis and not at all with chairpersons. Thirdly, if one finally gets around to this most obscure and secondary meaning of *hail* as a verb, it carries with it generally negative connotations for, after all, "Heil Hitler" is in English "Hail Hitler!" Finally, on methodological grounds, it is impossible to defend the use of this phrase in an introduction to basic English, in a textbook for advanced students, or even in a postgraduate seminar on the use of English in politics. Take the primers used by Berlitz in their internationally famous and overpriced language schools used to teach a wide variety of languages. Like most beginning-level language books the world over, they begin with simple grammar, using simple words that deal with the visible world of the here and now. "What is this? This is the pencil. Is this the pencil? Yes, this is the pencil" is how my beginning Berlitz text starts its first lesson in Russian. Not very thrilling stuff, but neither I contend is "Hail Chairman Mao" for Chinese pupils who have heard and said this phrase in Chinese for all of their young lives.

Mao was similarly present in even more advanced materials. One of the texts prepared by our institute and was used by our college-aged students began with a description of the Chairman by Edgar Snow, the American journalist whose writings portrayed both Mao and the Communist revolution in a most positive light.

> Whatever extraordinary there is in this man grows out of the uncanny degree to which he synthesized and expressed the urgent demands of millions of Chinese, and especially the peasantry—those impoverished, underfed, exploited, illiterate, but kind, generous, courageous and just now rather rebellious human beings who are the vast majority of the Chinese people.

Lots of good vocabulary here with an apt use of authentic language and pedagogically light-years ahead of "Hail Chairman Mao!" But context is everything. Irrespective of whether Snow's excerpt was useful in helping our students acquire English, contrast this quote from the students' textbook with what happened in China to their parents' generation. Due to Mao's superpower campaign to export food in exchange for military equipment and technology twenty years before, the "kind, generous, and courageous" peasants were forced to subsist on starvation diets while producing export crops to feed Mao's national ambitions. At least twenty million died during this period, and some estimates are almost double that number. It was Mao who impoverished, underfed, exploited, and in essence, murdered those courageous human beings. Once more, history is turned topsy-turvy, and the perpetrators of genocide are lauded and, yes, even hailed!

This same textbook ends with a little lesson on intonation, the way our voice rises and falls as we stress certain words in spoken English. A poem is used here as the text, a good choice since the cadence of traditional poetry is an excellent illustration of how intonation works in English, but rather than choosing from any of the hundreds of poems and songs that salt and pepper English foreign language textbooks around the globe, the teacher who composed this exercise chose a slightly ungrammatical translation of a hymn of praise to the Great Helmsman. Here it is as it appeared in our institute's textbook without the notational system marking the stress, cadence, and intonation used to teach the students how to recite this verse in English.

> The Reddest's the Sun; Our Dearest's Chairman Mao.
> Your brilliant thought forever illumes my heart.
> The Warmest's the east wind. Our dearest's Chairman Mao,
> Our course'll always be guided by your line.
>
> Your merits are indeed great. Your love's really deep.
> You're the sun never setting in our hearts.
> Ah, your heart beats in unison with ours.
> Ah, your heart beats in unison with ours.

It's you smashed up our iron fetters.
Former slaves have become masters of the land.
It's you dispersed dark clouds and thick mists.
Spring's set in and the Sun's shining over the land.

It's you have brought happiness to us all.
We'll live happily forever.
It's you opened up the new bright highway.
We'll march firmly on and on.

The reddest's the Sun, our dearest's Chairman Mao.
Your brilliant thought forever illumes my heart.
The Warmest's The East Wind, our dearest's Chairman Mao.
Our course'll always be guided by your line. Ah!

Ah, where to begin! Let's ignore the strange punctuation, unusual use of possessives, misspellings, and fractured syntax. Let's also dismiss any stylistic criticism concerning the use of mangled metaphors, hackneyed phrases, and catalectic cadence. After all, the original piece is in Chinese, and obviously, much has been lost in translation. My brilliant colleague at the institute, Lao Jin, could have churned out a Shakespearean equivalent of this in a few minutes had he been asked to do the translation. But forgetting how miserable this piece is as a means to help Chinese university students acquire English, it conveys most clearly the political atmosphere that surrounded the nation at that time as well as during the decades preceding our arrival. This kind of maudlin adulation permeated the air the Chinese people breathed at home, at play, and in this particular example, at work. Substitute the name of Hitler, Stalin, or Kim Il Sung and you get a sense of how extremely and extensively this adulation pervaded society.

So ardent was the fealty to Mao that any willingness to disbelieve was suspended, and there was no attempt to appeal to logic, common sense, or reasonable doubt in describing the man and his accomplishments. Take his epic swim in the Yangtze on July 16, 1966. Mao chose to take a dip in the river at a time when there was a dip in his own popularity among the Party leaders and when the Cultural Revolution was beginning to erupt, so it was a demonstration that despite the fact that he had turned seventy-two, he was still China's strong man. Indeed, if one is to give credence to the official account, he was by far the strongest swimmer of all time. He allegedly swam about ten miles in roughly sixty-five minutes, floating some of the time and relying mostly on the sidestroke (unfortunately, not officially sanctioned by any swimming authority). Factoring in the favorable current, it has been estimated that for him to have swum that far in that amount of time, he must have averaged about fourteen minutes for every metric mile (1,500 meters). I am the same age as Mao was as I write this, and being a mediocre masters swimmer and having swum the mile in competition as well as longer in open-water swims, I am amazed that a pudgy smoker my age with almost no training could swim ten times farther than I at such an incredible speed and accomplishing this with the leisurely and unsanctioned sidestroke. Today, the world's fastest swimmers still can't match Mao's 1966 record even with the help of intensive training, goggles, fast suits, and a wall to push off of every fifty meters, and naturally, the master's record for the seventy to seventy-five age group is about six minutes slower than Mao's alleged time per mile. Just as incongruous, the best known photograph of Mao's historic swim shows his head sticking prominently upright like a man struggling in quicksand superimposed so badly on to a background of water that the picture almost dares you to imagine that it is a genuine depiction of the event. After her fall from grace, Mao's wife was notoriously airbrushed out of a photo with her husband more deftly than the Chairman was airbrushed into this famous snapshot. Nevertheless, the attempts to glorify him remained so relentless and assiduous that accuracy, plausibility, and credulity were never an issue. Mao was the truth, the whole truth, and nothing but the truth.

Several months after we had settled in and after we were better acculturated to our new environment and our Chinese friends and colleagues had grown more familiar with us, they started to share stories of their recent pasts over tea or meals when they could spend more private moments in our company. Partly because we were not overtly political and did not appear to be either leftist-leaning "friends of China" or "ugly Americans" who felt compelled to defend the United States both politically and socially, they began to open up to us. Without any solicitation on our part, they spontaneously began to talk about their personal lives and especially about the Cultural Revolution, which had severely affected almost every one of them. Janene has always been a good listener and projects a sense of empathy and trust, so she was exceptionally privy to many of these private and often anguished accounts, but either with her or sometimes alone, I too was privileged to hear these stories. There was another reason our friends felt free to talk to us about such deeply personal matters. By and large, these conversations were conducted in English since most of our friends were English language teachers, and because it was a foreign language, hotel staff or others lingering nearby would have difficulty eavesdropping on our conversations. But I think even more significantly, the fact that they were sharing these secrets in English and not in their mother tongue created a certain distance and sense of security in them, and several of them told us that they had never mentioned some of the anecdotes they shared with us even to their wives or husbands. Many of these sessions made us feel like priests at confessionals, and though we were almost never asked for advice or assistance, it was frequently apparent that our interlocutors left with a sense of relief, as if a hidden guilt had been assuaged or a deep longing had been satisfied. We came to China as political neophytes, but by the time we prepared to leave at the end of the year, we knew a great deal more about the country we lived in, the manner in which Mao and the Party controlled their lives, and the pain so many of them had endured. This was a China I never knew. Naturally, we had heard only the stories of the survivors. My, what tales the dead could have shared!

For at least a century, competing forces tore China apart. Initially there were the imperialistic powers from abroad and then the ever-increasing internal struggles culminating in the eventual victory of the Communists over the Nationalists in 1949. But social unrest and political turmoil did not end even after the Chinese could finally reclaim their land and rule their own country. In quick succession after Liberation, there were large-scale campaigns that mobilized the entire society in revolutionary reforms, often contradicting the one immediately preceding: the Hundred Flowers Campaign, the Anti-Rightist Movement, the Great Leap Forward, the superpower program, and so on. Mao loved five-year programs, but most of these movements lasted far less. Back and forth, up and down it went, all an excuse for making revolution and creating an artificial dialectic spun from Hegel's formula for revolutionary history: thesis plus antithesis equals a new thesis, which is opposed again in a never-ending cycle. In Mao's China, recyling was in decades before it became part of the green movement in other nations, only Mao kept coming up with a way of trashing ideals instead of an ideal way to deal with trash. In the summer of 1966, this concept of making revolution reached its most damaging and most prolonged extreme for this is when Mao launched the Great Cultural Revolution (*wen hua da ge ming*; literally, the culture great revolution). Most Sinologists ascribe the origins of this campaign to both top-down and bottom-up forces. Mao was constantly battling to maintain his supremacy of the Party and the nation throughout his political life, and by fomenting unrest throughout the countryside and in every city, this turmoil would serve as a distraction to any of his political competitors. He was quick to accuse almost anyone of taking a capitalist path and was always plotting to ensure that this was the road not taken. In the midsixties, there were many Chinese who had then lived almost a full generation under Communism and saw little change from the bad old days under the Nationalists. Many Party leaders had misused their power and had appropriated the luxurious lifestyle of their prerevolutionary predecessors, a case in point being the British Club in Tianjin whose colonial amenities were exclusively reserved for only the top Party officials in the city. Thus the Cultural Revolution squeezed most of society in a gigantic vice where they were caught between the vicious policies of the Party on top and the rebellious and revolutionary fervor of the youth on the bottom.

Especially during the first three years of this decade-long struggle, the People's Republic was torn apart by its own people, by the Red Guards who roamed the nation leaving teenage mayhem in their wake, and by adults as well who vilified family, friends, and colleagues as well as themselves in self-criticism sessions. Everyone at some time was victimized and the unfortunate more than once. Torturers ended up tortured, and like the French Revolution, executioners often met the ultimate fate they had exacted from others. In many places, pitched battles took place between competing political gangs, each claiming to be more anti-Rightist and to love Mao Zedong thought more than the other. Thank God the Chinese were unarmed because the combatants during these skirmishes were limited to rocks, clubs, and knives. Had they been bearing arms, the casualties would've been dramatically higher. Our institute colleagues described some of these encounters in vivid detail, and I could more clearly appreciate the siege mentality that had been adopted by our librarians and the curator of the museum whose buildings were in the middle of this battleground. Mao's little red book became China's bible, and the entire nation became consumed with "Bible study." I have a Thai and an English version of the *Quotations from*

Chairman Mao, and these are filled with commentaries about such thrilling notions as ideological revolutionization, struggle for the great cause of socialism, and down with US imperialism, down with Soviet revisionism, down with all reactionaries. Everyone spent hours reading and memorizing this drivel and even more time in mind-numbing meetings discussing Mao's thoughts and engaging in accusations. In those early years of the Cultural Revolution, China was swept by waves of mass migrations by Red Guards traveling to the farthest hinterlands to carry their unique form of criticism and vandalism to every province in China (fortunately, the province of Taiwan was mysteriously spared) while many of their city-dwelling fathers and mothers were sent to the countryside to perform corvée labor and to be rehabilitated. It goes without saying that the Confucian virtues of filial piety and social harmony were thrown out the window of almost every domicile.

> Don't believe your neighbor or trust your friend. Be careful what you say even to your wife. In these times sons treat their fathers like fools, daughters oppose their mothers, and young women quarrel with their mothers-in-law; a man's enemies are the members of his own family.
> Micah 7:5–6, Good News Bible

This is a perfect description of China in the late sixties although it doesn't come from Mao's bible but from the prophet Micah, who was lamenting the social decay of Judah some twenty-six centuries before the Cultural Revolution. There were all kinds of accusatory labels that were thrown about, and as long as there was an iota of plausibility about the slander, the labels stuck on the beleaguered victim like a giant Kick Me sign on their rear ends. Castigations like being antirevolutionary or anti-Rightist were vague enough to sling at anyone with some degree of accuracy, but there were also laundry lists of alleged enemies that could easily be interpreted to accuse anyone. Our teachers often mentioned being labeled one of the *chou lao jiu* (the stinking old nine): landlords, rich peasants, counterrevolutionaries, bad elements (mercury? arsenic?), rightists, traitors, spies, capitalist roaders, and intellectuals. "How terrible," our teaching colleagues lamented. "We were the worst since we were the very last of the stinking nine!" True to the Chinese proclivity to use numerical naming, besides the *chou lao jiu*, numbers were used for other criticisms: one-man viewpoint (individualism), two-faced elements, three dos and three don'ts, and so on. Sometimes, it was a silly act and not a label that brought punishment. We heard one story of a young woman who inadvertently projected Mao's picture upside down during a slide show and was summarily sent to the countryside for many years. Later, the very leader who had condemned her was also sent packing because he had wrapped his shoes in a newspaper that happened to have Mao's picture on it. What's good for the goose is good for the gander. People were browbeaten with ideology, literally beaten by mobs brandishing Mao's little red book, and most cruelly of all, beaten to a bloody pulp often in front of family and loved ones as both an object lesson and a form of torture by observation. An unthinking and dispassionate groupthink was pummeled into the populace. As one of the teachers we talked with put it, "Everything must be done by Chairman Mao's saying. It ossified the people's thinking. If Chairman Mao said plant your rice very closely, then in *every* part of China they planted rice closely, and if he said plow deep, then *every* part of China ploughed deep." To sum it up, it was Marxist-Leninism on steroids.

I was born into a Chinese society where some women's feet were still tethered, but now I was living in a land of tethered minds, where everyone, women, men, and children, were bound tightly by the thoughts of Chairman Mao. This incessant psychological pressure, a collective Chinese waterdrop interrogation, if you will, naturally created a society of broken wills and minds as well as broken hearts and bodies. Suicide was a dishonorable way out since according to the Party, it was the ultimate admission of guilt, but it was taken often. More people ascended Tai Shan during those years than returned down the seven thousand steps. Even worse than suicide was the horrible fate of those who unluckily survived attempting it. During one of my trips to Shandong University, as I was strolling back to the lecture room with a group of teachers, I asked my companion why one of the teachers in front of us walked with such a profound limp. My companion replied almost casually that during the Cultural Revolution, this teacher had been so viciously criticized that he tried to commit suicide by jumping off a building. "This one here," he said as he gestured, pointing ahead to the very building where I was about to give my talk, and he went on to add that this unfortunate wretch survived with a severely damaged leg. The Cultural Revolution thus created three categories of victims: the living, the dead, and as in the case of this poor man, the undead. On our campus, on that one, and in almost every institution throughout China at that time, there were stories like this. Because of the divisions, collusions, betrayals, and sometimes torture that took place within these institutions and the fact that everyone from our youngest students to the oldest faculty members were separated from those tumultuous days by only a few years, victim and victimizer met day after day. They often met in the same room or building where the atrocities took place, so the worst moments of the Cultural Revolution may have passed by into the sad chronicles of contemporary Chinese history, but the mental wounds remained raw and bleeding. It then became more apparent to us why so many of our faculty were ill, unable to teach at times, and why some were barely on speaking terms with others.

Visit after visit, person after person, story after story, the laments about the Cultural Revolution cascaded continually. Jennie Xu, our elderly Christian friend, told how she, her husband, and her mother were imprisoned in 1967 and all their furniture and books were confiscated. After over a year, she was released and confined to a room at her school, where she spent the next two years studying Mao Zedong thought and Marxist-Leninism and writing self-criticisms. Her apartment was never returned to her, and at that time in Tianjin, she, her husband, and her brother lived in one room, sharing kitchen and toilet facilities with her neighbors. Another teacher complained that there was no academic progress all those years. "All that energy and waste spent on rubbish. I wasted 60–70 percent of my energy on that rubbish between 1966 and 1974. Meetings, six days a week, [and we] teachers regarded as monsters." Another teacher who was sent to the countryside got special permission to return to Tianjin after getting word that the Red Guards had ransacked his home. At the Beijing Railway Station, while he was switching trains, he had to step over the naked corpses of women and men and was told they were capitalists, landowners, and rich peasants. A year later, he heard his sister had committed suicide, but he said he heard nothing more, no news, no ashes. Of course, educators were not the only ones who were treated adversely. Sharing train seats with a neurologist from Shanghai on one trip, we listened to him talk for over an hour about what had happened to him. Here is part of what he shared with us and what Janene was able to write down as a direct quote.

> You can't imagine the Cultural Revolution! Tourists coming through see only the best and certain things when all the other bad was going on. Many specialists, top cadres, leaders, experts, etc. were killed or committed suicide. Each unit killed some, so you can imagine the numbers. There were gang fights. Everything was shut down for ten years. I worked one year at a time on different farms for three years total, and I couldn't practice medicine.

We were approached one evening by a small group of teachers with an unusual request. Their former university teacher had been imprisoned since the early days of the Cultural Revolution on some generic charge of sedition and had been recently released in Tianjin. This man has nothing, they told us, and since he was soon to be reinstated at a university in another city, our friends wondered if we could give him any books we had to help him restart his life as an English teacher. A week or so later, we were able to meet Lao Wang and spend some time with him, and though limited in what we could provide, I was able to give him a few extra books we had brought with us from Pittsburgh. He was frail and blind in one eye and insisted in speaking English with us, his first opportunity to use the language in about a decade. Though reluctant to talk about his incarceration, he did describe a few of the worst details.

Lao Wang was arrested in 1966 and placed under house detention for two years and then imprisoned for nine in a cell about fifteen square meters with thirty other inmates. They shared two brick beds huddled together in the winter for warmth so that when one turned over, all the others had to move in concert. Like most inmates, he had to perform forced labor during the day, and it was at the prison factory where he lost the use of his left eye when a piece of machinery struck him in the face. Industrial accidents were common in China at that time even outside of prisons and forced-labor camps as two sources of evidence seemed to suggest. For one thing, many of our textbooks had stories about the horrors of industrial accidents in capitalist countries where workers were slaves to unrealistic production quotas. Reading accounts like this made us wonder if the index finger the Party was pointing in one direction only magnified the fact that the other three fingers in that gesture were pointing back at the accuser. The other piece of evidence was that in a few major cities such as Shanghai, surgeons were exceptionally experienced and adept at vascular microsurgery, especially of fingers and thumbs, and this made me assume that they must have had a steady stream of patients with mangled hands, giving new meaning to the digital divide. Lao Wang made one comment that brought home with vivid impact the suffering so many endured during this decade of despair. As soon as he was incarcerated, he was placed with the many other political prisoners and throughout his internment, in the internal hierarchy that emerges within the confines of a prison, they were dominated by those jailed for criminal offences. It was shocking to realize that antirevolutionaries ranked lower than thieves and murderers during that period of unrest. The criminals were rewarded with extra food or reduced sentences if they assisted in torturing the political prisoners. Once Lao Wang had to strip naked and get down on all fours and balance a pail of urine and feces on his head. Then he was taunted and kicked until the pail spilled, covering him in excrement. *Wei renmin fu wu!*

In mid-November, I arranged a visit to Shijiachuang to give two lectures at Hebei Teachers University, and there we met Lao Wang for the last time. By then, he was fully settled into his renewed life as a university professor and, except for his blinded eye, showed little evidence of the pain he had endured for the previous decade. Poor though he was, he insisted on giving us a gift to remember him by, a lovely silk print tapestry of a classic Chinese scene: nine red-crested Manchurian cranes against a bronze background. Cranes have always symbolized longevity in China, and they were emblazoned on the ceremonial robes of the imperial court in the past as an auspicious blessing for eternal rule. And nine has long been an auspicious number, and in Chinese history, one can go far back to the nine bronze tripods, the nine classics, and the nine gifts of investiture. Lao Wang was imprisoned for being one of the stinking nines, but to us, he symbolized the best of China, a fragrant symbol of eternal freedom.

I was always bothered by the inequity of the caste system in India when I lived there during my high school years. Though leaders like Gandhi and Nehru were opposed to the tradition, caste permeated most of Indian society, and if you were born a Sudra (the lowest caste of all), you remained a Sudra irrespective of your life's achievements. Your parents' DNA determined your fate. After Liberation and especially during the Cultural Revolution, a quasi-caste system dictated who were considered to be among the privileged and who were deemed enemies of the state. When universities opened up again and began accepting students at the end of the Cultural Revolution in the midseventies, students whose parents were workers, peasants, and soldiers filled the rolls. These young people were exceptional to be sure since they were chosen from a cohort of applicants who had waited years for tertiary education, but strange as it may sound, I don't recall a single student at our institute whose father was a landlord, capitalist roader, or counterrevolutionary.

Wang Zhanmei, our good friend from the Tianjin Teachers College, is an example of how "the fathers have eaten sour grapes but the children's teeth are set on edge," to quote the Good Book. I have already related how because of his alleged antirevolutionary heritage, it was only late in his life that Wang was finally accepted into the Party, and this gave him a modicum of status and privilege before he died. At his funeral, he was lauded as an excellent CCP member and loyal Marxist fighter but not for his lifelong service as a brilliant and productive scholar and dedicated professor. There was another twist after he died demonstrating that the indelibility of the stain from an unclean past tainted an individual from womb to tomb. He was not accorded the full rank of a professor but classified at a lower rank that prevented him from receiving a memorial service and only a "farewell to body" ceremony. Even his cremation was done at a site for the general public despite the fact that technically, because of his Party status, Zhang should have been cremated at the senior cadre building. As his son so accurately and acidly observed, "Even in death, one could not escape the Party's caste system." Caste was alive and well in the People's Republic, but unlike India, where it is was always through bloodlines, in China, a bloody label could be cast on anyone.

Mao's policy of fomenting political turmoil and keeping all of society on edge affected not just individuals but entire institutions. The deleterious effect of his various programs and pogroms on the national economy and on the construction and destruction of entire industries is well documented, but I was witness to a small but revealing sample of how the Party's machinations determined the fate of an entire profession. Before Liberation, psychology enjoyed the same reputable status as other academic fields, and influenced by scholars trained abroad despite the constraints of the protracted civil war and conflict with Japan, Chinese psychologists had an active association, conducted conferences, and pursued research and publications in this young and popular academic discipline. For reasons I could never uncover, Mao and the Party did not approve of the study of mental life, however, and some time in the fifties, psychology was banished, and psychologists were asked to pursue other things. Recall my account about the problem of getting an American textbook on psycholinguistics because the censors at the post office were psyched by the prefix *psycho*.

China's banning of psychology struck me as odd since the USSR had poured millions of dollars into aiding the CCP from its inception through the founding of the People's Republic and a decade thereafter up to Mao's falling out with Khrushchev and the final dissolution of the rocky marriage between the two Communist giants. The influence of the Soviet Union was everywhere, in the military, industry, agriculture, economic programs, city planning, and systems of education, including the social sciences. I recall being aghast to learn that the Central Institute of Minorities that I visited during my first week in Beijing used an essay by Stalin to categorize ethnicity, thus explaining some of the strange classifications I encountered about who was or was not a Han Chinese. Although hampered by the same oppression that all other disciplines faced during Stalin's long reign of terror, psychology was a prestigious science in the Soviet Union, and during that time, Russia gave the world three of the twentieth century's greatest psychologists: Ivan Pavlov, Lev Vygotsky, and Alexander Luria. Even the study of paranormal behavior was tolerated and had more prestige in the USSR than it did in the United States, yet the Chinese showed little interest in following the Soviets in this field. Psychology was banned, and the Chinese Psychological Society was dissolved not long after the founding of the People's Republic. As one of my Chinese graduate students remarked, "Before the Cultural Revolution, psychology was put on the back burner. During the revolution, things went from bad to worse: it was simply thrown out of the kitchen!"

Shortly before we were to return to the States, I got word that the Chinese Psychological Society was finally given permission to convene again right there in Tianjin on November 28, and after a hasty negotiation, I arranged to give a paper on recent trends in neurolinguistic research to the medical psychology group at this historical conclave. With Lao Jin as my accomplished interpreter, I spent a day at this meeting and enjoyed the opportunity to make a presentation and, even more, to participate in the question-and-answer session afterward. On entering the room that morning, however, I was caught by the sight of my audience. Scanning the room as I walked in, except for a reception with the city council that ruled Tianjin, I had never seen so many old men in one place. Those assembled must have been close to double my age, and it was immediately obvious that when these scholars were just reaching their professional prime, they were around forty, like me, but that was exactly when they and their profession became politically extinct. It would take another generation of Chinese before young minds would begin to study the mind again, and like so many other areas of life in China, society had been forced to take two strides backward while the rest of the world was racing ahead. The reactionary forces that held the nation back in 1979 and kept them continually one step behind the developing world underscores the amazing manner in which the China of today has rocketed phoenixlike from the ashes of its past.

One of the most powerful forces binding the People's Republic and chaining the populace in fear and mental oppression was the Party's ability to control information. Even today, China's firewall around the Internet is much more impermeable than the fabled Great Wall of its past, and for their leaders, IT is more about an information trap than transfer. Though we were foreign guests of the Chinese government and treated royally and paid handsomely by them, at least in contrast to our colleagues, we were subject to the same censorship as everyone else, perhaps even more stringently in some cases. Those were the days before the Internet, and even international phone calls were a rare luxury, so snail mail correspondence was our primary means of personal and professional contact with the outside world. Both Janene and I have always been prolific correspondents, and between us, we posted over four hundred letters to some fifteen countries that year, virtually all via airmail. Early on, we realized that some of our mail was taking much longer than a week to reach its foreign destination though it was easier to recognize the delays affecting our incoming correspondence more than the delays hampering the letters we sent out. Maybe planes flying westward across the Pacific were slowed by the jet stream. True, but at most, they are slower by only an hour or so compared to eastbound flights to the States. Maybe Chinese workers at the post office had trouble reading our Tianjin address in English. Perhaps, although mail from abroad was always initially streamed to postal employees who knew English, and it seemed odd that it would take two months to translate a simple address into a Chinese destination. Besides, most letters came to us within a week of the US postmark. Why did some letters take eight times as long? The obvious explanation was that they were delayed at our end in China, case in point—my problems in getting textbooks on psycholinguistics shipped to me on time.

A sad example of this delay was one of the weekly letters my parents faithfully sent us throughout our stay. It was dated July 15, 1979, and began and ended with descriptions of unremarkable summer activities, but the central gist of the letter described the sudden death and sad aftermath of a very close friend of ours from Thailand who just happened to be in the same town as my parents north of New York City. We knew she had been battling breast cancer for years and had been well enough to visit America with her family, but she had a sudden relapse, prompting her husband to call my father whom he knew was a physician and lived in that same town. My father signed the death certificate and arranged for a hearse while my mother tried to console our friend and his three young children. My parents even helped to arrange a memorial service and bought rosebuds for the altar signed "From Tom and Janene." This somber and important message was just the kind of information one would want to receive as soon as possible, and nowadays it would've been instantly telecommunicated to us even if we were in China. The aerogramme (yet another anachronism) came September 25, more than two months after my parents had mailed it to us, and like other random pieces of mail we received that year, it had been resealed with the same kind of mucilage that we used to seal letters when we went to post correspondence at the central post office in Tianjin. When I launched one of several complaints to the postal authorities about our mail being opened and censored, I routinely received the same answer. There was no censorship in China, especially for respected foreign guests like Janene and me. Perhaps the letter was delayed because the antirevolutionary elements working for the US Postal Service routed this (and all the other mail we complained about) first to Taiwan. According to them, it was a well-known fact that some of the mail to the People's Republic was diverted to the province/nation of Taiwan, opened, censored, resealed (with Tianjin mucilage), and after this unfortunately long delay, finally sent to the central post office in Tianjin, where it was immediately whisked to us. These explanations were delivered with a straight face and oozed in sympathy. They became more convoluted and sympathy oozed less later in the fall when we were to engage the censors once again in a more contentious conversation.

One Thursday in late October, I received notification that two people from the customs department of the post office wished to see me, and a while later, two older men cycled up to our classroom building and came up to my office, each carrying the small black briefcases that all cadres seemed to covet as necessary accessories. Xiao Zhang was asked to interpret, so I knew this was serious business. After fidgeting nervously through polite introductions, they finally got around to the point of their visit, saying they had "some things from Hong Kong" they wanted me to look at. They reached into their bags and pulled out two packages wrapped, or I should say rewrapped, in brown paper addressed to me in neatly printed English. "Is this your name and address?" they asked in a style of inquiry that is rarely used in normal chitchat but is the manner lawyers employ when interrogating a witness on the stand. "Yes," I replied, stating the obvious. They then asked me to open the packages. I resisted the temptation to appear too flippant by pointing out that I was actually reopening the mysterious bundles, and to no one's surprise, except Xiao Zhang's, there in front of us lay a dozen Chinese New Testaments fresh in their black leather covers. We had brought a Bible with us for personal use throughout our stay, but as the months progressed, various Chinese friends, some Christian, some not, expressed a keen interest in obtaining a Chinese or English Bible. The true believers obviously wanted to own a Bible in Chinese to use personally, but there were also many who were intrinsically curious about Christian Scripture, recognizing its important role in English literature, hence they were interested in obtaining one in English. We had purchased a copy of the 1978 PRC Constitution (handsomely bound in red silk), and despite the absence of any overt religious activity whatsoever, Article 46 clearly stated that "Citizens enjoy freedom to believe in religion and freedom not to believe in religion and to propagate atheism." The devil appeared to lurk in the details since freedom of religion was permitted, but unlike its antithetical counterpart, religious faith could not be propagated, meaning, it seemed, nor could it be promulgated, practiced, or pursued. Citizens could go around hailing the jewel of the flowering lotus, believing Allah was great, or petitioning God to be merciful to them as long as they did it individually and under their breath. Hence, we knew we were flirting with regulations when we wrote to friends abroad for copies of the Good Book both in Chinese and English. What began as a simple conversation with these two cadres had now evolved into a deposition. The questioning continued.

"Are you going to use these Bibles for your personal use?"

"No," I responded, "I'm going to give them to some friends."

"Hmm, and do these friends live in Tianjin?"

"They live in China" was my not so informative retort.

"Where in China? What are their names?"

As my responses grew vaguer and vaguer, they finally informed me that there was a certain regulation that only two Bibles were permitted per person, and even if my wife, two children, and I were capable of reading a Chinese edition comfortably, we had in essence exceeded our quota. We talked back and forth for almost two hours intently but always in a polite and formal manner following courtroom decorum. I showed them Article 46 in my handsomely bound PRC Constitution, suggesting that their regulation violated rights to freedom of religion, but this counterargument was dismissed as irrelevant. After much discussion, I was left with two choices: either rewrap the Bibles (yet again) and mail them back to Hong Kong or they would take the Bibles with them, and I could invite my Chinese Christian friends, whoever they were and wherever they happened to reside, to come to the central post office and pick them up. They seemed pleased with my decision to go for the second option, assuming that no fellow citizen, Christian or otherwise, would dare walk into a government office and ask for the very book that was burnt by the thousands or that served as evidence of being a counterrevolutionary during the preceding decade of political turmoil.

Although it started off poorly, this little event had a happy ending. We had already been introduced to Pastor Liu Qingfen, the remarkably brave and energetic leader of the local Christian Patriotic Association, the officially sanctioned but still heavily restricted group of Christians in the city, and during the next of his periodic visits to our hotel, we told him that we were able to secure a dozen Chinese New Testaments for him and other friends but that the censors at the post office had in turn secured them from us. "No problem," Pastor Liu replied. "I'll go over and get them myself. Thank you so very much!" At his next visit, he told us how he had cycled over to the central post office, announced his name and intentions, and after some discussion with the two cadres who had come to see me, he insisted that they relinquish the Bibles to his custody, promising that not only would he ensure that no members of his flock would get more than two copies each, he assured the cadres that no one would get more than one copy of this precious book! No one involved lost face, and among other things, this anecdote demonstrated the remarkable courage some Chinese exuded even in the face of oppression, but it also showed how our city was becoming more open. An incident that would have been inconceivable four years earlier now took place with only a minimal amount of fuss.

Annoying as the random acts of censorship were, most of our correspondence got through to us speedily and without interruption, but several times, letters were delayed because of a peculiar kind of reverse censorship; that is, there was unmistakable proof that someone involved with the Chinese postal system interfered with our mail, but by the same token, it was obvious that the postal authorities who read our letters or blocked our Bibles and psycholinguistic textbooks were clearly not involved. From time to time, a letter would arrive that manifested superficial signs of tampering: it took longer than the usual week to ten days to arrive, the envelope was uneven or slightly torn at the top, and there were the telltale smudges of Chinese mucilage, sometimes lathered on quite liberally. When opened, these envelopes always revealed a little surprise, a small slip of paper ranging from about a quarter to half the size of a sheet of regular letterhead, containing a photocopied message in Chinese sometimes handwritten and sometimes printed. The contents always concerned some form of political protest and were signed and dated at the bottom by anonymous groups from various provinces. To me, they appeared to be a kind of *xiao zi bao* (little character posters), and when we showed these slips to Chinese friends whom we felt comfortable entrusting with such information, they concurred that these were genuine notes of dissatisfaction apparently intended to be disseminated surreptitiously. Most were terse and printed neatly in verse form like one that was slipped into one of the letters we received from the States late in the fall.

> Chopping off heads is not important,
> Seek only for the people;
> After Wei Jingsheng is slaughtered,
> Many others will disappear.
>
> Fudan University Human Rights League
> 12 November 1979

Although I did not know this until well after we had left China and had done some reading about contemporary Chinese history, Wei Jingsheng was, according to many scholars, China's most famous dissident who was tried for criticism against the Party that October and was imprisoned with a fifteen-year sentence.

Fudan University is located in Shanghai and was and still is one of China's premier educational institutions.

One of the first of these secreted broadsides we received was, in contrast to the verse above, a fairly lengthy lament handwritten in prose style about all the young people who were scattered to the countryside during the Cultural Revolution but were still stuck out there, unable to return to their homes and families in the cities and to resume their formal education.

> The peasants are unsatisfied—the educated youth have occupied some of their land, divided and shared their grain, and have increased the contradictions in the countryside. Families are unsatisfied—children have been dispersed everywhere, their knowledge is left unused, the parents have tried their very best to bring up their children but in the end they are unable to help their parents in shouldering any family responsibilities and have caused parents to send money to the countryside for their children to survive. The nation is unsatisfied—a waste of knowledge learned—ten years or more of education not being used by anyone anywhere but the educated youth are forced to use hoes "to fix up good old mother earth."

The critique ended with a series of slogans, which you could almost hear being chanted by a crowd of disgruntled youth.

> We want food to eat!
> We don't want to be called new farmers!
> Down with the Gang of Five!
> Back to the cities and make revolution!

At the bottom, it was signed in the same handwritten black ink characters as the rest of this document, "Northern Guangdong, The Educated Awakened Society Propaganda Team, February 1979." The Gang of Five was a distinctly politically incorrect reference to the Gang of Four, the alleged leaders of the Cultural

Revolution that included Mao's wife and that were the villains of the day during the time we lived in China. Without explicitly naming him, they added Deng Xiaoping, who was conversely cast as the official hero of the day, rescuing the republic from its leftist past and propelling it on its path toward modernization. Deng certainly was a revolutionary in this regard, but he was also a reactionary in his oppression of dissent as was evident a decade later during his role in the Tiananmen incident. The writers of this protest longed for more than just the economic trappings of modernity.

Heavy and depressing as these messages were, there was something refreshing about reading descriptions of Chinese society that were almost the polar opposite of the constant and consistent propaganda that bombarded our eyes and ears every day in the media and in all public pronouncements. It was heartening to know that at least *some* Chinese had an alternative view of the universe and, even more, that they were willing to risk expressing that view in the open albeit via the few *xiao zi bao* that appeared occasionally in our foreign correspondence. Here was a tiny harbinger of how dissent could be disseminated publicly in the future via the Internet and social media, but back in 1979, the only tools of mass communication available to protesters were brush and ink and slips of paper slipped into an opportune envelope. Another thing that struck me when I read this particular document was the way in which traditional Confucian ideals emerged despite the fact that the young author(s) had spent their entire life in an anti-Rightist republic and had just survived a civil revolution viciously attacking Confucian ideals. Education and knowledge are valued over ideology. Note too the strong sense of filial piety and the distinctly hierarchical but harmonious perspective on society. Dissatisfaction at the proximal level gives rise to dissatisfaction at the more distal level that in turn creates dissatisfaction throughout the whole nation. You can take the boy out of the civilized city and into the countryside, but you can't take Confucius's view of a civil society out of the boy.

A more benign and humorous form of censorship and information control was exemplified by Janene's attempt to involve her students in community service. On the face of it, all of Chinese society was mobilized to serve the greater good, and non-academic communal labor was part of our institute's weekly curriculum. As foreign experts, we got off easy for we were not obliged to take part, but on several Saturday afternoons, we would join the students and faculty anyway in these collective endeavors, such as picking up trash or sweeping the dusty campus. However, Janene wanted to engage the students in attacking a more pressing and pungent problem, the smelly bathrooms that stunk up our building especially during the heat of late spring through early autumn. The men's lavatory was bad enough, and like Janene, unless nature's call was unrelenting, I tried to avoid using the squat toilet, and for most of the time, it remained only the "number one" restroom for me. But the women did not have the luxury of using a mildly malodorous trench as a urinal and were forced to employ the squalid stalls. She took me into the ladies' room one warm afternoon when no one was around, and the sight and stench of a miasma of bloody rags and unflushed excrement was revolting enough to make us doubly appreciate the flush toilet, soap, clean sink, and tepid water back at our hotel. Inspired by the *da zi bao* (big character posters) popular at the time as a way of public protest, Janene came up with the clever idea of having her students create posters in English to display in the halls and bathrooms and inspire cleanliness. The rats and flies had allegedly disappeared under Communism, so the next logical step would be to tackle the public toilets. The students leaped at this opportunity to blend their learning of English with a form of community service more effective than moving the campus dust every weekend, and within a day, attractive posters in English encouraged everyone to be more socially responsible.

This little campaign didn't go quite as far as the admonishment hikers are encouraged to follow (pack out what you packed in) but did produce slogans more colorful than the Party's. "We aim to please: you aim too please!" was one I suggested and served, I would go so far as to claim, as a better motto for learning English than "Hail Chairman Mao!" The institute's cadres were immediately alarmed. For one thing, *da zi bao* were somewhat acceptable if posted outside public buildings at appropriately designated spots, but not inside and upstairs and all over the English department. More alarmingly, these protest posters were in English, so they had to be translated immediately for the leading cadres to decipher. The posters were taken down soon after they were put up, and as far as I could tell, within a few days, the girls' bathroom remained a putrid cesspool and the boys' aim was as bad as ever.

Much has been written about the Cultural Revolution, and over the decades, there are many eloquent and heart-wrenching stories about the personal tragedies that unfolded during this particularly bleak period of contemporary Chinese history. However, back then in 1979, none of these narratives had been published, and within China itself, at least in public, there was a general tendency to foster a collective amnesia. From the very top, Deng Xiaoping, Chairman Hua Guofeng, and most of the Party leadership raced to distance themselves from what had just transpired, and Deng in particular was eager to replace the Gang of Four, the official scapegoats for all of Mao's excesses during those days, with the Four Modernizations. In effect, the Party was telling the people to forget what happened yesterday and look to tomorrow. But the populace itself was eager to put the past behind them, at least publicly. Just as the Cultural Revolution was ignited by both top-down and bottom-up forces, now both sides seemed to unite in extinguishing any remaining embers of the conflagration. Embarrassment, guilt, depression, and pain are not frequent and spontaneous conversation starters, and like victims of rape, it is less painful to keep the festering agony trapped inside or even to pretend that it didn't really happen that way if at all. But privately, during the many confessionals shared with Janene and me, the stories spilled out, and there was almost an emotional transfer at the end of these conversations where our Chinese friends left feeling relieved, leaving us encumbered with yet another example of the depravity of it all.

I recall one evening, when I was musing about the way in which the Chinese and the citizens in the Soviet Union called their country the motherland in contrast to fascist nations like Germany during World War II, which referred to themselves as fatherlands, a strange juxtaposition emerged. Thinking of all the slaughter that had occurred around the world in my lifetime, especially in China, it seemed ironic that despots ruling fatherlands killed mostly foreigners whereas dictators of motherlands killed more of their own. In Hitler's mind, the millions of Jews he exterminated were not true Germans, but there was never an iota of doubt in Mao's thinking that the tens of millions of Chinese who died under his rule were not his own flesh and blood. I am not for a minute suggesting that there is a comparative scale of morality in play here, and the murder of one single soul that I will describe in a moment is an unfathomable loss, but there is something chilling when a nation's leader, like Mao or like Cambodia's Pol Pot, whom the Great Helmsman supported, can order the massacre of millions of his very own people and keep it a secret for so long and, worse yet, elicit the praises of foreign visitors at the very time the executions and exterminations are taking place!

We were living in Northern Thailand in the early seventies when selected groups of American students, teachers, union leaders, academics, and health experts visited China on short tours in the wake of the initial rapprochement inaugurated by Nixon and Kissinger's diplomacy. They all shared nearly the same itinerary, visiting the same No.1 nurseries, hitting the same

Friendship Stores, and if they were lucky, securing a last-minute audience with Zhou Enlai, a man who could charm the rattles off a snake and found that mesmerizing idolizing Americans was mere child's play. One American public health official whom we met during his visit to Thailand after one of these tours encouraged me to try to link up with such an excursion after learning of my background and was so lyrical in his account of his China visit that he seemed to have momentarily lost all professional judgment. I was amazed to hear from him that rats and venereal diseases had probably been eliminated under the Communists, and his evidence for this bold claim was that this is what everyone had told him and, further, he had seen none during his entire three-week stay! Like most of the world outside China at that time, I did not know the depth of the atrocities that had taken place before and during this period, but I was still bemused by his account. Because he was a stranger, I did not want to begin an argument about what constituted evidence but started wondering to myself if he, a professional health care worker, was willing to suspend that same disbelief during the time that we met in Thailand. After all, there were no rats or venereal disease in the room where we were conversing, and depending on his luck with rodents and whether (unlike many foreign visitors) he avoided the infamous sex houses, he could return to America with the same claim about Thailand that he had made so confidently about China. An experienced Chinese-American academic who was able to visit his relatives and several Chinese cities for over a month in 1975 wrote, "Everywhere, men and women of all ages move with a confident optimism and a unity of purpose that is at once simple and ennobling." Among most of my fellow graduate students at the University of Michigan in the late sixties and among our American academic and missionary friends in Thailand during the seventies, there was often a common blurring of very legitimate anti-Vietnam War sentiments with sympathy for Communist regimes in Asia, and so at an intellectual level, one can almost understand the desire to see China as a new Israel and Mao as a resurrected Moses. In fact, the report from which I just quoted made almost this exact comparison.

> People who have visited Israel at the most ardent moments of that new nation like to compare the two societies. But social reconstruction in China, of course, proceeds on a much grander scale.

Indeed it did! Thanks to Mao and the Party, the "reconstruction" took tens of millions of lives on a scale of truly inhuman grandeur!

My final childhood home in China was the large duplex we shared with a Chinese doctor's family in Canton. As I described in the previous chapter, this house and the surrounding compound were the most luxurious accommodations my missionary parents enjoyed, and that is why the events after Liberation seemed so especially cruel. A well-landscaped compound loses its beauty if it is the target of random bombings, and the site of malicious rumors and accusations only enhances the magnitude of man's inhumanity. An attractive house becomes a hovel under house arrest, and the healing comfort of a well-maintained hospital is transformed into a chamber of death if it serves as the stage for the kangaroo trial and execution of an innocent man. We shared our house with the family of Dr. Ross Wong, an American-trained doctor and a Christian, and as director of the Hackett Medical Center, he served as my father's friend, colleague, and boss. I have vague recollections of Dr. Wong since he devoted most of his time in the hospital across the courtyard as an administrator, surgeon, and as a teacher of surgery to the young interns who followed him dutifully. I do remember his daughters, however, both almost a decade older than I and beautiful enough to attract a steady stream of suitors, especially on weekends. As is the habit of many Chinese educated either in English or abroad, the Wong family used English given names, and Viola, the younger daughter, taught my sister and me piano, and despite the attractiveness of my tutor, Judy's lessons lasted longer and turned out much more successfully than mine. When Chinese troops crossed the Yalu River to engage in the Korean conflict and my parents suddenly became political pariahs and our family was placed under house arrest, our contacts with everyone, including the Wong family next door, were curtailed. Dr. Wong elected to stay in Canton and continue his medical work as best he could, but his wife and two daughters, like thousands of other Chinese citizens, fled to Hong Kong while they were still able to avail themselves of this rare opportunity. Years later, when Janene and I were teaching in Thailand, whom should we meet but Viola and her husband, David, who had emigrated to Bangkok and eventually moved on to Honolulu. So bitter were their memories of Canton after Liberation that I can't recollect ever being able to elicit any anecdotes from them about those days beyond a few platitudes about our piano lessons and familial friendship.

After they returned to the States, my parents were able to gather bits and pieces of Dr. Wong's fate more than fifteen years later when the Cultural Revolution was at its initial feverish pitch. Like millions of others, he was castigated by the Red Guards for his contemporary antirevolutionary attitudes and behavior. And like the president of Shandong University and so many other Chinese who had been educated abroad but had decided to return to China shortly after Liberation, he was interrogated incessantly about the reasons for his return. Love of the motherland and wanting to serve the people simply didn't cut it; the real motivation lurking behind these patently absurd answers was that he was a capitalist roader or, worse yet, a spy sent by the Americans as an antirevolutionary to destroy the new republic. The longer the denials persisted, the more merciless the interrogations became although confession and self-criticism, whether concocted or sincere, wrought immediate punishment, so the accused were caught in a Catch-22 purgatory. Adhere to the truth and endure increasing torment or break down and confess and endure increasing torment. Under this relentless and hopeless psychological assault, it is no surprise that suicides were common for although they were interpreted as implicit admissions of guilt by the torturers, at least they gave the hapless victim eternal amnesty from the torment that they had been facing. After days and weeks of agonizing interrogation and beating, my parents heard that their friend and colleague could stand this torture no more, and one night, he broke free from his confinement at the hospital and, climbing to the top floor, leaped to his death, thus justifying in the eyes of his revolutionary young captors their belief in his complicity.

There remained one small but chilling detail about Dr. Wong's death that helps illustrate how sordid that era in Chinese history had become. Dr. Ross Wong, the skilled surgeon who had left the comforts of America to return to revolutionary China, was found facedown on the pavement beside the hospital where he had worked, allegedly having committed suicide, but oddly, both of his hands had been freshly chopped off. *Wei renmin fu wu!*

After receiving this shocking news, my mother felt moved to write a long poem that she published in book form using illustrations taken by a Canadian photographer who toured China just as the Cultural Revolution erupted. It was titled "Red Is No Longer a Color" (*hong xianzai bu shi yanse*). It was dedicated "to the memory of a beloved doctor who gave his life for his students in whom he believed." This is how the poem begins.

> I remember the curve of a red lacquer bridge through Chinese willows...
> Suddenly winds of change blew violence across the land.
> The smoldering tinder of the patient past took fire.
> Brother fought brother; child fought mother and father
> for the clean breath of a new day.
> I saw these people caught in the winds of change—
> The old, fearful of change,

The young who believed that change in itself
is always a change for the best;
the young, the old, and the middle-aged
who knew that change must come
who believed that this was a change worth dying for...

—Myra Scovel, 1967

Writing this chapter has brought me no joy, and I imagine it is just as morose to read, so it seems fitting to conclude with a counterpoint to the political tyranny, violence, and even death that the Chinese people were forced to face even after they had won their freedom from the outside oppression of imperial powers. The Cultural Revolution left millions scarred, cynical, and disillusioned, and now that the former Red Guards are approaching the age of their grandparents back then, those three bitter fruits they helped seed among their own people as well as among themselves are not quite so astringent; indeed, for many Chinese, those days are best left simply forgotten. But amnesia is no panacea, neither is forgetfulness equivalent to forgiveness. We would have left China in the same mental and emotional state as many of our Chinese colleagues had we not been blessed with the opportunity to meet members of the Christian community in Tianjin and witness the resurrection of their church just before we left. Here were the very people my mother had written about in her tribute to Dr. Wong. They were the people who endured because they believed, and because of them, we left China with hope.

I have already noted that the way the constitution of the People's Republic of China was written, under the section titled "The Fundamental Rights and Duties of Citizens," all Chinese could "enjoy freedom to believe in religion" but that Article 46 went on to say, in effect, "or not!" That is, only nonbelievers had the right to propagate their unbelief. On March 15, there was an editorial in *Ren Min Ri Bao* (*The People's Daily*), the Party's primary medium for disseminating policy and information, on religion and feudal superstitions, and it began with the sweeping claim that "all worship of mysterious supernatural powers can be called superstition. Religions are superstitions." The editorial went on to stake out a very orthodox Marxist view, talking about how religion is the opiate of the people and insisting that Marxists consistently oppose any form of religion. It is not surprising, therefore, to see that in the China we lived in, a China that had just begun to recover from the oppression of the Cultural Revolution, a China that was firmly ruled by a Communist Party rooted deeply in traditional Marxist-Leninist ideology, the promise of freedom of religion entertained by the first clause of Article 46 was as vacuous as outer space. No Buddhist, Taoist, Muslim, or Christian house of worship was fully open at that time (with a tiny exception that I will describe in a moment), and except for an underground community of believers, religious belief was at best in the heart but not in the temple, shrine, mosque, or cathedral. In addition, as we witnessed in our encounters with the supposedly nonexistent censors at the Tianjin Post Office, religious literature and scriptures were either banned or severely curtailed. As far as I could see, the closest the Party came to promoting any form of religion was during the heyday of the Cultural Revolution, when Mao himself was conferred an almost divine status and was worshipped and idolized. And since he lived right next to the Imperial Palace in Beijing, like the ancient emperors, he wore the Mandate of Heaven and served as the sole intermediary between heaven and earth, in fact, between life and death.

After eight months of holding informal family worship services in our hotel room each Sunday morning, in early September, during a weekend trip to Beijing, we finally got to worship in the only government-sanctioned Christian service in China. Each Sunday from 10:00 a.m. to 11:30 a.m., the Beijing International Christian Fellowship gathered at the Sino-Japanese Youth Exchange Center. Our Shandong cabbie who drove us to our downtown destination from the International Guesthouse in the northwest quadrant of the city made a couple of wrong turns and, at one point, barreled down an alley that was blocked by a parked truck. There was no place to turn around, and by this time, two cars came up behind us to prevent a retreat. Time was wasted trying to locate the truck driver, more time for our driver to squeeze his vehicle up on to the narrow sidewalk, and even more expended by our now very frustrated cabbie trying to needle through the remaining aperture without losing his side-view mirrors. We arrived at the Youth Center barely in time for the beginning of the service. From their faces, the hundred or so worshippers seemed to be predominantly older Chinese with foreigners of various nationalities comprising the rest: tourists, businesspeople, and diplomats. We learned later from an American embassy family that attended regularly that until Easter, the ratio had been the reverse, but gradually, more and more Chinese were coming to worship. The service was led in Chinese by an elderly Pastor Yin. There was a half hour of prayers, hymns, and Bible readings followed by another half-hour communion service, an apparent coupling of Reformed and Anglican traditions. Missing from the liturgy was a sermon, so preaching was taboo even for this unique and highly scrutinized service. Except for the lack of coffee and cookies, the friendly mingling among the congregants after worship reminded us of similar experiences on Sunday mornings in Thailand and back home in the States. We met three other elderly pastors who rotated leading worship with Pastor Yin. We were delightfully surprised to bump into an American couple who were touring China and were friends of ours when we lived in Thailand together. Their tight itinerary precluded their taking a spontaneous side trip to see us in Tianijn, but over the course of that year, we must have entertained about half a dozen American friends or acquaintances who were able to include Tianjin on their tours and who were taking advantage of being among the first large wave of Americans to visit the exotic land that had been hidden from them for so long behind the Bamboo Curtain.

We had returned home to work from our weekend in Beijing for less than a week when, through our friendship with Jennie, we were introduced to Pastor Liu Qingfen, one of the leading lights of the Tianjin Christian Patriotic Association. A large, almost plump man with a round face and quick smile, had he a white beard and red suit, he could have almost doubled as a Chinese department store Santa. He was in his midsixties, but he moved vigorously and with purpose, and later, when we heard his story about cycling over to the central post office to demand the Bibles that had been confiscated from us, that single episode captured the essence of the man. He spoke little about himself though we did learn that because of his faith, he had been singled out for rehabilitation long before the Cultural Revolution broke out. For twenty-two years he labored in the countryside and only recently was allowed to return to Tianjin, where he was permitted to do social work with young people. As he sipped tea in our second floor sitting room at the hotel, he told us that just a week earlier, on September 1, the association was allowed to regroup in Tianjin and was given permission to resume public services of worship in the city. This was an astounding piece of news for us as by then we were well aware of the empty churches and cathedrals we had seen in our cycling around the city as well as on our travels to various provinces. Whether abandoned or converted into warehouses, they stood like skeletons amid the crowded buildings surrounding them, with no hymns or prayers breathing life into those hollow halls, and like the dry bones of the Negro spiritual, they lay lifeless, longing to hear the Word of the Lord. We were equally aware of the social, political, and psychological trauma that all believers were forced to endure, and for many, this oppression had left them like their former houses of worship, mere spiritual skeletons. So Pastor Liu's news was truly good news to us, but imagine how the Chinese faithful felt. We had to wait only eight months before our chance to join with other Christians in communal worship; they were forced to endure almost double that number in years. At the very most, we were slightly inconvenienced now and then by the censors; at the very least, they were harangued by the Red Guards, ostracized by their colleagues and community, and had their Bibles confiscated and burned. Back home in America, our friends had the choice of attending any of a wide variety of churches or of attending none. American citizens also enjoyed the constitutional rights of a completely balanced version of Article 46: freedom to believe in religion, freedom not to believe, and freedom to propagate either. Here in China, at least up to that moment, for well over a decade, our Chinese believers didn't even enjoy the protection that the first half of that article supposedly guaranteed. It was the single most positive news we received that entire year; it was the first hint that maybe there was a bridge through the haze of willows.

Pastor Liu became a fairly regular visitor after that, and one evening, he brought the exciting news that the ownership of the former Methodist church downtown was officially transferred to the Tianjin Christian Patriotic Association, and he invited us to attend the first public worship held in the city for many years in early December. It was through him that we first learned about the Christian community in Tianjin after Liberation. Initially, there was relative religious freedom, but like all Chinese people and institutions, Christians experienced the same waxing and waning of hope, the same waves of political campaigns, the same periods of economic improvement and devastating famine, and the same relentless political control of their destinies. But unlike most of their fellow citizens, they were subject to unusual discrimination, especially during the Cultural Revolution that had preceded our arrival. An additional challenge for the Christian community was dealing with the fractious denominational differences that remained as a legacy of comity and the contrasts among the foreign missionaries coming to China from different countries representing a multitude of denominations and reflecting a wide range of theological beliefs. United by their Christian faith, these groups differed widely in their interpretation of liturgy, doctrinal beliefs, church polity, and acceptable cultural norms. For many of these foreign proselytizers, slight contrasts in culture almost overshadowed theology. Most American Protestants eschewed alcohol, so unlike the English Anglicans, who celebrated the Eucharist like the Catholics with wine as Jesus did, Presbyterian communicants drank grape juice, which Jesus didn't. It was bewildering enough for a Chinese acculturated to the three indigenous "religions" of Confucianism, Taoism, and Buddhism to be introduced to a new religion proclaiming that a man named Jesus was the Son of God and was resurrected from the dead to save them from sin. Furthermore, how confusing to receive this message from different traditions: Anglicans, the China Inland Mission, Jehovah's Witnesses, Lutherans, Mormons, Quakers, Seventh Day Adventists, and Southern Baptists. And to top this all off, these different versions of the faith were preached to them by Americans, Scotsmen, Australians, Swedes, Danes, and Germans all in their individual and often highly accented renditions of Chinese. It is truly a miracle that after Liberation, the majority of Chinese Protestants were able to unite into a single ecclesiastical body with a common theology though the fractures of the past still lingered on. Pastor Liu told us about a group of Christians in Tianjin called the Little Flock and spoke wistfully of the hope that they would seek fellowship with his association. While we resided in China, I never heard of the house churches, but after leaving China, I learned of how many Chinese Christians distrust the state-sanctioned church and worship as independent congregations. To this day, again usually following denominational lines, many believers in the States distrust the officially sanctioned church in China and surreptitiously support the house churches or seek their own ways to sidestep the Three-Self Patriotic Movement, the government-approved Protestant church.

A case in point is a flight I took in the States some years back when I happened to be sitting next to a very well-dressed and attractive middle-aged woman, and we got to talking about China. It turned out that she and her husband had a successful televangelism ministry in Colorado, and their large evangelical congregation had a practice of sending members to China on tours, but their primary goal was not sightseeing but organizing night raids on apartment complexes to place leaflets by as many doorways as they could. At first, I thought she was pulling my leg, but she seemed absolutely sincere in her account, and brazen though their actions were, they seemed congruent with a missiology that is predicated on Americans being the best if not the only disseminators of God's Word to the world. Her description of getting an ally in Hong Kong to print up "repent and be saved" pamphlets in Chinese, hiring taxis in the middle of the night, and returning to their hotel to share stories about how many floors they had to climb or how they managed to escape detection all sounded more like a fraternity night escapade than missionary zeal. When faced with such actions by foreign groups of Christians, it is no wonder that the average Chinese still considers us to be barbarian invaders.

Christianity was first introduced into China by Syrian Nestorians way back in the middle of the seventh century AD during the Tang dynasty, well after Buddhism but before Islam. It began to grow only after the arrival of European Catholic missionaries and, much later, of American and British Protestant missionaries in the early nineteenth century. Not unlike the foreign powers who started to carve out the major port cities into concessions, various Protestant mission agencies agreed on dividing up various areas of China so that they would not compete directly against one another in their proselytizing of the faith. Accordingly, the American Presbyterian Mission Board, which was the sending agency for my parents, had responsibility for most of Shandong, and that province became a bastion of Presbyterian mission work. Unlike most other denominations and in direct contrast to the Southern Baptists who were present in the same area, the missiology of the Presbyterians cast a broader net than straightforward evangelism, and following the example of Jesus, the main call for most American Presbyterian missionaries was teaching and healing the sick. Most of my American friends are amazed when they have asked about my Chinese upbringing and family, that my parents had no theological training nor were they hellfire and damnation preachers. Another surprise is when I reply in the negative when Americans ask if I knew their great aunt, their next-door neighbor's cousin's grandfather, or some other acquaintance who had been a missionary in China before Liberation. First of all, China is a huge country, so like the United States, it is highly unlikely that two foreigners would be living in the same part of that large nation. Second, due to comity, the divvying up of different provinces to different denominations, unless the person asked about was Presbyterian, they would almost invariably have lived in a different province. Even if this individual was the same denomination as my parents, there were at least seventeen hundred Americans who served in China for our board during the century or so preceding Liberation, so rarely could I please my inquisitor with a favorable reply. For these reasons, although their time in China roughly overlapped with my parents, our family never met or knew several famous Americans raised in China by missionary parents: Nobel laureate Pearl Buck, Audrey Meadows (Jackie Gleason's wife in *The Honeymooners*), Ruth Bell Graham (Billy Graham's wife), or Henry Luce (founder of *Time, Life, Fortune,* and *Sports Illustrated* magazines).

Seeing the handwriting on the wall (to use a Biblical metaphor), most foreign missionaries left China in the late forties, and by Liberation, few remained, and my parents were one of the last American missionary families to leave. For the first time, most Chinese Protestants were united into an indigenous church, *zhongguo jidujiao sanzi aiguo yundong* (the Chinese Protestant Three-Self Patriotic Movement). Self-support, self-governing, and self-propagating formed the trinitarian foundation of this new organization although these pillars of a self-sufficient national church had been promoted by some foreign missionaries for decades. Following the zeitgeist of the day, the Three-Self Movement quickly distanced itself from its missionary past and, in many cases, quite rightly criticized foreign missionary efforts for their imperialistic behavior. Even in 1979, the official view was that all missionaries were stooges working hand in hand with the imperialistic powers, and most leaders of the Chinese church hewed to this same perspective when speaking ex cathedra although they were more temperate in their criticism in nonpublic conversations. In all our private meetings with Pastor Liu and other Christian friends, we never heard any direct criticism of American missionary efforts, and during our summer travels to my parents' two mission stations in Jining and Huaiyuan, the locals sang my father's and mother's praises albeit without ever directly acknowledging that it was their Christian faith that brought them to China, and this is what motivated their service to the Chinese people.

In this regard, it vexed me to no end that the foreigners who the Party publicly extolled as true friends of China were, without exception, virtual unknowns in their native lands and to the world at large, yet were household names in China. Thus, you would've thought that it was Edgar Snow who had won the Nobel Prize in literature and had movies made of his works starring Ingrid Bergman rather than Pearl Buck. Who on this good earth was Pearl Buck anyhow? In the fall, during our weekend lecture trip to Shijiazhuang, a large city south of Beijing, as part of the obligatory sightseeing, we were taken to the Revolutionary Martyr's Cemetery to view the grave of Dr. Norman Bethune. Norman Bethune? Surely you recognize the name, the famous

Canadian surgeon who joined the Communist Party, enlisted in the partisan resistance during the Spanish Civil War, and then ended up in China to serve Mao's forces for almost two years before dying of an accidentally induced infection while operating on a PLA soldier. Even within the small domain of Canadian surgeons who had visited China, I could come up with a better candidate for lionization than Bethune. Take Dr. Wilder Penfield, the Montreal neurosurgeon who was a specialist in treating epilepsy who helped pioneer the mapping of language functions in the human brain and who later was an ardent advocate for early bilingual education in Canada. Among the places he visited was the hospital in Tianjin where I was able to observe brain surgery performed by Chinese doctors who had been trained by Dr. Penfield during his visit in the 1960s. But most of all, it galled me that throughout all the places I saw in China, there was not one single public acknowledgement of the medical work hundreds of missionary doctors performed, most of whom had devoted decades of service to the Chinese people, like my father. Of course, none of these foreigners were members of the Party.

This miscasting of history calls to mind a later visit to China when I happened to be in Chongqing in Southwest China. I was strolling with two young Chinese teacher friends through a city park when they pointed out a monument to the brave Soviet airplane pilots who helped the Chinese people defeat the Japanese during the last few days of World War II. I couldn't resist asking if somewhere in this same park there was a monument to the American pilots who had served for many years against that common enemy, and in all innocence, my Chinese friend queried, "Were there American pilots in China during World War II?" Like Norman Bethune, the Soviet pilots scant fifteen minutes of fame as friends of the Party superseded any reasonable reading of Chinese history, and obviously, even a decade and a half after Janene and I lived in the PRC, the Flying Tigers, like my father and many of his fellow missionaries, simply never existed.

The most important story, however, is not the benign neglect or intentional disrespect foreign missionaries received in the writing of modern Chinese history. It is the uplifting account of the Chinese Christian community and its brave witness through years of political turmoil, through the repressive decade of the Cultural Revolution, and its resurrection and significant growth as a spiritual and social force in contemporary China. Like many of their compatriots, all Christians faced varying degrees of persecution at some point in post-Liberation China, but it was no accident that Chinese Protestants were less restricted than their fellow believers who were Catholic. An illustration of this bias is the relative speed with which Pastor Liu and his flock were able to resume public weekly worship in Tianjin whereas, even though the Catholic Christians in the city were given official permission to worship at that same time in early September, it took years before the congregants of the deserted French cathedral Janene and I had visited on Easter Sunday were able to obtain permission to open. Even the Chinese names for these two religious traditions indirectly give the more recent branch of Christianity higher status than the mother church: *ji du jiao* is Christianity and, by default, Protestant Christianity in Chinese, but *Catholicism* is a completely different name, *tian zhu jiao*. Although some ignorant Americans might come to a similar conclusion, this difference in nomenclature leads most Chinese to believe that Catholics aren't Christian. The problem is not just linguistic. Because Catholics are catholic in that they all belong to one universal church that acknowledges the pope as their titular leader and because the Holy See is a political entity with embassies scattered around the world reporting to Rome, the Party obviously has a problem with Chinese pursuing a dual allegiance. It is one thing for a Chinese to harbor superstitious thoughts about a heavenly father, but it is completely unacceptable to be a good citizen while simultaneously pledging loyalty to a holy father in Rome.

During those cold winter months after our arrival, the spiritual climate around us seemed as intemperate as the weather, and we had no intimation that before we left for China we would witness the resurrection of the Chinese Christian community in Tianjin. Although we knew that individual Christians were present, few of our colleagues or contacts would admit to being believers. In fact, just the opposite occurred when Lao Wang, our academic chair, confessed that he grew up in a Christian family and that his given name was Su Lai (Jesus comes), but after Liberation, he dropped both his faith and the first syllable of his Christian name and adopted the name Wang Lai. If faith is the substance of things hoped for, the evidence of things not seen, as the author of Hebrews so eloquently describes it, there was little empirical confirmation to support our hope that the small but long-standing tradition of Christianity in China was still vibrant until one afternoon in late March. I was sitting in my frigid office and turned to look out the third-story window at the same monotonous scene that had remained unchanged since my very first day at the institute. Row upon row of dusty shacks and smoky factories flowed out across the flat landscape, painting the earth in shades of brown and gray, complementing the dull color of the hoary sky. But on that late afternoon, toward the end of Lent, I saw something quite unusual. In a subdued but distinct contrast to the dull scene I had grown so accustomed to, three willow trees in the yard across the wall from ours bore sprays of budding green. That greenness, the color of new rice, was a sudden reminder that winter was passing and spring was eminent, the season of rebirth. I had not noticed the trees before for without color, their bare branches were lost in a sea of monotony, but now they stood out like the three crosses on Calvary as silent symbols of things hoped for. It was only much later that we would witness direct evidence of a church restored, but on that cold day in late March, I caught a glimpse of hope, and my faith was renewed.

As the bleak midwinter faded into spring and the days became longer and brighter, we had the opportunity to meet more

American visitors as more and more tourists started to pour into China and grace even our unsightly city with their presence. In contrast to our rare chance meetings with foreigners in our hotel, like the group of Texan businessmen we met in late January and who were as clueless as we about the outcome of the Dallas-Pittsburgh Super Bowl, friends from the States started to write us about plans to tour China so that by the end of our stay, we had entertained at least a half dozen Americans with meals in our hotel, tea or drinks in our sitting room, and best of all for them, cycle tours around the streets of Tianjin. Many of these friends were fellow believers, so some of our discussions revolved around our knowledge of the local Christian community, and sometimes we were able to arrange them to meet with Chinese Christian friends. One such tête-à-tête took place in August between a respected Chinese-American professor friend of ours who was visiting Tianjin and our son's piano teacher, the first Chinese to share his faith with us. I was struck by the strong American bias our professor friend displayed in his take of the situation despite the fact that he was of Chinese origin, that this was his second visit to China, and that he was a highly educated bicultural, bilingual scholar. Individual freedom and outspokenness were sacred values to him irrespective of the cultural context. By the same token, I was also struck by the way he seemed to echo my own views when I first arrived in Beijing, and I began to appreciate the manner in which our interaction with our Chinese friends the preceding months had led me toward a greater appreciation of the life they led.

American Professor: "China needs a new face—Christianity!

Chinese Christian: "They will call you a reactionary."

American Professor: "You must carry the cross. If you don't, who will?"

Chinese Christian: "It is easy for you to say because you are American, but it is not easy for us."

"It is easy for you to say." What telling words, and how sobering for me to reflect on them when I think back on all the complaints, criticisms, and condemnations that I voiced over and over again that year. Like Conrad's Lord Jim, another white man lost in an Asian setting who discovered that only the smallest of margins distinguishes between being viewed a hero or a coward, I found myself thinking that there is an equally slim border between empathy and arrogance. Whatever your national or cultural background, it is difficult to distinguish between seeing the world through your own eyes, a natural and normal psychological state, and seeing the world *only* through your own eyes. Our interactions with the Chinese Christian community that autumn forcefully reminded me that compassion can never permit the latter.

Our last Sunday in Tianjin dawned fresh and unusually clear. Gone, at least temporarily, was the polluted air of a normal winter day fouled by the dust from a million stoves burning bituminous coal. It was one of the rare mornings when shafts of clear sunlight angled across the streets and buildings, and the sky was unmistakably blue. The four of us dressed in our Sunday best, not suits and ties nor dresses and heels but dressed best for the long, cold walk ahead of us. Janene wore her warm, fuzzy hat with tassels, Derick his khaki PLA cap with the flaps tied down, Christine had a bright pink, knitted skullcap, and I had the black and gold of the Pittsburgh Steelers pulled over my ears. With our down jackets and running shoes, we looked more like motley mountaineers than churchgoers. It was a mile and a half walk downtown to 163 Hebei Lu, where the former Methodist church had lain dormant for so many years, and with the exception of a white sign newly fixed to the brick entryway, the building had the same dismally deserted appearance it always had whenever we chanced to cycle by. Written boldly and traditionally in vertical and neatly squared characters, the freshly painted sign announced the location of the Tianjin Christian Church (*tianjin ji du jiao hui*). Pastor Liu was at the door to greet us along with a stream of about 220 other worshippers, mostly older people and substantially more women than men. Sprinkled throughout the congregation were several young people, and it seemed as if almost every other grandmother had brought their little granddaughter along to participate in the first public worship service in the city in thirteen years. The building was as decrepit inside as it looked like from the street, and the streams of sunlight pouring through the dilapidated windows caught thousands of sparkles of dust hovering above us. The liturgy seemed quite familiar though obviously it was all in Mandarin; there were prayers, hymns, scripture readings, announcements, and as Pastor Liu had promised us earlier, a sermon. Only during the hymns, when the tune slowed the language down syllable by syllable, could we keep up with the cadence of our fellow Chinese worshippers. Most moving for us was the reading of Psalm 23 that Pastor Liu used as the Scripture lesson for his homily.

> The Lord is my shepherd: I shall not want.
> He maketh me to lie down in green pastures:
> He leadeth me beside the still waters.
> He restoreth my soul:
> He leadeth me in the paths of righteousness for his name's sake.
> Yeah, though I walk through the valley of the shadow of death,
> I will fear no evil: for thou art with me...
>
> Psalm 23:1–4, KJV

Although the congregation had a relatively short time to prepare for this service, members were able to round up a choir of about two dozen voices, and despite their age, the uncertain accompaniment on a stridently untuned piano, and the quivering of voices left unheard for so long, this intrepid choir began to sing joyfully and vociferously. They hadn't completed more than a measure or two of their anthem when one of the windows to our right fell completely out of its frame, shattering glass and bits of wood and mortar to the floor of the church. Fortunately, the debris landed close to the wall where no one was seated, and the choir, undeterred after having had to wait for so many years for this opportunity, sang lustily on. I had heard that sopranos were capable of shattering a champagne glass with a high C, but that aged and unpracticed choir that December morning in Tianjin one-upped even the most operatic diva; they took out a whole window! A skeptic might claim that the event was caused by an already weakened frame hit by a gust of wind, but for those of us fortunate enough to be present at that morning service, it was clearly the working of the Holy Spirit that blew into the sanctuary at the first sound of praise after so many years. Afterward, we stayed to greet some familiar faces and many new ones and explained reluctantly that we would not be back the following Sunday for we were about to depart for America. Janene and I have worshipped in thousands of services, in many different churches, and in a variety of languages around the world, but that December morning in Tianjin was by far the most memorable. God's presence was palpable, and the light of Christ shone in the brave faces of those who were present that day. The poem that my mother wrote during the height of the Cultural Revolution ends with the following refrain, and to me, she expresses an almost presentient vision of what we witnessed a dozen years later among the Chinese Christians we had been privileged to meet.

> Here are a people caught between past and future.
> Fire purges but it also destroys. Wind sweeps away chaff
> but the bulk of a heritage three thousand years long cannot
> be moved.
> Or can it? Here are a people enduring, believing, hoping.
> Somewhere through the haze of willows, there is a bridge.
>
> —Myra Scovel, *Red Is No Longer a Color*

CHAPTER 8

心有灵犀一点通

xin you ling xi, yi dian tong

Hearts which beat together are linked.

Economics is the lifeblood of any nation. Income and imports are the arterial flow, pumping fresh life in while expenses and exports course out, and at the heart of this circulation of wealth is the political system governing this commerce. Communism, like any political system, is as much economics as it is politics, perhaps more so since in essence, it is a government that is dedicated to a centrally planned economy. The key message of Marx's *Das Kapital* is follow the money, and where that trails leads tells you a great deal about a society. By the time autumn rolled around and we had begun a new academic year of teaching, we had a clearer understanding of what it was like to live in a country where the Party, not profit, dictated the cost of living. From a microeconomic perspective, the centralized control of the market was evident in everything we bought, whether it was carrots or bicycles, jackets or train tickets, toothpaste or fountain pens. For staples and frequently purchased commodities, the amount of goods available for individual purchase was controlled through the distribution of coupons (*piao*), and this rationing dictated what could be bought or sold more stringently than the price itself. When we first arrived, we couldn't buy used bicycles until we were given the appropriate coupons for such a purchase; similarly, before we headed to the department store to acquire some winter clothing, we had to be given the necessary number of cotton coupons allowing us to make this purchase. Coupons could not be bought, at least legally and officially; they were distributed by your dan wei according to each worker's monthly or annual allotment, so ours came via our institute's wai ban. We were fortunate to purchase our daily meals via our hotel, so we didn't have to worry about exceeding our proportion of rice or meat coupons, but for our colleagues, not only did they have the typical concerns of budgeting for the cost of feeding their families each month, they also had to worry about not exceeding their monthly allotment of coupons for their food staples in order to make certain that they could even spend their money for food in the first place. This is why our friend, the Korean Jin, attracted unwanted and unwarranted jealousy from his colleagues. Through no fault of his own, the government decreed that since he was Korean and not pure Han and since it was a well-known fact that Koreans ate more rice than Chinese, he was given extra rice coupons each month allowing him to purchase more than his colleagues, creating the very racist discrimination that the government was intending to compensate for. A cynic might go so far as to claim that this was the underlying intention of this peculiar policy all along.

Central planning was even more conspicuous at the macroeconomic level because, largely due to Deng Xiaoping's leadership, there was a major shift in Chinese economic policy that summer. As a way of furthering Deng's goal of accelerating China's pursuit of the Four Modernizations, in June, the Party's central committee established special economic zones (SEZ), where many of the normal constraints on foreign investment and business would be suspended and where outside capital and expertise would be encouraged. The initial and model site for these SEZ was a small town (at least back then) smack on the border of China and the new territories of Hong Kong called Shenzhen. After Liberation, I often heard Americans express the concern that some day China would take over Hong Kong, but beginning with the first wave of Hong Kong businessmen who began to flock to Tianjin and stay in our hotel as winter thawed to spring, it seemed to me that the reverse was more plausible, that capitalistic Hong Kong was already moving north to take over China. The unmitigated economic success of SEZ over the years since 1979 has proven that rather than China taking over Hong Kong by military force, it has now overtaken Hong Kong by virtue of its commercial and entrepreneurial strength. Shenzhen is the perfect exemplar. It has grown into a modern city with skyscrapers, high-tech industries, research labs, and it even has a law school that grants American JDs. Of course, Hong Kong is now officially China through Deng's policy of one nation, two systems, and Janene and I, who happened to be in Budapest when this transpired in June 1997, watched the transition from British rule to Chinese sovereignty on Hungarian television with great interest. We couldn't help but remember how, almost twenty years earlier, we had to walk across the unimposing bridge that symbolized the enormous economic chasm that separated the bustling free enterprise capital of Chinese capitalism in Hong Kong from the undeveloped socialist giant to the north. Now the two economies are joined at the hip, and Hong Kong is indistinguishable from Shenzhen, Shanghai, and most of metropolitan coastal China. Though not geographically contiguous, these cities in effect form one continual commercial megalopolis from Hong Kong in the south to Shenyang in the north. Communism did not take over the former British colony nearly as much as the capitalism of Hong Kong has overtaken China, and as obvious nowadays, it has done so with a vengeance. Thanks initially to Deng's policy of permitting first marketization and then privatization, China's economic growth rate, which was similar to other Communist nations when we were there and kittenish compared to the developed world, accelerated to a tigerish 10 percent annually and has only recently slowed down.

Another key principle governing a Marxist approach to economics is the well-known phrase that sounds suspiciously like it was lifted from the book of Acts in the New Testament, "From each according to his ability; to each according to his need." Clearly, this sentiment is antithetical to capitalism whether it wears an American or Chinese face, but when we were living in China, it was a laudable and important goal and was ostensibly a major economic policy of the Party, but often it seemed to be a rule honored in the breach. Take our pay for example. We went to China without a contract, not even a handshake, not even a ballpark figure of what we would be paid. In my phone calls with the Chinese liaison office in Washington the previous December, the woman's voice on the other end of the line promised to pay our round-trip airfare, accommodations, and a salary; she further informed us that once we got to China, we would be given a contract that would spell out our duties and specify our wages. At the end of March, two months after we had been teaching at the institute and after having received our monthly pay, we were given contracts to sign. Both were hardbound in somber brown and spelled out our pay and duties in both languages. Due to the compactness of Chinese orthography and the fact that English tends to use about one and a half syllables for every one in Chinese, as typical of bilingual documents, the English version took six pages to spell out what was contained in four in Chinese. By that time, anything in writing was a fait accompli, so we readily signed the documents even though there were some quirks in what the contracts specified and what we could deliver. For instance, the very first clause was that our term of service was from July 1, 1979, to June 1, 1980, even though we began teaching six months earlier and everyone knew we would be leaving by mid-December. I was paid ¥600 a month and Janene ¥550, both exorbitantly high salaries in China. Although given the then current exchange rate of ¥1.53 to $1.00, we individually earned less than $400 a month or together had an annual salary of about $9,000, a pauper's income in the United States even in the late seventies. But in Chinese terms, we were paid more than anyone else in our institute and, as my friend in the Foreign Experts Bureau in Beijing told me, as much as the top Party leaders. Clearly, our Chinese hosts saw us as people in desperate need!

In the same vein, the normal laws of supply and demand often did not seem to apply in the Chinese marketplace that we had grown accustomed to, and again, the needs of the citizens were not met even when they each had given according to their ability. As documented earlier, bicycles were the heart and soul of Chinese transportation, and after Liberation, hundreds of millions of them were bought, sold, used, and reluctantly discarded only when the wheels could no longer make a single rotation. Given the demand and the need and also considering that bikes were cheaply made of heavy steel and lacked gears or any other luxuries, one would assume that they would be a relatively cheap and accessible commodity in a Communist society. Not so! Like other popular goods, it was necessary first to acquire a coupon in order to make a purchase, no simple feat since, unlike tickets for rice, those for bikes weren't distributed monthly but basically once per worker per lifetime of service at one's dan wei. Then there was the cost. We purchased our three Flying Pigeons secondhand, but a new one cost ¥123 ($80) or more. Considering that the average teacher's wage was about ¥35 a month, a bicycle was equivalent to about three and a half month's wages, roughly comparable to the cost of a new car for a normal wage earner in the United States. Luxury items were astronomically expensive. A decent wristwatch or cassette tape recorder cost ¥115 ($75), a new black-and-white TV would set you back almost a year's pay at ¥383 ($250), and at ¥1,000 ($654), a modestly sized fridge was the stuff that only dreams were made of.

With no competition, prices were consistent throughout the country, but that did not mean they didn't change. In October, the use of coupons to ration food and other necessities was discontinued, and simultaneously, there was a dramatic spike in prices. Chicken, fish, shrimp, and pork cost 10 to 30 percent more, and our Chinese friends were told that on January 1, vegetable oil, clothes, and the price of other commodities would also increase. Our hotel, ever ready to overcharge its foreign guests, attempted to triple and, in some cases, quintuple all meat dishes, interpreting a 30 percent increase as mathematically equivalent to the original price times three. At the end of that month, wages for everyone were increased to compensate for inflation, but as you might have surmised, they went up about 10 percent and came nowhere near compensating the average worker for the sudden spike in prices. I wondered whether our hotel staff were gravely disappointed when they discovered that their monthly pay didn't treble in concert with their attempt to triple the prices in the dining room. We didn't realize it at the time, but during the fall of 1979, there was a major change in the way the Chinese economy was structured. The modernizing reforms that were being instituted at the macroeconomic level had now trickled down to the homes, shops, streets, and right under our very noses; the People's Republic of China was turning into a market economy, capitalism with Chinese characteristics.

With no free market, everyday prices for most goods and services were fixed for the Chinese, but we quickly discovered that we were often being overcharged. It was as if the sight of our faces created instant inflation. One way was legitimate and simply became a minor nuisance, but the other was not officially condoned by the authorities but neither did it appear to be prohibited. Right from our first week in Beijing, we discovered that for most public excursions, such as entering parks, zoos, or museums, or when we attended plays, movies, or exhibitions, we had to pay twice the normal fee as Chinese citizens. In all these cases, the extra cost was posted at the entrance or ticket office: children at half price, adults at full price, and foreigners at double. Sometimes the last category was referred to euphemistically as nonresidents, but after initial grumbling about the fact that we didn't have such a two-tier system back in the good old USA, we swallowed our pride and accepted this as a teensy sacrifice for being paid such a ridiculously high salary compared to Chinese standards. However, the constant unofficial overcharging grated on our nerves, and even during our last few months, we found it annoying to be constantly on our guard about prices since many commodities were expensive for us. I suspected that the Chinese had the same perception that residents in other nations do: all Americans are considered rich. We constantly had to be vigilant about any bills we were presented with, and this demand for wariness included our children. Once, Derick ate lunch alone in our hotel dining room and, after finishing a bowl of rice and vegetables, was charged ¥3.16 for his frugal meal. After much protest, he signed a tab for the normal charge of ¥0.80, one-fourth the original bill. During one of my Shandong visits, I was browsing through the Shandong Antiquity Store for foreign tourists in Jinan and, unable to believe the prices listed, I pressed the clerk to determine if some of the items had been mispriced. No, she insisted, the pair of tiny jade earrings was indeed ¥10,000 ($6,536), and the small gem of polished jade was ¥22,000 ($14,739)! "Would you like both of them?" she inquired innocently. Moments like these gave me the impression that store owners were so inexperienced with pricing and marketing, especially for non-Chinese customers, that for them, it was basically a game of Monopoly and all foreigners apparently walked around with wads of golden-colored five-hundred-dollar bills in their pockets.

In some ways, our stay that year did resemble a game of Monopoly because during that era, as a way of controlling both foreign visitors and residents as well as their own citizens, the Party used two types of currency, regular currency used by the Chinese and *wai hui* (foreign exchange certificates), which came in slightly larger, usually newer, and always more colorful bills than ordinary currency and which had Chinese on one side and English on the other. Ten yuan in what we called funny money was exactly the same as ten yuan in real Chinese money, and though they were monetarily equivalent, their use created two parallel systems of monetary control. Except for those working at banks, Friendship Stores, hotels for foreigners, and the like, no Chinese was allowed to have wai hui; conversely, no foreigners were allowed to possess regular Chinese currency nor could they bring the same into or out of the country. Thus the use of this dual system allowed for tight control of goods and services, making certain, for example, that ordinary Chinese citizens couldn't purchase the luxury goods foreigners enjoyed buying at Friendship Stores and, conversely, foreigners couldn't purchase unofficial goods or bribe or entice services from Chinese citizens with currency only they were legally allowed to own. Although he didn't come up with this practice, Deng Xiaoping probably would've called this policy one nation, two currencies. This strictly enforced system was a frequent inconvenience since much of the time, we dealt with chump change and street vendors, conductors on buses, people watching over our parked bikes, and other common folk in ordinary places never dealt with foreigners and did not have the change, and most of them doubted that the funny money printed by their very own government was real in the first place. By fall, we were adept at getting small amounts of real currency to use in these daily encounters, making everybody happy and endangering no one. Not even the most zealous protector of Party policies was going to hassle either the bus conductor or us for not paying our five-fen fare in wai hui. Besides, there was no wai hui note that small.

It is a testimony to the generosity of our Chinese salaries as well as our natural predilection toward a thrifty lifestyle that by the end of the year, despite having treated hundreds of students, teachers, and friends to meals and parties at our hotel, we had managed to save up the equivalent of $3,700 by the time we were ready to leave. In keeping with our belief that most of what was accrued in China should stay in China, we returned to the

Tianjin Carpet Factory, which we had visited during our first few days in the city, and purchased some lovely wool carpets for both our families and ourselves, and even after factoring the cost of shipping, we were still able to save a little over half our savings to take back out with us after it had been converted into US dollars. We were reminded that it was illegal to attempt to take any wai hui with us out of the country although we fully realized how foolish this would be for like ice in a hot oven, as soon as we entered Hong Kong, the value of our remaining salary would've melted away and vaporized into thin air as no foreign nation would convert valuable hard currency into useless yuan whether it was serious or funny.

Some of the lessons I learned in China during 1979 served me well in later years. In 1994, I was invited to spend a week in a small city in southern Hungary to work with a teacher training project sponsored by the World Bank. Although Eastern Europe was in the process of rapid political change, at the time, many vestiges of the Communist regime still remained in Hungary, including its monetary system. I spent the last night before my flight home at the Forum Hotel in Budapest, and because I was paid in Hungarian forints and because the exchange rate into hard currency (US dollars) was highly unfavorable, I tried to pay my hotel bill with my wad of leftover forints. I was told that this was not possible when I attempted to check out in the morning and that my bill could be paid only in dollars. Remembering our experience in China, I knew exactly what was going on. The hotel wanted to get reimbursed in foreign money (I was told that deutsche marks were also acceptable) and not in their own currency, which was next to worthless. I persisted on trying to use my remaining Hungarian currency, knowing that as soon as I cleared immigration and entered the international terminal at the Budapest airport, my forints would be as valuable as toilet paper, actually, less so given their coarse texture. I appealed to the clerk's spirit of nationalism, protesting that we were in Budapest, not

San Francisco and should not kowtow to the Yankee greenback, but he remained intransigent. Noticing that a local guest next to me was shelling out forints to pay his bill, I asked why I couldn't do the same, and the clerk replied that, well, yes, I could use the local currency, but my bill would be double what it would cost me in dollars. I quickly counted my forints and was delighted to find that my overnight stay would exhaust almost all of them. The erstwhile reluctant clerk was delighted to allow me to pay twice as much for my room, and as I checked through immigration with only a few worthless forints in my pocket, I was even happier than he. If someone had told me in 1994 that in a decade or so the Chinese yuan would be as valuable as the US dollar as a medium of international exchange, I would have thought they were on hallucinogens. If they had said the same back when we were in China in 1979, I would have replied, "Yeah, sure, and next you're going to claim that some day Germany will be reunited and there'll be no more Soviet Union!"

Funny money, the exchange rate, and the illegality and impropriety of exporting Chinese currency out of the country were only concerns of foreigners and the few citizens able to travel abroad. For the Chinese people, however, their economic system brought certain limitations, but it also provided enormous benefits, provisions that Americans have only dreamed of. All housing was subsidized by the state, and remember that China is divided into provinces, so the state means the national government, which in effect means the Party. Granted, Xiao Zhang had only one room with minimal facilities but he paid only a yuan a month for his accommodations, just sixty-five cents! To be sure, this was relative to the cost of living in China in 1979, but in effect, he spent about one twenty-fifth of his monthly salary for room, literally a tiny fraction of what almost any American shells out for a place to sleep. Even better, let's consider the two third rails of contemporary US politics that polarize the two major political parties. Depending on your political leanings, citizens of the People's Republic of China lived in a utopia unimaginable to any American. They dwelt in a Republican paradise or, if you will, a Democratic hell, for they paid absolutely no taxes—no sales taxes, no excise taxes, no corporate taxes, no individual income taxes, none whatsoever! However, to reverse the American political perspective, they enjoyed the fruits of a Democratic Garden of Eden in contrast to a Republican view of Hades; thanks to the central government, all Chinese had free and universal health care. This curiously created tax-free welfare state was possible of course in a Communist country where the state owns or controls all major facets of the economy. To stand the catchy capitalist phrase on its head, what's good for the country is good for General Motors. If the Party was the banker in a national game of Monopoly and, in addition, had complete control over each player's money, who needs taxation to pay for any subsidies the state provides? With a quixotic kind of reverse logic that an American Marxist friend once explained to me, department stores in China, East Germany, and the Soviet Union looked so drab and barren compared to their counterparts in Hong Kong, West Berlin, and New York because the only things you see inside them are the few commodities that the state does not provide for free!

After living in China for almost a year, we became fully acquainted with another system of governance that in one manner was like the politics and economics of that Socialist nation and was at least partially attributable to the way a Communist state functions, but in other ways, it did not seem at all related to the history and culture of the Chinese people. Superficially, it mirrored the two-tier, one government, two-systems bifurcation of government that controlled the monetary and economic system taking place as part of Deng's reforms, but in actuality, it was a completely separate and much more complex phenomenon. Throughout our stay, the word and the nation that kept popping up in mind whenever we were confronted with this social behavior was the apartheid of South Africa. I know this sounds far-fetched, but bear with me as I try to lay out my case.

Exhibit 1: From our very first night in Beijing, we could see that Chinese and foreigners lived in two separate and unequal worlds. The Beijing Friendship Guesthouse was not simply a hotel and restaurant complex; it was a fortress built to house only foreigners, and except for the Chinese staff and office workers, such as members of the Foreign Experts Bureau, no Chinese were allowed to enter, eat, or reside there. I already described how on a subsequent visit to China, due to a near air disaster, my flight to Beijing was delayed by many hours, so when I eventually got to Beijing late in the evening, I and Wang Zhanmei, our Chinese friend awaiting my arrival, were forced to seek accommodations at the Guesthouse late that night. There was no problem getting a room; one with two beds was available even though it was past midnight. The problem was that he was Chinese and not allowed to overnight in a hotel for foreigners. Like so much of the infrastructure of China, the tourism business was set up like the Soviet model in the early fifties where foreigners shopped, dined, and slept in special facilities catering only to them. These stores, restaurants, and hotels were invariably better than local establishments and served partly to impress foreign tourists, partly to secure that hard currency from abroad fell into the right pockets, and partly to ensure there was a minimal amount of mingling between freethinking foreigners and right-thinking natives. Every place in China open to foreign visitors at that time had a Friendship Store, and it was inconceivable that tourists could hit a city even for one night without being taken to one of these establishments. Long before Deng Xiaoping's goal of socialism with Chinese characteristics, the slogan in China seemed to be, "Tourists of the world unite. You have nothing to lose but your hard currency!" Except for Party fat cats and some of the staff, these stores were closed to all Chinese citizens, and if a commoner had the temerity to attempt to do some shopping inside one of these venues, a very unfriendly security guard would make sure that friendship was only extended to people with non-Chinese names and faces.

Exhibit 2: Like apartheid in South Africa, the Chinese system had three categories of racial discrimination. It was generally easy to distinguish Chinese residents from foreigners (mostly whites and Japanese, but occasionally visitors from Africa or South America), but what about *hua qiao* (Chinese visitors living abroad)? Except for their clothing, they were indistinguishable from the local population, and because many of them grew up bilingual, they were often fluent in one of the Chinese dialects. Due to the vagaries of this strange classificatory system, these visitors had their own hotels, restaurants, and stores separate and apart from those reserved for other tourists. Thus you would have the unusual situation of an American tour group composed of whites and maybe a few African-American and Japanese-American tourists visiting the same city as a tour group of Chinese-Americans, but the two contingents would be staying in different hotels and shopping at separate Friendship Stores, and they would only meet up if their tour buses happened to take them to a selected tourist site at the same time!

I once tried to test this system of separation in Tianjin, mostly motivated by an attempt to purchase canned vegetables for a colleague of Janene's whose blood disease restricted him to a diet free from any animal fats, a cruel joke in Northern China, where even bai cai is usually served drowned in lard. I'll admit, however, that I also wanted to see if I could penetrate what I viewed as a racist barrier. *Hua qiao* were defined as either people born in China and then moved abroad or children of the same. "Aha!" went my palindromic reasoning; by this definition, I am qualified to enter our local overseas Chinese Friendship Store and purchase a large supply of canned vegetables with my wai hui. I didn't make it past the front door. "Yes," the guard agreed, "it's obvious from your passport that you were born in Shandong and now live in the United States, but you can't purchase products from this store." He went on to elaborate that there was a Friendship Store a few blocks away, indirectly implying "For people like you." I explained that my wife and I had shopped at that establishment many times, indirectly implying, "Yes, I know I'm white," but they didn't have the canned vegetables I heard were available in this store so that's why I wanted to shop in a place set up for people exactly like me, born in China but now living abroad. I even used my Chinese name. By now, the usual crowd had assembled, and as they heard my argument, smiles turned to chuckles, and chuckling merged into laughter. What a great sense of humor I had! What a cute story to tell when I get home! Imagine a *hua qiao* with light brown hair, blue eyes, and white skin, and to top it off, his Mandarin is better than many overseas Chinese! The encounter vexed me only slightly for I knew full well how preposterous my little venture was to begin with, and after cycling over a couple of blocks to the store for my kind of people, I was able to get vegetables for our friend though not the type that he really wanted. What intrigued me was the subtext in all of this. Race was never mentioned explicitly, and unlike the tragic history of the United States, it was quite rarely the source of any vicious behavior or traditions. Yet it was there, as visible as the large billboards seen in every Chinese city depicting four different human races marching in integrated solidarity with their right fists upraised, forged into one world brotherhood under the slogan, "Workers of the world unite. You have nothing to lose but your chains!"

Exhibit 3: Irrespective of race, religion, citizenship, or ideology, we are all social animals, and this is abundantly evident when it comes to eating. The modern tendency of overly preoccupied Americans to gulp down a morning coffee while driving to work or to wolf down a quick bite at the office alone at noon is an aberration both historically and demographically. Most people eat together most of the time, and our more important moments in life are celebrated by social feasting. Race, religion, citizenship, and ideology often drive us apart, but food brings us together, or should. Whenever we hosted dinners for our students, fellow teachers, or friends at our hotel or elsewhere in China, mealtimes were an opportunity for everyone to gather around the same round table; young or old, women or men, foreign or Chinese, all were enclosed in a circle of hospitality. Whenever the Chinese hosted us for any simple meals and especially for formal feasts, the social inclusion was similar: children or adults, the young or the elderly, ladies or gentlemen, bureaucrats or their drivers, Americans or Chinese all squeezed together in happy harmony. However, for everyday meals in our hotel, in restaurants, and especially whenever we traveled, meals were a time when the races were separated. Excluding the specially hosted dinners just mentioned, every time we had breakfast, lunch, or dinner together as a family, we whites ate separately and far better than the locals.

At the larger accommodations, like the Beijing Friendship Guesthouse or our hotel, there were separate dining rooms or areas: the more attractively appointed one with a greater variety and quality of dishes for foreigners and the less attractive one with fewer choices and more common food for the Chinese. Besides the overt inequality of this system, I always preferred the common Chinese cuisine I had grown accustomed to as a child and would have gladly given up every multicourse dinner for a simple bowl of *miantiao* (wheat noodles) and *mantou* (steamed bread), but these were considered much too plebian to serve to foreigners. In smaller places, especially in the towns and cities we visited that year, since usually there was only one dining room, Janene, Derick, Christine, and I would sit around one small table, enjoying a multicourse dinner, even for lunch, while Xiao Zhang or whoever happened to be accompanying us that trip would be eating simple fare on the other side of a screen. Before and after meals, we all rode in the same minivans, attended the same lectures, or toured the same parks, museums, or factories, but as soon as the moment arrived for us to sit down and eat together, we didn't. We always ate separately. Initially, we protested vigorously, dragging Xiao Zhang or our other Chinese companions to our side of the screen and pulling some extra chairs to our table to accommodate them as part of our extended family, but we soon perceived that this was more embarrassing to them than the status quo was to us. Very quickly, like the Chinese who had already done so long before us, we eventually caved in and adhered to established behavior.

During that rare trip to my birthplace in Jining, where no foreigners had visited since Liberation and where we had to stay at the Party guesthouse, the separation was particularly embarrassing. All our meals were served in a small dining room divided by a folding screen made of white cloth. Xiao Zhang and Lao Long (our China Travel Service guide from nearby Qufu) ate noodles and a few simple dishes on one side of the barrier, and the four of us were stuffed with course after course of fish, pork, beef, assorted seafood, and occasionally vegetables while glasses of soda, beer, and *mao tai* were constantly filled even when they had been barely touched. The incessant chinking of tableware and the clinking of glasses on our side—let alone the wafting aromas of each new dish—contrasted with the virtual silence and absence of scent on the other side of the makeshift curtain. That flimsy sheet of cotton was more than a screen; it was an impenetrable barrier once again far more effective than the Great Wall of China, for its function was not to keep the barbarians out, it was designed to wall out the native Chinese. And yet again, there was evidence that the Party impinged and infringed on the life of its own countrymen more than they did on us foreigners. How strange, I thought, that in some ways, the people of China are more segregated from foreigners now in their own republic than fifty years earlier when their coastal cities had been carved into concessions by the invading imperialists.

Exhibit 4: One early autumn weekend, Xu Laoshi, Derick's piano teacher, got permission to accompany Janene and the kids to Beijing so that he could introduce Derick to his former music teacher. By now, Janene was adept at handling the travel permits, purchasing return tickets to Tianjin, hailing taxis, and getting around the capital city so that these brief excursions to the Big Persimmon had become pleasant adventures rather than tedious ordeals. On this trip, she wanted to do something special for Xu Laoshi, who had now become almost an extended member of our family. Knowing that it was verboten to take him into the large Friendship Store on Dong Chang An Jie just a few blocks east of the Imperial Palace and knowing that he would adamantly reject any gift she might attempt to buy him anyway, she convinced him to accompany her and the kids to the top floor of the famous Beijing Hotel nearby and treat him to a drink on their outdoor restaurant on the fourteenth floor. On our first visit to this establishment early in the year, we had a chance to check out some of the accommodations. Each guest room had wall-to-wall carpeting, a clean bathroom, and marvels of all marvels (especially for the kids), its own color TV! The hotel even had Otis elevators and not the jerkier and less dependable Tianjin-made lifts that we had become used to. Naturally, this was *the* place for foreigners to reside during their visit to Beijing, and we wondered about the celebrities who may have stayed there during our tenure in China: Seiji Ozawa, Bob Hope, Issac Stern, Vice President Walter Mondale, or that year's NBA champs, the Washington Bullets. Janene had no trouble getting Xu through the front door, lobby, and into the Otis elevator to the top floor, but as soon as the four of them exited on the fourteenth floor, they were stopped by the fu wu ren at the entrance to the terrace restaurant. Janene, Derick, and Christine were warmly welcomed; the Chinaman was not. Janene protested mightily. They were not going to eat a meal but only sit down for half an hour for some drinks; Xu Laoshi was like little Christine, who, as our adopted Thai daughter, was distinctly non-Caucasian in appearance, and an adopted member of our family; he had spent countless hours teaching our son to become a better pianist and should be respected as Derick's laoshi. All of these arguments and the increased intensity of her protestations failed to dissuade the hotel staff from their assignment of making sure that none of their own kind crossed the bar. Defeated at last, Janene took them downstairs and out to a public restaurant for snacks. She was in tears when she left, and she remained inconsolable when the family returned to Tianjin the next evening. Because she had not spent her childhood in China, she found the inequities much harder to bear than I did, and this particular incident anguished her. Coming toward the end of our stay, it compounded all the other injustices that we had witnessed, and like a nail pounded again and again, this moment in Peking pierced her very soul. We came to China with many questions, but we left with even more, and this system of apartheid raised one of the most profound queries of all. Thirty years had passed since the Chinese Communist Party had freed China from foreign imperialists; why then did the Party choose to continue to favor foreigners and discriminate against its own people?

The new academic year had begun, and autumn, which invariably falls early in Northern China, was already in the air, and though we saw a considerable amount of the country during our summer circuit of travel, there was still one place I longed to visit before the year and our time in China were complete. Having spent my high school years in the foothills of India on the other side of the Himalayas, I've always loved mountains and since boyhood have nurtured dreams of visiting imaginary haunts like Shangri-la. With only three months left and the specter of winter approaching, I would have to act quickly to secure the chance to visit that most exotic of all mountain retreats, Xizang Zizhiqu (literally, the Western Depository Autonomous Region), or what the rest of the world refers to as Tibet. By this time, I was fully aware of how difficult it was to secure permission to travel anywhere in China. A simple round-trip visit to Beijing involved getting the blessing of our institute's wai ban, a travel permit from the local police, arranging for transportation to the railroad station, buying a one-way ticket to the capital city, showing the travel permit to the police on arrival in Beijing, rebooking a return ticket, clearing the police checkpoint upon returning to Tianjin on the evening train, and finally arranging for an institute car or taxi back to the hotel. Imagine the logistics of trying to get to Tibet, sixteen hundred statue miles away and located in a different political galaxy from the rest of China.

My childhood dream was initially nurtured by an incident that occurred in the late spring, when, despite the geographical and cultural distance that separated Tianjin from that autonomous region far to the southwest, our institute was enlisted as part of a national campaign to recruit Chinese faculty to teach in Lhasa. Ostensibly, this was a laudatory goal on behalf of the Party to upgrade the educational level of minority people in that part of China, but following the Soviet model, there was a darker side to this policy. From the moment Tibet was liberated from the supposedly oppressive yoke of religious superstition and imperialistic feudalism by the kindly uncles of the PLA in October 1950, there was the general intent by the government in Beijing to move in large numbers of Han settlers so that the region would be Chinese both politically and demographically. Living on the southern slopes of the Himalayas in the early fifties and having done some climbing in the mountains around Dharamsala, where the newly deposed Dalai Lama lived along with thousands of other Tibetan refugees, the accounts I heard as a high school student in India were very different from the Party line we were given in China. Words like *liberated, religious superstition*, or *feudalism* were not the descriptors the Tibetans themselves used to portray the Chinese invasion of their homeland. Regardless of what happened way back then in early

May, the Tianjin Foreign Language Institute was asked to send an English teacher to the Teachers Training College in Lhasa to contribute to the education of the Tibetan people, and one of our younger teachers, Li Laoshi, was tapped by the institute's cadres for this three-year assignment. On an unusually hot Sunday morning in May, we cycled down Revolutionary Avenue to the main square to catch the elaborate send-off ceremonies celebrating the departure of the "volunteers" for the glorious task of teaching in Tibet. One hundred teachers had been dragooned into this assignment from our region of China. There were bright red posters, ribbons, bows, drums, cymbals, martial music, and speeches, and then the selected century were bustled into a row of waiting buses to be taken to the railway station where trains would take them to Sichuan, and from there, they'd be bussed to Lhasa. Li and his fellow conscripts did not appear enthusiastic at all, and after saying good-bye to his wife and family, he clung to us until the very last minute in vain hopes that somehow our alien status could protect him. Once on the bus, he crawled over the bus driver to lean out the window for a last round of handshakes to prolong his departure, and the driver, thinking he was attempting to bolt out of the vehicle, shoved him rudely back into his seat.

The day before, our institute had hosted a farewell party for Li, and instead of a festive atmosphere of candy, music, and warm wishes, the institute's cadres held a dull meeting where they read memos of praise for Li's volunteer spirit and promised to take care of his wife and family while people milled about the room, chatting among themselves. Six of these were teachers who had been selected along with Li as potential candidates, and they acted equally relieved and embarrassed over what was transpiring. We found out later the quid pro quo arrangements that had led to Li being selected and willing to be exiled to Tibet. For one thing, he had been one of the few English teachers at our institute who had been granted the luxury of studying abroad, having spent two months in Canada at a summer institute the year before, so this was his payback to our dan wei for having enjoyed a plum overseas assignment. In effect, two months in Canada was equivalent to three years in Tibet. His new bride of four months had been teaching in a middle school in a tough district on the outskirts of Tianjin, so part of the compensation deal arranged was that she was now transferred to teach at our institute while her husband was in the hinterlands. We heard that similar scenarios had been drawn up for the other volunteers that had been chosen. As the buses pulled away with their despondent passengers, I began to think of how Li's unhappy fate could play into my good fortune. Wouldn't it be logical to have a foreign expert visit Li and his comrades in Lhasa after they had settled in and consult with them about their work as English language teachers? Fall would be a perfect time for such a visit if only such an expert would volunteer.

Knowing that ultimately the Foreign Experts Bureau in Beijing would be responsible for granting me permission to make an official visit to Tibet, I contacted them during a visit to Beijing in October, and they were supportive of my proposal since they already were impressed with my willingness to give lectures at a wide variety of institutions and places during the spring and summer and because they saw the logic of my being able to help a Tian Wai colleague and his Chinese compatriots in their daunting task of training Tibetan English teachers. As I was willing to pay for the airfare to and from Tibet, the Beijing office had nothing to lose, and I left Beijing happy to have received their blessings. The reluctance quite naturally came from the other end of the bureaucratic chain of command. Yes, it would be nice if Li ensconced in Lhasa had some help from me as a Tian Wai colleague, but our institute was reluctant to have me gone for a week or so especially since Janene and I would be leaving for good in a little over two months. A more selfish and less logical factor came into play, however, one that I was now quite fully aware of. Recall that your dan wei, your work unit, had replaced the ancient Confucian concept of clan. In times past, your allegiance was to your clan, and the elders demanded and deserved your loyalty and obedience, and your successes or failures brought pride or shame to your family name. In modern China, filial piety was paid to your dan wei, and the leaders of your work unit were your titular mom and dad, a form of in loco parentis. Add to this a kind of dog-in-the manger syndrome where the dan wei was so possessive of its workers that they were reluctant to share them with another work unit even if it cost them almost nothing. A quick story adopted from *Chinese Wit and Humor* is instructive here.

Somewhere in northern China, there lived two rich families belonging to different clans. It was early autumn, the time of the eighth moon, when tradition dictated the sharing of moon cakes. These two families were known not only for their wealth but also for their stinginess, qualities that often go hand in hand, and the villagers were curious about how miserly each of these clans would be given the dictates of the holiday. "Come here, son," said Mr. Li. "I want you to take this moon cake to give to Mr. Wang," and he handed him a piece of rice paper with only a circle inked on its surface. As the younger Li paraded across the village proudly showing off his father's gift to Mr. Wang, all the villagers smiled and shook their heads at the remarkable stinginess of the Li clan. Not to be outdone, Wang called his son over after receiving Li's "moon cake" for instructions about how to present his gift in return. He told the younger Wang to put the thumbs and index fingers of both hands together to make a tight, little circle and instructed him to show this to all the villagers as he paraded over to Li's house, demonstrating that the Wang clan was not to be outdone when it came to miserliness. The villagers roared with laughter at the sight of the miserly moon cake from Wang, and Wang Junior was happy to report back to his father. In excitement, he spread his fingers apart as he showed him the "gift" and told his father how the entire village agreed that the Wangs once again exceeded the Li clan in cleverness at this autumnal festival. "No, no," his father retorted almost in horror, "you made your moon cake too big." And curling his hands into a tight circle, he scolded his son. "I told you to make it small like this!"

The direct and didactic message of this little fable is to demonstrate how silly it is to be selfish, but there is indirect information about Chinese culture packaged into this episode as well. Cleverness is clearly commended here, but the Confucian values of filial piety and loyalty to the clan are upheld as well. In post-Liberation China, the rivalry is much less between the Lis and the Wangs and much more between work units, especially those that live, so to speak, in the same institutional village: between the famous Nankai University and our less famous institute or between our own Tianjin Foreign Language Institute and the ignominious Teachers Training College in Lhasa. So to give me permission to travel from the former all the way down to the latter would, in a sense, bring dishonor to my dan wei. Why should a work unit in far off Lhasa, a teachers' training college teaching Tibetans not Chinese, enjoy lectures, advice, or expertise, from our American foreign expert? After weeks of back and forth between the institute's wai ban and administration and mixed messages over worries about my health given the distance to Tibet and the altitude of Lhasa and other concerns, some genuine and some superfluous, the institute finally nixed my request to go to Tibet, and like a good Confucian son, I had no recourse but to accede. There is a semihumorous coda to add to this little incident, however, that harkened back to what had transpired way back in May.

Janene and I were bustling through a normal day of classes and special lectures in mid-November when we saw what we first took to be a ghost. There in the hallway in front of us one morning was none other than Li from Lhasa! It was no apparition, and though he looked slightly thinner than he did when we had last seen him on that hot Sunday morning in May, trying to squirm out of the bus that was taking him to never-neverland, there was no mistaking his presence or his almost giddy demeanor. It turned out that he allegedly never could acclimate to the high altitude of the Tibetan plateau and was reputedly constantly sick. So ill, in fact, that he hardly ever taught, teaching so very little, in fact, that he was next to useless, and being so utterly useless, in fact, that his dan wei in Lhasa decided to ship him back to Tianjin. And there he was returned to sea level in his home city, remarkably recovered from his near-death experience in the thin air of Tibet, back to his old job with his bride secure in her new job, and as far as I know, they lived happily ever after.

About the same time I was angling to visit Tibet, an opportunity opened up to give a guest lecture at Beijing University. From a Chinese perspective, no one in his right mind (let alone his left) would pick a chance to speak at the Teachers Training College in Lhasa over that most golden of opportunities, an invitation to deliver a lecture at the most holy of all academic holies, Beijing University. Why make the arduous trip to a benighted non-Chinese Himalayan desert when the effulgent honor of visiting China's most prestigious university was only an hour's train ride away? Tea or champagne, *miantiao* or Peking duck, sweet potatoes or sirloin, get real! I had already given almost fifty talks at various institutions with an average attendance of three hundred, so of course I was willing to go to Beijing to speak, especially at the most famous university in China, but looking back, if I really had a choice that fall and could do it all over again, I would've picked the tea, *miantiao*, and sweet potatoes in an instant. Given the enormous discrepancy in status between the tiny institution in Lhasa and Bei Da (North Big, the Chinese abbreviation for Beijing University), I expected absolutely no problems in securing permission from my home institute to give some talks at the academic apex of China, but once again I was surprised. Permission was granted, but it did not come quickly or easily. There were suspicions about why such a lofty institution would be interested in someone from such a lowly place as Tian Wai even if that certain someone were an American expert. Was Bei Da trying to humiliate the institute in some perverse manner, a kind of Wang-over-Li type of one-upmanship? At the time, I thought this rumor was silly, but after my visit to Bei Da, I had second thoughts.

Permission granted and travel arrangements quickly booked and seizing a chance for a final joint venture to Beijing, the family joined me on a Friday morning train to the capital city. The night before, October winds had gusted throughout the region, strong enough to knock out some of the windows in our hotel, so when our train pulled into Beijing, the skies were sparkling. The miracle wasn't that the Western Hills were clothed in autumnal majesty but that they could be seen at all. The dismally polluted metropolis that greeted us so reluctantly in January was transformed into the eternal city of Chinese civilization. After we settled in to the Beijing Friendship Guesthouse, I got a ride out to the northwestern section of the city where Bei Da was located. Unlike most institutions that had been influenced by inelegant but functional Soviet-style architecture, Beijing University still had many traditionally styled buildings with tiled roofs topped by the distinctive Chinese finials, and there was a lovely pagoda overlooking a small lake surrounded by willows and maples. Ironically, this architecture had also been influenced by foreigners, not by Russians but by the American missionaries who founded what was then known as Yenjing University. Bei Da, like Tian Wai and many other educational institutions in secular China, had roots that were both foreign and religious.

My Friday afternoon lecture was for the English department, and so I was asked to speak on the role of grammar in the teaching of English. A topic like this sounds stultifying to

Americans, but most Chinese English teachers love grammar. Grammar rules, though arcane, are finite, thus easier to learn than vocabulary, idioms, and pragmatics. More importantly, as our Chinese colleagues readily pointed out, unlike vocabulary or reading texts, grammar was politically safe. No Red Guard ever persecuted any English teacher for claiming that verb phrases using prepositions tended to be followed by gerundive complements. I was disappointed by the perfunctory greeting from a sparse group of participants in an uncomfortable room in what seemed to be an attic. Of all the talks I gave in China, this was the smallest audience I had, and it seemed they were also the most apathetic. To top it off, it took over an hour for my hosts to arrange for a university car to take my Tian Wai companion and me back to the guesthouse. The next morning, I returned to the university, this time to talk to their fledging program in psychology on current issues in psycholinguistics. That fall semester, I was teaching psycholinguistics at our institute, the first time this course had ever been taught in China, and my Tianjin graduate students were genuinely intrigued with the subject, but once again, the Beijing University audience was small, and their interest appeared to be tepid. This time, there was no chance of getting a university car to take me back to the guesthouse no matter how long I waited. No one had contacted the transportation office, and it was Saturday afternoon, and the drivers were leaving for the weekend. In the socialist hierarchy of the time, drivers trumped university professors in status, even at Bei Da. Again, at no other institution did I encounter such difficulties with transportation, and to be frank, it almost seemed as if the amount of interest and hospitality directed toward me was inversely proportional to the prestige of the university. After a long wait and seeing that for my hosts, once I was out of sight, I was also out of their minds, I walked outside the university gates and, in a most unhappy mood, managed to crowd on to two different buses and finally reached the guesthouse for a late supper. The visit to China's acme of education was worth one good story, however.

After my Saturday talk on psycholinguistics, I had tea in the school cafeteria with several students who had attended. In the course of our chitchat, one of them, the only girl, described a remarkable incident when we started talking about some of the venerable professors who taught at Bei Da. She and four male students met once a week with one of the most ancient of these scholars for an afternoon seminar. He moved slowly, spoke in a whisper, and had a habit of dozing off in front of them, prompting the oldest student to nudge him gently back to semiconsciousness. One day, their professor nodded into somnolence yet again, and once again, the class leader prodded him gently, whispering, "Teacher, teacher." Only this time, their most esteemed Beijing University professor did not move. It took the students a few minutes to realize that their distinguished mentor had delivered his last lecture, so to speak, and it took them even more time to decide what to do with the body. After dismissing the most tempting but least moral alternative of leaving him ensconced in his now eternally endowed chair and skipping out of class to celebrate the weekend early, the five decided to transport his corpse to the university infirmary since, as far as the students knew, the campus had no morgue. They lifted him up and carried him off, each of the four boys grasping a limb and, to quote the teller of this story almost exactly, "And, Dr. Scovel, I was left with the head!" I've heard several good jokes about college professors including two involving their demise, but the anecdote shared by this lively student during my visit to Bei Da beats them all. Reality trumps fiction every time.

The gusting autumn winds and falling temperatures presaged other changes in the air. Like the weather, the transformations most obvious to us were those most visible in our day-to-day encounters. In late August, our hotel restored an old dining room, and from then on, we ate in a cleaner and well-lit space that boasted window tables from which we could watch street life through the sheer, white curtains. We were also surprised by the quick service, at least on the first day the dining room opened; our breakfast came on time, at least on that opening morning, but by the next day, the fu wu ren relapsed into their lackadaisical and desultory ways, forgetting once more what we had ordered the day before. For nine months, our hotel housed a few permanent residents like us but for the most part accommodated rare groups of foreign businessmen or occasionally clusters of tourists, but by autumn, the place bustled with tour groups. Small armies of them came flooding in from Japan, this time toting cameras rather than rifles, and they were reluctantly welcomed for their hard currency despite the brutally harsh memories of yesteryear. Because we spent so much time cycling, even the slightest changes in street life were the ones first noticeable. Traffic lights at several major intersections now operated automatically without being abruptly switched by the cop at the kiosk, and the street signs were neatly repainted in red and white. Along the larger avenues, low chain fences now separated bike lanes so cyclists could no longer meander in and out of the vehicular traffic. Janene and I both noticed that the bike riders were more aggressive, frustrated perhaps by what may have seemed to be infringements on their civil liberties, and they still seemed startled to see a foreigner suddenly appear in their midst. One late afternoon, when Derick and I were running along the road bordering the river, on two separate occasions, cyclists either ran into each other or into a utility pole when staring back at us as they sped by. It was if they could not believe what they just saw!

As already mentioned, there were marked improvements visible during any of the train trips we took that fall. The Tianjin station had been repainted inside and out, fresh flowers were planted, and new food stands were put up, selling a wider variety of snacks and drinks for the milling passengers. Even the uniformed railway attendants were more solicitous, constantly replenishing our hot water thermoses and, instead of grumbling about it, offered us new tea bags whenever we ran out. The former German restaurant Kiessling, conveniently located halfway between our hotel and our institute, began serving more than pastries and ice cream. Much to our children's delight, in mid-September, they began purveying chocolate chickens and Easter bunnies, six months premature yet appreciated all the same, and all of us enjoyed their new offer of deluxe sundaes at ¥1.20 (an affordable 78¢). The former "Rose Garden" during the days of British occupation that had been crammed with temporary shelters and provided vignettes of daily life for so many months from our upstairs window across the street from our hotel had now been completely cleared of shanties and had become a park again. Small children continually lined up to barrel down a slide made to look like an elephant, and the elderly now had space to practice their morning exercises or take a gentle evening stroll.

Although we were totally oblivious of the enormous macroeconomic transformation that was starting to take place, beginning in late August and increasingly prevalent throughout the fall were street markets that began to sprout up downtown on weekends and evenings. From the very beginning, there had been so-called farmers markets where a few peasants would pedal in from the surrounding countryside with a bike load of vegetables for sale, but what they peddled was meager in both quality and variety. These new open markets consisted of rows and rows of stands selling shoes, clothes, household necessities, and small manufactured goods. Fruit and vegetables were also available as in the past, but their amount and quality had significantly improved. The apples and pears were not so shriveled; large and tasty peaches made a brief appearance during the month of August, and by October, oranges and peanuts were plentiful, treats we had rarely seen for sale before. Neon lights were strung up along these makeshift stands as the evenings began to darken, and Janene pointed out that the downtown department stores were much less crowded as shoppers shifted their attention away from the state-run businesses to the growing private enterprises that began to surround them. Without any overt realization on our part, or for many of our fellow Chinese citizens for that matter, the virus of capitalism was beginning to infect the Marxist model that the People's Republic had heretofore so desperately attempted to protect.

Lingering from earlier days and right up to our arrival at the beginning of that year, almost anything American was viewed with suspicion, derision, or contempt. Autumn brought signs of subtle attitudinal changes, however, and there was growing evidence that the already globalized American pop culture was starting to seep through the Bamboo Curtain. Three male teachers asked Janene (and tellingly not me) if she could procure a copy of *Playboy* for them. Tour groups and special visitors from the States were increasing monthly. Within one week, the Philadelphia Boys Choir and the Washington Bullets professional basketball team visited Beijing and other cities. Two weeks later, we saw a Chinese play, *A Chinatown Legend*, that was set in San Francisco's Chinatown and which portrayed life in America from an apolitical if not favorable perspective. These little changes percolated into our austere institute as well. Sun, ever the iconoclast, showed up to teach one morning in a light blue turtleneck sweater, and until we recognized how startled we were by this choice of dress, we didn't appreciate how used we had gotten to the dark blues and khaki cotton outfits that had become the unofficial uniform of every teacher. Emboldened by the teacher's sartorial change, one of Janene's students showed up the following week in a turtleneck himself. Lao Chen, the most open-minded of our administrators, had danced with Janene on one of the institute-sponsored weekend excursions and, after some pressure from the students, decided to allow student dances to be held once a week. These were nothing like high school proms in the Sates but very subdued gatherings where a few girls ballroom-danced with each other and occasionally with a few brave boys. Still, mild and modest as these occasions were, they stood out in stark contrast to the virulent antiforeign and antibourgeois zeitgeist of the nation just a few years earlier. Like a homeowner only dimly cognizant that the shrubs and trees are gradually inching upward in the backyard garden, we weren't overtly aware of all these slight changes in our landscape, but looking back on them, they were all interlinked, and the Communist kingdom we had entered in January was a different place from the nation we would leave at the end of the year.

More dramatic and contentious was the change in housing for our Chinese colleagues. Devastated by the catastrophic Tangshan earthquake of 1976, many of the residents of Tianjin lost their apartments and had been living in temporary shelters for more than three years. As I chronicled earlier, these flimsy shanties crowded out all the available open spaces: parks, sidewalks, gardens, campuses, and even our institute's swimming pool (although I still maintain our institute did not have such a facility at that time). Workers tended to reside in shelters erected around their own dan wei, and consequently, most of our colleagues lived in the shacks built on and around our campus or on the site of their spouse's dan wei. There were some exceptions: Sun resided in a small basement-like flat off campus, and one of the leading cadres of the English department lived in an apartment for the faculty of a fine arts school, but he had to bike almost six miles round-trip to commute to our institute. Like visitors to the PRC nowadays, we were constantly struck by the amount of building that was going on. From its inception, one of the main organs of communication for the Party to visitors and the outside world was the magazine *China Reconstructs*, and the constant tearing down of the old to be replaced with the new was not only a mantra of revolution, it seemed to be the goal of every Chinese contractor and civil engineer. All the pounding and clanging was an ever-present part of the soundscape that enveloped us that year. In other words, even if we were blind to all the building going on, our ears could tell us that apartments were going up all around us, bringing hope for new homes for our shantytown colleagues. Alas, as the Chinese frequently observed, usually with a sigh and a shake of the head, "*Ren tai duo, difang tai shao* [So many people, so little space]," and thus ugly decisions had to be made about who would be allowed to move into a new home and who wouldn't.

Although my mother has a chapter describing our family's life in the Weifang Internment Camp set up by the Japanese during World War II in which some two thousand Allied civilians were incarcerated, Langdon Gilkey, who was interned for the entire operation of that camp, devoted a complete book to that experience in his excellent and copiously detailed account entitled *Shandong Compound.* As a young, single, male academic, Gilkey immediately began to observe the events that transpired during his confinement like an anthropologist studying an alien culture, and his comments about prisoner housing under those crowded conditions are telling. Because the internees were civilians, the Japanese guarding us displayed none of the extreme brutality they exhibited toward the Allied military prisoners so vividly chronicled in such books as Eric Lomax's *The Railway Man* or Laura Hillenbrand's best-selling account of Louis Zamperini's incredible life, *Unbroken: A World War II Story of Survival, Resilience, and Redemption.* For the most part, the internees of our camp controlled the day-to-day activities with Gilkey in charge of housing issues. Initially, he held the rationalist and humanistic perspective that these well-educated and reasonable people would unite in a commonwealth of good will given their common plight and enemy, but how wrong he proved to be! When it came to the basics, such as food and housing, he soon discovered that humans, like nature itself, are "red in tooth and claw." When the Japanese commandant ordered his committee to find new quarters for a contingent of Belgian prisoners being shipped in, Gilkey was unable to extract anyone from their rooms even when it was clear that they had more space than any other prisoners. And after discussion, reason, and appeal to the common good failed to move a group of men to smaller quarters to accommodate the new internees, Gilkey basically had to ask the Japanese commandant for the authority to enforce such a move, leaving many of the men to label him a traitor and threatening to sue him after the war's end. This and similar incidents led Gilkey to an epiphany where he began to see that reason and humanism alone were insufficient to justify human behavior. "Why *should* a man wish to be reasonable or moral if he thereby lost precious space? Do men *really* value their own moral excellence more than they value their own comfort and security?" he asks so tellingly (p. 78, *Shandong Compound*). During our summer visit to Weifang when I was the first former prisoner to return to the site of that camp, recall that Janene had counted up all the middle school families and staff that now resided there and observed that there were as many, if not more, people living in that compound in 1979 than there were prisoners of war in the days of the Japanese occupation. Given that, with a population of about seven million souls, Tianjin was also overpopulated, you can begin to understand that when people are packed together in tight quarters, one of their most salient and primitive drives is to seek a better place to live, and this is why the allocation of new apartments for our colleagues at Tian Wai became such a controversial issue.

Our daily commutes to and from the institute took us right past the municipality office and like the big-character posters, the number of protesters waxed and waned throughout the course of the year. With construction completed on much of the new city housing by October, the steps of the town hall swarmed with hundreds of protesters, and there were posters plastered all over, lamenting the delay and the availability of homes for all the many residents who, a full three years after the earthquake, were still living in temporary squalor. The fighting for one of the new flats erected on our campus was fierce, and compounding the problem was that Hebei University, whose main campus was on the far outskirts of the city, seemed to have a historical claim to some of our land. Thus their faculty, eager to be housed inside the city rather than out in the boonies, coveted the same new quarters that our teachers were fighting for. Due to the limited number of new units available and the seemingly limitless number of people needing new housing, only 40 percent of our faculty could be accommodated. A directive from the Ministry of Education in Beijing decreed that seniority ruled: teachers with the most experience and status would be given the best apartments first. Rumor had it that the first, best situated, and most spacious apartment went to none other than Mr. End of the Month! The young teachers, especially those who were unmarried, were out of luck. One of the sayings popular at this time went something like "If you want to get married, find a room first and then look for a girlfriend. It's easier to find a bride than an apartment." In a reversal of tradition, Chinese men in effect had to buy a bride from her family with a dowry; a promise of a place to live had become the modern equivalent of this form of marital barter.

Our friends and colleagues felt freer to visit us in the fall, and after supper, we often welcomed visitors; some were expected, and some came unannounced. One of the older teachers asked to visit one evening and told of his struggle to get into one of the new buildings. "I asked the institute for a new apartment. There are seven of us living in a shelter just seventeen meters square. I was refused. What can we do?" Another evening, one of the younger teachers came to our hotel room ostensibly for some idle chitchat, but she started to cry as she told Janene how betrayed she had felt when her family was denied the promise of one of these prized apartments. Her crying melted into sobs as she lamented the prejudice directed against her because of her age, gender, and lack of *guanxi* (connections). We saw Xu Laoshi often, and by now, he was almost a brother and much more than just Derick's piano teacher. Having seen his small room in the dirty and dilapidated building that housed the staff for the music school and having visited with him and his family during our summer stint in Qingdao, we knew that his life was constrained much more than just concerns over housing. One evening, he listed some of these limitations. Unlike Tian Wai, his institute had no new apartments available for the staff that fall, so he didn't even face a 40 percent chance of getting a better place to live. As was typical of many couples at that time, he had been separated from his wife for three years, and he could see her only once or twice a year, visiting her in Shandong in the summer or she him in Tianjin during the Spring Festival. I thought about how prisoners in the States had more conjugal opportunities than him. Despite the fact that he was the most accomplished pianist at the music conservatory, due mainly to his unclean past, he was relegated to teach only middle school students and was not a member of the more prestigious conservatory faculty. For us, his misfortune was our gain since Derick learned much under his tutelage, and we gained a dear Chinese friend. Finally, Xu Laoshi was not free to worship and had been persecuted greatly during the Cultural Revolution for his bourgeois training and love of classical music and for his Christian faith. What could we say in the face of such anguish sitting in the cozy luxury of our hotel? "Don't worry, everything will be all right"? "Just wait patiently, your day will come"? "I'm sure things will work out in the end"? Janene uttered none of these platitudes but simply hugged him, whispering how sorry she was and telling him how much he was loved. More than all the lectures, classes, seminars, and consulting, I think these profoundly personal encounters with our Chinese colleagues left the deepest impression and stood perhaps as the most significant legacy of our tenure in China.

The rapid changes taking place all around us were so conspicuous that they almost obscured the fact that much had not changed one iota. The continual pollution, the congested living conditions, and the constant pressure of work all conspired to weaken our immune systems and to make us susceptible to a mix of minor illnesses. Compounding the situation was the problem of heat. Although China has mountains of coal reserves, it was still a limited commodity, so for our area of China, all institutional heating was turned off in the early spring and not turned on again until the late fall. Our hotel had special compensation since it housed foreigners, so we started to have heat in our rooms on November 1, but our institute office and classrooms remained unheated until December 1. On September 10, Janene recorded in her diary that it just so happened all four of us were afflicted at once: Christine had a cold, Derick had a sore throat, Janene had a scratched cornea, and I had a bladder infection. Janene was able to see an ophthalmologist, who gave her some salve for her eye and a prescription for regular glasses, and from then on, she biked with glasses instead of wearing contacts, and this saved her eyes from further damage from the daily grit. In October, during our marvelous opportunity to spend a weekend by ourselves in Qufu, the birthplace of Confucius, Derick, whose birthday we were celebrating, came down with the flu. Shortly after returning to Tianjin, Derick was sick again and missed school for a couple of days with vomiting and diarrhea. Simultaneously, Christine had yet another bout of conjunctivitis. Each morning, we would wash away the pus that had congealed her eyes shut and add antibiotic ointment before dressing her for the day. A fortnight later, she was sick again, this time with vomiting and a fever while I came down with another cold. Throughout my adult life, I have been blessed with good health and, except for an occasional cold, enjoyed an active and strenuous, disease-free life whether in the States, Thailand, or during many international trips, so the cascade of illnesses in China began to get me down. In early December, when my academic load was probably heaviest and when we were being feted almost every other night with farewell feasts and parties, I succumbed to yet another respiratory infection, and Janene wrote, "Poor Tom is so ill he doesn't care about anything. I've never seen him in such a mean mood!"

Another constant were the minor but daily hassles facing us at the hotel and the institute. All in all, they involved petty little activities, such as getting breakfast on time, urging the English department office to have class materials ready, convincing the wai ban to have a car take us to or from the railroad station, or trying to extract books from the impenetrable confines of the library, but they added up little by little, day after day so that their collective impact ended up much greater than their combined sum. In a sense, they were trifles, but as Xiao Zhang had wisely observed much earlier, in China, there were no trifles.

Of all these skirmishes, the one that took the greatest toll on Janene were her incessant struggles to reserve car transportation for our family. Starting with the new academic year, we barely saw Lao Shen, the smiling head of our institute's wai ban who had hosted us our first week in Beijing, for he had taken on greater responsibilities as new foreign experts had arrived at Tian Wai, and there were plans to develop an international program where foreign students, initially from Japan, could come to Tianjin during the summer to study Mandarin. We saw Xiao Zhang constantly, of course, but now he reported to a new man, a certain Fu whose given name was not Manchu but who we still quickly began to perceive as not simply inscrutable but irascible and obstreperous too. Because Janene made most of the arrangements for car travel, she was the one who dealt with Fu most frequently, and what began as a simple feud over the spring and summer escalated into skirmishes, battles, and all-out war by autumn.

As part of its contractual duties, the institute was responsible for all our transportation, so theoretically, they had to provide a car to take Janene and me back and forth to the institute each day. At the very beginning, we wanted to bicycle as much as possible and chose to commute by bike except on rare occasions when the weather was uncommonly bad or when Janene had films and materials to ferry from the hotel to the institute. Thus, from our point of view, the dan wei was indebted to us for not monopolizing one of their cars and drivers each day and should have been happy and willing to respond with alacrity and enthusiasm to any of the requests we made for car transportation. It is hard for me to imagine what was the point of view of the intractable Mr. Fu, but it may have run something like this. "The strange Americans chose not to use the car pool for daily commuting, so that was their own decision, and thus there is no linkage to any other negotiations. When they do demand a vehicle, it almost invariably involves business with another dan wei, to take their daughter to the Tianjin nursery, their son and his music teacher to the conservatory, or to go to the railroad station in order to travel to yet another dan wei in some distant city. As a cadre working for the Foreign Experts Office, my allegiance is to the Tianjin Foreign Language Institute and not to any nursery, conservatory, or Mao forbid, teachers college in some far-off city, and it certainly isn't to the Scovels! Xiao Zhang had it worst of all for he was the intermediary between Janene and Fu, and like a table tennis ball, he was ping-ponged between the two every time there was a request for transportation. By November, entries about her encounters with Fu appeared more frequently in Janene's diary, and in none of them was he portrayed in a charitable light. Even Xiao Zhang was siding with us, telling how Fu refused to reimburse him for the chintzy price of his bus tickets when running errands for the wai ban. On the Monday after yet another weekend run-in with her nemesis, Janene arranged to talk with Lao Chen and then Lao Wen, the president of our institute, about the problems we had encountered. They both listened attentively and astutely agreed to talk the wai ban into giving Xiao Zhang more responsibility in handling our affairs, judiciously letting both Fu and us off the hook while relieving Zhang of much of the strafing he took in the middle of this duel.

Whether it was a family illness, another squabble with Fu, the unexpected lack of water or heat, a sudden change in plans at the institute, or another late breakfast to be gobbled down before rushing off to work, again and again I reminded myself that in contrast to every single one of our Chinese colleagues, our situation was far better than theirs. We had to put up with all of this for only a year; in fact, in a few months, we would be returning home to the States. We would soon gain a permanent reprieve from the pollution, the decrepit housing, the constant fights with bureaucracy, the haphazard availability of goods, services, and utilities, and the infringements on so many of the freedoms Americans take for granted. Our Chinese friends were far worse off than we in every respect, but worst of all, they weren't going anywhere at the end of December; there was no light at the end of their tunnel. They were permanently imprisoned within the system. No wonder that so many of our colleagues asked us to help them get a scholarship or secure some other opportunity for them to go to America. No wonder that after our return to the States in the early eighties when thousands of Chinese visiting scholars won an opportunity to study abroad that so few of them returned to China. Most of them were middle-aged teachers, engineers, scientists, physicians, and administrators, and at first blush, it seemed odd that the Chinese government was sending experts toward the end of their careers rather than young people just beginning their career trajectory, but from what I saw back in China and then after our return to the States, this was the generation, and these were the professions that were most severely persecuted during the Cultural Revolution. For those who suffered, a year abroad was a tacit admission of guilt by the Party and an indirect attempt to expiate what the Party had done. Burned by the bitter memories of the past and having tasted the forbidden fruits of American materialism and democratic freedom, the majority of these visiting scholars seized upon their opportunity as something far greater than a chance for professional enrichment; it was for all intents and purposes a card to get out of jail free.

Having said all this in an attempt to be open and honest about what we experienced and how we felt, I don't want to leave the impression that our year in Tianjin left me constantly peeved and churlish, for along with these challenges and disappointments came many happy events, and I'd go so far as to say that our last few months brought us a great deal of enjoyment. Much of this came from the simple fact that at no time in our lives before or after did Janene and I spend so much time together and with our children. I don't believe in quality time, that euphemism used by Americans to conceal the fact that ultimately, they have other priorities that are more pressing. It wasn't that our family had quality time together that year; it was that we enjoyed a massive quantity of time with one another. With little competition for entertainment, I spent part of almost every evening reading out loud to the kids with Janene listening nearby. Growing up as a child in a China with resources more limited than ours in Tianjin, I can recall my father reading to me at bedtime books like *The Stars for Sam,* and as part of a long-standing family tradition, every December my mother would read the unabridged version of *A Christmas Carol.* I can still hear her voice begin to break down as she came to the part where The Ghost of Christmas Future projects what might happen if Scrooge does not repent and Tiny Tim dies. She would hand the book over to my father to conclude that unhappy scene before regaining her composure and resuming her role as reader. During those evenings together in Tianjin, I read *The Wind in the Willows, Huckleberry Finn,* and *A Connecticut Yankee in King Arthur's Court.* The latter seemed particularly apt, for more than once we felt as if we were time travelers, inhabitants of the twentieth century thrust back into an earlier era to struggle with the clash between ancestral and modern values. In mid-December, with only a week before we were to leave, Derick and I would cycle over to the institute for several evenings in a row where I read an abridged version of Dickens's Christmas classic to him and any students wishing to sit in. On the penultimate night of reading, when I came to the poignant part in the narrative where Tiny Tim dies, at least for that moment, I couldn't help but think that the roles from my childhood days were reversed and that my mother and father were listening in.

Unlike English speakers who view the head as the fount of cognition and the heart as the source of emotions, the Chinese divides neither the body nor the concepts in two. The word *xin* refers to both heart and mind, thus it is the root for *psychology* (*xinlixue*), the study of the mind, and simultaneously, the stem for words like *beloved* (*xinai*). As we drew near to the end of our stay, we had developed enormous respect and empathy for our Chinese friends for we could now better understand the physical constraints and political limitations that framed their world. Working side by side with our colleagues and students and interacting with them day by day and often evening after evening, we began to sense the rhythms of their daily life. To be sure, we were always foreigners, transient and distant in many ways, but by the end of the year, we felt that our hearts were joined both by common thoughts and uncommon affection, and in rare but exhilarating moments, we felt as if our hearts were truly linked and beat as one.

CHAPTER 9

路遥知马力，日久见人心

lu yao zhi ma li, ri jiu jian ren xin

Over distance, you learn the
strength of your horse; over time,
you learn what's in a person's heart.

All year long, we were invited to plays, movies, concerts, and other programs all generously planned, booked, and paid for by our wai ban. These continued throughout the fall, and they all served to break the tedium of work and routine. One Saturday night, we were treated to about our fourth trip to a performance of a Beijing opera. The Chinese genre differs from the European version about as much as the tango differs from the waltz. Despite the cigarette smoke, drumming, and incessant clanging of cymbals, Janene and the kids started to doze off, but only toward the end of the three-hour performance. Unlike European opera that has little live action, the Chinese version is closely allied to the martial arts, and each one contains at least some scenes of acrobatic fireworks. In this one, as the drumming and clanging increased in tempo, the heroine defended herself against an attack by a gang of thieves and deftly deflected the real-life spears they threw at her with swirling kicks and athletic spins. Though quickly turned off by the long periods of shrill and highly nasalized singing between protagonists, like car chases and firefights in movies, the kids always got a kick out of the fight scenes.

From childhood, I have always enjoyed sports as a participant and spectator. Regardless of the weather and well-trafficked streets, I tried to run between three to six miles as many times a week as I could, and sometimes Derick would join me on these late-afternoon jaunts. As pointed out earlier, by running mostly on the backstreets and along the river, I frequently saw people and scenes that were rarely observed along the more stately Revolutionary Avenue that ran in front of our hotel. The disadvantage of exercising at this time of day was the rush-hour traffic of bicycles and the chance of being struck by one of them or, worse yet, by a projectile of phlegm suddenly discharged by a passing cyclist. Janene took up jogging faithfully a few miles almost every morning and had no traffic to contend with, but it was hard to get up on the many frigid mornings and easy to stumble in the predawn darkness. Both of us gained some release from this exercise for these runs gave us a few moments alone to ponder, pray, or simply daydream as we plodded along the pavement in front of us.

I missed participating in the annual race held by the city each fall because I was out of town, but in mid-October, Derick and I cycled over to the Physical Education College, and I competed in a ten-thousand-kilometer run with some of the students there and was pleased to be able to break a seven-minute-mile pace for that six-mile event despite my succession of ailments and limited training. During our visit, I first became aware of how sports were downgraded during the Cultural Revolution, and this seemed to account for China's poor performance on the international stage. I noticed that Eric (*Chariots of Fire*) Liddell's winning time in the four-hundred-meter dash at the 1924 Olympic Games still bettered the Chinese record some fifty-five years later. Except for table tennis and diving, Chinese athletes fared poorly in international competition at that time, and I never dreamed that China would one day dominate the medal count in the Olympics.

We attended a couple of volleyball and basketball games as a family, and one evening, Derick and I joined the fu wu ren to watch the visiting Washington Bullets play the national PLA team on TV. The American NBA champs struggled at first for the Chinese side was aided by two ponderous but virtually unstoppable seven-and-a-half-foot giants, and the referees, who tried hard not to disappoint the home team with their calls, had obviously not memorized the popular slogan from the days of Ping-Pong diplomacy, "Friendship first, competition second." By the second half, with an improved midcourt game, steals, and soaring dunks, the Bullets won not only the game but the crowd, and at the end of the contest, I was impressed with the grudging appreciation displayed by the Chinese team, the audience, and our circle of hotel workers.

Such decorum was not present a few days later when one of our teachers took me to a professional soccer game. What was intriguing about this experience had virtually nothing to do with sports, however; it was the fact that, unlike in almost all of our other encounters in China, I was not mingling with a class of older, educated teachers of both genders but milling about with young men who seemed to be either factory workers or unemployed street toughs. The real athletic contest did not take place on the field itself but in the stands when getting into and out of this event. The stadium supposedly held twenty thousand people, but there appeared to be double that number of fans squeezing through the six narrow entry doors that formed the only egress into the match. We fought to ooze through the entrance, fought to mount the stairs up to our section of seats, and fought to find our seats among the rows and rows of fans squished together. All seats were numbered and reserved, but the three young men packed into the two places that had our ticket numbers on them did not seem interested in the discrepancy between their butts and our stubs and were unwilling to move. Only after shouts from neighboring spectators who couldn't see the field because my friend and I were standing in front of them did the trio move, and we two slid into a space that had immediately shrunk further in size. During the game, there were shouts, jeers, random squabbles, and a couple of fistfights among the fans, and at the end of the game, the spectators were left fit to be tied with the final score, Tianjin 1, Hebei 1. Now my friend and I had to reverse the process and struggle down the steps, through the doors, and eventually get to our bikes and cycle homeward along with the masses. The encounter reminded me of a flashbulb memory from my childhood. Our family was about to board a train, and as we were shoved and jostled as we made our way to the door of the carriage, I stopped to let an elderly Chinese woman step in front of me, and in that tiny gap, it seemed as if a tsunami of passengers swept by in front of me. My tall father, used to the rules of the Chinese road, instantly grabbed me, lifted me above the swarm, and shoved me through an open window, shouting a command to hold a seat for the rest of the Scovel clan. Then, as now, Confucius and Communism were forgotten when it came to crowds. *Ren tai duo, difang tai shao!*

We were feted and feasted from our first night in Beijing, during our visits to cities and schools throughout our travels, and on every holiday and special occasion in Tianjin, but as we entered our final two months of residence, the banqueting began in earnest, and had it not been for our simple meals, bouts of illness, and our daily regimen of exercise, we would have left China considerably heavier. For Americans, whose culture still seems unduly wedded to Europe, French cuisine stands out as the acme of culinary experience, and just one indication of this is the way certain foods seem to increase in both prestige and price if they're named in French rather than in English. Anglo-Saxon meat is more delectable and expensive when it is taken from a dead cow and called beef (the Anglicized pronunciation of *boeuf*, the simple word for *cow* in French), and it is transformed into a pricey delicacy when referred to by the French loanword *filet mignon*. Admittedly, given my natal heritage, I am not an unbiased observer here, but I would argue that Chinese cuisine surpasses its Gallic equivalent in virtually every way except when it comes to desserts. As pointed out earlier, things Chinese have a longer unbroken history than any other culture, so while Asterix and Obelix were running around the forests in northern France, eating burnt game, the Chinese were already enjoying exquisite meals served in porcelain. Given its size and disparate geography and climate, China also cradles an enormous variety of food and ways of preparing it. Even daily staples vary: wheat in the North, and rice in the South. In sum, despite the lethargic service in our hotel home, we did not go hungry, and if I could've kept up with all the different kinds of food that went into our stomachs that year, this gustatory list would be as lengthy as it would be diverse.

Like people the world over, the Chinese love to eat, and like all cultures, as a guest, if you've not eaten everything heaped in front of you or, even worse, turn down the food the hosts have prepared, you have in effect rejected their hospitality, culture, and affection. But unlike the food eaten by most people around the world, Chinese cuisine is almost endless in its variation and delectability, at least for the rich. In the rural and war-torn China that I grew up in, it was extremely rare that people could actually overeat and get fat. It was a compliment back then to be called *pang* (fat) for it really meant healthy, and my sole memory from infancy is that of people pinching and shaking my chubby cheeks and saying "*xiao pangzi* [little fatty]," one of the kindest forms of flattery a proud (and rich) mother could ever hear. By 1979, our friends and colleagues had survived the famines of the past and, under three decades of socialism, had reasonable access to food, at least in our city, and though few were chubby, few were gaunt, fine food and feasts were rare luxuries, so any chance to celebrate an occasion with the Scovels where the government picked up the tab was one not to sneeze at but to seize upon. During our first few months, we realized that multicourse banquets were almost as much about honoring us as they were about grabbing an opportunity to feast upon some rare morsels. This explains, for example, why at almost every one of these occasions, sea slugs were served despite the fact that from the very first time we politely swallowed and managed to hold down a few slivers of this slimy seafood, it was obvious that we found them less than appetizing. The kids were more transparent in expressing their distaste: they simply spat it onto their plates when inadvertently biting into a slug that some oversolicitous Chinese host had deposited into their bowl. However, our hosts and friends were not gluttons, for despite all the courses of food that came in ceaseless waves and left us longing to see the soup that always signaled the end of the banquet, it became increasingly apparent that the meal was just an excuse, a catalyst, if you will, for a prolonged and uninterrupted period of delightful intercourse. Though some of our conversation dealt with what was in front of us or what we had just ingested, food itself was secondary to the delightful colloquy and social interaction that emanated from these occasions. The mother of all banquets, both in terms of amount and diversity of food and as measured by the eminence of our hosts, came on National Day.

October 1 marked the thirtieth anniversary of the founding of the People's Republic of China, and the transitional status of the leadership and policies of the Party as well as the generally weak state of the economy militated against the fireworks, giant parades, and display of military hardware one might have expected. The city square was decorated with fresh flags, billboards, and sparkling lights each evening, but these were the only visible tributes to the holiday. It was a tradition for the Tianjin Revolutionary Council to invite foreign guests to their annual banquet celebrating National Day, so we were taken to the former British Club along with a gaggle of guests representing all of the foreign experts and residents who worked at various institutions around the city. As soon as we stepped out of our car, I was whisked off into a separate room where a small reception was taking place hosted by the leading cadres. We sat down, introduced each other, and made small talk over tea, nuts, and candied apples. After a few pleasantries, we were ushered into the large dining room to our assigned seats along with the rest of the guests. There were introductions, speeches, and an official toast given by the secretary of the Tianjin Revolutionary Committee that must have taken five minutes and was punctuated by salutations to *pengyoumen* (friends, the foreigners in the audience) and *tongzhimen* (comrades, the Chinese present). Janene and the kids sat at a table with President Wen of Tian Wai while I was escorted to the head table surrounded by old men, none of whom I recognized. Only after all of the celebrations were concluded did I discover why I was the only foreigner at the head table. I had been chosen as the model foreign expert and thus, for at least a few fleeting moments of fame, served as the right honorable ambassador plenipotentiary for every alien resident of the city.

Chinese feasts usually begin with nuts and sweets and conclude with soup (here it was a melon consommé), prompting the overly glib cross-cultural generalization that since the Chinese write from right to left (not really true incidentally), they also reverse the "everything from soup to nuts" sequencing of food customary at an American banquet. Because I was struggling to sound both polite and coherent in Chinese given my august and venerable hosts, it was hard for me to keep count, but about fourteen dishes appeared and disappeared before us, and all of them were various kinds of meat; there were plates of pork, beef, mutton, chicken, duck, goose, sea fish, shrimp, squid, crab, eel, fish stomach, stuffed snails, and of course, for such an extraordinary occasion, sea slugs, the pièce de résistance that I strived mightily to resist. All of these were presented on well-decorated platters with differing mixtures of sauces, and each dish wafted a fresh bouquet of aromas to our table. I was reminded yet again of the long tradition of Chinese gastronomy that is aptly described in the Chinese formula for any successful cuisine: *hao kan, hao wer, hao chi* (if it looks good, then it will smell good, and thus it will naturally taste good). As splendid as this cornucopia of gluttonous delights was, I would've been more than happy with just one of the dishes (except the last) augmented by a bowlful of wheat noodles or plain rice, but anything less than a carnivorous orgy would have insulted the select group of friends, our esteemed comrades, and the nation itself on that special day.

In a strange sort of role reversal, Janene and the kids enjoyed a far better meal than I because they did not sit at the head table. All the other guests in the room attacked a buffet of food lining an entire wall that was loaded with both national and European fare from end to end. In the fashion typical of Chinese when they find themselves en masse in the relative anonymity of being in public, it was every man for himself. Nevertheless, there was enough food for all, and when Janene and the kids finally filled their plates after the men who had crowded ahead of them were done, they had the luxury of choosing both what and how much they wanted to eat, so their sly glances and grins directed toward me throughout the evening demonstrated that they had indeed gotten the last laugh on their haughty emissary for the day. Along with this continent of food came an ocean of drinking. There were carbonated beverages for the kids and the few teetotalers in the room, but beer, sweet red wine, and *mao tai* was served for the majority. In between courses, some of us at the head table would get up with our glasses and wish each of the other tables *gan bei* (cheers) as a welcome respite from eating. By now I had learned not to swallow what was given me at these occasions but to barely sip any drinks for as soon as anyone saw that my glass wasn't full, they would immediately grab a bottle and fill it back up to the brim. From the very beginning, Janene and I avoided the *mao tai* since we avoided strong liquor at home and found the astringent Chinese brand distasteful, so I stuck to beer, but like some of my older hosts, I nursed my glass carefully throughout that long celebration. The rest of the room got noisier and more amiable as the drinking continued, but I noticed that since I was surrounded by men, almost all of whom were about twice my age, the weight of food and drink had a soporific effect, and several of them started to nod off.

Although it is not impolite to inquire into someone's age in China, as the youngest by far at the head table and a foreigner and capitalist to boot, I did not want to appear nosey and ask personal questions, but of the six members of the ruling committee that surrounded me at the head table, four appeared to be in their seventies, and two must have been even older. The secretary seemed to be the oldest and most senile for he was almost deaf, and after giving the opening toast, he had trouble staying awake for the rest of the meal. Here in essence was the ruling council for a metropolitan area of seven million people, and none of them struck me as vigorous or charismatic leaders. They seemed more like members of a veterans-of-foreign-wars association, attending a luncheon in their honor and alternately bemused and bored with all the attention. One of the dramatic changes that took place in China very shortly after our departure was a policy that forced anyone over sixty to retire. There were some exceptions to this draconian move, but at that banquet table, I could readily see the wisdom of this decision and assume that all the fresh blood pumped into the workplace by this policy played an important role in the rapid modernization of the nation's economy and growth. But at that celebratory moment, I was struck once more by the stark contradiction between the values of a supposedly revolutionary society (youth must be served) and the nation's long-standing Confucian tradition (venerate the elderly).

The National Day feast seemed to herald an open season for parties, special trips, and as the date of our December departure neared, a succession of farewell dinners. It just so happened that the weekend after the celebrations of the thirtieth anniversary of the People's Republic marked a far more ancient holiday, the Mid-Autumn Festival, which is held on the fifteenth of the eighth month according to the traditional Chinese calendar. Following Chinese cosmology, the large, hot sun represents the *yang* or male forces of nature that are twinned with the small, cool moon that symbolizes the female forces of *yin*, and thus this lunar holiday celebrates the ascension of the more feminine forces of nature when days are colder, shorter, and darker. Less than a week after the enormous banquet in honor of a modern political holiday, we were now to be feted once again with a weekend trip in honor of a much more ancient festival. The Foreign Experts Bureau arranged a weekend trip to Jixian, a small town about eighty miles from Tianjin just within the northern tip of the city's large metropolitan district. Early Friday afternoon, about forty-five of us clambered into three minibuses for the weekend excursion. With the growing importance of modernization in every sphere of the nation's central planning, more foreign experts were being recruited, so in addition to the half dozen of us already teaching at Tian Wai, about a dozen more foreigners were hired in the fall: a single American woman, a married American woman with her baby and stay-at-home husband, a French woman with her son and stay-at-home husband, a Japanese woman, a Japanese man with his two kids and a stay-at-home wife, and a Peruvian man with his two children and stay-at-home wife. Typical of Chinese bureaucracy and its penchant for overemployment, in addition to the twenty of us foreigners, there were twenty-five Chinese to take care of us: drivers, members of the wai ban (including smiling Shen and unhappy Fu), translators (including Xiao Zhang), several professors, department chairmen, and Lao Chen, our former chair but now vice president. Naturally, these extra cadres were also motivated by the opportunity to accompany the foreign guests on a free excursion compliments of the state, for their iron rice bowls were tinged with silver.

We drove out of the city proper past innumerable brick factories that ringed the suburbs, and soon our macadam road narrowed into a dusty single lane that took us by the mud houses and open sewers of the rural area that is home to most of the Chinese populace. Peasants were out harvesting the last of the corn and replacing it with winter wheat, and occasionally, we'd see a few two-wheeled tractors, but for the most part, the heavy work was done by animals, oxen and horses straining at harrows or little donkeys tugging stone rollers to tamp down the dusty earth before planting. The road too was almost devoid of mechanization but was crowded with pedestrians, bicycles, carts pulled by mules or oxen, and people straining with loaded wheelbarrows or tethered to handcarts bulging with cornstalks or straw. The fields were never empty but speckled with people, sons and daughters of toil, daughters and sons of the soil. These were the unseen hands that labored so hard to provide our daily meals. Magically, their wheat, corn, barley, fruit, and vegetables were transported into the city each night and transformed into the tasteful meals we almost always took for granted. No accomplishment impressed me so much during our year of touring the nation than the miraculous way in which food was planted, grown, harvested, and transported so that over a billion people could sleep without hunger each night, at least the majority of these masses. And this all began with the faceless figures I was watching from the comfort of my moving window. As I saw them laboring, a feeling of respect and admiration came over me, and though I have absolutely no confirmation of this, from what I witnessed, these rural folk seemed much more ardent about their work than the teachers and cadres we lived with in the city. Their lives were extremely simple, and it was obvious they enjoyed few amenities, and as I've remarked before, compared to the city dwellers, it seems as if their lives had changed very little over the past century or two let alone after thirty years of liberation. They were good workers toiling away at the good earth.

The late autumn sun was already low by the time our entourage pulled into Jixian, and as we checked into the only guesthouse, we immediately became the town's Friday night's attraction. After crowding together to wash up in the few sinks in the single unisex bathroom that would serve us the next two days, we stepped outside into the already darkened evening to gaze at a splendid full moon rising a dark yellow in the east but turning whiter and brighter as it arched across the southern sky as the night progressed. We were led into a central dining hall and were fed a huge feast that almost rivaled the one hosted for us in Tianjin exactly a week before. We retired to an upstairs room for tea, fruit, and moon cakes. Chinese *yue bing* are a pastry but less of a cake than a round, crusted biscuit filled with a semisweet confection of spices and fruit. The crust is usually imprinted with Chinese characters or figures, traditionally a rabbit, since the Chinese (and any impartial observer, I would argue) believe the full moon depicts an upright hare. Unlike the Shandong story of stingy Mr. Wang and miserly Mr. Li, our hosts were generous in supplying us with an ample supply of the real confection. Not long after we dispensed with the moon cakes, someone had brought a cassette recorder, and soon, the air was filled with dance music. First the foreigners and then some of the more daring Chinese began dancing, among them was Lao Chen, who surprised all of us with his graceful ballroom moves. By now, the locals had surrounded the guesthouse and craned their necks to catch sight of the bizarre behavior of their strange visitors partying away and celebrating the confluence of *ying* and *yang*.

The next morning, as we were driven to the site of some Qing dynasty tombs, we passed through several small villages, and since it was Saturday, each of them were filled with people shopping at the weekend market. Again, it seemed that rather than traveling forward several miles in distance, we were actually regressing backward in time and were now in the middle of a medieval marketplace. Gone was the modernity promised by Deng's Four Modernizations. Fresh produce lay on both sides of the roadway for sale; nervous piglets were tied up next to bamboo baskets of anxious chickens, ducks, and a few geese. Several tables held bolts of cloth, the only splash of bright color in that otherwise dusty scene. Vendors squinted at their weighted stick scales as they carefully balanced out their transactions. The tombs and surrounding monuments seemed emblematic of the nation itself for they lay in a state of transition after being vandalized by invading armies, ransacked by warlords, and intentionally defaced by the Red Guards during the Cultural Revolution. Now they were undergoing a state of renovation so that everywhere we visited, workers on bamboo scaffolding were replastering, painting, and restoring the glories of China's heritage. Even a new monument commemorating the guerillas who had resisted the Japanese invasion was under restoration. In the afternoon, we all hiked up a hill overlooking the larger site to a Buddhist temple and monastery built during the much earlier Tang dynasty. Given the destruction evidenced among the monuments below, there was relatively little damage to these buildings and the images they contained. Inside was a giant Buddha and behind it, a smaller and more graceful *Guan Yin* (the Goddess of Mercy), my favorite Chinese deity. Even though this temple was also being renovated, there was an aura of stability and peace surrounding the hilltop, and as we rested in the shade outside, it was the ideal moment for contemplation. Looking out across the valley and enjoying the unusual quiet, I couldn't help but notice the bold contrast between the incessant noise and rhetoric that encompassed our daily life in Tianjin and the serenity of that special moment. The best-crafted slogans in the world cannot inspire a people who live in a dispirited land.

After another huge meal and another soiree of dancing that night, we toured some more on Sunday morning before finally heading back toward Tianjin in the afternoon. Because this was a rare opportunity for our kids to interact with other foreign families, it was an unusual and exciting experience for them as well. Christine seemed to enjoy the chance to escape the discipline of both her nursery and her life under our tutelage in the hotel and got into mischief more than once. She somehow managed to slice her finger with a knife during dinner our first night, but despite the profusion of blood, it was not a serious wound. Derick had never danced, but by the second night was the life of the party and could scarcely sleep from the excitement. Pierre, our French foreign expert and resident joie de vivre, kept the children entertained with spontaneous fits of drama. His best moment came during a lull in the afternoon of the second day when he either fell or intentionally jumped into a pit of powdered lime and emerged from behind one of the tombs, terrifying both kids and adults. He was the true epitome of a *yang guizi*! We left Jixian Sunday afternoon, and as the autumn sun dropped rapidly in the west and as all of us sat dozing in the minibus, Bruce, the husband of the new American teacher, organized a wager on the exact time we would arrive at the institute after collecting five fen from those of us willing to contribute to the pool. Derick guessed ten after five, and the weekend excursion ended perfectly for him when we reached home at five eleven on the dot.

Were I to rely entirely on my memory, I would concede that our family trip to Qufu did indeed take place some time in the fall but would claim that it transpired at least a month before or after the midautumn venture to Jixian; nevertheless, our letters, the calendar, and Janene's copiously recorded diary do not lie, and they all document that the Friday after the wai ban sponsored excursion and a fortnight after the National Day gala, we set out for a weekend visit to Qufu, Confucius's hometown, our first trip completely on our own. Much of the timing and motivation for this excursion was that Derick became a teenager on that Friday, so this was a birthday present to be unwrapped by the entire family. As I recorded in my earlier account of this weekend, even though Derick was sick with the flu, the weather, the travel connections, our chance to tour the birthplace of classic Chinese culture, and mainly that we were traveling independently, all combined to make this a perfect culmination to all our travels throughout the nation that year. Never shy about seizing the chance to give a lecture and thus secure a free night's accommodation, we stopped in Jinan on our way so I could give my final lecture to the faculty at Shandong University. Thus, our trip also gave me a chance to say good-bye to President Wu, the Russian Lao Jin, and several other people whose friendships I valued. It also gave us an opportunity to go over to the hospital to visit the Shandong American who was convalescing there from a broken hip.

We had not been in China more than a few weeks when I started hearing about this mysterious Shandong American, and initially I was miffed that people were not talking about me; after all, was not this the perfect appellation for me? However, like all foreigners who become household names in China, this American had a close association with Communist politics. The fame enjoyed by this particular individual goes back to the Korean War, when Chinese and American soldiers fought each other for the first and hopefully final time. The PLA volunteer led by Peng Dehuai overwhelmed the United Nations forces supporting South Korea, but they did so at a terrible loss of life. In July 1953, at the conclusion of that conflict, prisoners on both sides were exchanged though fourteen thousand PLA soldiers adamantly refused to return home to China and eventually ended up in Taiwan. All but a handful of American POWs were happy to go back to the States, but a few of them, almost all African-American, accepted an invitation to live in China, where they were promised a home and freedom from prejudice. Within a few years, almost every one of these defectors defected back to America, preferring to live in the comfort of family and capitalism despite the racism. Two men remained, both living in Shandong and both, interestingly enough, among the very few white defectors. We met them both during our visits to Jinan. One was a quiet Texan, a guy by the name of Howard, who was still married to a Chinese and taught English at the Shandong Medical University. The other was Jim Veneris, who originally hailed from Pittsburgh, our American home at that time, and for reasons even he himself couldn't explain, he was the Korean War vet singled out as the famous Shandong American. Still speaking with a Western Pennsylvania accent and clearly a man of working-class roots, Jim delighted in getting firsthand information from us about his hometown and learning that his Pirates and his Steelers managed to win the World Series and the Super Bowl that year. Jim taught English conversation at Shandong University but had worked for many years in a factory and had suffered a variety of political and health-related afflictions over the decades and always seemed out of place among the well-educated and intellectual faculty members who were ostensibly his colleagues. Divorced and now hospitalized from a fall, he appeared frail and was understandably less lively. We felt sorry for him, especially since, like the other Chinese hospitals we visited, this place was unsanitary and depressingly decrepit, and his ward seemed more like a morgue than a place for healing. Both Howard and Jim reminded me of the two expatriate Thais that I met that year in China. They, like the Shandong Americans, had also chosen to live in China for political reasons, but even if you take the boy out of his country, you can't take the country out of the boy, and I empathized with all four of these men. They were the un-Chinese, living in limbo, condemned to die in neither a heaven nor a hell but in a human purgatory of their own choosing. How terrible to be a man without a country!

This was to be our last long train ride in China, and we savored the improved service and the privacy of our own soft-seat compartment. As a classless Communist society, the People's Republic rejected the notion of first-, second-, or third-class seats, so there were basically two types of tickets one could purchase to ride the rails: *ying xi* or *ruan xi* (hard seats or soft seats), and as the names imply, it is easy to guess where the foreigners, cadres, and fat cats sat. We rode hard-seat a couple of times when all the first-class tickets had been booked, and by and large, even though the carriages were crowded and noisy, except for the incessant staring, we didn't mind being downsized. However, there was one hard-seat ride that left me longing for an upgrade. On my return to China from the quick winter trip I took to attend an academic convention in Boston, I could only get a hard-seat ticket for the two-hour ride from the Hong Kong border to Canton, where I would catch a flight to Beijing and then a train back to Tianjin. It was my double misfortune to fly into Hong Kong just at the start of Spring Festival, when it seems like everyone in China is traveling back to home and family and the nation's entire transportation system turns into a giant game of musical chairs. To compound the crowding, it was the first year that the PRC allowed relatives visiting from Hong Kong to bring in gifts of electronics and appliances. I would've been delighted to have enjoyed a seat as hard as rock on that trip, but I was lucky just to have been able to fight my way up and into a car with one hand and lugging a heavy suitcase in the other, and because all of us standing were squeezed together virtually cheek to cheek, I ended up with only one leg to stand on with the other foot perched on top of my suitcase, which was propped vertically in order to fit in among the tape recorders, TVs, microwaves, and refrigerators that my fellow passengers managed to pry on board. I thought of some of my parents' stories about train travel back during the war with Japan when refugees overwhelmed every horizontal space of every car, when my father once rode straddling the coupling between two freight cars, or when my mother survived an adventuresome train ride, carrying explosives through the teeth of battle.

It was the late thirties, and my parents had just returned to China by ship after a year's furlough in the States. My father had gone ahead to Jining to help meet the pressing demands of the mission hospital since the entire province of Shandong was seesawing with battles between various Chinese factions and the invading Imperial Army of Japan. My mother, the children, and my grandmother who had come to live with us in China remained in the relative stability of the large port city of Qingdao, where they had disembarked, waiting to join my father in Jining when the train line was demonstrably safer. Because Jining was relatively small and isolated, medicine and hospital supplies were difficult to obtain, and one day, my mother received a desperate telegram from my father.

HOSPITAL FULL OF WOUNDED SOLDIERS
NEEDING OPERATION.
NO ETHER.

My mother was a small woman, but she had a big heart if measured by both courage and compassion. She went around Qingdao buying as many cans of ether as she could and set out by herself on the perilous journey over hundreds of miles into the interior, uncertain if the train would ever be able to cross through several battle zones or escape air attacks from the invading army. Sure enough, during the long first leg west to Jinan, the train would intermittently come to a stop, and all the passengers would hurtle left and right off the cars as Japanese planes swooped overhead, sometimes strafing, sometimes ignoring the string of cars. After overnighting in Jinan, my mother with her precious suitcase of inflammable cargo tried to get on a train south for the second leg to Jining, but there were so many refugees milling about that she couldn't even reach the station. After finally being able to get word to the stationmaster of her plight, a squad of policemen came back and squeezed her through the masses and onto the only train heading in that direction, a hard seat in a carriage packed with KMT troops deploying for battle. As the only woman on board and with her suitcase propped on her lap, my mother typically tried to make the best of a desperate situation. "Please stop smoking," she said at one point to the young recruits puffing away around her. "I'm carrying ether in this suitcase, and it would be easy for the fumes to blow us all up!" "Who cares, *tai tai*," they replied cavalierly, "we'll either die here or on the battlefield." Ever quick with a retort, my mother replied. "There's a very big difference, my friends. I won't be with you on the battlefield!" As I mulled over these memories, my standing-room-only ride didn't seem quite so intolerable, and soon I was able to disembark in Canton and catch the smoke-filled flight to my family and home up north, but even that wasn't so bad. After all, I was now traveling soft-seat, and I wasn't carrying any ether either.

The banquets, excursions, and special occasions did not replace our normal workload at the institute, and it seemed as if the latter even increased in indirect proportion to the number of days we had left, and the greater demand on our time and energy may explain why our physical ailments seemed to afflict us more frequently that fall. Janene helped her class produce the institute's first student publication, the inaugural and only edition of *The Tianjin Tattler*, which the department chair edited assiduously to ensure that it was politically correct. She also helped her class write and produce a skit for the institute's talent show in which she played a naïve American tourist impressed with all the great changes transforming China but discombobulated by the English the students used. "Carter? Do you mean President Carter?" she inquired, when one of her students who was pretending to be her tour guide talked about the institute's cadre, which the Chinese pronounced *Carter* in English. Following Janene's lead when she volunteered to give a talk to the three hundred pupils at the middle school associated with our institute and from which many of our university-age students had graduated, I cycled over one November Tuesday to the same site and tried to make a talk on the daily life of teachers and students in America interesting and intelligible to the large audience of young people. After speaking to Janene's students on the importance of sports in American culture, in order to be fair to the other classrooms of the '77 grade, I agreed to repeat the talk for the other '77 students who were not members of Janene's elite classroom. Smart as Janene's students were, there was evidence that the narrow focus on English language training throughout their later education led to a lack of learning about other basic aspects of general education. They knew quite a bit about England and America, the countries that were closely tied to their English education, but they were surprisingly ignorant about other parts of the world and had trouble reading the maps we brought because they differed slightly from the Chinese ones they had been weaned on.

Several students struggled with any problems that relied on rudimentary arithmetic for an answer. Reviewing a passage her students had read on the American Revolutionary War, Janene asked one member of her select class when that conflict ended if the war began in 1775 and lasted seven years, and this problem proved too difficult for him to solve without resorting to pencil and paper. On a written quiz testing their comprehension of the assigned passage, her students were completely thrown off by a question that asked them to choose something George Washington was *not*. Both of us introduced our students to different testing formats to help prepare them in the future for standardized examinations, such as the Test of English as a Foreign Language, and they were confused and very reluctant to tackle multiple-choice questions, and matching questions gave them fits. Learning in any culture is not simply the acquisition of facts, skills, and values; it is also the accretion of metacognitive skills: learning how to learn, study, test, and so on. The new formats we used to evaluate our students were naturally challenging for them yet all indirectly part of the process of modernization espoused by their government.

Throughout the year, visitors to China and many of the foreign expert teachers we met commented on the superb level of English our students and other Chinese majoring in the language commanded, especially given the relative isolation they had endured from access to modern materials and contact with native speakers. Certainly, there was truth in this generalization, but having lived and worked with English learners there for almost a year, we could immediately qualify this claim. First and foremost, with miniscule exceptions, only the crème de la crème of English learners served as tour guides or travel agents for foreign visitors, and unlike India, where English serves as a national language, or Thailand or even Japan, a foreigner interacting with the average city dweller can frequently find someone who knows English. At that time in China, however, without the assistance of one of those highly trained English interpreters, a foreign visitor would be hard-pressed to find any Chinese citizen able to communicate with a stranger in English. Finally, as Janene and I discovered in our daily contact with these students, a curriculum that focuses narrowly on training specialists in English does not create a well-rounded education. Just as the attached middle school and our institute produced terrific language learners, at least for the most part, Derick's middle school and its attached conservatory trained accomplished musicians but both fashioned graduates who knew very little about geography, history, science, math, or any other subject outside of their specialties. Once more you can see the way that Chinese institutions were independent, vertical structures. If you want a translator, go to Tian Wai. If you need a violinist, go to the Tianjin Conservatory of Music. If you need a mechanical engineer, try Tianjin University. Even at Nankai University, the city's only comprehensive university and the most prestigious institution of tertiary education in town, if your major was accounting, you studied that subject for four years and did not dabble in such trifles as electives. At the time, it was impossible for me to foresee any possible changes in this narrowly focused curriculum. Anyhow, where would Chinese students go in the future if they wanted a more balanced, liberal-arts type of education? Certainly, they would never flood American colleges and universities! Would the PRC ever develop such institutions itself? What a preposterous speculation!

We were honored to have won a surfeit of friends during our stay, and as we approached the time for our departure, most of them tried to arrange a visit before we left, so over and above the banquets, final trips, and added teaching duties, our hotel room turned into a reception center practically every other evening late that fall. In keeping with the realization that each of these was most likely our ultimate time together, our Chinese friends were even more open and ardent about sharing their lives with us, and in turn, we became much more aware of just how remarkable these people were. Take Lao Chen, for instance. As the Party commissar for the English department, he was our direct boss when we first arrived, and he was the one who had startled us by his uncanny resemblance to Ho Chi Minh down to the waving cigarette in his hand whenever he gestured. We immediately developed a close relationship with him, and after his surprise request for us to lecture on the legacy of George Washington in early February, we could see that, unlike the hackneyed use of the terms in the propaganda immersing us, he was a true revolutionary. Lao Chen had visions for the future and was not trapped by the reactionary narratives of the Long March, the Great Leap Forward, or the Cultural Revolution. After his promotion to vice president of our institute, we had fewer direct contacts with him, but rarely a week would go by without a chat with him while at work, and we were honored to be his sounding board when he paid an occasional visit to our quarters at the hotel. Considerate of our distaste for cigarettes, he would hold off from his favorite smoke for a whole hour during these visits, speaking loudly and easily in English in his deep and commanding voice. Now that he was enmeshed in the politics of central administration, he would lament the favoritism, dissent, incessant fighting over housing and all of the turmoil that we simple classroom teachers were so lucky to avoid. We plied him with tea, sympathy, and appreciation, and it upset me to see how, even within the Party hierarchy, seemingly good people with apparently good ideas were often ignored.

Some of these visitors were friends of friends and came from outside of our institutional circles of contact. Lao Pang was one of these, a professor from Nankai University and someone we met late in our stay. He was a specialist in English literature and one of the most fluent English speakers we encountered that year. A gifted raconteur, he was the one who among other anecdotes had shared with us the story about the girl who was sent off to the countryside during the Cultural Revolution for having inadvertently put Chairman Mao's picture upside down during a slide show. His buddy and our dear friend Wang Zhanmei brought him to our hotel on a Wednesday evening in the middle of October, and they filled the time with fascinating narratives and insights, and had it not been midweek or us being so tired, they probably would've stayed on till dawn. Lao Pang had a keen intellect and a gift for language, and he was not shy about drawing generalizations about people, cultures, and ideas nor was he modest about his own abilities, an unusual trait for a Chinese if I myself can make a bold generalization. Toward the beginning of our discussion, he claimed, "I have lived all of Chinese history within my lifetime." I sensed he was not as brash as he sounded for I knew he wasn't implying he had experienced four thousand years of reincarnations but rather something like that he was old enough to remember pre-Liberation China and had vivid memories of all the vicissitudes of life since the revolution. To a survivor then, it must have felt like an eternity. When our conversation began to meander on to whether or not there was a uniquely Chinese character, Pang had hit his element, and fortified only by weak tea and without strong drink, he felt free to share some uninhibited and insightful observations about his fellow countrymen.

Chinese are constrained by space but not time; Americans are just the reverse. Happiness is not as important in China as being content. Americans, on the other hand, seek happiness but never seem to be content. Here is where he shared the story about the boy who had caught a sparrow during the time Pang had been sent to the cowshed (a euphemism for the rehabilitation camps set up during the Cultural Revolution). Every time the bird attempted to fly away, the boy would rudely yank on the string tethered to its leg, but as long as it stayed within the radius of that string, the bird remained unbothered. "Contentment," Pang concluded, "is living within the confines of your constraints."

At this point, Wang Zhanmei entered in with another observation. "In China," he remarked, "we learn never to look up at what more you could have but to look down at how far you have come." I wondered if this is what Pang meant by contentment, and again I thought of an overdrawn yet easy comparison to the American pursuit of happiness versus lives of discontent. The conversation finally turned to a generalization made often about the Chinese people: they are patient, tolerant, and long-suffering. Here Janene and I added our own generalizations, once more contrasting these characteristics with our view of Americans, who, in this respect, seem to be a very impatient people. For a year, we observed Chinese patiently waiting in line (well, except at bus stops and railway stations) whereas Americans often fume if someone is too slow to respond to a green light or if the old lady in line in front of them at the supermarket takes a few seconds too long fumbling for the correct change. On the other hand, we pointed out that many of the false accusations leveled during the unremitting witch hunts and kangaroo courts held throughout the Cultural Revolution would not have been tolerated in an American setting, especially in the less public meetings among colleagues who worked together. I can't imagine my academic colleagues in the States sitting quietly at a department meeting, agreeing through their silence to ludicrous false charges screamed at a fellow professor. To cite a historical example, there was a great deal of criticism of Senator Joe McCarthy even during his moment of fame at the height of the Cold War, and since then, that excess of political slander has been universally scorned in public discourse, the media, and in American history books.

Janene and I were exhausted, and it was only midweek, so our time together was over. It was late when I walked Lao Pang and Zhanmei out of the hotel to where their bikes were parked. Following the old tradition, I always enjoyed accompanying our guests to the front gate, and on the way down the stairs and out the front door, they both politely protested, "*bie song, bie song* [there's no need to send us off]." But what better way to end an evening and to show your appreciation and hospitality than to join your guests in their first few steps on that long and dark journey home.

In preparation for our own send off back to the States, our Chinese friends and acquaintances—in their typical display of generosity—were not going to let us leave Tianjin without showering us with farewell gifts. We had already gotten a liberal dose of their munificence during our many visits to other cities and institutions, and we never left even the shortest and most informal talk some place without being acknowledged with a gift. These came in all shapes, styles, and sizes and were often souvenirs of the place we had visited, so when it came time to start thinking about packing up for our return, we had already accumulated a variety of bric-a-bracs, most of which we would've gladly unloaded on someone else before our departure. In keeping with our intent of trying to keep most of the salary we earned in China by spending it during our tenure, we had purchased carpets and a few other household items to be crated and sent back to the States, so we had an opportunity to ship a few of the more valuable gifts we wanted to keep and even some of the less valuable but unique objects. My favorite among the latter was a cute ceramic panda that naturally won over the kid's affection as something to keep. What captured my heart, however, was its function: it was not a toy or keepsake but a Fire Micky. Yes, the name was intriguing and only obliquely hinted at its intended use. Clearly marked as an item marketed to foreigners, it was a forerunner of the massive flood of goods designed and produced for export to the United States.

Although it may be hard to imagine, back in 1979, there was barely a trickle of Chinese goods being produced for export to America, and those that were being manufactured were generally of poor quality. Contact with American businessmen and corporations had just begun, and the Chinese had very limited acquaintance with US consumers and American culture. Because they were familiar with Disney's first and most famous character at that time, my guess is that this ceramic panda was named after "Mickey Rat" since the Chinese have always felt free to borrow (or is it steal?) brand names, copyrights, and intellectual property with impunity. Thus given its cute appearance and famous name, the manufacturers of this cuddly mammal hoped it would sell like hotcakes given that every home should have one for, you see, the panda was more than a decoration, it was a fire extinguisher, and more than that, an especially adorable one! The English instructions for its use are telling evidence of the primitive state of export products manufactured in China at that time.

OPERATION INSTRUCTIONS

Attention Scope: This FIRE MICKY can put out initial house fires caused by general material inflammable gasses, combustible liquids and domestic electric equipment, etc.

Directions For Use: For furniture or domestic electric equipment, etc., be sure to find, at the source of the fire, a hardly spot at which to hurl the MICKY so that the extinguisher breaks and the agent diffuses right there to put out the fire. For liquefied gas utensils or frying pans etc. on fire, throw the MICKY high so that it breaks and puts out the fire: or take the agent from the MICKY and energetically spread it over the source of the fire.

Remarks: To meet an emergency, this MICKY should be placed handy and kept away from humidity. Keep more than TWO MICKY ready for use in case the first one is missing. If a number of fires concur or an indoor fire spreads out, do not wait in expectation. In such circumstances, the FIRE MICKY can guarantee escapes such as entrance, exit and staircase, etc. The agent filled in the FIRE MICKY is non-poisonous, non-corrosive, and non-conductive. It is effective for 3 years.

Fortunately I never had to hurl my Fire Micky at any conflagration, and now, decades after his inner agent has lost all its mojo, he still sits proudly in my office. A little medallion hanging from a chain around his neck attests to his anti-incendiary powers, and his black-circled eyes look dolefully at me from his distinctively oversized head. Who would've guessed that he was one of the first of thousands of pandas, millions of action toys, billions of Christmas lights and decorations, and a gazillion other products ranging from nanotechnology to massive steel bridge parts ferried by ships built specifically to carry them that would one day flood the US market in tsunami after tsunami of exports. My little Fire Micky, you were the first of a kind!

We implored our friends that we needed no gifts, that we had no room for them in the first place, and that the greatest present was the simple memory of our friendship, but I knew none of our protestations would be heeded. They were not unlike the way we begged our Chinese hosts not to keep heaping new dishes on to our already full plates at banquets and that we had already *chi baole, he zhule* to use, the Chinese equivalent of stuffed to the gills. All of our pleading went for naught, and it was as if all our friends could hear was "Hit me again." After pleading for them not to give us any gifts then, I went on to add that *if* they felt absolutely compelled to leave us with a memento, a modest scroll would be acceptable. Scrolls were small, lightweight, and easy to pack. More importantly, from the first one that was given to me as a child, I've appreciated their aesthetic blend of art and language. Most are painted to be hung vertically, announcing at the very outset that art is a link between earth and heaven. Typically, they depict natural scenes, usually of *shan* (mountains) and *shui* (water in rivers, lakes, or streams), thus the Chinese word for scenery is *shanshui*. Most have a human visitor or two somewhere within the natural scenery not as central figures dominating the landscape but as humble interlopers overwhelmed and entranced by the harmony of their surroundings. And most have a short poem, a doublet or quatrain followed by the artist's name, written down the side in a distinctive style of calligraphy, and this is as much of the scroll as the painting itself. To an alien eye, one used to the effusive use of color and space by the European masters, most Chinese scrolls appear to be half empty, for above the flowers, trees, or mountains that crown the top of the painting, there is nothing but space. But just as music is as much about the silence between notes, the emptiness in a Chinese scroll is as important as every stroke of the brush. Scrolls we asked for, and scrolls we got, so many in fact that to this day, we rotate the many hanging in our home so that the rolled up ones do not lie neglected too long. Most of these were painted for us by artists known by our friends, so the calligraphy contains a personal dedication making the gift all the more meaningful and adding to the provenance of each scroll.

There were one or two pleasant exceptions to our fiat about scrolls only. Pastor Liu gave us a Chinese Bible, an extraordinarily generous act given their rarity at that time but what better symbol of the remarkable faith of the Christian community we met than the Word of God spoken to them in their mother tongue. Nevertheless, there was one farewell present that directly defied our pleas for restraint and, in contrast to the scrolls we received, violated all standards of aesthetic sensibility. It came from Derick's music school, and it came as a complete surprise. The weekend before we were scheduled to leave Tianjin, a representative of the conservatory knocked on our door and, with great relish, announced that at that very moment, their institute's gift was being carried up the stairs behind him. From the grunting of the two men even before I caught sight of their monstrously overgenerous present, I knew we were in for trouble. The panting duo swung through the door and pivoted so we could see the front of the large, rectangular object they had struggled so hard to bring up to us. There in front of us was a depiction of the Da Gang oil fields made out of seashells. Janene and I were stunned, literally shell-shocked. From our slackened jaws, bulging eyes, and complete silence, our three visitors could only assume that we were speechless with delight. "Well, what do you think?" they asked. We both had almost exactly the same response. "You shouldn't have," we gasped. "You really shouldn't have!" After sending them off with perfunctory handshakes and thank-yous, we turned to each other to discuss what we were going to do with this monstrosity. Its size alone was a problem since at roughly three by five feet, it was far too large to squeeze into the small spaces still available in the crate containing our carpets. It also weighed a ton since it was made up entirely of seashells encrusted on a wood board, and even the frame was covered with shells. But even if it were a tiny replica and only the size of a book, it was such a tasteless piece of kitsch that you wouldn't want to pawn it off on an acquaintance even as a joke. What then should we do? I finally thought of a perfect way to recycle it when I remembered that we still hadn't given a present to Christine's nursery to thank them for the year of loving care they had devoted to our daughter. The next morning, our entire family trundled off to her nursery, Janene with Christine on her bike and Derick and I balancing this massive objet d'art on mine. The staff was surprised to see all of us arrive together and were amazed when we turned our gift around so they could see what it was. Their jaws slackened, and their eyes dilated, and they emitted a collective gasp of astonishment. Clearly they were speechless with gratitude. "You shouldn't have," one of the ladies said. "You really shouldn't have."

There is a little coda to this story. In 1991, Janene and I led a group of our church friends from California on a marvelous tour of China that included Tianjin. Because Christine accompanied us on that trip, we scheduled a visit to her old nursery on our itinerary, and we were fortunate to do so for, like so many other places in the city, it was about to be replaced by a larger building, so it was already in the process of being closed down. One of her former teachers happened to be there, even though twelve years had elapsed, and it was touching to see her reunited with little Christine, now a young woman. We did a quick tour for we wanted our group to see what a Chinese nursery looked like. When we walked into her old classroom, I was pleased to see our gift—the familiar depiction of the famous Da Gang oil fields carefully crafted out of hundreds of sea shells. It was a picture quite literally heavy with symbolism of the success of the petroleum industry under the leadership of the Party.

Among the details of our invitation to go to China discussed in my phone negotiations with the then Chinese liaison office in Washington the previous fall was the promise to pay our family's round-trip airfare. The Chinese were almost always faithful in meeting their commitments, and I often got the sense that the spoken word carried even more weight than a written contract. There was a tiny hitch in the details conveyed to me over the phone back in Pittsburgh about our air travel, however, and this was the fact that the liaison office would only pay our way to China. I could understand the reluctance of the Chinese official in Washington to cover the cost of round-trip fares for our family all at once, but innocent as I was back then, I foresaw the possibility of problems arising once we tried to arrange a return flight back to America. Now it was time to do just that, and now the problems started to emerge. Ever trustworthy and faithful in his duties, Xiao Zhang set off for Beijing on November 22 on business for our wai ban, including purchasing and booking tickets for the Scovel family. Usually, these trips lasted a day or two, but three then four days went by and Zhang didn't return. He came back on the fifth day, angry and depressed, and a major cause of his despondency was the inability to get anything accomplished concerning our return tickets. There was no problem with funding, for the Foreign Experts Bureau in Beijing took care of that efficiently, but the trouble lay with Civil Aviation Administration of China. At that time, CAAC was the only commercial carrier for all air transport in the country, and as a government-owned-and-run monopoly, it was responsible for all flights foreign and domestic. I've already cited illustrations of their poor service, but booking flights for tickets already paid for should have been relatively easy to accomplish, especially when Zhang was visiting their head office in Beijing personally, so I hadn't anticipated him running into any trouble. Obviously, he needed backup. We had a slew of parties and other engagements to meet, but a little over a week later, Janene arranged to go to Beijing with Zhang to take care of the matter directly.

They took the six-forty morning train on the first of December and, upon arriving at the capital, headed straight for the CAAC office, where instead of service with a smile, they encountered agents that were, in Janene's polite words, unbelievably rude. The sticking point was trying to reserve flights from Hong Kong to the United States. After considerable discussion, the woman supposedly helping Janene finally agreed to book flights for our family and asked our preferred itinerary. We had close friends in Hawaii whom we wished to visit en route, but we also wanted to make certain that we'd be home in time to spend Christmas with our families. Janene gave a suggested date for our departure from Hong Kong and another one two days later from Honolulu, and the CAAC agent took out a blank ticket form and began furiously filling it out. Suspicious by the ease with which the agent was able to so quickly choose a carrier, flight, and convenient departure and arrival times, Janene realized that the agent was simply writing down whatever itinerary Janene provided so that she'd leave with her bogus tickets and the agent would've gotten rid of the pesky foreigner. Exasperated, Janene headed to the United States Embassy with Xiao Zhang in tow. It was a much larger, finer, and more secure establishment than the temporary liaison office we had checked into upon our arrival in early January. Stapleton Roy kindly came down from his upstairs office to greet Janene and introduce her to a staff member who immediately called their travel contact in Hong Kong, and within a few minutes, he was able to promise four bona fide air tickets for us back to the States, something that CAAC was unable to do even after two long visits to their Beijing headquarters. David, the embassy staff member who helped Janene, explained that beyond the surly intransigence of the CAAC agents and their general reluctance to provide service to customers, CAAC had not yet joined International Air Transport Association partly because China refused to conform to a single standardized pricing structure for all passengers. In other words, CAAC would've had to have given up charging non-Chinese customers more, part of the dual-pricing policy we witnessed and had been subjected to. But as the bard observed, all's well that ends well, and Janene was able to get back to Tianjin Sunday in time for a yet another farewell dinner, this time hosted by Wang Zhanmei's family. Xiao Zhang was no longer morose, and for the first time in weeks, Janene fell asleep without any worries about whether we'd ever be able to be home for Christmas.

That following week, Janene's class held a farewell party in her honor supervised by Da Ni, her Chinese counterpart who had partnered with her for most of the year and for whom she had served as both a personal and professional mentor. The institute's red Fiat came to take us through the evening fog to Ni's house, and we crowded together inside with her class. The electricity was out that night, so the candlelight added a holiday warmth to the winter chill. After a little prodding, we got the students to sing some Christmas carols, which Janene had taught them, and there were a couple of awkward speeches of gratitude, but emotions got the better of some of the students, and Janene couldn't hold back the tears herself as she stood to thank them for the scroll they had brought for her. We stood in a circle and sang "Auld Lang Syne," and then Janene hugged each one, surely the first time any teacher had ever embraced them, and they all gathered around outside to see us off as we drove away into the night mist.

By and large, we found our friends and acquaintances more romantic than inscrutable, and this was especially true of Janene's students, whose same youthful emotions just a few years earlier fueled their adoration of Mao and vitriolic excesses against capitalists and perceived counterrevolutionaries, but now this ardor was directed toward us, admiration and affection toward their teachers from the very heartland of antirevolutionary capitalism. We received notes of gratitude from many of them, and some were so cloyingly maudlin that I could barely wade through them without wincing, but others were refulgent with appreciation without being over the top. Consider this touching poem Janene received.

> Time was flying by when we were together,
> Our eyes were swollen with tears when we depart,
> Who knows in which year and on which day we'll meet again,
> But our hearts on both sides of the great ocean link together.

The next morning, we crossed the bridge to the other side of the city to Derick's music school for the last time. The completion of his study at the conservatory was punctuated by a final examination for which he had prepared hard during the final months and over which he had sweated bullets. It was actually a recital, an unusual one at his institution because unlike the Chinese students, he studied two instruments, so he had to be assessed on both. When we chatted with Xu Laoshi and Yu Laoshi, we quickly discovered that his piano and trombone teachers were more nervous than their pupil. In China, a teacher is directly responsible for a student's success or failure, and because Derick was the first and only foreign pupil at the school, there was additional pressure on him, and this stress was thus magnified for his instructors. As an American teacher, I like our tradition better for I could readily accept credit for any of my students' successes and simultaneously blame them as sluggards were they to do poorly. Derick did a superb job, playing pieces on both instruments from memory in front of a troika of stern-faced older teachers who served as judges. At the end, his fellow students roundly congratulated him and his proud parents and his two mentors, who were almost giddy with relief. The school's librarian was also present, an Indonesian-Chinese who had managed to escape the bloodbath against Communists and Chinese in that nation during the late sixties and eventually married and settled in Tianjin. She took a special liking to our son and now had a unique request for us. She had talked this over with her husband, she began, and she wanted to secure our permission for her ambitious enterprise. Derick had made remarkable progress in his musical training and had even learned some Chinese, she went on, but she felt that if he could stay on for another year, his progress would accelerate considerably, and he could then return to join us in the States as a more competent bilingual and a better trained musician. He could live in their apartment, and she and her husband would take care of all of Derick's expenses. The sincerity and magnanimity of her offer overwhelmed us, and it was one more illustration of the incredible personal bonds forged that year and the generosity that so many Chinese extended to our family. It was hard for us to convince her that we were genuinely impressed with her liberality but equally resolute that Derick had to return with us, and we left the conservatory that night with the same mixture of emotions with which we would leave China a few days later.

Friday, December 14, came very early for us. I had been up until 2:30 a.m., packing suitcases and making certain that all our papers were in order. As I went to bed to catch a few hours sleep, Janene got up anxious about facing all our friends for the final good-bye. We ate our last breakfast at the hotel and gave each of the fu wu ren a small gift then took their pictures with the kids. The tallest girl was now a young woman; her short, bobbed hair replaced the two pigtails she wore when we first met her, showing she was now married. I cycled Christine over to her nursery and then gave my final two-hour lecture to my postgraduate class. Xu Laoshi came over to the hotel to visit Janene and his prize pupil one last time and once more pleaded for our help in arranging for his wife and him to go to the States. Off and on throughout the year, many of those close to us asked quite directly for assistance in obtaining some sort of scholarship or financial aid to study in America, an oblique attempt to emigrate to the nation where tens of thousands of Chinese had sailed for a difficult but ultimately better life the century before. Like passengers desperate to lighten the load of a swamped boat, we tried to jettison everything we didn't need in our final packing, so Janene and Derick spent the rest of the morning distributing these goods. Xiao Zhang got one of our most prized possessions, the portable typewriter, and Lisa, the new American foreign expert, bought our last remaining bike. After lunch, Janene cycled over to the institute to teach her beloved students for the final time, and as the two of us hurriedly ran our last errands, an angry winter wind whipped the dust up and down the streets, billowing it as high as the treetops as if nature herself was protesting our departure.

In the late afternoon, the fu wu ren fought for our suitcases and hauled them downstairs and out the front door to where the entire hotel day staff had lined up smartly to *song* us on our journey. Two cars came from the institute late as usual, and we wove in and out of the bicycles on Liberation Avenue to the train station, where representatives and teachers from Christine's nursery, Derick's music conservatory, and about fifty teachers, administrators, and all of Janene's students from Tian Wai were already assembled. Mercifully, we were short on time, so there was no painful lingering over our parting. Nevertheless, tears still began to flow as Janene embraced her students for the last time, and the children's teachers said farewell to them. The entire entourage accompanied us into the station up and down the stairs that led to the track for Beijing, and everyone fought for a final handshake through the window of our car once we had boarded. The boys in Janene's class ran alongside as the train gathered speed pulling out of the station, and Derick, inspired by one of his boyhood military heroes, leaned precariously out the window and shouted backward at the sea of waving hands, "We shall return!"

Our final day in Beijing was a recapitulation of our arrival a year earlier although in reverse. After we settled in at the International Guesthouse, we were feted with spicy Hunan cuisine for our last banquet by the leading cadres of the Foreign Experts Bureau, an experience that was more of an ordeal than entertainment given our state of exhaustion and our distaste for opulent dining with bureaucrats who seemed to materialize only during lavish ceremonies. In the morning, I had a final meeting with the people who I knew at that office, like our good friend Gao Luduan. There they debriefed me about our experiences, and I took the opportunity to express our gratitude for the initial invitation to come to China and for their unswerving support for our work and travels throughout our stay. Then it was off to the airport for the flight south to Canton and one final visit to a childhood home and a valiant attempt to fulfill a promise I had made to my parents before we left on our China venture.

Our plane descended past White Cloud Mountain and landed at the same airport I remembered as an eleven-year-old boy when we took the bumpy flight from Bengpu to Canton on the overloaded C-47. After a long wait, the minibus the Foreign Experts Bureau had reserved for us arrived and the four of us checked into a small hotel, doubling up on the twin beds in an unpretentious room. Despite snoozing on the flight south, we were still exhausted from the activities and emotions of the previous weeks, so we ate only jiaozi for dinner, but they weren't nearly as tasty as the hundreds we had devoured during our year up north. During this brief sojourn in transit to Hong Kong, we were on our own and for once had free time on our hands, and since the next morning was Sunday, we called a cab to take us to the east side of the city for church. It turned out the service did not begin until noon, so we strolled around a nearby market, intrigued by the variety of food and goods compared to what was available on the streets of Tianjin. Arriving so early, we had a chance to chat with the four elderly pastors who led this large congregation, and two of them remembered my parents. There were well over a thousand congregants packed into and outside the sanctuary when the service began. It was standing room only, and there were many more young people than I recall from the service in Tianjin. The one and a half-hour worship was conducted entirely in Cantonese, so I understood virtually nothing, but the liturgy was familiar, and because it was Advent, all of us recognized the Christmas carols and sang them out lustily in English. Like Tianjin, we were uplifted from the spiritual experience of being surrounded by hundreds and hundreds of Chinese of all ages and stations who, for the first time in many years, could express their faith in public and celebrate exultantly in word and song.

But time was growing short, and we still had two more important errands. Guided by a map, my memory, and the helpful advice of some church members after the conclusion of the service, we took the number 3 bus westward to the other side of town to the No. 2 Municipal Hospital. The old gate was still there, arched by the same tiled roof, and after we walked through it, immediately in front of us was the familiar circular driveway ringed by potted poinsettias blooming bright red for Christmastide. Here was the entrance to my home for my last three years in China, what was then called Hackett Medical

Center. My parents began their work here in 1948, when the nation was still under the control of the Nationalists, but when they were finally granted permission to leave the country and the people they had grown to love in 1951, they left a new land called the People's Republic. We walked around the right side of the hospital buildings past a dirt yard, once the green lawn where I used to play war and fly kites with my Chinese friends. We walked over to the last house on the right, the duplex shared by the Wong and Scovel families. Canton was more open than the North, so we weren't stopped at the gate, and the residents of the duplex were happy to show us inside once I explained the purpose of this sudden visit by these strangers from the East. Like our summer visit to my former home in Huaiyuan this house was far smaller and less palatial than I remembered, and it was more crowded and far grimier than the time when it only had to accommodate our small family. I showed the kids the tiled drain spout I used to shimmy down as a kid, and from the second floor veranda, I pointed over the wall to where the PLA had placed their noisy and consistently inaccurate antiaircraft gun. The canal in the back was still there but narrower than before and hedged with more houses, and I could've sworn that the water was a milk chocolate brown back then; the water we saw was oil black. As we retraced our path to the front gate, I felt a twinge of emptiness, knowing that I would never return to this place, and had I known at that moment about Dr. Wong's horrible death by the hands of the Red Guards from the main hospital building we passed as we were walking out, I'm sure my feelings would have been much more convoluted and heart-wrenching.

My father was an only child, and after my grandfather died of a heart attack in midlife and long before I was born, my parents arranged for my grandmother to come to China to live out her life with them there. Grandmother accompanied us on the flight to Canton, but by then, age and Parkinson's disease had gradually transformed her into a frail shadow, and after a few months, she succumbed to age and illness. I can vaguely remember the memorial service at the Anglican church on Shameen Island, where we sang "Abide With Me," but because I always loved boats and ships, I have an unusually strong memory of people carrying Grandmother's coffin on to a small riverboat and put-putting southward down the Pearl River for a mile or two then landing on the left bank at the British Cemetery, where she was buried. Our last act in China was to fulfill a promise I had made to my parents before leaving the States, and that was to try to find Grandmother's grave.

We returned to the hotel for an orange soda and a quick rest, and it was already late afternoon when we called another cab and headed off on our quixotic venture along the road paralleling the east side of the river. It was readily apparent that this was an industrial area of town, and it stood to reason that factory after factory had been constructed within easy reach of river transportation and yet a distance from downtown. We were in a strange city with no trusty local guide or faithful Xiao Zhang to assist us, and besides, dusk had already fallen. We stopped at a customs house, thinking officials there might know of where foreign devils might have been buried, and though no one had heard of the British Cemetery, one of the younger cadres jumped into the cab to assist us. Impressed by his offer to help and believing that his uniform might open doors for us, we continued south, stopping at about every other factory gate with our peculiar inquiry. At one of these, a young woman worker thought that there was indeed such a cemetery, which she believed might be next to a bicycle factory further downstream. We soon reached the bike factory, but the night manager there said that it wasn't his place but a cement factory just down the road where the foreigners once buried their dead, and he was happy to show us the exact spot. Our cab driver was adamant that no one else clamber into his overcrowded vehicle, and what with Janene and me squeezing him in the front seat and the two kids half on the laps of the customs officer and woman worker filling up the back, the manager hopped on his bike and pedaled furiously in front of us as our headlights lit the way.

A few minutes later, we all piled out in front of the gate to the cement factory, and between our own contingent and a gathering crowd of locals curious to see what was disturbing their quiet Sunday evening, there soon was a mass of us pressing against the factory gates. The clamor eventually drew the reluctant gateman out, and he seemed stunned and confused at the sight. Yes, this was more liberal Canton, but rules were rules, and when he saw the foreign faces in the middle, he was confronted with one of modern China's most enduring and disturbing scenarios, barbarians at the gates! The factory manager explained our quest and begged him to open up so we could see what remained of the cemetery. The woman worker argued we would only be there a few minutes and meant no harm. The young customs officer vouched for the authenticity of our story and bravely accepted responsibility for any problem that might arise from our visit. By now, the assembled crowd chimed in, most of it in Cantonese, so it was impossible for me to follow, but the communal force of the collected voices finally persuaded the gateman to reach into his pocket and put the key into the padlock, and a millisecond after it clicked open, we all burst through and flooded the courtyard, looking for signs of a graveyard. Someone shared a flashlight with me, and among the rubble scattered all over, I found pieces of headstones with fragments of English on them, and it soon became apparent that the factory had been built on the site of the cemetery after the headstones had been crudely but effectively dismantled. I would hazard the guess that the cemetery had been vandalized some time during the Cultural Revolution, and land being so valuable in China, especially in a metropolitan area, this plot was soon swallowed up by the string of factories constructed to feed the needs of the Four Modernizations. I found nothing with my grandmother's name on it, and it was clear that even in bright sunlight, it was likely we might never recover any hint of her tombstone were we to search all day. We walked back out to the street, and the gateman locked the gate behind us greatly relieved.

Janene and I thanked all of our new comrades who had generously and spontaneously pitched in to help, and tired from the adventures of the day and drained from a decade of experiences all compressed into one momentous year, we returned exhausted to our hotel. From the moment the train pulled out of Tianjin a few days earlier, Janene began crying because she missed her students so desperately, and each night she would fall to sleep in tears. "At some point, you have to say your last good-bye," I tried to console her. "The tears have to stop some time. How about tomorrow when we leave China for good?"

Except for meeting us at the airport the night before, the cadres supposedly in charge of our Canton stay never reappeared, so the bad news was we were stuck paying all our expenses ourselves, and I was forced to exchange ten dollars I happened to have into *kuai* to cover our bill at the hotel. It was worth the trouble of going at it alone, however, for attending church, visiting the former Presbyterian hospital compound, and searching for Grandmother's grave all by ourselves gave us a feeling of freedom and independence that we rarely enjoyed the entire year, and this experience was also a fitting preparation for the old life we were about to return to in a few hours. There was no need to go to the train station to travel south or to disembark and cross the border bridge into Hong Kong as I had done with my family twenty-eight years earlier or as we had done in reverse when we entered China that January day that now seemed so very long ago. For our departure, it was possible to fly swiftly and in comfort to Hong Kong, and as we boarded our plane for our final journey in China, I thought of how the preceding twenty-four hours had captured the essence of our experiences and what we had learned during that long year.

Great changes were indeed taking place epitomized by our flight from Canton to Hong Kong. No longer were we earthbound travelers confined to the inconvenient train trip hyphenated by the bridge at the border. Now we soared into the heavens on a modern aircraft. And yet there was the experience of the previous night still haunting me. What motivated all those strangers to join us in that strange quest to find my grandmother's grave? Why would they inconvenience themselves on a Sunday evening to help an American who all of them had been taught to despise only a few years earlier? It was the pull of filial piety, the Confucian ideal that all relationships are ultimately founded on those that are familial, and again, even though these helpful strangers had been taught to detest the teachings of the sage, those ideals had endured.

How fortunate we were to have lived in China that year—the year China changed. We were also fortunate to have been challenged in so many ways, to have been inspired by the courage and nobility of so many lives, to have been honored with the gift of friendship from so many people, to witness the birth of modernization in the world's oldest continuous civilization, and yes, even to have learned about the terrible suffering wrought by the misguided policies of the Party. Indeed, the latter provided the context through which everything else we experienced became so meaningful. It is abundantly evident that the Chinese people now live in a better nation than that war-torn land of my childhood. It is equally clear that they live in a society that is unquestionably superior to the China we experienced in 1979, but the Chinese people deserve better. What this means and how it is achieved is up to the future and up to them. As for us, we left China enriched beyond measure.

GLOSSARY

airen	爱人	loved one: spouse
baicai	白菜	Chinese cabbage
baozi	包字	steamed bun stuffed usually with meat
bie song	憋送	"There's no need to see me off."
bingguer	冰棍	popiscle: ice lolly
bu xing	不行	not satisfactory
Chang Jiang	长江	the Yangtze River
Chaoxian zu	朝藓族	Korean nationality
chibaole, hezhule	吃饱了，喝住了	"I'm stuffed to the gills!"
chou lao jiu	臭老九	"the stinking old nine:" nine categories of counter revolutionaries persecuted during the Cultural Revolution
chunjie	春节	Spring Festival: "Chinese new year"
danwei	单位	administrative unit: work unit
dazibao	大字报	big character posters
didi	弟弟	younger brother
duile	对了	correct
erhu	二胡	a two-stringed Chinese violin
faxiangdi	发详地	birthplace
furen	妇人	wife
fuyuren	服务人	hotel or restaurant staff

fuzhong	附中	a middle school attached to a tertiary educational institution
ganbei!	干杯	Cheers!
gege	哥哥	older brother
Gongchan Dang	共产党	the Communist Party (CCP)
gong nong bing	工农兵	workers, peasants, soldiers
guanxi	关系	(personal) connections
guo lai!	过来	"Get over here!"
Guomin Dang	过民党	the Nationalist Party (KMT)
haokan, haower, haochi	好看，好闻，好吃	"If it looks good, it'll smell good, and if it smells good, it'll taste good."
he	河	river
hongweibing	红卫兵	the Red Guards (of the Cultural Revolution era)
hua qiao	华侨	Overseas Chinese
Huang He	黄河	the Yellow River
jiaozi	饺子	dumplings
Jidujiao	基督教	Christianity
Jiefang Lu	解放路	Revolutionary Avenue
jiefang ri	解放日	the day of Liberation (October 1, 1949)
jin	金	gold: a common surname ("Kim" in Korean)
jisuanji	计算机	computer
keyi, keyi	可以，可以	can do, can do

konglong	恐龙	"fearful dragon:" dinosaur
Lao	老	Old: a respectful address form for older people
laojia	老家	ancestral home (where your father was born)
laoshi	老师	teacher (used after a name as an address form)
mantou	馒头	steamed bread
maotai	茅台	a popular Chinese distilled alcoholic drink
meiguo bin	美国宾	American guest
meiyou	没有	(we) don't have (any)
miantiao	面条	noodles
pang	胖	fat
pengyoumen	朋友们	friends
piao	票	coupons: tickets
qi	气	spirit: morale
qizi	妻子	wife
renminbi	人民币	the unit of exchange for regular Chinese currency
rentaiduo, difangtaishao	人太多, 地方太少	too many people, too little space
rou	肉	meat
ruanxi	软席	soft seat (business class)
san min zhuyi	三民主义	the three principles of the people
shan	山	mountain

shanshui	山水	scenery (with mountains and water)
shaobing	烧饼	sesame seed bun
song	送	to see someone off
ta	他	third person singular pronoun (he, she, it in spoken Chinese)
taijiquan	太极拳	traditional Chinese shadow boxing
Taiping Yang	太平洋	Pacific Ocean
Taitai	太太	Madam: wife
tiandi	天地	heaven and earth
Tianjin R Bao	天津日报	The Tianjin Daily
Tian Wai	天外	"Tian Foreign:" abbreviation for the Tianjin Foreign Languages Institute
Tianzhujiao	天主教	(The Roman) Catholic (Church)
tiefanwan	铁饭碗	iron rice bowl
tingzi	厅子	pavilion: "tea house" (usually octagonal)
tongzhi	同志	Comrade: a generic address form popular in 1979
tongzhimen	同志们	Comrades
waiban	外办	Foreign Affairs Office; member(s) of such an office
waiguobin	外国宾	foreign guest
waiguo zhuanjia	外国专家	foreign experts
Xiao	小	Little: an address form used for younger people
xiaopangzi	小胖子	little fatty

xiaozibao	小字报	little character posters (contrasted to *da zi bao*)
xigua	西瓜	watermelon
xinlixue	心理学	psychology
yang	阳	the masculine, positive, light force in nature
yang guizi	洋鬼子	foreign devil
yi lu ping an	一路平安	"Peace on your journey." (traditional Chinese farewell)
yin	阴	the feminine, negative, dark force in nature
yingxi	硬席	hard seat (coach class)
yuebing	月饼	moon cake
Zhongguo Jidujiao Sanzi Aiguo Yundong Weiyuanhui	中国 基督教 三自爱国 运动委员会	the Chinese Christian Three Self Patriotic Movement Association
Zhu Jiang	珠江	the Pearl River

ANNOTATED BIBLIOGRAPHY

Allen, George. 1910. *It tickled him: Around the world with George Hoyt Allen.* Clinton, NY: Occidental and Oriental Publishing Company.

An eccentric cousin on my father's side of the family made and lost considerable amounts of money in the furniture business in upstate New York a century ago. He was a prodigious world traveler (when wealthy) and produced a number of self-published and colorfully written books filled with remarkable pictures of his travels in Asia. These books were part of our family library and may have had some influence on my father's decision to go to China as a medical missionary. Ironically, although they were written by an American traveler and a rather odd one at that, his books gave me a picture of the very land I grew up in, although his descriptions were from a China two generations distant from the one I knew as a boy. One very gruesome account in this book is the description "Uncle George" gave of a mass execution he witnessed in Canton where a skillful but heartless executioner sliced off the heads of fourteen Chinese criminals in the matter of two minutes. His photograph of one headless victim with blood spurted out from the severed neck haunts both the book and my memory!

Bredon, Juliet & Igor Mitrophanow. 1927. *The moon year: A record of Chinese customs and festivals.* Shanghai: Kelly & Walsh Limited.

The authors of this rare volume meticulously chronicle all the traditional festivities and customs surrounding each month of the Chinese lunar calendar. Many of the traditions of the eighth or "harvest" moon in this calendar are still observed by Chinese both in the PRC and those living abroad and were the foundations of the celebrations which we enjoyed during a weekend trip north of Tianjin in the early autumn.

Brinkley, Alan. 2010. *The publisher: Henry Luce and his American century.* New York: Vintage Books.

Like my older siblings and me, Henry Luce was born in Shandong and raised by Presbyterian missionaries, and like us, he left his parents to further his education and seek his fortune in America. Unlike the Scovel siblings however, Luce found a huge fortune by establishing a publishing empire that began with *Time, Life, Fortune,* and *Sports Illustrated* magazines and that evolved into a multimedia conglomerate that still thrives today, long after his death. Although Luce's missionary heritage had only a partial impact on his adult life, his China heritage played a major role in his work as one of America's most influential media moguls. As Brinkley's well-documented biography attests, Luce's enthusiastic support of the Nationalists and Chiang Kai-shek steered the "China Lobby" and government leaders from the President on down away from any rapprochement with Mao and the Communists and helped to create a political chasm between the PRC and the U.S. until Nixon's presidency. Of special interest to me is the brief first chapter of this book that describes Luce's father's work in helping to develop missionary schools and hospitals in Weifang and Jinan. The Luce home in Weifang housed the Japanese soldiers who guarded our internment camp during WWII. Luce's father was instrumental in raising funds in America to build the Presbyterian mission's medical college in Jinan where years later two of my siblings were born and which Janene and I visited in 1979.

Brown, G. Thompson. 1997. *Earthen vessels and transcendent power: American Presbyterians in China, 1837-1952.* Maryknoll, NY: Orbis Books.

"Tommy" Thompson's book is a detailed history of the American Presbyterian missionary presence in China and a marvelous compendium of all the mission stations established and all the missionaries who served in China for over a century. Included are the stations which my parents worked and where I lived as a boy: the Hunter-Bachman hospital in Jining, the Hope Memorial Hospital in Huaiyuan, and the Hackett Medical College in Canton.

Brownell, Susan. 1995. *Training the body for China: Sports in the moral order of the People's Republic.* Chicago: University of Chicago Press.

Though it's difficult to believe nowadays given China's supremacy in so many Olympic sports, there was a time when the Party had a policy of downgrading all athletic activities. According to Brownell, an American athlete who lived and competed in the PRC, Mao's wife, Jiang Qing, led a movement during the Cultural Revolution to suppress sports and to persecute sports officials. As a consequence, I was surprised to discover in 1979 that despite the size of its population, Chinese national records paled in comparison even to many other Asian nations. For example, Eric Liddell's gold medal time in the 400 meters at the 1924 Paris Olympics easily surpassed the Chinese national record when we were residing in China fifty-five years later, and it wasn't until the late 1980's that Chinese athletes and sports teams began to dominate, first in the Asian Games and then in the Olympics.

Butterfield, Fox. 1982. *China: Alive in the bitter sea.* New York: Bantam Books.

A well-trained China scholar, Butterfield arrived in Beijing the year after we left to cover the PRC for the New York Times. Filled with insightful observations and many personal stories, his work was the first by an American to portray China openly and honestly after a decade of mostly laudatory but limited reports by foreign tourists who wrote about their carefully controlled travels around the country at the end of the Cultural Revolution.

Chang, Jung & Jon Halliday. 2005. *Mao: The unknown story.* New York: Anchor Books/Random House.

At over eight hundred pages and based upon forty-eight pages of Chinese and non-Chinese references and relying on hundreds of interviews with people from thirty-six nations (from Albania to Zaire), this dynamic duo of authors has produced the most comprehensive and authoritative biography of Mao. It is also controversial in the eyes of some China watchers in that it is a less than flattering portrait of the Great Helmsman. Indeed, this tome is a fascinating but deeply disturbing account of the life of one the contemporary world's greatest megalomaniacs. To be fair, Fenby's biography of Mao's rival, Chiang, is also unflattering.

Chin, Robert & Aili Chin. 1969. *Psychological research in communist China.* Cambridge, MA: M.I.T. Press.

A rare account of the limited work in psychology carried out after Liberation during the short period of time before social sciences like psychology and sociology were downgraded and the Chinese Psychological Society was disbanded.

Ditu Chubanshe. 1977. *Zhonghua Renmin Gongheguo Fen Sheng Dituji.*

I purchased this official PRC atlas in Beijing during my first week in China in 1979 and have relied on it heavily ever since. It not only provides political and topographic maps of every province (including Taiwan) and lists thousands of villages, towns, and cities in Pin Yin and Chinese characters, this atlas is a window to the political views of the Party back then. For instance, it's difficult to find Hong Kong since this major city in the south is marked as an insignificant town; furthermore, it's hard to discern that it was at that time a British colony and not Chinese territory.

Edell, Dean. 1999, *Eat, drink and be merry: America's doctor tells you why the health experts are wrong.* New York: HarperCollins.

A popular media expert on medical affairs and incidentally a collector of Chinese snuff bottles, Dr. Edell describes mass sociogenic illness (MSI) and lists historical examples of how groups of people can be led to experience similar psychosomatic symptoms. Watching the maudlin wailing of mourners in the film of Zhou Enlai's funeral and glimpsing similar reactions among our students during the movie suggested that their behavior was a manifestation of MSI. It struck me that MSI may have been a common phenomenon when Mao and Zhou were venerated.

Fairbank, John. 1982. *Chinabound: A fifty-year memoir.* New York: Harper & Colophon Books.

One of America's most famous Sinologists and a mentor to many China scholars, Fairbank's comprehensive autobiography is an account of his abiding interest in Chinese history and modern politics and his work as an academic and as a government advisor.

Fairbank, John. 1986. *The great Chinese revolution: 1800-1985.* New York: Harper & Row.

Although most people might claim that the Communists were the first and greatest Chinese revolutionaries, Fairbank (and other scholars like Spence) demonstrates that a historical perspective proves otherwise. Here America's great Sinologist shows how the Taiping Rebellion a century earlier laid the foundation for the series of revolutionary movements in the twentieth century that ultimately culminated in the creation of the modern nation we recognize today.

Fenby, Jonathan. 2003. *Chiang Kai Shek: China's generalissimo and the nation he lost.* New York: Carroll & Graf Publishers.

If readers of Chang and Halliday's biography of Mao believe that book is too biased against the leader of the Communists, they should read Fenby's copiously documented biography of the leader of the Nationalists. Chiang Kai-shek is portrayed as a man sincere in his efforts to forge a modern nation but ruthless and relentless in his quest for power. As a young boy who had just moved to India from China in the mid fifties, I was sometimes asked about what I thought of Mao and Chiang, and my naïve reply back then does not seem completely off target even today. My conclusion was other than one was fat and messy and the other thin and well-dressed, there wasn't much of a difference. Reading the two biographies of these two enemies leaves one with essentially the same observation.

Foreign Language Teaching & Research Press. 1978. *A Chinese-English dictionary*. (I also have used the slightly revised edition published in 1998.)

Like my trusty Chinese atlas, I was fortunate to purchase this dictionary when it was first released during the week we arrived in China, and I have relied on this dictionary to provide nearly all of the transliterations and definitions cited in my book. Like the atlas, this reference reveals the subtle influence of Chinese politics back then, but it still remains an accurate and useful work. The Chinese pay attention to details and love translation, and this work attests to both of these cultural strengths.

Fung, Raymond. 1982. *Households of God on China's soil*. Geneva: World Council of Churches Mission Series.

This rare little pamphlet is a collection of fascinating first-person accounts mostly by members of "house churches" of the difficulties they faced after Liberation. Their testimonies are reminiscent of the accounts recorded in the New Testament epistles describing the nascent congregations of the early church. Fung interviewed these Chinese Christians shortly after our year of residence so the responses demonstrate both the bravery of the interviewees to talk about the persecution they faced but also their restraint in criticizing the Party's policies too stringently.

Gilkey, Langdon. 1966. *Shandong compound.* New York: Harper & Row.

Like almost all male internees, Gilkey was incarcerated at the Weifang camp for the duration of WWII. Several have written about their life in this camp, including my mother who has a chapter in her first book about our family's experiences, but Gilkey's book is the most detailed account. As a prominent theologian, the author reflects on the spiritual journey he traveled during his years of imprisonment and the ways in which their collective experience brought out the best and the worst of the internees. I took this book with me to China, and the simple sketches and map drawn by prisoners were helpful when I visited the site of the camp as the first former prisoner to return. The camp's most famous resident was Eric Liddell, hero of the 1981 Academy Award winning film, Chariots of Fire. Liddell died in the camp hospital my father helped to establish shortly before American paratroopers liberated the Weifang prisoners at the end of the war.

Ginsbourg, Sam. 1982. *My first sixty years in China.* Beijing: New World Press.

It was a privilege to have been friends with Sam, the "Russian Jin," who taught at Shandong University and who had lived in China for over half a century. Like many "White Russians," Sam's family emigrated from the Soviet Union and ended up in Shanghai, but unlike virtually all of them, including the Ginsburg family, Sam remained in China, married, and raised a family. He was a steadfast supporter of the Party despite mistreatment from time to time, and I was honored when he asked me to edit part of his manuscript even though he knew I held a less than charitable view of the Party's role in modern Chinese history.

Gittings, John. 2006. *The changing face of China: From Mao to market.* Oxford: Oxford University Press.

Compared to thirty years ago, there is now a plethora of books written by foreigners and Chinese alike about the PRC, so it is impossible to keep up with this continuous stream of publications. Gittings served for many years as a reporter and editor of Chinese and Asian affairs for the Guardian, so this book provides a nice British balance to the American correspondents such as Butterfield or Hessler whose works I've also cited. The author does an excellent job of covering recent political and economic changes in the PRC and salts his accounts with reports from interviews with common citizens.

Gonzalez-Crussi, F. 2007. *A short history of medicine.* New York: The Modern Library.

I relied on this work to document the early medical advances by the Chinese.

Goodrich, L. Carrington. 1962. *A short history of the Chinese people.* London: George Allen & Unwin.

Though obviously dated in terms of contemporary events, this is an abbreviated but helpful account of Chinese history written by a respected Sinologist. It is impossible to cover four thousands years capably in any single volume but Goodrich comes close in fewer than three hundred pages.

Green, William, Gordon Swanborough, and John Mowinski. 1987. *Modern commercial aircraft.* New York: Portland House.

I used this reference to identify the Soviet civilian planes flown in China during our year of residence. On several subsequent visits to China to 1979, it was comforting to see improvements in civil aviation, especially in air safety and quality of service. Much of the former was the result of reliance on newer aircraft, most of them fleets from Boeing which replaced the older Soviet planes and which also gave the Chinese access to modern flight and maintenance training.

Hillenbrand, Laura. 2010. *Unbroken: A World War II story of survival, resilience, and redemption.* New York: Random House.

Louie Zamperini's life is fascinating enough, but in the hands of a masterful writer like Hillenbrand, the author of *Sea Biscuit*, his story makes for riveting reading. Much of *Unbroken* describes the brutality Zamperini faced as a military prisoner in concentration camps in Japan, barbarism and cruelty my family fortunately never experienced during our time of incarceration as civilian prisoners in China. After the war, Zamperini was born again after attending a Billy Graham rally back in the States and became an inspiring speaker and youth leader. We had the privilege of hearing him speak as a charismatic ninety-year-old while I was writing this China book. (see Lomax)

Hessler, Peter. 2001. *River town: Two years on the Yangtze.* New York: HarperCollins.

Written twenty some years after the time I taught in China, this captivating account of a young American teacher's experiences in a remote town on the Yangtze River was reminiscent of many of my experiences. Even as a young writer, Hessler displays a nimble ability to weave words together, an impressive skill for acquiring Chinese, and a precocious ability to understand contemporary Chinese culture. Unsurprisingly, he has since become a keen and prolific reporter of developments in contemporary China.

Holmes, Leslie. 2009. *Communism: A very short introduction.* Oxford: Oxford University Press.

It is indeed "very short" as this slim volume in a series by Oxford can easily slip into your back pocket. Holmes gives a terse description of the rise and fall of international communism and the rocky relations between Russian and Chinese leaders and was a resource for my book when I needed historical information, comparative statistics, or specialized vocabulary (e.g. Comintern).

Issacs, Harold. 1958. *Images of Asia: American views of China and India.* New York: Harper & Row.

Because it examines American perceptions of the two nations I grew up in and because it was published just after I came to the States to further my education, this collection of random comments, reports, and cartoons is of idiosyncratic interest to me. Issacs cites Ripley's "Chinese marching 4 abreast..." which I remember when reading *Believe It or Not* as a young boy in China.

Kao, George. 1946. *Chinese wit & humor.* New York: Coward-McCann, Inc.

This anthology of jokes, fables, and short stories records two of the jokes I included in my book: the ones about the tea connoisseur and the two selfish families. Like so many of our childhood memories, I am hazy about where I first heard these. I have the vague notion that my parents or Chinese family friends told them to me when I was quite young, but I might have also gotten them from this book when I was around twelve.

Kaplan, Robert. 2012. *The revenge of geography.* New York: Random House.

Sweeping in scope both historically and globally, the author persuasively demonstrates how geographical factors have shaped cultural and national histories in the past and will continue to do so in the future. Kaplan devotes an entire chapter to "The Geography of Chinese Power" and makes intriguing predictions about China's future relationships with her neighbors and with the United States. Ironically, where I have tried to show how Chinese geography is constraining, Kaplan contends just the reverse and goes so far as to claim that "China, as Eurasia's largest continental nation with a coastline in both the tropics and the temperate zone, occupies the globe's most advantageous position." (p. 189)

Kramer, Martha. 1945. Seen in North China. *Journal of the American Dietetic Association* 21:7, July-August.

Kramer was interned at the Weifang camp, but like almost all the women initially detained there, she was released before the end of the war, and after returning to the States, she wrote up this informal account of the dietary needs of the internees. In this article, she describes how eggshells were gathered, cleaned, and ground into a powder in an attempt to provide calcium for the children and for pregnant mothers. This supplement was vital to the health of the Scovel family with five growing kids and my mother pregnant with a sixth.

Lam, Agnes. 2005. *Language education in China: Policy and experience from 1949.* Hong Kong: Hong Kong University Press.

Obviously I'm biased since the author is a former and brilliant doctoral student of mine, but as a University of Hong Kong researcher who has conducted extensive surveys of language learning and use in the PRC, Lam has produced a rigorous and helpful review of China's policies regarding the teaching of Mandarin and foreign languages after Liberation. She also documents one of the Party's most significant achievements: it took a vast land of divergent "dialects" and minority languages and created a nation unified by a single lingua franca (Mandarin) and by a writing system made easier to acquire because of a simplified system of characters and the adoption of the Pin Yin alphabet.

Leys, Simon. 1978. *Chinese shadows.* New York: Penguin Books (originally published in French in 1974 as *Ombres Chinoises*)

This was the first book written by a foreigner published after the Cultural Revolution that was critical of the Party's policies. The reader is given immediate evidence of the direction of Leys unusual views on the cover page where he quotes the author Lu Xun. *Thus, if a foreigner could be found today who, though admitted to the Chinese banquet, would not*

*hesitate to rant in our name against the present state of China, him
I would call a truly honest man, a truly admirable man!*

Lomax, Eric. 1995. *The railway man: A POW's searing account
of war, brutality, and forgiveness.* New York: W.W. Norton &
Company.

This moving autobiography is very similar in substance
and theme to Zamperini's story (see Hillenbrand), and again
it documents in vivid manner the cruelty the Japanese military
inflicted on Allied prisoners of war, a distinct contrast to the
relatively benign treatment my family and others received
at the Weifang civilian internment camp in China. Like
Zamperini, Lomax was able to overcome his intense hatred
of his Japanese captors and was moved to forgive them, so
his book and Hillenbrand's are ultimately uplifting stories of
remarkable individuals whose lives were transformed.

Luo, Weihong. 2004. *Christianity in China.* Beijing: China
Intercontinental Press. (translated by Zhu Chenming)

I found this short account an exceedingly selective and
ignorant view of Chinese history (e.g. the Taiping rebellion
which had Christian roots goes unmentioned) and lacking
any genuine understanding of Christianity and the Chinese
church today. I cite this as an example of how even at present,
official views of Christianity are largely ignorant or biased.
This work is a distinct contrast to Fung, Wickeri, Yao, and the
many other publications now available describing the history
and role of Christianity in China.

Mathews, R. H., 1960. *Mathew's Chinese-English dictionary.*
Cambridge, MA: Harvard University Press. (Revised
American Edition: first published in 1931).

Although the authoritative Foreign Language Teaching &
Research Press served as my central source for contemporary
Chinese vocabulary usage and English translations, I used this
older reference several times to verify or to revise citations

from the modern dictionary I relied on. One of the many examples of how writing systems often reveal sociopolitical contrasts is immediately visible in the phonetic alphabets used in various Chinese dictionaries. Mathew's work relies on a "Western" Wade-Giles transcription system whereas the modern Beijing work uses the "Chinese" Pin Yin, and though the two transcribe exactly the same syllables, the transcriptions can look quite different (e.g. *hsien tsai* vs. *xian zai* "now").

Oxford University Press. 2003. *Pocket Oxford Chinese Dictionary (English-Chinese: Chinese-English)*. Third Edition.

Like the Mathews dictionary, I sometimes relied on this source to confirm or supplement a citation I first referred to in the Foreign Language Teaching & Research Press text.

Pan, Philip. 2008. *Out of Mao's shadow: The struggle for the soul of a new China*. New York: Simon & Schuster.

Another book on contemporary China by a foreign journalist, this one by Pan, who reported for the Washington Post, is a series of vignettes about brave Chinese who courageously spoke out against Party policies and attempted to redress injustices. The most famous of these individuals, at least at the time of this writing, is Chen Guangcheng, the blind lawyer who had the temerity to protest against local authorities for their policy of forced abortions. He created quite a political stir during the summer of 2012 when he appealed to the U.S. for help and after tense diplomatic negotiations between the two super powers, he and his wife were allowed to go to the U.S. Like many other notables, both Chinese and foreign, Chen comes from Shandong.

Peters, Ted. *God- the World's future*. Minneapolis, MN: Fortress Press.

This weighty philosophical treatise has absolutely nothing to do with China but serves only as the source from which I found the definition for the theological concept of prolepsis that I used in the prologue.

Pollock, David & Ruth Van Reken. 2001. *Third culture kids: The experience of growing up among worlds.* Yarmouth, ME: Intercultural Press.

Pollock was not the originator of the term "Third Culture Kids," but his many talks and workshops on the subject demonstrated his expertise and led to this book, one of the first studies of the social and psychological consequences of growing up in a culture very different from one's parent's native land. Given the pervasive globalization that has taken place over the past few decades, TCK's abound in most developed countries, and nations like Japan and Korea have special high schools designed to re-acculturate the children of expatriate citizens living in countries as diverse as Canada and Indonesia to the culture and educational systems of their parents' homeland. Naturally, this "third culture" affected the six of us Scovel children to different degrees and in different ways depending on our temperament, the events that transpired while we were young, and the age of departure from China or India. I cannot speak for my siblings, but overall, my TCK experience had a powerful and salubrious effect on my personal and professional life, but not without cost. Feelings of loneliness, aimlessness, and a sense of not belonging pervaded my college life after I immigrated to America and demonstrate that bilingualism and biculturalism can be both a gift and a limitation.

Reichelt, Karl. 1951. *Religion in Chinese garment.* New York: Philosophical Library.

As a China missionary with an interest in interfaith dialogue back in the 1920's, the author had a long career as an interpreter of the traditional religions of China: Buddhism, Confucianism, and Taoism. His extensive contacts with Chinese religious leaders give him a sympathetic yet scholarly perspective on these great traditions.

Scovel, Myra. 1962. *The Chinese ginger jars.* New York: Harper & Row.

As described in my book, my mother had limited formal education, but in her fifties, after having moved to India from China where she had to learn a new language and culture, she sat down at a portable typewriter and pecked out her China memoirs for the six of us children. Without any initial inclination to publish her work, she was urged by my father and friends to mail the manuscript to the States, and in relatively short order Harper & Row accepted her work and so successful was this first attempt, they went on to publish five more of her books. For the rest of her life, my mother enjoyed a productive and fulfilling life as an author, poet, and public speaker. During the year Janene and I were in China, her book was an invaluable guide during our visits to sites where our family once lived, and I have relied upon her work for several of the autobiographical details referred to in my book.

Scovel, Myra. 1967. *Red is no longer a color.* New York: Friendship Press.

Successful as my mother was as a writer of prose, her first and dearest love was poetry. This illustrated volume of a single poem came out just after the Cultural Revolution had begun, and my mother wrote it in honor of one of my parent's closest friends and colleagues in China, Dr. Ross Wong. Like far too many loyal Chinese citizens, Dr. Wong lost his life during this time of upheaval. The black and white pictures in this book were taken by a Canadian photographer, Richard Harrington, during his travels in China in 1965 and 1966.

Shaefer, Silvia. 1979. *Chinese and the gold rush.* Mariposa, CA: Journal Publications.

This paperback is one of many sources that document the prejudice and abuse Chinese immigrants faced in California over a century ago.

Spence, Jonathan. 1991. *The search for modern China.* New York: W.W. Norton.

At almost nine hundred pages, this is a masterful and comprehensive look at the last two centuries of Chinese history, aptly illustrated with maps and photographs. All things being equal, the more recent a nation's history, the greater the impact it has on contemporary national events. Spence's excellent overview gives the reader a deeper understanding of today's China and her people, especially regarding the "barbarians at the gates" world view that I mention several times in my book.

Spence, Jonathan. 1996. *God's Chinese son: The Taiping heavenly kingdom of Hong Xiuquan.* New York: W.W. Norton.

To my mind, trying to understand revolutionary China without appreciation of the impact and legacy of the Taiping Rebellion would be equivalent to trying to examine recent contemporary Japan without any knowledge of the Meiji Restoration or trying to comprehend the present day cuture and politics of the U.S. without knowing anything about the Civil War. The Taiping Rebellion took place roughly the same time during the nineteenth century as the two major events just cited, but it was far bloodier than either of those and left an enormous historical impact on relations between China and foreign powers. Spence is America's most prominent and productive scholar of Chinese history, and in this book he gives the definitive account of the tragic but extraordinary Taiping revolution.

Spurling, Hilary. 2010. *Pearl Buck in China: Journey to The Good Earth.* New York: Simon & Schuster Paperbacks.

This recent biography of Pearl Buck relies on extensive quotations from the author's many manuscripts as a window to her personality and inner psyche. Like another Pulitzer Prize winner, Thornton Wilder, she was born and raised in China by Presbyterian missionaries although Buck gained further fame by winning the Nobel Prize, only the third American at that time to achieve this honor. Even into her adulthood and her eventual move to the U.S., Buck spoke fluent Chinese and unlike most China-born expatriates, she also was a competent reader of Chinese and was closely associated with several Chinese intellectuals as a young woman. Spurling's work describes how Buck ultimately became dissatisfied with the fundamentalist doctrines of her missionary father and grew distant from her religious heritage, although throughout her life she was a passionate supporter of the poor and established the Buck Foundation to support orphanages, a legacy which remains to this day. In her later years, Buck's life became mired in failed or strange relationships and like an American "Empress Dowager," she spent her final years dressed in the finest Chinese regalia so that people could take pictures of the once popular novelist. Despite the fact she was only a decade older than my parents and lived in parts of northern China where they were stationed, their paths never crossed though naturally, Pearl Buck and her award-winning novel were well known in our family.

Terrill, Ross. 1972. *800,000,000: The real China.* London: Heinemann.

This book came out before Simon Leys published his revealing book that claimed "the emperor had no clothes." Though a veteran Sinologist, Terrill was one of several visitors to China during the Cultural Revolution who often failed to see what was actually happening. For example, toward the end of his work he concludes with "the revolution has been good for workers and peasants but problematic for intellectuals" (p. 233). Given that millions of Chinese of all social positions were killed directly or indirectly due to the Party's policies since 1949, it is difficult to swallow claims such as these. Many Americans, especially those in academia, were so excited by the prospects of the rapprochement with China initiated by

President Nixon, even seasoned China watchers seemed to have temporarily suspended any sense of disbelief. I was a graduate student at the University of Michigan from the late sixties through 1970 and active in the various centers of Asian studies. I was stunned and often annoyed at how many of my fellow students and some faculty members viewed the PRC as a political utopia and Mao Zedong as an emperor dressed in the finest regalia.

Towery, Britt. 1990. *Churches of China: Taking root downward, bearing fruit upward.* Waco, TX: Baylor University Press.

Originally published four years earlier, this paperback edition describes how Chinese Christian communities grew deep indigenous roots after Liberation that allowed them to survive and now flourish because of their independence. Towery was the first China Liaison Director for the large Southern Baptist church whose missionaries were much more theologically conservative than my parents. A Southern Baptist missionary who was a contemporary of my parents and who was sometimes a guest in our home in Jining lamented that she would not see my father in heaven because he was a Presbyterian!

U.S. Government Printing Office. 1978. *Peking street guide.* Washington: U.S. Government Printing Office.

This was one of several materials we bought from the U.S. Government Printing Office before we left for China, and I relied on this pamphlet for several details of our visits to Beijing. We also purchased American city maps of Tianjin and Shanghai that were helpful in augmenting the Chinese maps that we had.

Wang, Rongpei & William Puffenberger. 1991. *Laotse.* Liaoning: Liaoning University Press.

Less well known than Confucius, Laotse is almost as influential. As the founder of Taoism ('the Way"), his teachings emphasized virtuous conduct and are filled with simple insights ("accomplish a great deed by attending to small details") or revelations based on contradictions ("the softest thing under heaven overcomes the hardest thing under heaven"). Taoism relies a great deal on models from nature and accounts for the pervasiveness of landscapes in Chinese art and natural metaphors in Chinese poetry.

White, Theodore. 1978. *In search of history.* New York: Harper & Row.

> *Time* magazine's "man in China," Theodore White, later became famous in national politics during the Kennedy era. White relates his experiences covering Mao and other leaders of the Chinese Communist Party when they were still clearly the underdogs in their war with Chiang's Nationalists troops. Among the many stories of Zhou Enlai's charm with foreigners is the author's account of the "Chinese chicken" incident.

Wickeri, Philip. 2007. *Reconstructing Christianity in China: K.H. Ting and the Chinese church.* Maryknoll, NY: Orbis Books.

> No American theologian is more professionally familiar with the established church in China than Wickeri, but because of his years of working with Bishop Ting and contacts with the Three-Self Patriotic Movement and the China Christian Council and his ordination by the Chinese church, he also has enjoyed a personal relationship with contemporary Chinese Christian leaders. This is a lengthy, scholarly, and balanced review of Bishop Ting's legacy as well as a history of the modern "registered" church in China.

Williams, S. Wells. 1883. *The Middle Kingdom: Volumes I & II.* New York: Charles Scribner's Sons.

> I'm not sure how these aged volumes ended up in my hands, but they are a fortuitous acquisition for they are filled with descriptions of historical sites, temples, traditions, and

Chinese history. The second volume devotes several pages to the Nestorians, who were the first Christian missionaries to China and whose well-documented visit and influence took place in the early part of the sixth century. This book is a trove of information about almost every aspect of Chinese life a century and a half ago, often resorting to fine print to squeeze in pages and pages of translated documents. The foreign and alas sometimes Christian bias of the author occasionally reveals racist attitudes that unfortunately are still in evidence today. Despite Williams' overall admiration of China's people and civilization, there are embarrassing sections, such as one on the "mendacity of the Chinese." Among other things he writes, "More uneradicable than the sins of the flesh is the falsity of the Chinese, and its attendant sin of base ingratitude; their disregard of truth has perhaps done more to lower their character than any other fault" (Volume I, p. 834). Attitudes like this have naturally fueled legitimate resentment, anger, and distrust of foreign missionaries from the nineteenth century right up to the present.

World Almanac Books. 2011. *The world almanac and book of facts: 2011*. New York: World Almanac Books.

For random demographic, geographic, and historical details, I generally eschewed the Internet and have relied on this single source for information. Because there was no Google or Internet during our stay in China in 1979, that year's edition of the almanac was a godsend as the Chinese, who are inveterately curious, peppered us with questions about America and the world. The almanac also proved useful in preparing for our classes and special lectures, like the time we were suddenly asked to give a public talk about George Washington. Between Janene's training in history and the information gleaned from the 1979 almanac, we were able to prepare a ninety-minute lecture overnight.

Wu, Nelson. 1963. *Chinese and Indian architecture.* London: Prentice-Hall International.

This is an excellent introduction to the symbolic and cosmological aspects of Chinese (and Indian) architecture. The table of contents alone is a succinct summary of the way simple forms stand for complex cultural beliefs: The Square and the Circle, The Indian Mountain of God, The Chinese City of Man, and Outside the Square and Inside the Circle.

Xu, Guoqi. 2008. *Olympic dreams: China and sports 1895-2008.* Cambridge, MA: Harvard University Press.

Because of my love of sports, I found this volume a bit disappointing in that it is mostly about the history and politics of international sports and contains precious little about Chinese athletes and their achievements. C. K. Yang is never mentioned for example, despite the fact he came very close to winning a gold medal in the grueling decathlon at the 1960 Rome Olympics. Yang competed for the "province" of Taiwan: at that time, the PRC was excluded from the United Nations and the Olympics. Xu writes about the political background for such policies as "friendship first" and "ping pong diplomacy." There are a few gaps for a book that intends to cover China's Olympic dreams. For instance, no mention is made of how the experience of the women's swim team turned into a nightmare when they were sent packing at the 2000 Games because performance enhancing drugs were found in the athlete's luggage upon their arrival at Sydney. Americans should not feel too smug about this incident however since several of our athletes have competed illegally with more dramatic consequences. Marion Jones won gold medals in both the 100 and 200 meter dashes at those 2000 Olympics but lost them seven years later when it was discovered she had been taking performance enhancing drugs.

Yao, Xinzhong. 1996. *Confucianism and Christianity: A comparative study of Jen and Agape*. Brighton, U.K.: Sussex Academic Press.

In general, Confucianism and Christianity are viewed as contrasting and rather unrelated belief systems, but in this work, Yao demonstrates that Christian love ("agape") and the Confucian concept of *ren* ("humaneness") are indeed quite different, but they do share some similar characteristics. Yao is a Chinese-educated academic who teaches and publishes in Great Britain and thus bridges both cultures and world views. The author is a Fellow of the Royal Society of Arts.

Yao, Xinzhong. 2000. *An introduction to Confucianism*. Cambridge: Cambridge University Press.

Confucianism not only is the foundation of Chinese culture, it also spread to influence China's neighbors, especially Korea and Japan. The author tackles the longstanding argument of whether or not this belief system can be classified as a religion. Yao's book is an excellent introduction to the core characteristics of Confucianism and its historical legacy as well as to its contemporary practice.

PHOTOS

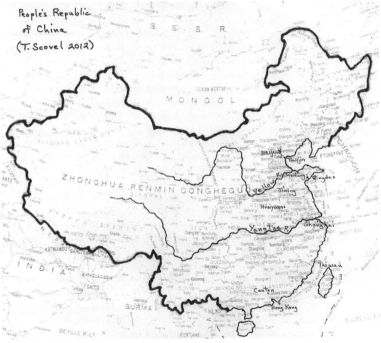

Map of China

Fred and Myra Scovel at their home in Huaiyuan, 1947

Tom, aged two, with Zhang Dasao at the beach in Qingdao

*Janene, Derick, and Christine, ready to
enter China in January, 1979*

Tom at the Great Wall on his fortieth birthday

Our home for all of 1979, The Tianjin Hotel

Tom at the gate of our institute. The inscription on the
red sign reads, "Study, study, and again, study!"

Tom biking to work on a winter morning

Lenin and Stalin stare down runners in
the central square in Tianjin

*Temporary shelters, home to tens of thousands of Tianjin
residents after the devastating Tangshan earthquake*

Janene with a sign in Qingdao restricting access to all foreigners

Our family flanked by the Tianjin police in their May Day whites

*Christine with her nursery classmates and
teachers ready for a performance*

*Our family hosting a party for Janene's
teaching group in our hotel room*

*Yang Bing, offering good "cheers" at party for Janene's
student at the Gou Bu Li Restaurant in Tianjin*

Lao Shen, of the Foreign Experts Bureau (center) flanked by a driver (left) and the "Korean" Jin (right) in front of the "Flying Bai Cai"

Jin Di, Tom's colleague and eminent scholar and translator

Jenny Xie with Janene and Christine and a feast of succulent jiaozis

*Our family with Birch Wang, newly freed
from years of unjust imprisonment*

*Pastor Liu Qingfen with our family in front
of the newly opened Tianjin church*

*Zhang Jintong and Tom describing the
Jining visit to a group of teachers*

Derick standing on the steps of the house in Jining where I was born

*Our family and the crowds at the old hospital
in Jining where my father worked*

Lao Li with our family in Jining. Despite his age and poor health, he was able to relate the story of when my father was shot by a drunken Japanese soldier in 1938

Our family using the map in Gilkey's book for orientation at the site of the former Japanese internment camp at Weifang

Our family standing in the communal kitchen at the site of the former Japanese internment camp in Weifang. My first memory of life is of my mother stirring gruel at this spot.

Fred and Myra Scovel with their three youngest children in front of their Canton home in 1948

The former Scovel home in Canton thirty years later when we visited it in 1979

Tom with the customs agent, factory manager, and driver who helped him try to find his grandmother's grave in Canton our last night in China